Asia Bible Commentary Series

MATTHEW

Asia Bible Commentary Series

MATTHEW
A Pastoral and Contextual Commentary

Samson L. Uytanlet

with
Kiem-Kiok Kwa

General Editor
Federico G. Villanueva

Old Testament Consulting Editors
Yohanna Katanacho, Tim Meadowcroft, Joseph Shao

New Testament Consulting Editors
Steve Chang, Andrew Spurgeon, Brian Wintle

© 2017 by Samson L. Uytanlet

The following topics © 2017 by Kiem-Kiok Kwa: (1) Family Matters; (2) Following Jesus in the Sermon on the Mount; (3) Living Out the Kingdom; (4) Welcoming People in the Church; (5) Confrontation in Hierarchical and Shame-Based Culture; (6) Church and Caesar; (7) The Suffering of Jesus; (8) Resurrection, Authority, and Mission.

Published 2017 by Langham Global Library
An imprint of Langham Publishing
www.langhampublishing.org

Langham Publishing and its imprints are a ministry of Langham Partnership.

Langham Partnership
PO Box 296, Carlisle, Cumbria CA3 9WZ, UK
www.langham.org

Published in partnership with Asia Theological Association

ATA
QCC PO Box 1454 – 1154, Manila, Philippines
www.atasia.com

ISBNs:
978-1-78368-171-6 Print
978-1-78368-274-4 ePub
978-1-78368-276-8 PDF

Samson L. Uytanlet and Kiem-Kiok Kwa have asserted their right under the Copyright, Designs and Patents Act, 1988 to be identified as the Authors of this work.

All rights reserved. No part of this publication may be reproduced, stored in a retrieval system or transmitted, in any form or by any means, electronic, mechanical, photocopying, recording or otherwise, without the prior written permission of the publisher or the Copyright Licensing Agency.

All Scripture quotations, unless otherwise indicated, are taken from the Holy Bible, New International Version®, NIV®. Copyright ©2011 by Biblica, Inc.™ Used by permission of Zondervan. All rights reserved worldwide.

British Library Cataloguing in Publication Data
A catalogue record for this book is available from the British Library

ISBN: 978-1-78368-171-6

Cover & Book Design: projectluz.com

Langham Partnership actively supports theological dialogue and an author's right to publish but does not necessarily endorse the views and opinions set forth, and works referenced within this publication or guarantee its technical and grammatical correctness. Langham Partnership does not accept any responsibility or liability to persons or property as a consequence of the reading, use or interpretation of its published content.

In memory of my parents
Juanito Uy (1928–2010) and Felisa Liao Uy (1932-2016)

and my two eldest siblings
Aurora Uytanlet Yang (1950–1999)
Wilson Uytanlet (1952–2009)

CONTENTS

Commentary

Series Preface xi

Acknowledgements xiii

List of Abbreviations xv

Introduction 1

Commentary on Matthew 11

Recommended Works 279

Topics

Family Matters 19

Whose Golden Rule Has More Karats? Confucius' or Jesus'? 77

Following Jesus in the Sermon on the Mount 80

Filial Piety and Some Asian Burial Practices 92

The "Blasphemy against the Holy Spirit" and Cessationism 133

Use of Parables and Confrontations in a Shame-Based Culture 139

The "Expansion" of God's Kingdom:
   Does God's Kingdom Really Need to Expand? 148

Living Out the Kingdom 152

Filial Respect and the *Qorban* 165

Welcoming People in the Church 174

Selling One's Possession to Receive Eternal Life:
   A Theological Reflection on Evangelism 207

Confrontation in Hierarchical and Shame-Based Cultures 219

Church and Caesar 227

Evangelism as a Means to Hasten Christ's Return 243

The Suffering of Jesus 273

Resurrection, Authority, and Mission 276

SERIES PREFACE

In recent years, we have witnessed one of the greatest shifts in the history of world Christianity. It used to be that the majority of Christians lived in the West. But now the face of world Christianity has changed beyond recognition. Christians are now evenly distributed around the globe. This has implications for the interpretation of the Bible. In our case, we are faced with the task of interpreting the Bible from within our respective contexts. This is in line with the growing realization that every theology is contextual. Our understanding of the Bible is influenced by our historical and social locations. Thus, even the questions that we bring into our reading of the Bible will be shaped by our present realities. There is a need therefore to interpret the Bible for our own contexts.

The Asia Bible Commentary Series addresses this need. In line with the mission of the Asia Theological Association Publications, we have gathered Asian evangelical Bible scholars in Asia to write commentaries on each book of the Bible. The mission is to "produce resources for pastors, Christian leaders, cross-cultural workers, and students in Asia that are biblical, pastoral, contextual, missional, and prophetic." Although the Bible can be studied for different reasons, we believe that it is given primarily for the edification of the Body of Christ (2 Tim 3:16–17). The ABCS is designed to help pastors in their sermon preparation, cell group leaders or lay leaders in their Bible study groups, and Christian students in their study of the Bible, and Christians in general in their efforts to apply the Bible in their respective contexts.

Each commentary begins with an introduction that provides general information about the book's author and original context, summarizes the main message or theme of the book, and outlines its potential relevance to a particular Asian context. The introduction is followed by an exposition that combines exegesis and application. Here, we seek to speak to and empower Christians in Asia by using our own stories, parables, poems, and other cultural resources as we expound the Bible.

The Bible is actually Asian in that it comes from ancient West Asia and there are many similarities between the world of the Bible and traditional Asian cultures. But there are also many differences that we need to explore in some depth. That is why the commentaries also include articles or topics in which we bring specific issues in Asian church, social, and religious contexts into dialogue with relevant issues in the Bible. We do not seek to resolve every tension but rather to allow the text to illumine the context and vice versa, acknowledging that in the end we do not have all the answers to every mystery.

May the Holy Spirit who inspired the writers of the Bible bring light to the hearts and minds of all who use these materials, to the glory of God and to the building up of the churches!

Federico G. Villanueva

General Editor

ACKNOWLEDGEMENTS

I consider it a privilege to be one of the contributors for the Asia Bible Commentary Series. It took me a while to finish the work, and there are many people who helped me in the process. I am thankful to our seminary president, Dr. Joseph Shao, and our academic dean, Dr. Chiu Eng Tan, for allowing me to take a few weeks off from the seminary so I could concentrate on writing. I appreciate the flexibility of my students in New Testament 1 and Greek 1 (S.Y. 2015–2016), and for allowing me to "compress" our schedule so we could finish the class at an earlier date. This allowed me to focus on this work for several weeks. Moreover, through the partnership of the Asia Theological Association (ATA) and Asbury Theological Seminary, and with the facilitation of Dr. Mark Royster, I had a chance to spend my leave at Asbury (Wilmore, KY) for research and writing. Elder Allen Lim and Dr. Craig Keener have also provided helpful inputs for this work. I deeply appreciate the contribution of Kiem-Kiok Kwa who wrote several contextual applications (Topics) in this work. I am thankful to my wife, Juliet, and our son, Johann Sven, for their constant prayer and encouragements.

Samson L. Uytanlet

Biblical Seminary of the Philippines

Summer 2016

I am grateful to ATA for this opportunity to write contextual applications for the Gospel of Matthew. This has forced me to spend time to reflect deeply on the text as well as context, and not just my own context in Singapore but also that of Asia. For that I appreciate the constant interactions with students at East Asia School of Theology who shared their stories and experiences and so challenged my hermeneutics, provoking me to a deeper and richer understanding of both the text and context. Hence I dedicate my contributions to my students, especially those who took my course on Contextualization. I have learned much from you.

Kiem-Kiok Kwa

January 2017

LIST OF ABBREVIATIONS

BOOKS OF THE BIBLE
Old Testament
Gen, Exod, Lev, Num, Deut, Josh, Judg, Ruth, 1–2 Sam, 1–2 Kgs, 1–2 Chr, Ezra, Neh, Esth, Job, Ps/Pss, Prov, Eccl, Song, Isa, Jer, Lam, Ezek, Dan, Hos, Joel, Amos, Obad, Jonah, Mic, Nah, Hab, Zeph, Hag, Zech, Mal

New Testament
Matt, Mark, Luke, John, Acts, Rom, 1–2 Cor, Gal, Eph, Phil, Col, 1–2 Thess, 1–2 Tim, Titus, Phlm, Heb, Jas, 1–2 Pet, 1–2–3 John, Jude, Rev

BIBLE TEXTS AND VERSIONS
Divisions of the canon
NT	New Testament
OT	Old Testament

Ancient texts and versions
LXX	Septuagint
MT	Masoretic Text

Modern versions
NASB	New American Standard Bible
NIV	New International Version
NRSV	New Revised Standard Version

Journals, reference works, and series
ACCS	Ancient Christian Commentary on Scripture
AfTS	African Theological Studies
AnBib	Analecta Biblica
ANR	*Andover Newton Review*
ASE	*Annali di storia dell'esegesi*
ASMS	American Society of Missiology Series
ASNU	Acta Seminarii Neotestamentici Upsaliensis
AThR	*Anglican Theological Review*
BA	*Biblical Archaeologist*
BBR	*Bulletin for Biblical Research*

Bib	*Biblica*
BibInt	*Biblical Interpretation*
BlTh	*Black Theology*
BR	*Biblical Research*
BRS	Biblical Resource Series
BSac	*Bibliotheca Sacra*
BZNW	Beihefte zur Zeitschrift für die neuentestamentliche Wissenschaft und die Kunde der älteren Kirche
CBQ	*Catholic Biblical Quarterly*
CdT	*Cuadernos de Teología*
ChrCent	*Christian Century*
ChrEJ	*Christian Education Journal*
Colloq	*Colloquium*
CTM	*Concordia Theological Monthly*
CurTM	*Currents in Theology and Mission*
CV	*Communio Viatorum*
Dial	*Dialogue*
Enc	*Encounter*
ETL	*Ephemerides Theologicae Lovanienses*
EuroUS	European University Studies
FC	The Fathers of the Church
GOTR	*Greek Orthodox Theological Review*
Hor	*Horizons*
HTR	Harvard Theological Review
Int	*Interpretation*
JAAR	*Journal of the American Academy of Religion*
JBL	*Journal of Biblical Literature*
JES	*Journal of Ecumenical Studies*
JETS	*Journal of the Evangelical Theological Society*
JLAT	*Journal of Latin American Theology*
JPCC	*Journal of Pastoral Care and Counseling*
JPT	*Journal of Pentecostal Theology*
JPTSup	Journal of Pentecostal Theology Supplement
JRT	*Journal of Religious Thought*

List of Abbreviations

JSNT	*Journal for the Study of the New Testament*
JSNTSup	Journal for the Study of the New Testament Supplement Series
JSPS	*Journal of the Society for Pentecostal Studies*
JTAK	*Journal of Theta Alpha Kappa*
JTS	*Journal of Theological Studies*
JTSA	*Journal of Theology for Southern Africa*
Kairós	*Kairós*
LNTS	Library of New Testament Studies
MAJT	*Mid-America Journal of Theology*
Matrix	Matrix: The Bible in Mediterranean Context
MBC	Mellen Biblical Commentary
Missio	*Missiology*
MiSt	*Mission Studies*
MW	*Muslim World*
NCBC	New Cambridge Bible Commentary
Neot	*Neotestamentica*
NICNT	New International Commentary on the New Testament
NovT	*Novum Testamentum*
NovTSup	Supplements to Novum Testamentum
NTD	Das Neue Testament Deutsch
NTL	New Testament Library
NTS	*New Testament Studies*
OJT	*Ogbomoso Journal of Theology*
Paideia	Paideia Commentaries on the New Testament
PNTC	Pillar New Testament Commentary
PRSt	*Perspective in Religious Studies*
RefJ	*Reformed Journal*
ResQ	*Restoration Quarterly*
RevExp	*Review and Expositors*
RTR	*Reformed Theological Review*
SBEC	Studies in the Bible and Early Christianity
SBR	Studies in the Bible and Its Reception
ScEs	*Science et Esprit*
SCJ	*Stone-Campbell Journal*

SEÅ	*Svensk exegetisk årsbok*
Semeia	*Semeia*
SNTSMS	Society for New Testament Studies Monograph Series
Spring	*Springfielder*
StBibLit	Studies in Biblical Literature (Lang)
StBL	Studies in Biblical Literature (SBL)
Str-B	Strack, Hermann L., and Paul Billerbeck. *Kommentar zum Neuen Testament aus Talmud und Midrasch*
Théoph	*Théophilyon*
ThTo	*Theology Today*
TJ	*Trinity Journal*
TKNT	Theologischer Kommentar zum Neuen Testament
TOTC	Tyndale Old Testament Commentary
Tradition	*Tradition*
TS	Theological Studies
TUGAL	Texte und Untersuchungen zur Geschichte der altchristlichen Literatur
TynBul	*Tyndale Bulletin*
UTSQR	Union Theological Seminary Quarterly Review
VC	*Vigiliae Christianae*
Vision	*Vision*
VT	*Vetus Testamentum*
Worship	*Worship*
WTJ	*Westminster Theological Journal*
WUNT	Wissenschaftliche Untersuchungen zum Neuen Testament
WW	*Word and World*
ZNW	*Zeitschrift für die neutestamentliche Wissenschaft und die Kunde älteren Kirche*

INTRODUCTION

Before I started attending school, my mother, who only speaks our native Chinese dialect *Hokkien*, would wake me up in the morning by making the sound of a rooster's crow, "*Kok-korok-kok*! It's time to wake up!" For this reason, I thought that roosters crow by making the sound *kok-korok-kok*, until I started to read English and Tagalog literature. The confusion begins when I read that the cock in English books crows *cock-a-doodle-doo* and the *tandang* (Tagalog for rooster) of the local books cries *tik-tilaok*. Roosters from different countries do not make different sounds, but why is there a variety in representing the same sound? This is because people from various cultures *hear the same sound differently*. Of course, not all representations of the same sound are equally valid, because roosters can never make the sound *moo-moo* or *quack-quack*, but there is more than one correct way of *hearing* the rooster's crow. This principle is true, not only in hearing audible sounds, but also in listening to messages. There is always something about the listeners that make them hear the same message differently.

It is important to stress that not all ways of hearing are equally correct (I am not suggesting that biblical truth is relative). To cite an example, there is a teacher ministering in Central Philippines who taught the local children to say the English expression, "God is so good!" The children said instead, "God *isog gyud*!" (*isog*, in the local dialect *bisaya*, means "valiant" or "fearless," and the closest equivalent of the expression *gyud* is "indeed").[1] Although what the children said is still true as the Old Testament (OT) sometimes portrays God as a warrior, it is not what the expression says. Turning back to the earlier illustration about the rooster's crow, one may say that although not all interpretations are equally valid, there can be more than one correct way of hearing and interpreting the same thing, and that the way to biblical truth is "wider" than many Evangelicals would acknowledge. To use Jesus' metaphor in a different way, we journey towards biblical insights by entering the narrow door, not by walking on a tightrope.

The sociopolitical, cultural, and religious backgrounds of the readers allow or prevent them from seeing certain dynamics at work in the writings they read. The more the similarities between the readers' background and that of the writers and his original audience, the more the readers should be

---

1. I am indebted to one of my colleagues at the Biblical Seminary of the Philippines, Rev. Dennis Yam, for this illustration.

able to relate with the stories being told. This means that the historical setting of the Gospel of Matthew is important in understanding its message, but readers today can bring with them their own backgrounds and worldviews that may enrich their understanding of the gospel's message. Thus, Asians can read it in ways that may be different from readers from other continents. In fact, even among Asians, there may be differences in the way we hear the Bible's message.

ARE THERE NOT ENOUGH COMMENTARIES ON MATTHEW?

Many students of the Bible have benefitted from the commentaries that have already been written in the past, so it is only right to ask whether there is still a need for more commentaries to be written now. Aside from the fact that interpreters from various cultures can hear the same message differently, there remains a continuous need to listen to the Bible's message in various times and locations.

A simple way of understanding the message of the Bible is to follow these three steps: Observation – Interpretation – Application. Even in a more academic setting, scholars also use these steps (or at least the first two), except that the amount of materials outside the Bible which they include in their *observation* and the expertise they bring in their *interpretation* makes the process more tedious for them. This means that although the steps may be simple to remember, the process itself requires a lot of work. One thing is often missing in commentaries like these – the application part. The Bible is always relevant, and there is nothing we can or need to do to make it *more* relevant, but we can always do something to conceal or distract readers from seeing its relevance. How God's word can transform people (both individuals and communities), challenge and change worldviews and cultures with its various expressions, are often missing in these works. In recent decades, scholars are beginning to renew their interest in reading commentators from the first few centuries. If there is one striking difference between commentators from earlier centuries and those from the last two centuries it is that the latter usually make a clear distinction between interpretation, theological reflection, and application. No wonder many seminaries in various parts of the world see the need to emphasize the relationship between the head, the heart, and the hands. We are now trying to reintegrate in our study of the Bible some things that should not have been separated, and the fact that we are trying to do so means something went wrong along the way. We cannot continue with the

Introduction

kind of biblical scholarship that separates interpretation from application, and historical information from spiritual insights.

Moreover, the three-step process (Observation – Interpretation – Application) is often seen as linear rather than cyclical (see Figure 1). By "linear" I mean the first step to understanding the Bible's message is to do *observation*. Once we have gathered enough data from observation, we are ready for the *interpretation*. After which, we can think of the *application*, the ultimate goal of observation and interpretation. Hearing the Bible's message does not always work this way, because our attempt to apply God's word in various contexts enables us to observe things we may not been able to observe before. In other words, the application can inform *what* we observe, inevitably affecting our interpretation of the text.

Figure 1: Linear or Cyclical?

Observation → Interpretation → Application

Linear

Cyclical

READING MATTHEW THROUGH MODERN ASIAN LENSES

The historical setting of the Gospels is important in understanding their message, but some of the issues typically discussed in commentaries do not really affect the way the text should be understood. Take authorship as an example. Knowing that the author of the Gospel of Matthew was a former tax collector who later became an apostle of Jesus may help us understand why his work was readily accepted by early believers as authoritative (because of his apostolic authority), but it does not help us in understanding the message of the Gospel. Likewise, knowing the original recipients of the Gospel of John or Mark may explain why Mark uses Latin terms and translates Aramaic expressions, or why John needs to explain Palestinian geography, local customs or idioms. These data do not help us better understand the Gospels' message.[2]

---

2. R. T. France, *Matthew: Evangelist and Teacher* (Grand Rapids: Academie Books, 1989), 77–78.

Matthew

The authors of some books of the Bible may be unknown (for example, Hebrews), and some writings may have been written for a wider audience (for example, Ephesians), but not being able to identify the author and the specific audience is not essential in understanding the message of these writings.[3] Some historical information, however, is more important to know. It is generally accepted that Matthew was written to a group of Christians in Antioch (Syria) who had conflict with Jewish groups associated with the Pharisees. The use of fiery language such as "hypocrites," "woe," and "brood of vipers" shows the extent of the strained relationship between the Jewish Christians and the Pharisaic Jews.[4]

Laurence Culas lists several reasons that may have led to the crisis experienced by the believers:[5] (1) The death of James, who had been key to preserving the Jewish traditions among early Christians; (2) The death of Peter, who had been a unifying factor in Antioch; (3) The failure of Christians to support Jewish interest in their war against Rome; (4) The destruction of the temple, which had been interpreted by Matthew as a consequence of the Jews' rejection of the Messiah and their treatment of Christians; (5) The Roman imperial presence in Antioch, which was a constant reminder of their sovereignty, and its degrading effect on Jewish society; (6) The Christians' separation from the synagogue; and (7) The failure of their mission to the Jews.

Knowing the historical setting of Matthew is undoubtedly important, but as modern readers, we also bring our present experiences with us as we read the Scripture. They can either aid or distort our understanding of Matthew's message. Our aim, therefore, is not to disregard our present contexts as if it is useless in our interpretation, but to lay them out and let it be open for scrutiny and dialogue. The best starting point is to identify what we share with Matthew's ancient audience that could aid us in understanding his message.

---

3. For more discussion, see the collection of essays in Richard Bauckham, ed., *The Gospels for All Christians: Rethinking the Gospel Audiences* (Grand Rapids: Eerdmans, 1997). Two helpful essays that discuss this topic in relation to Matthew are included in David E. Aune, ed., *The Gospel of Matthew in Current Studies* (Grand Rapids: Eerdmans, 2001); Donald Senior, "Direction in Matthean Studies," 5–21; Richard S. Ascough, "Matthew and Community Formation," 96–126.

4. Augustine Stock, *The Method and Message of Matthew* (Collegeville: Liturgical Press, 1994), 10–15.

5. Laurence Culas, *Good News Amidst Crises: Antioch and the Gospel of Matthew* (Delhi: Indian Society for Promoting Christian Knowledge, 2010), 92–106.

Introduction

Persecution of Believers

The book of Acts informs us how the followers of Jesus suffered persecution from both Jews and Gentiles alike, and the various reasons for such persecution. Religion, politics, society, and culture are interrelated factors that result in persecution. The priests and Sadducees, for example, considered the disciples' teaching about the resurrection as incorrect (Acts 4:1–2; see also 23:8). Doctrine was the major issue for them, and this was partly the cause of their persecution of the apostles. Politics also had something to do with the persecution of Christians. The Thessalonian Jews considered the Jewish Christians in Thessalonica as rebellious people because they were teaching that there was another king named Jesus (17:6–7). Many of the Christians in the city were Jewish, and for Christians to proclaim that there was another king other than Caesar would put the rest of the Jewish people in danger. Self-preservation was the reason for the non-believing Jews in stopping the growth of Christianity. Economics is another reason for the persecution. The master of the fortune-telling slave girl (16:16–24) and the craftsmen of Ephesus (19:24–41), who were likely Gentiles, complained against Paul because his ministry was causing their businesses to collapse.

The kind of persecution that the early believers experienced was something which many Asian believers until now could identify. There is religious opposition in Asian countries where Islam, Buddhism, or Hinduism is the dominant religion. Christians are being watched by the government in communist countries where religion is prohibited, or at least not encouraged. In more prosperous countries, Christians may also be in danger for the ethical practices they promote. In the Gospel of Matthew, there are hints that the Christians were undergoing persecution. The nature of the persecution is hinted at in some of passages in the Gospel: some Christians were slandered (Matt 5:10–12), and some were killed (10:28; 23:37). The reason may have to do with their preaching of the gospel (10:23; 13:21), but we can only speculate about the pertinent historical details.

The presence of colonial powers in the New Testament (NT) is something Asians can understand. The rule of some Western forces remains fresh in the collective memory of most Asian countries. In the same way that the ancient Jews had various responses to their colonizers or even to national tragedy like the exile,[6] Asians today also respond differently to Western coloniza-

---

6. Nicholas Perrin, "Exile," in *The World of the New Testament: Cultural, Social, and Historical Contexts,* eds. Joel B. Green, and Lee Martin McDonald (Grand Rapids: Baker Academic,

tion. Some Asians see it as beneficial, while others focus on its oppressive elements. The primary difference is that preaching the gospel in the first century Roman Empire could easily be misunderstood as treason, while the imperial rule in modern Asia had been, to some extent, instrumental in the spread of Christianity in the region. Although preaching that Jesus is king is acceptable in many parts of Asia, many Asians remain unreceptive, or even hostile, to this idea because some still consider Christianity as a "Western religion."

Society and Culture

David A. deSilva notes that "[the original] readers of the New Testament shared certain values, such as honor, and codes of forming and maintaining relationships, such as patronage and kinship, and ways of ordering the world, expressed frequently in terms of purity."[7] Much of what can be said about the culture of the NT world is also true of modern Asian culture. The term "Asian culture" is too broad, because even among Asians, there are elements of dissimilarities. Yet there are several cultural similarities among Asians, which is also comparable to that of ancient Jews and other Mediterranean people. As Asian readers, it would be beneficial to point out these parallels as we continue to seek God's message for us today through Matthew's writing.

First, there are many similarities between the modern Asian idea of kinship and that of ancient Israel. The family is the basic structure of any society. The definition of "family," however, may vary in different cultures. In a more individualistic culture, "family" includes only a father, a mother, and their children. Grandparents, uncles/aunts, cousins, and in-laws are part of the "extended family." Although the expression "extended family" is part of the vocabulary of English-speaking Asians, the concept remains foreign to many of them. Extended family is still "family." There is a *Hokkien* expression, *kai ki lang* (自己人) which means "one's own people." This is often used in situations when a person does a favor to non-relatives, the former would say, "*kai ki lang*," suggesting that the latter need not feel embarrassed for receiving a favor because the one who does the favor treats them as if they are his/her own people. Among the Tagalog speakers, there is a colloquial expression to refer to siblings, *'tol* or *'utol*, a shortened form of *kaputol* which means "the other portion," used often for long objects like a stick, or a rope. The idea of the *kaputol* is that one's sibling is the other part, the *kaputol*, of the umbilical

---

2013), 35.
7. David A. deSilva, *Honor, Patronage, Kinship, and Purity: Unlocking New Testament Culture* (Downers Grove: InterVarsity, 2000), 18.

Introduction

cord. The same can be said of the more formal expression *kapatid* (*patid* means "to cut," as in a string). For English speakers, the spouse is sometimes called, "better half," the other part of a marriage union; but for Filipinos, a sibling who had been in the same womb is "the other part." However, kinship is not only about biological relationship, but also about shared values and beliefs. The same could be said about ancient Israel's idea of kinship, thus abandoning family religion and values may lead the natural family to force deviating members to return to what they deem as the honorable way of living.[8] This makes Jesus' call to discipleship, which is a departure from the shared values and religion of the family, extremely challenging for the early believers (Matt 10:34–39).

Within this type of family system, honor is another thing that members of the family share with each other. Although rivalries within the family may exist, yet honor achieved by an individual member is considered honor of the family. Likewise, when one family member does something perceived as shameful and can potentially bring disgrace to the family or place it in danger, other members may act to stop this member from bringing dishonor to the family. No wonder Jesus' own family members were not his supporters during his earthly ministry (12:46–50). Jesus' call to discipleship included the formation of a community who shared the same belief in the kingship of God and the same desire to live a life of obedience to him.[9]

Second, parallels can also be observed between the social structure of modern Asian society and that of the society where Jesus lived. People are classified based on their wealth, political power, education, ethnic origin and language spoken, and gender. In modern Asia, possessing wealth or political power places a person in an honorable position. One's education or ethnic origin, and still in many regions, one's language proficiency or gender, are also sources of honor. It is true that the idea of honor is present in practically every culture of the world today, but the value one places on receiving or maintaining individual or corporate honor varies. This is like comparing dark blue and light blue, although we are talking about the same color (blue), the intensity is not the same. The value Asians normally place on one's honor is comparatively greater than the more individualistic cultures. This is seen in the practice of honor killings in some Asian countries, and the cases of suicide due to dishonor.

---

8. DeSilva, *Honor, Patronage, Kinship, and Purity*, 194.
9. Stephen Westerholm, *Understanding Matthew: The Early Christian Worldview of the First Gospel* (Grand Rapids: Baker Academic, 2006), 121–140.

In the NT world, the various classes or groups relate to each other through the system of patronage, or the *padrino* system, which "was an essential means of acquiring access to goods, protection or opportunities for employment and advancement."[10] This *padrino* system is also common in many Asian countries, wherein one gains favor or advantage, not for having the right skills and knowledge, but for knowing the right people. The person of influence is typically the ones granting favor to another who is expected to reciprocate by showing loyalty, or in some cases, by returning the favor. Related to this practice is grace and gratitude. The one who receives grace is expected to show gratitude. Filipinos use the expression *utang na loob*, commonly translated as "debt of gratitude." The *utang na loob* is more than just "feeling" grateful, it is about reciprocating. The best example in the gospel that reflects a similar cultural practice is the Jewish elders' request that Jesus heal the slave of the centurion of Capernaum. Their reason is that the centurion "deserves" Jesus' favor because he loves the nation and he built their synagogue (Luke 7:4–5). This cultural value can be both positive and prone to abuse. It is a good practice because it encourages gratitude that promotes harmonious interpersonal relationships; but it can be abused especially if the one who grants favor requires the receiver to reciprocate in ways that violate ethical and moral standards.

Religion and the Understanding of the Spiritual World

The belief in the spirits and their activity in the physical world is one thing modern Asians and ancient people share. There is no question that local myths and folklore influence one's belief and representation of spiritual beings. It is no wonder different cultures have different names and descriptions of these evil forces,[11] and that there are also various forms of superstition that result from these. However, these beliefs are not only shaped by traditional stories, but also by personal encounters with the supernatural. Although such experiences can be misinterpreted, they *cannot always* be explained using psychological categories. There are many examples of such encounters in the Gospel of Matthew which will be discussed later in relation to particular passages.

One feature of ancient religion that is noteworthy is their worship of heroes and political leaders. The closest equivalent to ancient hero and emperor cults in modern Asia is the veneration of leaders in countries like North

---

10. DeSilva, *Honor, Patronage, Kinship, and Purity*, 96.
11. For examples of the various beliefs about the spirit beings, see Rodney L. Henry, *Filipino Spirit World: A Challenge to the Church* (Mandaluyong: OMF Literature, 1986), 5–16.

Introduction

Korea. Comparative studies between ancient hero or imperial cults and its modern counterparts remain a virtually open field for study.

MESSAGE OF THE GOSPEL OF MATTHEW

Two of the more influential views regarding the structure of the Gospel of Matthew are: (1) the five-discourse structure popularized by Benjamin W. Bacon; and (2) the three-part outline proposed by Jack D. Kingsbury.[12] The statement, "When Jesus had finished (these things)" (Matt 7:28; 11:1; 13:53; 19:1; 26:1), is considered the transitional statement for the five-discourse structure. Each portion is said to have a narrative section and a discourse section. Critique of this view is presented by Kingsbury,[13] who proposes that the statement, "From that time Jesus began to" (4:17; 16:21), should be considered the pivot points of Matthew's writing. Thus, the Gospel of Matthew can be divided to three major parts that focus on the Person (1:1–4:16), the Proclamation (4:17–16:21), and the Passion (16:21–28:20) of Jesus the Messiah. This structure is helpful for the readers to see how the story of Jesus develops in the Gospel of Matthew, although the readers must remember that it is not only Matthew's discussion that focuses on the person of Jesus in the first section but the question of John the Baptist (11:1–6), the confessions of Peter (16:13–20), and the centurion (28:54) also present the person of Jesus the Messiah. Likewise, Jesus' proclamation prior to his crucifixion (16:24–28; 18:1–20:16; 21:28–22:14; 23:1–25:46), and his passion is already hinted at in the story of John's death (14:1–12).

It should be observed that the first story about Jesus in the Gospel (genealogy and birth of Jesus) concludes with the naming of Jesus as the Immanuel or "God with us" (1:23), which underscores God's presence with his people because of Jesus' physical presence with them. Similarly, the last story of the Gospel concludes with Jesus the Immanuel promising his disciples his continuous presence even in his physical absence (28:20). This suggests that the stories in between focus on God's presence through Jesus.

---

12. For a more detailed discussion on the various views regarding the structure of Matthew, see David R. Bauer, *The Structure of Matthew's Gospel: A Study in Literary Design*, JSNTSup 30 (Sheffield: Almond Press, 1988), 21–55; H. J. Bernard Combrink, "The Structure of the Gospel of Matthew as a Narrative," *TynBul* 34 (1983): 61–62; Jack Dean Kingsbury, *Matthew: Structure, Christology, Kingdom* (Philadelphia: Fortress, 1975), 1–7. See also Benjamin W. Bacon, *Studies in Matthew* (New York: H. Holt and Company, 1930).

13. Kingsbury, *Structure*, 4–7.

Matthew

Matthew's concern for writing the Gospel is threefold; he has spiritual concerns (e.g. the relevance of the law for the Christians), polemic concerns (e.g. the credibility of Jesus as the Messiah), and pastoral concerns (e.g. the quality of leadership in his church).[14] Throughout the Gospel, the readers are invited to recognize the presence of God.[15] The promise of God's presence is given to the believers who are undergoing persecution. Despite the challenges that Jesus' followers might have to face as they heed his call to discipleship, and the difficulty they may face even from their own family members, there is a promise of a new family to which the believers can belong if they follow Jesus. Considering the system of patronage present in the society within which they live, the believers are assured that God is the real giver of good gifts. As the believers face another challenge related to their health and well-being, their experiences of the supernatural, the evidence of God's presence is seen in the work of Jesus in their midst. With Jesus promise to his disciples of his continuous presence, the same message is given to his disciples as they continue to proclaim God's kingship, not just in Asia, but everywhere.

---

14. John Yieh, *Conversations with Scripture: The Gospel of Matthew*, Anglican Association of Biblical Scholarship Study Series (Harrisburg, PA: Morehouse, 2012), 16–21.
15. Warren Carter, *Matthew: Storyteller, Interpreter, Evangelist* (Peabody: Hendrickson, 2004), 8.

MATTHEW 1:1—2:23

The Human Origin of Jesus

There are many ways to trace one's genealogy. The surname or family name of a person is a good place to start. The names of Chinese males usually have three characters. Traditionally, the first character is the *xìng* (姓) or the family name; the second character is the *zì bèi* (字輩) or the generation name which is shared by the males of the same generation; the second and third characters together are the *míng* (名) or the given name, and the third character is the unique *míng* used to distinguish an individual from other males in the same generation within the family or clan. The *zì bèi* helps a person how to properly address a distant relative. Naming children according to the *zì bèi* is a practice that is becoming less popular, however. In Asian countries wherein Western influence is very strong, the closest equivalent to this is the use of name suffixes, like Sr., Jr., III, IV, and so on. For many Indians, genealogies are used to determine the caste to which a person belongs. The Filipinos use the expression, "*Taga-saan ang mga* (surname)?" or ("From where are the [surnames]"?) to ask the province of origin of a person with an unfamiliar surname. Knowing the land of origin is associated with tracing one's lineage. Modern historians and biographers trace a person's genealogy for the purpose of reconstructing historical accounts. One way to do this is by checking government records and archives. For modern historians, genealogy must be complete to be considered accurate, but their standard of accuracy may not be exactly similar to that of ancient writers.

Ancient biographers and historians also used genealogies for various reasons. Identifying family connections was one reason. For political historians, tracing a king's lineage to gods or ancient heroes was one way to boost the image of the king. Others identified their family of origin in order to claim ownership of lands. There are evidences that ancient Israel and Rome kept registries where one could trace a person's lineage.[1] However, many of the records in ancient biographies and histories are transmitted orally, and therefore, not as complete and accurate as those based on modern standards.

Paul observed that his contemporaries' fascination with genealogies distracted them from focusing on essential matters of faith (1 Tim 1:4), but

---

1. Josephus, *Life* 1 §6.

ancient genealogies can also be used in a positive way. Tracing one's kin is a way to keep a brief family history. Ancient rhetoricians sometimes included genealogies in their speeches to praise a person for belonging to a good family.[2] Usually, biographers used genealogies to show that a king was descended from a line of kings, and thus his kingship was legitimate.[3] Matthew's reason for including Jesus' genealogy appears to be similar; as a descendant of David, Jesus came from a line of kings. This is particularly important as Matthew discusses the kingdom of heaven in his Gospel.

In a culture that values honor and shame, a good family history is important. Jesus had the honor of being descended from the faithful Abraham and the king David. By beginning his Gospel with Jesus' genealogy, Matthew is saying that Jesus is someone whose life is worth knowing.[4] Unlike the genealogies used for political propaganda, which present either the illustrious or the virtually unknown yet honorable ancestors, there are some things in Jesus' genealogy that make it less honorable, such as the exiled kings and women with "questionable" background. These names not only suggest the truthfulness of Matthew's record, but also highlight the grace of God that can bring honor to what is deemed dishonorable.

1:1–17 THE GENEALOGY OF JESUS

1:1–6a Jesus, the Son of Abraham

Humans naturally like "winners," and not "losers." Unfortunately, we bring this attitude with us even as we interpret the Bible. No wonder it is easier to discuss about Jesus being the son of "winners" like Abraham, the great man of faith, or David, the man after God's own heart, but not of "losers" like Jeconiah, the defeated king exiled to Babylon.[5] However, according to Matthew, Jesus is the son of Abraham, son of David, and the son of Jeconiah (Matt 1:1, 6, 11).

---

2. Ancient rhetoricians like Quintilian taught that genealogies can be used in a formal public speech to compliment a person (*Institutes of Oratory* 3.7.10).
3. Ancient biographers like Suetonius includes genealogies of Julius Caesar (*Julius* 6.1) and emperor Otho (*Otho* 1.1–3) to show that they were legitimate kings because they were descended from prominent families. See Gerard Mussies, "Parallels to Matthew's Version of the Pedigree of Jesus," *NovT* 28, no. 1 (1986): 32.
4. Jerome H. Neyrey, *Honor and Shame in the Gospel of Matthew* (Louisville, KY: Westminster John Knox, 1998), 97.
5. Richard J. Erickson, "Joseph and the Birth of Isaac in Matthew 1," *BBR* 10, no. 1 (2000): 35.

First, Jesus is the son of Abraham (1:1–2, 17). Excluding the genealogy, Abraham is only mentioned three times in the Gospel: (1) he is the chief ancestor of the Jews whose lives exhibit the "fruit of repentance" (3:8–9), and not necessarily of those who are descended from him biologically; (2) together with Isaac and Jacob, Abraham will host the banquet for the faithful ones who will "come from the east and west" (8:10–12); and (3) together with Isaac and Jacob, he shows the certainty of life beyond the grave and future resurrection (22:30–32). On all three occasions, those who share his blessings are not limited to a particular ethnic group.

In the OT, the LORD promised to give Abraham four things: (1) descendants (Gen 12:2), (2) land for them (12:7); (3) a great name (12:2); and (4) a unique role as a channel of blessing to the families/tribes of the earth (12:3). God's presence with Abraham is implied in the promise to him and his offspring (17:7). The third promise was fulfilled together with the first two. Through Isaac (17:19, 21), and eventually through Jacob and his twelve sons (Exod 2:24), the LORD's promise of descendants was fulfilled. Through Moses and Joshua, God's promise of land came true (6:4; see also 3:6–10), which is part of God's plan to establish Israel as "a kingdom of priests and a holy nation" over which he would reign (19:5–6).[6] As a kingdom of priests, they are to serve as a "bridge" between the LORD and the "family of nations." This task was not accomplished completely. However, with Jesus commanding his followers to make disciples of "all nations" (Matt 28:18), Matthew seems to be saying that Jesus is the son of Abraham through whom God's fourth promise to Abraham would be fulfilled. Jesus is the fulfillment of the promise of blessing to the nations.

Matthew includes some female names in Jesus' ancestry. Although ancient Jewish genealogies typically contained names of males, Matthew is not the first to include women in genealogies (Gen 11:29; 35:22–26; 36:10, 22; 1 Chr 2:4; 7:24).[7] In 1–2 Kings, with the exception of Jeroboam (1 Kgs 11:26), only the mothers of the Judean kings are identified (1 Kgs 14:31, etc.). First Kings 22:52 and 2 Chronicles 22:3 hint that the matriarchs influence their sons either to despise or to walk according to God's commands; and this is perhaps the reason they are mentioned in those accounts. These records show that Matthew's inclusion of women in Jesus' genealogy is not unusual, even within a patriarchal culture.

---

6. Israel was also considered the "kingdom of the LORD" (1 Chr 28:5; 2 Chr 13:8).
7. John C. Hutchison, "Women, Gentiles, and the Messianic Mission in Matthew's Genealogy," *BSac* 158, no. 2 (2001): 163 n. 26; see also Erickson, "Birth of Isaac," 43, n. 22.

Interpreters of Matthew's Gospel use one of these five basic reasons to explain the inclusion of women in Jesus' genealogy.[8] First, the women are "sinners" and their inclusion shows the grace of God. The problem with this is that during the time of Jesus, the women were already considered heroines and not sinners: (1) Tamar was considered "more righteous" than Judah (Gen 38:26); (2) Rahab belonged to God's people (Josh 6:25; Heb 11:31); (3) Ruth was considered righteous (Ruth 1:16); and (4) David was blamed for the adulterous affair, not Bathsheba (2 Sam 12:7).

Second, the women had experienced God's extraordinary work to bear children: Tamar had a son with her father-in-law, Rahab had been a prostitute, Ruth was married to her dead husband's relative, and Bathsheba had an adulterous relationship. The problem with this is that in the OT, God's extraordinary work is seen more in the lives of barren women who bore children, like Sarah, Rebekah, and Rachel, but they were not included.

Third, the women had connections with Gentiles: Tamar to the Canaanites, Rahab to Jericho, Ruth to Moabites, and Bathsheba to the Hittites. This, however, does not explain why Mary was also included in the list.

Fourth, the women in the list were a challenge to the male-centered culture. Irene Nowell writes that the four women represent women "who have endured discrimination and false judgment, who have suffered through difficult pregnancies and childbirth, and who know how to use devious means to achieve their purposes."[9] Although it is true that Matthew was challenging some of the things that were considered normal in their culture, it is hard to see how Mary used "devious means" to get what she wanted.

Fifth, the women served as God's instrument at crucial points in Israel's history.[10] The first four suggestions may have some truth, but it seems that this one makes the most sense. Genesis 49:9–12 foresees a king coming from the descendants of Judah, and this became possible because Tamar bore sons for Judah after Judah's sons died. When Israel was about to take possession of the Promised Land, Rahab helped the Israelites enter Canaan (Josh 2:8–14).

---

8. Several studies were done in the past to explain why these women were included in Jesus' genealogy. For a brief summary of the previous works, see Edwin D. Freed, "The Women in Matthew's Genealogy," *JSNT* 29, no. 1 (1987): 3–5; Raymond E. Brown, *The Birth of the Messiah: A Commentary on the Infancy Narratives on the Gospels of Matthew and Luke* (New York: Doubleday, 1977), 71–74.
9. Irene Nowell, "Jesus' Great-Grandmothers: Matthew's Four and More," *CBQ* 70, no. 1 (2008): 15.
10. Wim J. C. Weren, "The Five Women in Matthew's Genealogy," *CBQ* 59, no. 2 (1997): 290.

Ruth's love and faithfulness to her mother-in-law and late husband was the reason she married Boaz, and eventually she gave birth to Obed, David's grandfather (Ruth 4:21–22). Bathsheba's relationship with David may not be ideal, but through the reign of her son Solomon, God's promise to David began to come true (1 Kgs 2:4). This is because God is faithful to Israel (1:37; 3:10–15). Finally, Mary gave birth to Jesus.

Often forgotten in the discussion is Uriah the Hittite, whose wife was Solomon's mother (Matt 1:6).[11] He was a loyal general of David who became the victim of David's selfish passions. In some ways, for Matthew to call Solomon's mother "Uriah's wife" (Bathsheba is not mentioned) is already a vindication for him, and a constant reminder that Jesus' human ancestry is far from ideal. For sure, Jesus did not choose who should be his ancestors, and there may be some things that are embarrassing in his family history. This shows the truthfulness of this record, and that Matthew did not clean-up Jesus' genealogy in order to make him look good. It is also clear that God is in control of history, and that despite those shameful things that happened in the past, God's presence remained with his people. In fact, it was through these embarrassments that God's power is made clearer. Jesus' genealogy is a testimony of God's work throughout history.[12]

1:6b–11 Jesus, the Son of David

Matthew has more to say about David the king than about Abraham. Among the Judean kings (or the "kings of the Jews"), only David was given this designation (1:6). The parables of Jesus suggest the kingship of the LORD (18:23; 22:2, 7, 11, 13). Aside from David and the God of Israel, only two other individuals are designated as king in Matthew's Gospel: Herod the Great, who ruled over the Jews on behalf of Rome (2:1, 3, 19); and Jesus, who is presented as the real king of the Jews (2:2; 21:5; 27:11, 29, 37, 42). Both Joseph (1:20) and Jesus (21:9, 15; 22:42) were designated as "son of David." Matthew recalls the incident when David ate the consecrated bread while escaping from Saul (12:3–4; see also 1 Sam 21:1–6). David was also acknowledged as the inspired author of the Psalms (Matt 22:42–45).[13]

---

11. For more discussions, see Jason Hood, *The Messiah, His Brothers, and the Nations: Matthew 1.1–17*, LNTS 441 (New York: T. & T. Clark, 2011), 119–138.
12. Peter Fiedler, *Das Matthäusevangelium*, TKNT 1 (Stuttgart: Kohlhammer, 2006), 38.
13. Jouette M. Bassler, "A Man for All Seasons: David in Rabbinic and New Testament Literature," *Int* 40, no. 2 (1986): 162.

It is noteworthy that Matthew uses the designation "son of David" in his narration of Jesus' healing ministry (9:27; 12:23; 15:22; 20:30–31), and not only in relation to his role as the Messiah (21:9, 15; 22:42). Like Abraham, David was also a recipient of God's promises (2 Sam 7:12–16; 22:51; Pss 89:29, 36–37; 132:11–17). To some extent, God's promises to David were an extension of his promises to Abraham: (1) a "great name" (2 Sam 7:9); (2) the land where Abraham's descendants could dwell peacefully (7:10–12); and (3) the establishment of David's descendants as rulers over God's people (7:13, 16). The kingdom over which David's descendants would reign is called the "kingdom of the LORD" (1 Chr 28:5; 2 Chr 13:8). Together with God's promises to David is a reminder of God's presence with him, "I have been with you wherever you have gone" (2 Sam 7:9), and his presence with Israel (7:7).

1:12–17 Jesus, the Son of Jeconiah

The phrase "son of Jeconiah" (Matt 1:11, 12) is not used by Matthew. Shame accompanies defeat and exile (see Esth 2:6; Jer 24:1; 27:20); and Jeconiah experienced humiliation because of the Babylonian invasion of Jerusalem. Compared to Abraham and David, Jeconiah seems to be less significant. Nonetheless, the period of Jeconiah's reign is an important turning point in Jewish history because he was at the beginning of the period of deportation. Early Jewish traditions show that Jeconiah was the reigning king during Nebuchadnezzar's military expedition to Jerusalem (1 Chr 3:16–17; Esth 2:6; Jer 24:1; 27:20; 29:2). More importantly, Jeconiah was the recipient of God's promise of the return of the exiles (Jer 28:4).[14]

Interestingly, Matthew presents only Judah (Matt 1:2) and Jeconiah (1:11) as representatives of their brothers. Perez and Zerah are mentioned together, but only Perez's descendants are named; Jacob's twin brother Esau is not even mentioned. It is difficult to be certain about the importance of the phrases "Judah and his brothers" and "Jeconiah and his brothers," but the similarity between Judah and Jeconiah is clear: they were both removed from their homeland to live in a foreign land, and in both cases, the nations

---

14. Writings outside the Bible also recount this Nebuchadnezzar's invasion of Jerusalem while Jeconiah was king (Additions to Esther 1:4). Other works say that Jeconiah, together with the other Judean princes in exile, gathered together with Baruch to pray and confess the sins of the nation before God as the latter read the words he wrote while in exile (Baruch 1:3–9). Jewish rabbis also present him as the one who led the people in repentance, thus, releasing them from the curse of their sins and securing a good future for the nation. Charles Thomas Davis, "The Fulfillment of Creation: A Study of Matthew's Genealogy," *JAAR* 41, no. 4 (1973): 530.

where they lived were super powers of their era that enslaved the Jews. Judah went to Egypt, Jeconiah to Babylon; but these super powers were not able to sustain their rule. Consequently, the Jews returned to their land.

The exile recalls the Lord's promises for obedience, which included abundance of harvest (Lev 26:4–5), peace in the land (26:6), dominance over their enemies (26:7–8), fruitfulness (26:9–10), and *God's continuous presence* (26:11). At the same time, it recalls his warnings against disobedience, the consequences of which include diseases (26:16), dominance by their enemies (Lev 26:17–18), inability of the land to yield crops (26:16, 20), death (26:22, 38–39), famine (26:26, 29), desolation of their land (26:22, 30–32), unnecessary fears (26:36), and exile or loss of land (26:33). Despite the severity of the Lord's punishment for their sins, he offered hope of restoration (26:40–42) and a renewed promise of his presence, "I will walk among you and be your God, and you will be my people" (26:12; see also 26:45).

At present, there are countless OFWs (Overseas Filipino Workers) scattered around the world. Many of them went abroad because of poverty and because they wanted a better life for their families; others could not find a job that fitted their skills. They live like exiles scattered around the world. Whatever the reason for being uprooted, whether their choice is out of priority or necessity, one thing is sure – God can be present in the life of those who trust and obey him, whether at "home" or otherwise.[15]

Matthew claims that there are three fourteen-generation epochs from Abraham to Jesus (Matt 1:17). From Abraham to David, from David to Jeconiah and the exile, and from the exile to Jesus. This means that there should be a total of forty-two generations between them. However, considering that there are only forty-one names in the list raises a question concerning the historical accuracy of the list and the significance of the three fourteen generations. What is the point of having three fourteen-generation eras?

Previous studies were done to explain the significance of this arrangement. Some say that Matthew was using *gematria*, a form of numerology practiced by ancient Jews, wherein each letter of the Hebrew alphabet is assigned a numerical equivalent. Incidentally, in Hebrew, the name David has three characters, *dwd*; and the numerical equivalent of *d* is 4 and *w* is 6, hence a total of 14. Others say that Matthew has the same understanding as the author 2 Baruch, an extra-biblical Jewish writing similar to the Book of Revelation,

---

15. For more readings about ministries to OFWs, see Ana M. Gamez, *Blessing OFWs to Bless the Nations: How to Set Up an OFW Ministry in Your Church* (Makati: Church Strengthening Ministry, 2012).

that divided history into fourteen eras.¹⁶ Matthew's reason for arranging the genealogy in this way is hard to ascertain, but God's continuous work in these three eras is clear (see Figure 2): God wanted his people to be a blessing to the nations and this was possible if they recognized his rule (Abraham–David); but his people refused to acknowledge his kingship and so they suffered its consequences (David–exile); yet despite their failure, God provided hope for them and this will be completed through Jesus (exile–Jesus).

Figure 2: Message of the Three Fourteen-Generation Eras[17]

Abraham–David	David–Exile	Exile–Jesus
⇧	⇘	⇧
God wants his people to be a blessing to others, but they have to obey him.	The people refused to be under God's rule; they suffered the consequences of their disobedience.	God provides them a hope of salvation through Jesus the savior.

---

16. John Mark Jones, "Subverting the Textuality of Davidic Messianism: Matthew's Presentation of the Genealogy and the Davidic Title," *CBQ* 56, no. 2 (1994): 266. See also 2 Baruch 53–74.

17. The genealogy reveals God's nature of mercy, justice, and faithfulness expressed in an "N-shaped" (ñøñ) record: (1) ñ Abraham-David – promise fulfilled (faithfulness); (2) ø David-Exile – sin and its consequence (justice); and (3) ñ Exile-Jesus – forgiveness and restoration (mercy). See also Frederick Dale Bruner, *Matthew: A Commentary,* 2 vols. (Grand Rapids: Eerdmans, 2004), 1:21.

FAMILY MATTERS

Just as Matthew starts his gospel with Jesus' ancestors and locates him in a family within time and space, so we all are part of extended biological families. The Chinese language captures and reflects the variety and richness of these relations: I call my father's sister "Gu Gu" but I call my mother's sister "Ee Ee," with additional words to determine if they are older or younger than my parents. In English these are all my "aunts." In Chinese the nuance of the relationship is revealed in how I address them. These relationships are important as they shape us.

We cannot choose our ancestors or extended families, but in God's sovereignty, this is our immediate context. Jesus did not "choose" prostitutes or foreigners to be his ancestors, but we see God's sovereignty and faithfulness: naming some worthy characters like Ruth but referring to Solomon's mother with the loaded term "Uriah's wife." As we look into our families, we will find relatives who are noble and good and whose characteristics we may wish to emulate. We may also find some black sheep, or we may be embarrassed about a cousin who is a criminal, or an aunt who gambles. Yet even in that situation we trust that God, who works all things for good, all our family's influences can be positive for us.

Often, there is religious diversity within one's extended family. This is partly because there are many other religions which are prevalent, and partly because many Christians are converted outside the home, such as in school. Hence our families become a microcosm of the larger context of religious diversity, and possibly economic diversity as well.

This diversity in the extended family leads to various challenges for Christians. Since family bonds are highly regarded and there are expectations for participation as family gathers for events, festivities and rituals, Christians have to decide when and whether they can participate. When a festival is cultural with minimal religious elements, such as Chinese New Year, celebrating a birthday or anniversary or a harvest festival, Christians can take part.

For example, the Taoists observe the *Qing Ming*, the annual event when the Chinese visit the graves of their ancestors to clean them, and make offerings and pray to their ancestors. Christians should be present to show their respect to their ancestors and may help in cleaning the graves, but will not pray to their ancestors. Presence at the event shows that they are part of the family, while non-participation in the ritual shows that Christians worship Yahweh. For rituals like these, Christians may consider substituting other practices which equally shows that they honor, love and respect their ancestors.

However, there are situations when a young Christian may face much pressure to take part in some rituals of other religions. In this case the body of Christ, as the spiritual family, should be there to support and protect that

> Christian, and not pass judgment on him. While taking part in such rituals is not ideal, in the short term there may be times when a Christian may need to participate in some rituals in order to preserve family harmony, with the long-term view of presenting the gospel in the future.
>
> Though family matters and family relationships are important, Jesus established a new family whose members are bound together by his blood; made up of those who do the will of his Father in heaven (12:50). In the kingdom of God, Christians have this family, sisters and brothers who are also followers of Christ in the power of the Holy Spirit. This Christian family transcends racial and cultural bounds and its members can show love and support in difficult and stressful times. That support is a powerful witness and testimony that the Christian family on earth tries to embody the teachings of Jesus.
>
> **Kiem-Kiok Kwa**

1:18–25 JESUS, THE SAVIOR

Every last Monday of August, the Philippines celebrate the National Heroes Day to remember the unnamed heroes of the *Katipunan*. Aside from this day, there are other days in the Philippine calendar marked to remember the heroes who fought against the colonizers like Spain, America, and Japan. These heroes are in many ways considered "saviors" who delivered the people from the hands of foreign rulers. The Jews during Jesus' days were no different. When they thought of a savior, they were very likely thinking of a hero who would liberate them from foreign rulers, in particular, from their Roman rulers.

However, being under Rome was not the root, but only a symptom, of a deeper problem. The OT, particularly the prophets, shows that foreign rule was one of the consequences of Israel's unfaithfulness, and many pious Jews saw that the way to be delivered from their foreign oppressors was through their repentance and through God's forgiveness. Matthew also emphasizes the necessity of repentance and forgiveness, but he makes clear that there is more to salvation than being liberated from foreign rule. Salvation is being free from foreign rule to be under God's rule (or to be part of the kingdom of God), and this story of salvation begins with the birth of the savior.

1:18–19 Betrothal and Plan to Divorce

The story of Jesus' birth begins with background information concerning Mary's betrothal to Joseph. Arranged marriage is still common in many Asian countries. This is done for various reasons. In some cases, the parents of the bride or groom may simply want to ensure that their child would be joined to a family that they trust. In other cases, the parents want to make sure their child marries someone that belongs to the same social class. Still others do so because of superstition. A fortune-teller may have informed the parents of the couple that the marriage would bring good luck and fortune, or a geomancer may have informed them that the birthdates of the bride and groom made them the best match.

In the OT, marriages were arranged among relatives. For example, Isaac married his cousin's daughter Rebekah (Gen 24:3–4, 15) and Jacob married his cousins Leah and Rachel (28:2). Race and religious beliefs were two distinct yet inseparable reasons for such practice (24:3; 28:1, 6–8; Deut 7:3; Josh 23:12) – parents arranged their children's marriage to make sure their future in-laws would not lead their children away from their beliefs. Thus, when Matthew says that Joseph and Mary were betrothed to each other, he may be suggesting that both of them were born to pious parents who wanted to ensure that neither of them would lose faith. Matthew also points to the piety of Mary and Joseph; Mary's virginity was mentioned twice (Matt 1:18, 25) suggesting her sexual purity, and Joseph's unwillingness to place Mary in a shameful situation shows his righteousness (1:19; see also Deut 22:13–21).

Matthew introduces Mary as "his (Jesus') mother" (Matt 1:18). He also consistently refers to her as "his mother" from the time of Jesus' birth until his death (1:18; 2:11, 13, 14, 20, 21; 12:46; 13:55). There are only three instances in the Gospel wherein Mary is not referred to as Jesus' mother: (1) to whom Joseph was a husband and by whom Jesus was born (1:16); (2) as the wife of Joseph (1:20); and (3) the mother of James and Joseph (27:61; see also 13:55). The description "his mother" is not really necessary after Mary is introduced in Matthew 1:18, except in 27:61 to distinguish Mary the mother of Jesus from Mary Magdalene and the other Mary. Matthew's use of such expression only suggests that in his Gospel, Mary's identity is dependent on her relationship with Jesus. The child in Mary's womb is said to be "through the Holy Spirit" (1:18). The reason it is possible to talk about Jesus being both human and divine is because his origin is both human (Mary) and divine (Holy Spirit). For Jesus to have been begotten by God suggests that he has a unique role in the fulfillment of God's plans (Ps 2:6–7). Joseph's abstinence further stresses that he was not the biological father of Jesus.[18]

Matthew does not provide details as to when and how Mary discovered her pregnancy; but he recalls how Joseph responded by planning to "divorce her quietly" (Matt 1:19). There is no question that honor of the *family* is at stake here,[19] just as it is in the case of "honor killings" that are practiced in many countries in the western part of Asia, even until the present. Joseph wanted to divorce Mary quietly for two reasons: first, because he was righteous, and second, in order not to shame Mary (1:19). In an honor/shame culture, one dishonorable act can permanently damage a person's reputation. At times, negative proverbs also develop based on one dishonorable act of a person.[20] It was scandalous for Mary to be pregnant before being married and it would have resulted in various forms of prejudice both for her and her child.[21]

The Jewish Law also contains provisions that protect rape victims; these provisions include protection for women who are already betrothed (Deut 22:23–27). However, as required by the provisions in the OT, Mary's untimely pregnancy might also have resulted in her execution if her pregnancy was with her consent (Deut 22:23–24), but there was no hint that this was the case. Yet even if Mary was spared, the reproach of having a child out of wedlock remained; and the just Joseph chose to protect Mary, and also her child, from a shameful predicament.

1:20–25 Divine Revelation through Dreams and Prophecy, and the Naming of the Child

The first instance of divine revelation in Matthew comes in the form of an angelic appearance in Joseph's dream (Matt 1:20).[22] This form of revelation

---

18. Andrew T. Lincoln, "Contested Paternity and Contested Readings: Jesus' Conception in Matthew 1.18–25," *JSNT* 34, no. 3 (2012): 214–215; Herman C. Waetjen, "The Genealogy as the Key to the Gospel according to Matthew," *JBL* 95, no. 2 (1976): 216 nn. 55–56.
19. Matthew J. Marhohl, *Joseph's Dilemma: "Honor Killing" in the Birth Narrative of Matthew* (Eugene, OR: Cascade Books, 2008), 34–37
20. There are proverbs that originated from a person's wrong deeds (Deut 28:37; Ezek 16:44; Hab 2:6).
21. For example, Sirach 23:22–26; Wisdom of Solomon 3:16–19. Illegitimate children were ostracized even though it was not their fault that they were illegitimate (4:3–6).
22. In the Ancient Near Eastern writings, such as the *Epic of Gilgamesh*, dreams have a literary purpose because they convey the message that there are predetermined future events or they are included to answer present practical concerns of the character in the story. In Greco-Roman and Second Temple writings, dreams are used to justify a political cause. Ancient rabbis have various ways of assessing the value of dreams, some thought it was just an extension

is also seen in the OT (Gen 15:1–16; 28:10–17; 37:1–17; Deut 13:1; Dan 1:17; 2:1–49; 4:1–37; 5:12; 7:1–28).[23] Dreams were considered a means of divine revelation in the ancient Mediterranean world.

Among the religions from Asia, Islam has valued dreams more than others with its numerous reports of people receiving divine revelation through night visions.[24] Christianity throughout the centuries lost interest in this topic (to our loss). Some even considered dreams as demonic in origin. For example, John Climacus (525–605), also known as John of the Ladder, writes: "The man who believes in dreams shows his inexperience, while the man who distrusts every dream is very sensible. Trust only dreams that foretell torments and judgments for you, but even these dreams may also be from demons if they produce despair in you."[25] Christianity today either responds in distrust, reluctance, or indifference towards this issue, with the result that there is not much investigation about the validity of dreams and its interpretation. Nonetheless, Christianity, in general, accepts the biblical writers' claim that divine revelation was channeled through dreams.

Like Joseph the son of Jacob and Rachel (Gen 30:24–25), Joseph the son of Jacob and the husband of Mary (Matt 1:16) was also a recipient of divine revelation through dreams (Matt 1:20–21; see also Gen 37:5–11). Angelic appearances in dreams are recorded in the OT (Gen 28:12; 31:11). The angel's command to Joseph, "do not be afraid," is an expression typically found in the announcements of the angels (Matt 1:20; see also Gen 21:17; 2 Kgs 1:17; Judg 6:23). The angel's address to Joseph as "son of David" once again

---

of one's thoughts during the day, while others see it in relation to prophecy. Dreams were also considered a means of divine revelation in the ancient Mediterranean world. This is evident among the Greek writers like Herodotus (*Histories* 7.12.1–19.3), Diodorus (*Historical Library* 34/35.2.7–8), Suetonius (*Galba* 4.3). Even Josephus claims to receive divine revelation through dreams (*Life* 42 §208). See Str-B, 1:53–54; Derek S. Dobson, *Reading Dreams: An Audience-Critical Approach to the Dreams in the Gospel of Matthew*, LNTS 397 (New York: T. & T. Clark, 2009), 133; William J. Subash, *The Dreams of Matthew 1:18–2:23: Tradition, Form, and Theological Investigation*, StBibLit 149 (New York: Peter Lang, 2012), 56–57, 126.

23. For more examples, see Craig S. Keener, *Miracles: The Credibility of the New Testament Accounts*, 2 vols. (Grand Rapids: Baker Academics, 2011), 2:872–875.

24. Bill Musk, "Dreams and the Ordinary Muslim," *Missio* 16, no. 2 (1988): 163–178. Oneiromancy (or the "science" of interpreting dreams) is considered a significant part of Muslim spirituality (Zeina Matar, "Dreams and Dream Interpretation in the *Faraj al-Mahmūm* of Ibn Ṭāwūs," *MW* 80, nos. 3–4 [1990]: 165–166; see also Keener, *Miracles*, 2:875–884). This was a practice generally accepted by ancient Jews.

25. John Climacus, *The Ladder of Divine Ascent*, trans. Colm Luibheid and Norman Russell. The Classics of Western Spirituality (New York: Paulist Press, 1982), 89–90.

underscores the royal lineage of Joseph's adoptive child, but his being "from the Holy Spirit" (Matt 1:20) points to the child's divine origin.[26]

The naming of the child is also part of God's revelation. It points to the child's vocation as the savior (Matt 1:21). Ancient Israelites named their children so as to remember the significant events/circumstances surrounding the child's birth (Peleg [Gen 10:25], Noah [5:29], Ichabod [1 Sam 4:21]). Names can sometimes reflect the person's character (Nabal [5:25]). Some names are predictive, showing what the person would become after he/she was given the name (Eve [Gen 3:20], Abraham [17:5], Sarah [17:15–16]). In the case of Jesus, the angels instructed Joseph to name Mary's child "Jesus" (or Joshua which means "the LORD saves") because the name reveals what would become of the child – the savior. Another name given to the child was Immanuel in fulfillment of Isaiah's prophecy (Matt 1:23; Isa 7:14). Isaiah's prophecy concerns the "house of David" (7:13), which was in danger of being destroyed because of the Assyrian's threat (7:17) and Ahaz's refusal to trust in the LORD. Although the Jews had been unfaithful to God and they were exiled as a result of it, God remained faithful to his promise to David. Matthew points to Isaiah's prophecy being fulfilled in Jesus, showing that the prophecy extended beyond the reign of Ahaz. Jesus' birth is the clearest evidence that God had not abandoned his people, and that his presence would continue through the birth of the savior.

God's presence can either be an assurance of his protection (Ps 46:7, 11) or the certainty of his judgment (Isa 8:8, 10). The promise of his presence assured his people that despite continuous foreign domination (Assyria and Babylon during Isaiah's days and Rome during Jesus'), God would continue to reign, and that this is manifested through the birth of the "son of David."

Matthew presents Jesus as the Immanuel ("God with us"), which means that God is present with the people through Jesus (Matt 1:23); and at the end of the Gospel, Jesus promised his disciples that his presence would continue to be with them "to the very end of the age" (28:20; see also Figure 3).[27] This suggests that Jesus' earthly life and ministry is the clearest evidence of God's presence with his people, so that in everything Jesus did, his teachings and miracles, God's faithfulness to his people is clear. Even after Jesus ascended

---

26. Philip A. King, "Matthew and Epiphany," *Worship* 36, no. 2 (1962): 92.
27. Ulrich Luz, *The Theology of the Gospel of Matthew* (trans. J. Bradford Robinson; Cambridge: Cambridge University Press, 1995), 4–5. David B. Capes correctly points out the need to examine how this theme developed in the individual episodes in Matthew ("Intertextual Echoes in the Matthean Baptismal Narrative," *BBR* 9 [1999]: 37–38).

to heaven, his presence continues with those who were and those who would become his disciples.

Figure 3: God's Presence in Matthew's Gospel

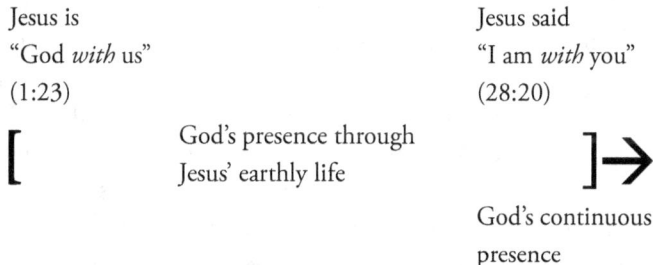

2:1–15 JESUS, THE SON

Many Chinese people are fatalistic and claim that whatever happens to them is because of *tiān yì* (天意) or "heaven's will." The Bible is clear that events do not happen by chance, but that there is a God behind the events that happen in the world. It is God who makes plans, reveals these plans through prophecies, and works in human lives and guides them so that what he planned may be brought to completion. God's work is accomplished within human history. This is illustrated in the story of Jesus' birth, how God revealed his plans through prophecies and how he orchestrated history to bring his purposes to completion.

2:1–12 The Magi Receive Revelation from God about Jesus' Birth

Jesus was born "during the time of King Herod" (Matt 2:1).[28] In the first century, the term "king" could refer either to Caesar or to the ruler he appointed

---

28. Note that there are six Herodian rulers mentioned in the Gospels and Acts: (1) Herod the Great or "King Herod" who ordered the killing of the infants (2:1; Luke 1:5), the King Herod mentioned in this story; (2) Archelaus the ethnarch, who is never called Herod in the Gospels (Matt 2:22); (3) Philip the tetrarch, also not referred to as Herod and whose former wife married his brother Antipas (14:3; Mark 6:17; Luke 3:1); (4) Herod Antipas, usually called "Herod the tetrarch" and who was responsible for the death of John the Baptist (Matt 14:1–12; Mark 6:14–29; Luke 3:1, 19–20; 9:17–21; 13:31; 23:6–17; Acts 4:27; see also Mark 6:14); (5) Agrippa I, who was also called "Herod the King" and was behind the death of James (Acts 12:1–13:1); and (6) Agrippa II or "Herod Agrippa" before whom Paul was tried (23:35; 25:13–26:32).

to govern a Roman province on his behalf, like Herod the Great. These governors were often called "client kings," who functioned like the emperor's puppets and carries out his orders.[29] Although Herod was acknowledged as king of Judea (Matt 2:1, 3), he was not "born king of the Jews" like Jesus (2:2). Matthew makes it clear that Jesus, the one born in David's city (2:2, 4; see also 1 Sam 17:12; Luke 2:4; John 7:42), was the real and legitimate king. The Herodians were no more than pretenders who reigned only because of their attachment with Rome.[30] Many Jews actually disliked the Herodians because: (1) they were Idumeans and not Jews, and (2) although they had many accomplishments, they were tyrants. Nonetheless, some treated them like gods and even considered them as a dynasty of messiahs.[31] In Matthew, Jesus is the real Messiah, not Herod the Great and his descendants.

Matthew witnesses to another form of divine revelation aside from dreams (Matt 1:20–23), the signs in the sky observed by the "Magi from the east" (2:2), whose origin recalls earlier diviners like Balaam who was also "from the eastern mountains" (Num 23:7). The identity of the magi remains unclear despite many attempts to discover it, but it is clear that they were Gentiles. The good news was proclaimed to non-Jews even at the time of Jesus' birth, and the magi were the first Gentiles in Matthew's Gospel who acknowledged the kingship of Jesus.[32]

Ancient accounts show that magi (Greek *magos* or *magoi*) from the east were interpreters of dreams; they also practiced magic and sorcery. Some church fathers considered the magi as kings, but many modern interpreters no longer hold this view, although the idea remains popular in many religious symbols such as the Christmas *belén*. Ancient magi were associated with the royal courts (Dan 2:10; 2 Tim 3:8). Thus, identifying the magi

---

29. Richard Vinson, "'King of the Jews': Kingship and Anti-kingship Rhetoric in Matthew's Birth, Baptism, and Transfiguration Narratives," *RevExp* 104, no. 2 (2007): 244.

30. See David R. Bauer, "The Kingship of Jesus in the Matthean Infancy Narrative: A Literary Analysis," *CBQ* 57, no. 2 (1995): 308.

31. Josephus tells us that the Pharisees was one of the groups that were against the rule of the Herodians because they were not Jews (*Jewish Antiquities* 17.2.4 § 41). However, there were loyalists who treat them like gods (Acts 12:22), and some even considered them as the messianic dynasty (Pseudo-Tertullian, *Against All Heresies* 1.1; Jerome, *Lucifer* 23). See also Joan E. Taylor, *The Essenes, the Scrolls, and the Dead Sea* (Oxford: Oxford University Press, 2012), 125; Savas Agourides, "The Birth of Jesus and the Herodian Dynasty: An Understanding of Matthew, ch. 2," *GOTR* 37, nos. 1–2 (1992): 139–141, nn. 17–21.

32. Dorothy Jean Weaver, "Rewriting the Messianic Script: Matthew's Account of the Birth of Jesus," *Int* 54, no. 4 (2004): 385.

as kings is understandable yet unnecessary.[33] Unlike the magi in the court of Nebuchadnezzar, king of Babylon (Dan 4:7; 5:15), those in Matthew's Gospel were not incompetent interpreters of dreams, but were skilled in understanding divine signs. All they lacked was the biblical knowledge that could be the basis for their understanding the revelation. Unlike the *magos* Elymas (or Bar-Jesus), the Jewish false prophet from Paphos who tried to dissuade the proconsul Sergius Paulus from believing in Jesus (Acts 13:6–8), the *magoi* in the First Gospel sought Jesus to worship him (Matt 2:2). Unlike the *magos* Simon, who sought Jesus for personal gain (Acts 8:9–24), the *magoi* showed sincerity in their search for Jesus (Matt 2:9–12).

Figure 4: Prophecies of Micah and Their Fulfillment in Matthew

Micah	Matthew
Birth of the ruler announced (5:2–3)	Birth of the ruler fulfilled (2:2, 5–6)
No revelation for the prophets and seers in Israel (3:5–7)	Revelation given to the magi, not to the chief priests and scribes (2:1–4)
End of sorcery, fortune-telling, and idolatry (5:12–13)	The magi came to worship Jesus (2:11)
Return from exile (Assyrian) as preparation for the ruler's birth (5:3–4)	Return from exile (Babylonian) as preparation for the ruler's birth (see also 1:11, 17–18)

When Herod heard about the birth of the "king of the Jews," he did not respond positively (2:3). The reason is obvious: if the king had been born, that only meant that his reign would soon end. Matthew comments that Herod was not the only one who was "disturbed" because of the birth of the king; "all Jerusalem" shared the same response (2:3). Matthew also contrasts Herod and the magi; Herod wanted to kill Jesus, but the magi wanted to worship him. This contrast all the more stresses the identity of Jesus as the

---

33. Ancient magi were known to have the ability to interpret dreams (Herodotus, *Histories* 1.132). They practiced magic and sorcery (Tacitus, *Annals* 2.27; 12.22, 59; Pliny, *Natural History* 30.2). Some church fathers consider the magi as kings (Tertullian, *Against Marcion* 3.13.8; Augustine, *Sermons* 200.2). Ancient magi were associated with the royal courts (Strabo, *Geography* 15.1.68; Xenophon, *Cyropaedia* 8.1.23-24; Cassius Dio, *Roman History* 63.1–7; Suetonius, *Nero* 13; Pliny, *Natural History* 30.6.16–17). Tony T. Maalouf, "Were the Magi from Persia or Arabia?" *BSac* 156, no. 2 (1999): 424-425; Mark Alan Powell, "Magi as Kings: An Adventure in Reader-Response Criticism," *CBQ* 62, no. 3 (2000): 467.

divine ruler.[34] Another contrast is between the magi in Micah's prophecy and those in Matthew's Gospel. Jesus' birth fulfilled Micah's prophecy concerning the birth of a descendant of David who would rule as king over Israel (Matt 2:5–6; Mic 5:2; see Figure 4). Micah also mentioned the diviners, prophets, and seers in Israel being disgraced because they had led God's people astray and they had not received any revelation from God (3:5–7). This implies that they had not turned to God, but Micah expected the end of fortune-telling and idolatry (5:12–13). In contrast, the magi in Matthew's Gospel received revelation from God (Matt 2:2). They were not disgraced; instead, they enjoyed God's protection (2:12). Their desire to worship Jesus may also suggest that they had set their hearts to seek God (2:2, 11).

The significance of the *magoi's* gifts is typically explained as follows (2:11): gold for Jesus' royalty, myrrh for his humanity, and frankincense for his deity. Gold, myrrh, and frankincense, however, were not exclusive symbols of royalty, humanity, and deity, respectively.[35] Nonetheless, the preciousness of these gifts show that the recipient was someone highly esteemed, and one presented by Matthew as God's Son (2:15). Matthew may also be playing with words so as to associate Jesus with Solomon, the son of David and his first successor. When Solomon became king, he used only gold vessels in the "House of the Forest of Lebanon (Greek, *Libanos*)" and received gifts of gold and myrrh (1 Kgs 10:21, 25; 2 Chr 9:20, 24). Jesus received gifts of frankincense (Greek, *libanos*), gold, and myrrh (Matt 2:11). If this is the case, it only strengthens Matthew's portrayal of Jesus as the Son of David, the anointed One (Ps 2:7), who would rule on the Lord's behalf. The gifts were all appropriate for a king.

God's revelation was given where it was least expected. Like the ancient magi who practiced things related to occultism, many Asians are involved in various forms of practices such as palm reading, geomancy, and numerology, among others. The story of the magi provides hope for people who may have been involved in various forms of evil practices like sorcery, fortune-telling, and magic. Turning away from these things to God is possible. The birth of the Messiah provides us with the reason to put an end to such practices (Mic 5:12–13). Moreover, Micah foretold that the birth of the ruler would signal the end of Israel's deportation to Assyria, and their return to their land would be the beginning of the Lord's reign over the survivors of the exile (4:7;

---

34. Bauer, "Kingship of Jesus," 323.
35. Edward J. Houdous, "The Gospel of the Epiphany," *CBQ* 6, no. 1 (1944): 83.

5:3–4). This description repeats God's promise to David and his descendants (2 Sam 7:10–16).

2:13–15 Joseph Brings Mary and Jesus to Egypt

Matthew quotes Hosea 11:1 as another prophecy in the series of prophecies fulfilled by Christ (Matt 2:13). Matthew's use of Hosea has been understood in various ways, and the diversity of interpretation shows the difficulty in understanding this passage. This difficulty has even led some to question the validity of the Christian faith.[36] It is worth noting that Hosea's statement is not a prediction of a future event, but it looks back to how the LORD rescued Israel from slavery in Egypt and how he set Israel apart to fulfill his plans (Exod 19:5–6). But Israel, God's son was unfaithful to God after they were called out of Egypt; they broke their promise to God by worshipping other gods. Thus, they were not able to meet the expectations of God (Hos 11:2).[37] God called his Son out of Egypt a second time, but unlike Israel, Jesus is God's obedient Son who would fulfill God's expectation of obedience.[38] Israel may have failed because of their unfaithfulness, but Jesus was victorious because he was obedient. This theme will be further developed in the story of Jesus' temptation (Matt 4:1–11).

2:16–23 JESUS, THE NAZARENE

After Joseph brought Mary and Jesus to Egypt, Herod the Great ordered the killing of the infants thinking that one of them was the "king of the Jews" (Matt 2:2, 16–17), and not knowing that the one who was "born king of the Jews" was already in Egypt (2:2, 14). Throughout history, there are numerous accounts of mass killing like this. More than seven decades ago during the Second World War, thousands of Filipino soldiers were brutally killed during the Bataan Death March (April 9, 1942). During the same period, millions of Jews were massacred in what is known today as the Holocaust. The reasons behind sufferings like these are not easy to explain. The Bible records instances wherein masses of people died because of sin. For example, Noah's

---

36. Julian the Apostate questioned the Christian faith because of this problem. For a summary of various explanations, see Tracy L. Howard, "The Use of Hosea 11:1 and Matthew 2:15: An Alternative Solution," *BSac* 143 (1986): 315–322.
37. Brandon D. Crowe, "Fulfillment in Matthew as Eschatological Reversal," *WTJ* 75, no. 1 (2013): 113.
38. Brandon D. Crowe, *The Obedient Son: Deuteronomy and Christology in the Gospel of Matthew*, BZNW 188 (Berlin: De Gruyter, 2012), 228.

contemporaries (Gen 6:5–8), the people of Sodom and Gomorrah (18:20; 19:12–13), and the people of Canaan (Exod 23:23–25) were cases in point; but this was not the case all the time. Matthew does not say that this was the reason for the death of the children in Bethlehem.

2:16–18 Herod's Attempt to Kill Jesus and Rachel's Tears

Matthew mentions two prophecies that were fulfilled by Jesus: (1) Rachel's weeping, and (2) Jesus' designation as a Nazarene. It did not take long for Herod to realize that the magi were not coming back to inform him where to find the "king of the Jews"; so he ordered children who were two years and younger to be killed (2:16). Josephus called Herod the Great a tyrant and recounted the crimes he committed during his reign. Herod also killed his brother Pheroras upon learning that the latter, according to a divine revelation, would replace him as king.[39] It was clear that the same fear motivated him to order the massacre of the infants (Matt 2:3, 7–8, 16).

Matthew considers the death of the children a fulfillment of Jeremiah's prophecy about Rachel weeping for her children in Ramah (2:17–18; Jer 31:15). At Mount Sinai, God warned his people that unfaithfulness would result in them being scattered abroad (Lev 26:33), and God would use this form of punishment after he had already exhausted all other means to make the people turn back (26:27, 41). In case Israel continued in their disobedience and they refused to repent despite his sending drought, famine, and plagues (26:1–26), then God would scatter them abroad. God, however, offered hope for them to return from exile (26:44–46). The prophet Jeremiah also expected the return of the exiles (Jer 31:7–14), and this would be preceded by a voice of "mourning and great weeping" in Ramah (31:15), where the Jews would be temporarily gathered before their exile to Babylon (40:1). The people might suffer intensely, but this also brings them hope that by the end of this period of punishment, God would renew his covenant with his people (31:16–34).[40] Even after the Jews returned from exile, they would still see themselves as exiles (2 Chr 29:15). With a new ruling empire, the Jews

---

39. Josephus, *Jewish Antiquities* 15.3.1 §§39–41; 15.8.4 §§289–90; 16.11.7 §§392–94; 17.2.4 §§42–44. Josephus does not mention the massacre of infants in his accounts, which led some to question the historicity of Matthew's account (for examples, see Richard T. France, "Herod and the Children of Bethlehem," *NovT* 21, no. 2 [1979]: 98, n. 1). This conclusion is unwarranted, just because Josephus did not recount an event does not mean it did not happen.
40. Eugene Eung-Chun Park, "Rachel's Cry for her Children: Matthew's Treatment of the Infanticide by Herod," *CBQ* 75, no. 3 (2013): 479. Some Jewish rabbis claimed that Jacob buried Rachel in Bethlehem so she can weep for the exiles when they later passed that way

remained under foreign domination; hence, even though they were occupying the land they previously owned, they remained as sojourners and exiles in their own land. Matthew may have understood the more recent tragedy (massacre of the infants) as a continuation of their misfortune as a nation; and just as Rachel wept for her children as they were brought to exile, she continued to weep for the slaughter of her children in Bethlehem. However, as Jeremiah foresaw, after the weeping at Ramah comes God's renewal of his covenant, and for Matthew, this renewal was made possible through Jesus, who taught that the Law is fulfilled not through blind obedience but through understanding its essential principle (Matt 5:21–48; see also Jer 31:33), and whose death made forgiveness of sins possible (Matt 26:28; see also Jer 31:34).

2:19–23 Joseph Brings Mary and Jesus to Nazareth

Divine revelation continued. Joseph was instructed through his dream to leave for Egypt because of Herod's threat and to return only after his death (Matt 2:13, 19), but was warned not to return to Judea because of Archelaus' taking over his father's place (2:20). Archelaus was no less brutal than his father. He overreacted to an uprising by killing 3,000 pilgrims in the temple, resulting in the brutal treatment of many Jews and Samaritans, and so the Roman Emperor Augustus banished him to Gaul.[41] God's control over history is made clear through these incidents. He protected Jesus in order that he might bring to completion what he planned to do for humanity.

Aside from Rachel's tears for her children at Ramah, the second prophecy that was fulfilled was Jesus' designation as the Nazarene. Jesus was called the Nazarene because he grew up in Nazareth, and this designation is also a fulfillment of a prophecy according to Matthew (2:23). In the Philippines, one of the most popular images of Jesus is the Black Nazarene of Quiapo. Devotees believe that if they use a handkerchief to touch the image, the handkerchief will have healing power (see also the discussion on Matthew 9:18–26). In the Gospel of Matthew, Jesus' designation as the Nazarene implies more than just his healing ministry; it has to do with God's forgiveness of his people. Jesus' title as the Nazarene may be related to the "Branch" that would come from the family of David and would rule peacefully (Isa 11:1).

(Genesis Rabbah 82:10). Matthew may have drawn the connection between Genesis 35:19 and Jeremiah 31:15 using Rachel as the common link (Craig S. Keener, *A Commentary on the Gospel of Matthew* [Grand Rapids: Eerdmans, 1999], 111–112).
41. Josephus, *Jewish Wars* 2.7.3 §111; *Jewish Antiquities* 17.13.2 §§342–344.

Matthew claims that Jesus designation as "Nazarene" was a fulfillment of a prophecy. The challenge for interpreters is to pinpoint which OT passage was fulfilled.[42] There are two terms in the NT that can be translated "Nazarene," referring to Jesus' place of origin. First, the term *nazōraios* (Matt 26:71; Luke 18:37; John 18:5, 7; 19:19; Acts 2:8, 22; 3:6; 4:10; 6:14; 22:8; 26:9), which refers to the group of Jesus' followers (Acts 24:5). The believers declare Jesus as king, and the Romans sometimes confused them with rebel groups who refuse to recognize Caesar as king (17:7). Rebel groups were sometimes identified by location of origin; for example, the "Galileans" (Luke 13:1–2). Leaders of the rebel groups were also identified by their place of origin, like, Judas of Galilee (Acts 5:37) and "the Egyptian" (21:38). The use of term *nazōraios* in relation to Jesus' place of origin cannot be ignored (Matt 2:23). Second, NT writers also use the term *nazarēnos* (Luke 4:34; Mark 10:47; 14:67; 16:6; Luke 24:19). Identifying someone based on his/her place of origin is not an unusual practice. For example, Mary was called "Magdalene" because she was from Magdala.

However, Matthew's use of the term Nazarene to refer to Jesus could be more than just a reference to his place of origin, but also to Isaiah's prophecy about "the Branch" (Isa 11:1). The Hebrew word for "branch" is *nezer*. Jesus the Nazarene is the (*nezer*) or "the Branch" (11:1): Matthew's audience, whether Jews or Greeks, should have had no problem hearing the word play. Isaiah was expecting a day to come when Israel's sins would be forgiven, and those who survive the exile would be considered holy (4:3–4), in the same way that those who entered the Promised Land were called "holy" (Exod 19:6). The reign of the Branch would be characterized by peace, and this would mark the return of God's people from exile (Isa 11:1–12).

The story of the miraculous birth of Jesus has similarities with some stories of the founders of other religion that originated from Asia. One example is the story of Rama in the Ramcaritmanas, a sixteenth century Hindu literary work.[43] A number of ancient biographies of emperors also include accounts of their miraculous birth.[44] These similarities should not blind us to the difference. Not only was Jesus' birth, and even his death, anticipated

---

42. For a brief discussion on the various interpretation of this prophecy, see Henry M. Shires, "The Meaning of the Term 'Nazarene,'" *AThR* 29, no. 1 (1947): 19–27.
43. Freek L. Bakker, "The Birth of Jesus and Rama in Christian and Hindu Sacred Texts: An Exercise in New Comparative Theology," *Exchange* 39, no. 2 (2010): 121–146.
44. For example, the supernatural events that surround the birth of Alexander was discussed by Plutarch (*Alexander* 3.1–4) and Aulus Gellius (*Attic Nights* 13.4.1–2), and Suetonius tells

by the prophets of the OT, his resurrection is God's clear affirmation of his identity as the true Messiah.

There is no doubt that the stories about these emperors made them look good in the eyes of the people, and the stories about how they defeated their enemies and how they conquered lands make them appear like gods and superheroes. Matthew's reason for discussing about Jesus' miraculous birth is different. The stories about Jesus' suffering later in the Gospel tell us that Jesus is not a superhero and conqueror like these emperors; but the prophecies that came true because of Jesus' birth show that he was the Messiah for whom the Jews had been waiting.[45] The purpose of the story of Jesus' birth is to introduce Jesus and make clear his identity. Matthew tells us three things about who Jesus is through these stories: (1) Jesus is the savior; (2) Jesus is the Son; and (3) Jesus is the king. All these point out that God is present with his people. The three episodes of Matthew's account of Jesus' birth share some common elements: (1) they present Jesus' identity, (2) they show God's rule through the instructions and various forms of revelation, and (3) they point to the fulfillment of prophecies (see Figure 5 for a summary).

---

the story of Emperor Augustus' miraculous birth (*Augustus* 94.4). Charles H. Talbert provides a list of parallels between Augustus, Romulus, and Jesus (*Matthew* [Paideia; Grand Rapids: Baker Academics, 2010], 319).

45. For longer discussions on what makes Christ's birth unique, see Andrew T. Lincoln, *Born of a Virgin? Reconceiving Jesus in the Bible, Tradition, and Theology* (Grand Rapids: Eerdmans, 2013).

Figure 5: The Identity of Jesus Based on Matthew's Account of His Birth

	1:18–25	2:1–15	2:16–23
Identity of Jesus	Immanuel (1:23) Savior (1:25)	Son (2:11)	Nazarene/Branch (2:25)
Revelation	appearance of angels in dreams (1:20)	appearance of angels in dreams (2:12, 13) celestial signs (2:2, 10)	appearance of angels in dreams (2:20)
Fulfilled prophecy	birth of Immanuel from the house of David (1:23; Isa 7:13–14)	birth of the ruler (2:6; Mic 5:2) God's Son return from Egypt (2:15; Hos 11:1)	Rachel's lament in Ramah (2:18; Jer 31:15) Jesus as the "Branch" or the Nazarene (2:25; Isa 11:1)

The OT quotations also share the same basic message: despite Israel's sin in the past which resulted in their exile, the offer of forgiveness remained. The various forms of revelation (prophecies, signs in heaven, dreams) show that God remains present with his people. The birth of Jesus is also a turning point in history, and his earthly ministry shows that God is at work even in this chaotic world. Jesus is the one who would rule on God's behalf, and the one through whom forgiveness of sins would be made possible.

MATTHEW 3:1–4:16

Preparation for Jesus' Public Ministry

The sending of messengers (envoys or ambassadors, or whatever we may call them) on behalf of the nation's leader prior to the latter's visit is a common practice today, and even in ancient times (Josh 9:4; 2 Chr 32:31). John, as Jesus' messenger, also "arrives" to announce the coming of the king.

Matthew's statement "in those days" (Matt 3:1) refers to the period three decades after the events in Matthew 1–2, which coincides with the latter years of Herod Antipas' reign in Galilee (2 BC–AD 39). Even after three decades, God's presence remained, and his presence was manifested in the life and ministry of John.

3:1–12 JOHN THE BAPTIST: THE MAN, HIS MINISTRY, AND HIS MESSAGE

3:1–2 John Calls for Repentance

John's message is the same message Jesus would preach later, "Repent, for the kingdom of heaven has come near" (Matt 3:2; 4:17). In Matthew, "nearness" may refer to closeness in time (21:34; 26:45) or space (21:1, 46). The "nearness" of the "kingdom of heaven" can also be understood in terms of both space and time. In short, John was telling the Jews that they could be under God's rule "here" and "now." This is the same message for us today; wherever we are, we can acknowledge God as the Supreme Ruler, and we can be under his rule.

Ancient Chinese use *tiān* (天) or "heaven" to refer to God. This practice of avoiding the use of personal name is one way to show honor. Even now, a typical Chinese will not call their pastors or teachers by their first name as a way of showing respect. The same can be said about many ancient Jews. The "kingdom of heaven" and "the kingdom of God" are two expressions that are essentially the same – both highlight the character (it is of "heaven," not merely of "earth"), and the origin and the one in authority (it is of God, not of human).[1]

3:3–4 John the Man

The physical description of Bible characters is provided only when they are significant. For example, the stature of Saul (1 Sam 9:2) and Zacchaeus (Luke 19:3), the built of king Eglon of Moab (Judg 3:19), the physical appearance of Leah and Rachel (Gen 29:17), the skin color of Solomon's Shunnamite wife (Song 1:5), and the garment of Joseph (Gen 37:3) are important details in their respective stories. In the case of John the Baptist, it is his clothing and diet that attract attention.

First, Matthew describes John's clothing: "clothes made of camel's hair and he had a leather belt around his waist" (3:3–4). This recalls Elijah's description. The Jews had been expecting the coming of Elijah before the Messiah (Mal 4:5–6), and Matthew is clear that John is the one they had been waiting for (Matt 11:14). More importantly, Matthew shows God's reign and power by arranging events in order to prepare for the coming of Jesus.

Eating certain food is often a matter of personal preference and availability, but some foods are associated with certain people groups. What one people group considers edible may not necessarily be appetizing for another group; and what one group considers exotic may be common in another place. For example, bulls' testicles are eaten in Afghanistan; fried tarantula in Cambodia; monkeys' brain in China; *sushi* (raw fish) in Japan; *beondegi* (silkworm larvae) in Korea; barbequed guinea pigs in Peru; *balut* (duck embryo) in the Philippines; chili scorpions in Thailand; squirrels in the USA; and paddy rats in Vietnam; and let us not forget that the ancient Israelites ate quails (Exod 16:13; Num 11:31–32; see also Ps 105:40). There are various reasons why certain groups eat certain kinds of food. Poverty, scarcity or availability of certain foods in a region, and religious beliefs are some of the reasons people eat or avoid certain foods. John's diet of locusts and wild honey, together with his clothing (Matt 3:1–12; Mark 1:5–6), are not mere trivia, but essential in understanding John's ministry. Interpreters from the

---

1. Jewish writings like the Mishnah can help us understand Matthew's use of the expression "kingdom of heaven." (The Mishnah is a collection of teachings of many 1st century Jewish rabbis that were handed down as oral traditions. The collection was produced in the 2nd century, but it provides us with some ideas about the practices of the Jews during the 1st century). In this collection, "heaven" is used as an alternative word for "God" (*Avot* 1:3, 11; 2:2, 12; 4:4, 11, 12; 5:17), and the expression "the Name of His Kingdom" also refers to the "Kingdom of God" (*Yoma* 3:8).

earlier centuries were inclined to underscore the simplicity of John's attire (for example, Chromatus, Maximus of Turin, Peter Chrysologus). They considered this as a symbol for repentance.[2]

More interpreters see John's clothing of "camel's hair and leather belt" (Matt 3:4; Mark 1:6) as a way of associating him with Elijah the Tishbite, who "wore a garment of hair, with a belt of leather about his waist" (2 Kgs 1:8; Zech 13:4).[3] Matthew uses exactly the same Greek expression *zōnēn dermatinēn* or "leather belt" as the Greek OT. John's physical description shows that he was the Elijah whom the Jews were expecting (Matt 17:10; see also Mal 4:5–6).[4]

The significance of using the skin of an unclean animal (see Lev 11:4; Deut 14:7) is unclear. It may be a symbol that John was identifying himself with the "unclean" Gentiles or the sinful humanity who need repentance. If this is so, it only points to the global extent of God's salvation. What is clear is that being "clean" or "unclean" does not depend on externals, such us touching or avoiding "unclean" animals (see Matt 15:10); the clean "fruits" come as a result of repentance (3:8).

Second, Matthew describes John's diet: locusts and wild honey. According to some early Jewish writings, some Judeans were able to survive eating only wilderness food, and in some cases, wilderness food was the staple for those who desired to avoid defilement.[5] John's diet of wild honey is closely related to his ministry as the voice in the wilderness (Matt 3:3–4; Mark 1:4–6), in the same way that Elijah was a prophet in the wilderness (1 Kgs 19:4, 15). Locust was in the list of "clean food" that the Israelites were allowed to consume (Lev 11:21–22); and ancient records show eating locusts was also common among the ancient Greeks.[6] Aside from locusts, John also consumed honey. In the OT, honey is associated with God's word (Pss 19:10; 119:103;

---

2. Manlio Simonetti, ed., *Matthew 1–13* (ACCS New Testament 1A; Downers Grove, IL: InterVarsity, 2001), 40–41; James A. Kelhoffer, "Early Christian Studies Among the Academic Disciplines: Reflections on John the Baptist's 'Locusts and Wild Honey,'" *BR* 50 (2005): 5–6.
3. For example, Leon Morris, *The Gospel according to Matthew*, PNTC (Grand Rapids: Eerdmans, 1992), 55; R. T. France, *Matthew*, NICNT (Grand Rapids: Eerdmans, 2007), 105–106; Grant R. Osborne, *Matthew*, ZECSNT (Grand Rapids: Zondervan, 2010), 112.
4. See also Sirach 48:10.
5. See Martyrdom and Ascension of Isaiah 2:11; Josephus, *Life* 2 §11; 2 Maccabees 5:27. Craig S. Keener, *The IVP Bible Background Commentary: New Testament* (Downers Grove, IL: InterVarsity, 1993), 52
6. See Herodotus, *Histories* 4.172; Aristophanes, *Acharnians* 870–871, 1114–1117. James A. Kelhoffer, *The Diet of John the Baptist: "Locusts and Wild Honey" in Synoptic and Patristic Interpretation*, WUNT 176 (Tübingen: Mohr Siebeck, 2005): 62–66.

Ezek 3:3) and wisdom (Prov 24:13–14); it denotes both abundance (as implied in the expression "land flowing with milk and honey" [Exod 3:8, 17]) and God's provisions for sustenance (Judg 14:8, 9; 1 Sam 14:25, 26, 29, 43). Honey was also part of the diet of the one expected to be born of a virgin (Isa 7:14–15), and was considered a delicacy that could be given as a worthy gift to dignitaries (Gen 43:11).

John's physical description is significant because it ties him to Elijah. The coming of John did not only fulfill Malachi's prophecy (Mal 4:5–6), his ministry also fulfilled Isaiah's prophecy as the "voice of one calling in the wilderness" (Matt 3:3; Isa 40:3).

3:5–12 John's Ministry

John fulfills the prophecy of Isaiah concerning the "voice in the wilderness" who prepares the way of the LORD (Matt 3:3; Isa 40:3). According to Isaiah, his coming includes: (1) God's plan to bring comfort to his people Israel (40:1); (2) his presence with his people (40:9); and (3) the promise of the LORD's coming both to rule (40:10) and to shepherd (40:11) his people. This means that John's primary work was to announce to the people that the LORD was coming and that they could once again experience his rule over them.

For four centuries, the Philippines was under a series of foreign rulers (Spain, America, and Japan). Throughout this period, there were countless number of revolts by local groups but they were not enough to bring the nation freedom. Some explain that this is because the Philippines is an archipelago, and so it is difficult for local groups from different islands to join forces against the foreign rulers. The conflicts among leaders of various groups constituted a factor, too. The ancient Jews had also been under a series of foreign rulers (Assyrians, Babylonians, Persians, Greeks, and Romans), but if someone was to ask a Jew from the time of Isaiah or Matthew as to why they were under foreign rule, their answer was likely to be very simple – disobedience. Ancient Jews considered foreign domination as a consequence of their disobedience (Lev 26:3, 6–8, 14–17, 32–39). Their refusal to acknowledge God's rule over them was the reason they were ruled by their enemies; hence, submitting to God was considered essential in gaining freedom. The Jews could once again experience God's rule if they repented (26:40–42), and this was the message John preached to them (Matt 3:11).

John's ministry extended from Jerusalem, to Judea, and the districts around the Jordan (Matt 3:5), and his influence was not limited only to one social class or one religious group. He preached to the crowd and to

Herod Antipas, he also addressed both the "Pharisees and Sadducees" (Matt 3:7). Considering the relationship between these two groups, the statement "Pharisees and Sadducees" is a very odd combination. Aside from having members who were part of the Sanhedrin (Acts 5:34; 23:6), the Pharisees and Sadducees did not have much to share in common. They had different theological views – for example, the Pharisees believed in the resurrection while the Sadducees did not (Matt 22:23; Mark 12:18; Luke 20:27; Acts 23:6–8). For a long time, they disliked each other; and this is why Matthew's statement "Pharisees and Sadducees" is somewhat unusual (3:7; 16:1, 6, 11, 12; 21:45). The expression is never used in the other Gospels. The only other instance outside Matthew where they appeared together is in Acts 23:7 wherein Luke talks about the disagreement of "the Pharisees and Sadducees" during Paul's trial. Why did Matthew use this expression? Perhaps the best way to explain this is to say that sometimes, even enemies can be friends if they have a common enemy. In this case, the Pharisees and Sadducees shared something in common; they were both opponents of Jesus.[7]

John had an unfriendly encounter with the "Pharisees and Sadducees"; that anticipated Jesus' confrontations with them. John acknowledged the Jews' repentance as genuine, as implied in his baptism (Matt 3:5–6), but he refused to believe that these religious leaders truly repented. This is seen in John's response to them: (1) calling them a brood of vipers (3:7); (2) requiring them to bring forth "fruit of repentance" (3:8); and (3) telling them they could not rely on their biological connection with Abraham to claim a share in God's kingdom warning them of the coming judgment (3:9–12).

First, the Pharisees were called a "brood of vipers." In the OT, vipers are sometimes agents of God's judgment (Num 21:6; Jer 8:17; see also Acts 28:3–4), but in Matthew, the vipers are the object of God's irreversible judgment (Matt 3:7; 23:33). Aside from Luke 3:7, the expression "brood of vipers" is found only in Matthew (3:7; 12:34; 23:33); and in all three instances, they refer to the Pharisees, either with the Sadducees (3:7) or the scribes (23:33). The expression also suggests the use of evil speech (12:34). In Tagalog (the dialect of Central Luzon), the word *ahas* (or snake) does not only refer to the crawling creature with split-tongue, it is often used metaphorically to refer to traitors. Ancient Greek writers used the term in a similar way; they associated

---

7. John P. Meier, "John the Baptist in Matthew's Gospel," *JBL* 99, no. 3 (1980): 390.

vipers with falsehood, whether referring to a false witness or a traitor. The expression is also used to refer to parent-killers.[8]

Second, the "Pharisees and Sadducees" were required to "[b]ear fruit in keeping with repentance" (3:8). The agricultural metaphor of "fruit" as a reference to actions/behavior is common in the NT. It will become more evident in the succeeding chapters of Matthew that righteousness included more than just external behavior (5:20), it should be a result of a change of heart.

Third, the Pharisees' biological connection with Abraham was not a guarantee that they belonged to the "kingdom of heaven." This means that being a Jew would not spare them from God's future judgment.

John's call to repentance was accompanied by his declaration of God's judgment. He used four images to present this message: (1) stones being raised to become children of Abraham (3:9); (2) the axe that cuts the tree that does not bear good fruit and which is eventually thrown to the fire (3:10); (3) the baptism of the Holy Spirit and fire (3:11); and (4) the winnowing fork that presumably separates the wheat from the chaff which is then thrown into the fire (3:12). The last three of these four images involve fire as a means of judgment.

John said that "out of these stones God can raise up children for Abraham" (Matt 3:9). The Jews were biological descendants of Abraham. In fact, even among the physical descendants of Abraham, they also enjoyed the special privilege of being descended from Isaac and not Ishmael (Gen 21:12), and from Jacob and not Esau (25:23). This means that as Israelites, they were the recipients of God's promise to Abraham (Exod 32:13). John's statement made it clear that being a biological descendant of Abraham, Isaac, and Jacob did not guarantee protection from God's judgment. The relationship between the members of the kingdom of heaven was not based on their natural relationship.[9] Hence, John's statement was more of a challenge against the Pharisees' false security because of their biological relationship with Abraham.

---

[8]. "Vipers" refer to false witnesses (Demosthenes, *1–2 Against Aristogeiton* 25.96), traitors (Sophocles, *Antigone* 531), and to those who kill their parents (Herodotus, *Histories* 3.109; Aelian, *Nature of Animals* 1.24; Pliny, *Natural History* 10.169; Philostratus, *Life of Apollonius* 2.14). See also Craig S. Keener, "'Brood of Vipers' (Matthew 3.7; 12.34; 23.33)," *JSNT* 28, no. 1 (2005): 6–8, 11.

[9]. In ancient times, Gentiles become part of the "people of God" through religious conversion, a process usually called "proselytism." These gentile proselytes become related to Israel, but their relationship is "fictive" rather than "natural." This idea of having a fictive relationship among Christians is not something new in the times of Jesus. See DeSilva, *Honor, Patronage, Kinship and Purity*, 157–240.

John also told the "Pharisees and Sadducees" about the axe prepared to cut down every tree that did not bear good fruit (Matt 3:10). The distinction in Matthew is not between the trees that bear fruits and those that do not (Luke 13:9; John 15:2, 4, 8, 16; Col 1:6), but between fruit-bearing trees that bear good fruits and those that bear bad ones (Matt 7:17, 19; Col 1:10).[10] Fire is the destination for the portion that is cut off (Matt 3:10b); Matthew alludes to eternal fire somewhere else (18:8; 25:41), and this may well be the case here ("unquenchable fire"; 3:12). It is clear that fire is the means of judgment.

John described the one coming after him as "more powerful than I" and the one "whose sandals I am not worthy to carry" (3:11a). This recalls the incidents wherein Moses and Joshua had to remove their sandals (Exod 3:5; Josh 5:15).[11] John further announced the coming of the one who would baptize the people "with Spirit and fire" (Matt 3:11b). Fire is consistently used as an image of judgment in the OT, especially in divine manifestations or theophanies (Exod 13:21; 19:18; 24:17; Lev 9:23, 24; Deut 4:11, 12).[12] The Spirit is also associated with the new covenant (Jer 31), suggesting that the one who would baptize them with Spirit and fire would be the judge and the instrument for restoration. The agricultural image of separating the chaff from the wheat suggests the separation of the repentant for the unrepentant,[13] – which is for the purpose of judgment.

John's role is not only to prepare the way for the coming of the one called Immanuel (Matt 1:23), but also to proclaim that God is faithful to his people. His message is clear: God's kingdom is beyond space, time, and ethnic and cultural boundaries. God's judgment is also real, and repentance is necessary in order for one to produce "good fruits" acceptable to God.

---

10. The cutting down of trees as a metaphor for divine judgment is used in earlier Jewish writings, and the roots that are left refer to the remnants who would return from exile to Jerusalem (see 1 Esdras 8:86).

11. Paul G. Bretscher, "Whose Sandals?" *JBL* 86, no. 1 (1967): 84.

12. J. Daryl Charles, "The 'Coming One'/'Stronger One' and His Baptism: Matt 3:11-12, Mark 1:8, Luke 3:16-17," *JSPS* 11, no. 1 (1989): 37–39. For a discussion on the various interpretations of John's statement regarding baptism "with Spirit and fire," see James D. G. Dunn, "Spirit-and-Fire Baptism," *NovT* 14, no. 2 (1972): 81–83.

13. The Greek word for "winnowing fork" is *thrinax*. Most English versions render the Greek word *ptuon* in Matthew 3:12 as "winnowing fork," but it can be translated "winnowing shovel." If this is the case, it may suggest that the wheat and the chaff have *already* been separated, and the clearing of the threshing floor using the shovel is for the purpose of bringing the latter to the place of "unquenchable fire." Robert L. Webb, "The Activity of John the Baptist's Expected Figure at the Threshing Floor (Matthew 3.12 = Luke 3.17)," *JSNT* 43 (1991): 107, nn. 2–3.

Matthew

3:13–17 JESUS' BAPTISM

The *tuli* (or circumcision) is a common practice in the Philippines but it is not a religious ritual. It is done for hygienic purposes. Since it is usually done when the boy is about to become a teenager, some consider it a sign of transition from boyhood to manhood. Hence, the expression, "*binata ka na!*" (or "you are now a man"). Anthropologists call ceremonies like this "rites of passage," wherein a person moves from one stage of his life to the next. Different countries have various practices. For instance, boys from the Maasai tribe of Kenya hunt lions as a sign that they are entering manhood, Jewish children celebrate the *bar mitzvah* (for boys) or *bat mitzvah* (for girls) as a sign that they are no longer children. Some ancients considered baptism and circumcision as forms of religious rite of passage.[14]

Matthew's statement, "From that time Jesus began to preach . . ." (Matt 4:17), after his baptism and temptation suggests that these were the "rites of passage" for Jesus.[15] Jesus was not just the Messiah for whom the Jews had been waiting. *He became a public figure* who preaches, teaches, and performs miracles as evidence that God is present, both with him and the people he served.

John the Baptist informed the people that someone was coming and he would be "more powerful than I, whose sandals I am not worthy to carry," and he would also baptize the people "with the Holy Spirit and fire" (3:11). There is no doubt that those who heard his words were wondering who this might be, and how they could recognize him. Perhaps they were also not expecting that the one who was to come would himself would go through water baptism.

Even in ordinary conversations, we sometimes switch topics for a while in order to give the other person the "bigger picture," then switch back to the main topic of the conversation. The story of John the Baptist (3:1–12) may also be considered a necessary digression; Matthew switches topic from Jesus (1:1–2:23) to John (3:1–12) then back to Jesus (3:13) to give us a "bigger picture" of God's work. From the OT prophets' pronouncements to the ministry of John, preparations were made for the coming of the Messiah. After John's introduction of Jesus (3:11–12), the focus shifts back to Jesus, who was

---

14. Harold O. Forshey, "Circumcision: An Initiatory Rite in Ancient Israel?" *ResQ* 16, nos. 3-4 (1973): 150–158; Roger Grainger. "Sacraments as Passage Rites," *Worship* 58, no. 3 (1984): 214–222.
15. Barry J. Beitzel, *Biblica: A Social and Historical Journey through the Lands of the Bible* (Hauppauge, NY: Global Book Publishing, 2007), 423.

last mentioned by Matthew as a boy living in Nazareth (2:22–23). In short, when Matthew says Jesus came from Galilee (3:17), he simply continues his story of Jesus of Nazareth, a town in Galilee (2:23).

Matthew mentions that aside from Jerusalem and Judea, people from "all the region about the Jordan" were coming to John to be baptized (3:5), and this included Galilee. Jesus was one of those who came to John to confess their sin, identified himself with sinful humans, and walked together with them to be baptized. Through Jesus' actions, he was saying to the people, "I am *with you*. I am one of you. Let us journey together and seek the righteous path God wants us to take." For the Jews who came to John, genuine repentance was expressed outwardly through baptism which include confession of sins, and life transformation – that is, the bearing of fruit was expected after baptism (3:2, 5, 8). John's response to Jesus clearly showed that he did not come to John to confess his sins and receive forgiveness (3:14). His baptism was in order to "fulfill all righteousness" (3:15); this expression means that Jesus is fully committed to obey God's requirement from him.

For the various Jewish groups, "righteousness" is something other people should see in one's action. Jesus taught something similar, "righteousness" may refer to a person's behavior, conduct, and actions; but he takes one step further by saying that "righteousness" also includes the person's thoughts and character. This is one of the points Jesus stressed in his Sermon on the Mount (Matt 5–7). In short, "righteousness" involves total obedience to God's purposes, plans, and commands.

Jesus "fulfills all righteousness" by undergoing baptism. The "Pharisees and Sadducees" also came to be baptized, but Matthew did not consider them or their actions "righteous." Matthew contrasts Jesus with the religious leaders. First, Jesus had a "righteous root." His ancestral record includes people called "righteous," like Abraham (Gen 15:6), Tamar (38:26), and David (2 Sam 8:15; 2 Chr 18:14). The Pharisees, however, were told that even though they were biological descendants of Abraham, their actions showed otherwise. This showed that Jesus' righteousness exceeded that of the Pharisees (Matt 5:20).

Second, the Pharisees and Sadducees were called to "produce fruit in keeping with repentance" (3:8). This implied that God's expectation of "righteousness" was not evident in their lives. In contrast, Jesus came to be baptized in order to "fulfill all righteousness" even though he did not need to be baptized (3:14–15). In this way, he met God's expectation of righteousness in full measure. In Matthew, the word *plēroō* ("to fill" or "to fulfill") is used 12 (out of 16) times to refer to prophecies that came to pass (Matt 1:22; 2:15, 17, 23; 4:14; 8:17; 12:17; 13:35; 21:4; 26:54, 56; 27:9). It may also mean to have full measure of something, for example, the fishes caught in a net (13:48) or sins reaching its full measure (23:32). The expression "fulfill all righteousness" seems to imply the same (3:15). Jesus brought his righteousness to its full measure by first undergoing baptism and identifying with sinful humans. He came as a representative of Israel by meeting the righteousness required by the Law.[16] In principle, he became a representative of sinful humanity by meeting the righteousness God required, and the clearest evidence of this was not only his baptism but his death on the cross.[17]

The baptism of Jesus was accompanied by several elements that are worth noting: (1) the opening of the heavens; (2) the descent of the Spirit as a dove; and (3) the voice from heaven that announced Jesus' identity. First, Jesus had a visionary experience of seeing the heaven opened immediately after he arose from the water (3:16). Incidents like this are common in ancient writings.[18] This story recalls Ezekiel's experience during the time when he was rejected by the people as he proclaimed God's message (Ezek 1:1–4; 2:1–10). Like Ezekiel, Jesus was God's legitimate spokesperson rejected by the people. The opening of the heavens also recalls Isaiah's prayer for God to "rend the heavens and come down, that the mountains would tremble before you" (Isa 64:1; see also vv. 2–3). In other words, the opening of the heaven points to Jesus as God's true messenger to Israel even if many of them refuse to believe him, and it emphasizes the presence of God with Jesus and with the people.[19]

Second, the Spirit descended like a dove on Jesus after he was baptized. In the Philippines, a dove is sometimes associated with prostitution, hence, the Tagalog expression *kalapating mababa ang lipad* or ("low-flying dove") is used to refer to prostitutes. Yet the same can be a symbol of purity, hence, two white doves are used in Filipino weddings to symbolize pure love between the bride and groom. For ancient Jews, however, doves represent various things. The dove recalls the end of the Great Flood (Gen 8:8–12), and God's salvation of Noah and his family. In later Jewish writings, the dove is

---

16. Jeffrey A. Gibbs, "Israel Standing with Israel: The Baptism of Jesus in Matthew's Gospel (Matt 3:13–17)," *CBQ* 64, no. 4 (2002): 521.
17. Anita R. Warner, "Fulfilling All Righteousness: The Death of Jesus in Matthew," *CThMi* 29, no. 2 (2002): 12.
18. For more examples, see David Matthewson, "The Apocalyptic Vision of Jesus according to the Gospel of Matthew: Reading Matthew 3:16–4:11 Intertextually," *TynBul* 62, no. 1 (2011): 93–98.
19. Capes, "Intertextual Echoes," 37.

associated with Israel's sufferings.[20] If Matthew is using the symbol of a dove in the same way, then this story points to Jesus' suffering as God's righteous Son. Ancient Jews also believed that the Messiah would be the main recipient of the promised Spirit.[21] In the baptism of Jesus, the Spirit descended upon Jesus like a dove which confirmed that he was indeed the Messiah they were expecting to come.

Third, the voice from heaven proclaimed Jesus to be God's beloved Son in whom God was well pleased (Matt 3:17). God's declaration is a quotation from Psalm 2:7. This verse is often quoted in the NT and they all point to the authority given to Jesus (see Figure 6). God's promise to grant even the "ends of the earth" as an inheritance for the king (Ps 2:8) partly explains why Jesus did not need to succumb to Satan's offer to grant him the kingdoms of the world in exchange for his worship (Matt 4:8–10).

Figure 6: How NT Writers Quote Psalm 2:7

NT Reference	Ps 2:7 quoted with	Jesus' authority
Acts 13:33	Ps 16:10; Isa 4:3	Jesus' eternal reign with God
Heb 1:5	2 Sam 7:4	Jesus' at the right hand of God
Heb 5:5	Ps 110:4	Jesus appointed the eternal high priest

4:1–11 JESUS' TEMPTATION

Trials and temptations are distinguished in many languages. "Trial" is *pagsubok* in Tagalog and *shì liàn* (試練) in Chinese; this refers to difficulties that mold a person's character. "Temptation" is *tukso* in Tagalog and *shì tàn* (試探) in Chinese; this refers to circumstances that may cause a person to sin. However, in the Bible, such distinctions are not that clear, whether in the Hebrew OT or the Greek NT.[22] Trials/temptations are difficulties that invite

---

20. One Jewish teacher, Rabbi Abbahu, said, "A man should always strive to be rather of the persecuted than of the persecutors as there is none among the birds more persecuted than doves and pigeons, yet the Scriptures made them [alone] eligible for the altar." His words are preserved in the Babylonian Talmud, *Bava Qamma* 38a–b. See also Psalm 74:19; 2 Esdras 5:21–6:34. Capes, "Intertextual Echoes," 48.
21. Both canonical and non-canonical writings show this (Isa 52:14–15; Testament of Levi 18:6–8; Testament of Judah 24:2–3). Dunn, "Spirit-and-Fire Baptism," 90.
22. For example, the Hebrew verb *nasah* can mean "to test" (Gen 22:1) or "tempt" (Ecc 2:1). In the same way, the Greek noun *peirasmos* can also mean "trial" (Jas 1:2) or "temptation" (Matt 6:3).

a person to sin, and winning against them is necessary in molding one's character. In the case of Jesus, his temptation showed that he was one who was tempted/tried, and "fulfilled all righteousness" not only through his baptism but also by overcoming temptation.

In the OT, accounts of victory over trials/temptations are usually turning points in the story; those who win against trials/temptations move from one stage of life to the next. So, for example, God renewed his promise to Abraham after his testing (Gen 22:16–19), God made Joseph ruler over Egypt after a long period of trials/temptations (41:39–44, 52), and God restored the fortunes that Job lost during his period of trial (Job 42:10–17). The story of Jesus' temptation in Matthew is also a turning point in the Gospel. Jesus' victory over temptations showed that he was indeed fit to fulfill the task of God's messenger.

The story begins with the Spirit leading Jesus to be tempted by Satan (Matt 4:1), and his role in the story is limited to this.[23] The wilderness is often associated with trials/temptations. In the OT, the wilderness is a reminder of divine help in times of danger (Deut 8:2), God's judgment, and hope (Pss 78, 105).[24] The account of Jesus' temptation records three confrontations between Jesus and the devil. First, the devil tempted Jesus to turn stones into bread (Matt 4:3). The 40-day period Jesus spent in the wilderness recalled the 40-year period the Israelites spent there (Deut 2:7; 8:2, 4; 29:5). The Israelites, having endured hunger, experienced seeing the dew on the ground turn to manna (Exod 16:3, 14–15). Likewise, Jesus was hungry after a period of fasting, and was tempted to turn stones into food. Jesus responded by citing Deuteronomy 8:3, which is part of God's reminder to the Israelites as to how they should live when they enter and possess the Promised Land (8:1). Moreover, the fact that the Israelites reached the point of entering the Land was a testimony to God's presence with them for forty years (8:2).

---

23. John T. Fitzgerald, "The Temptation of Jesus: The Testing of the Messiah in Matthew," *ResQ* 15, nos. 3-4 (1972): 153. During the 400-year period between the Old and New Testaments, the Jews produced many writings similar to the book of Revelation. In these writings, there are many instances where in the Spirit would lead a seer to places where they would see visions (1 Enoch 17:1–2; 71:3; 72:1; 75:1; 2 Baruch 6:3; 3 Baruch 2:1; Apocalypse of Abraham 15:2–3; Testament of Abraham 10:1; Apocalypse of Zephaniah 2:1; 3:1; see also Ezek 3:12; 8:1–3; 11:1; 37:1). Jerusalem is also the typical destination of visionaries. Matthewson, "Apocalyptic Vision," 104–105.

24. In the writings from Qumran, testing by both human and demonic enemies occur in the wilderness. William Richard Stegner, "The Temptation Narrative: A Study on the Use of Scripture by Early Jewish Christians," *BR* 35 (1990): 12.

Second, the devil tempted Jesus to throw himself down from the pinnacle of the temple (Matt 4:5–6). Satan justified his suggestion by pointing to God's promise in Psalm 91:12, and in response, Jesus once again cited God's command to Israel on how to live when they entered the Promised Land (Deut 6:16, 18). The Lord recalled the incident in Massah and Meribah where the Israelites demanded water from Moses (Exod 17:1–16), who interpreted this incident as the Israelites' expression of doubt about God's presence, "And he called the name of the place Massah and Meribah, because of the quarreling of the people of Israel, and because they tested the Lord by saying, 'Is the Lord among us or not?'" (Exod 17:17).

Third, the devil tempted Jesus to worship him in exchange for all the kingdoms of the world (Matt 4:8–9). The setting of the third temptation is on the "high mountain." In earlier Jewish literature, the top of the mountain is often associated either with God's presence or with the battle between the man of God and the devil.[25] Once again, Jesus responded using a passage from the OT (Deut 6:5), and as in the previous instances, this was part of God's statement as Israel was about to enter the Promised Land (6:1).

Jesus' victory over temptation contrasts him with Israel. Israel and Jesus went through similar testing, but where Israel failed, Jesus prevailed. Moreover, a comparison between Jesus and Moses is also implied. Jesus is not only the Son whose sonship was shown through his obedience, but also the heir of the Father's kingdom.[26] The story closes with the devil leaving Jesus and angels coming to minister to him (Matt 4:11). Stories of ministering angels can be found in the OT (see also Heb 1:13–14). Angels came to minister to Hagar after she left Sarah (Gen 16:7–16). Her encounter with the ministering angel assures her that God is *El-roi* who is watching over her (16:13). After Elijah's confrontation with the false prophets of Baal (1 Kgs 18), angels came ministering to him to prepare him for the task ahead (19:5–18). The same thing may be said about Jesus' experience. The angels came as an assurance that God was watching over him, and as part of his preparation for the task ahead.

---

25. Nicholas H. Taylor, "The Temptation of Jesus on the Mountain: A Palestinian Christian Polemic Against Agrippa I," *JSNT* 24, no. 1 (2001): 36.
26. Stegner, "Temptation Narrative," 15–16. For a comparison between Jesus and Moses, see Talbert, *Matthew*, 37–38.

4:12–16 JOHN EXITS, JESUS ENTERS

Matthew recounts John's ministry briefly (Matt 3:1–12), but Jesus once again enters the scene when he come to John for baptism (3:13–17). Jesus' preparation for his work continues with his temptation (4:1–11). John's imprisonment at this point in the story provides a good transition from John's ministry to that of Jesus. John's message, "Repent, for the kingdom of heaven is at hand" (3:2), is now the message of Jesus (4:17).

Jesus' move to Capernaum is considered a fulfillment of Isaiah 9:1 which talks about the people of Napthali and Zebulun seeing the light (Matt 4:14–16). The region of Galilee during the time of Christ, within which are the cities of Nazareth (where Jesus grew up), and Capernaum, Nain, and cities west of the Sea of Galilee (where he first ministered), belong to the tribes of Zebulun and Naphtali (Josh 19:10–16, 32–39). The light is "an image of divine presence and salvation in the midst of the political and socioeconomic hardship of imperial rule."[27] Isaiah's idea of Immanuel includes both a message of hope (Isa 7:13–17) and a message of judgment (8:5–8); yet amidst this gloom, he foresees the great light coming to Israel that includes freedom from their oppressors (9:4), and the reign of the child called "Wonderful Counselor, Mighty God, Everlasting Father, Prince of Peace" on the throne of David (9:6–7).

The baptism and temptation of Jesus are preparations for Jesus' public ministry. In both accounts, Jesus comes as a representative of Israel.[28] His oneness with Israel was seen in his willingness to go through baptism even though he did not need to do so. He distinguished himself from Israel, in that he was tempted in the same way as Israel was, yet he was victorious. Moreover, in both accounts, God's presence with Jesus was clearly presented.

Jesus' temptation may also be considered an example for Christian discipleship.[29] All of us are tempted like him, and just as God's presence was with Jesus during his temptation, his followers can expect the same thing.

---

27. Warren Carter, *Matthew and the Margins: A Sociopolitical and Religious Reading*, The Bible and Liberation Series (Maryknoll: Orbis, 2000), 112.
28. Gibbs, "Israel Standing with Israel," 522–523.
29. Fitzgerald, "Temptation of Jesus," 153; Mary E. Andrews, "Peirasmos: A Study of Form-Criticism," *AThR* 24, no. 3 (1942): 241.

MATTHEW 4:17–7:29

Jesus' Sermon on the Mount

The teachings of ancient Chinese sages were preserved through oral transmission, and later through writing. This is true for ancient Jewish sages as well.[1] For example, the disciples of Confucius kept his teachings by compiling them in the *Analects*,[2] Jewish rabbis produced the Mishnah, and the followers of Jesus preserved his teachings together with his biography in the Gospels.

Aside from the way by which their teachings are preserved, there are also similarities in some of their teachings, particularly in areas of ethics and morality. The Jewish teachers transmitted the *halakhah*, a set of teaching that told the pious Jews how they should live. The Confucians have the idea of the *rén* (仁) or "being humane," a set of standards that define what it means to be humans and how humans should relate to one another. Ethics is also an essential element in Jesus' teachings;[3] and his focus is not on the rigorous compliance to the Law, but an understanding and application of the "spirit," and not just the "letter" of the Law. These teachings are preserved in the Sermon on the Mount (Matt 5–7), which spells out the ethical standards of the kingdom of heaven (4:17). They were first given to his disciples; and stories of how some of them encountered Jesus were also recorded in Matthew.

4:17–25 THE FIRST FOUR DISCIPLES

Matthew clearly distinguishes between the "disciples" and the "crowd." These two groups were Jesus' audience when he delivered the Sermon on the Mount (Matt 5:1). Some of his disciples are introduced in Matthew 4:17–25, and they would later be part of Jesus' mission group (10:1–11:1). The first four

---

[1]. For a more detailed discussion, see Birger Gerhardsson, *Memory and Manuscript: Oral Tradition and Written Transmission in Rabbinic Judaism and Early Christianity* (ASNU 22; Uppsala: Villadsen, 1961), 324–335.
[2]. Wm. Theodore de Bary and Irene Bloom, *Sources of Chinese Tradition*, 2nd ed., 2 vols. (New York: Columbia University Press, 1999), 1:42.
[3]. David Flusser, *The Sage from Galilee: Rediscovering Jesus' Genius* (Grand Rapids: Eerdmans, 2007), 66–75; see also Elaine Mary Wainwright, "Reading Matthew 3–4: Jesus – Sage, Seer, Sophia, Son of God," *JSNT* 77 (2000): 40–41.

disciples were two pairs of brothers, who were all fishermen from Capernaum in Galilee (4:13, 18).[4]

Their description suggests the kind of commitment they had: Peter and Andrew "at once... left" their nets to follow Jesus (4:20), and James and John "immediately... left" their father and boat to do the same (4:22). The stories in the other three Gospels suggest that this was not the first time they met Jesus. Luke recounts Jesus' healing of Peter's mother-in-law prior to this incident (Luke 4:38–39; 5:1–11), and John recalls how John the Baptist introduced Jesus to his follower Andrew, who eventually brought his brother Peter along with him (John 1:35–42). Although this was not their first meeting with Jesus, their willingness to abandon whatever they have is commendable, and according to Jesus' promise, this would later be rewarded (Matt 19:27–30). Such kind of commitment is also seen in many parts of Asia especially in places wherein preaching the gospel is restricted.

Andrew does not play an important role in Matthew's narrative; he is mentioned in passing just twice throughout the Gospel (Matt 4:18; 10:2). Andrew's brother Peter has a more prominent role (see comments on Matthew 16:16–18). Peter's original name was Simon,[5] but most of the time, Matthew refers to him as Peter. Together with Peter, the two sons of Zebedee, James and John, were with Jesus in some of the more important events in Jesus' life (Transfiguration [17:1], Gethsemane [26:37]).[6]

The first four disciples of Jesus were fishermen. Given the nature of their business, it is not surprising that Jesus used the metaphor of fishing to talk about their task of proclaiming the kingdom of heaven (10:7; 13:47–50). This is an important lesson we can learn from Jesus on how to share the Gospel, namely, how we can communicate the same truth to various kinds

---

[4]. Capernaum is known as a fishing village north of the Sea of Galilee. Josephus describes the Sea of Galilee as a lake with pure and cool drinkable water, with many kinds of fish (Josephus, *Jewish Wars* 3.10.7 §§ 506–513).

[5]. Note that there are five Simons in Matthew: (1) Simon, also known as Peter (4:18; 10:2; 16:16, 17; 17:25); (2) another disciple who was a Zealot (10:4); (3) one of Jesus' biological brothers (13:55); (4) the leprosy patient who owned the house in Bethany where Jesus was anointed (26:6); and (5) Simon of Cyrene who helped Jesus carry his cross (27:32).

[6]. There are three persons named James in Matthew: (1) James the son of Alpheus, one of the Twelve (10:3); (2) one of Jesus' biological brothers (13:55; 27:56); and (3) the son of Zebedee (4:21; 10:2; 17:1). There are also two men named John in Matthew: (1) the son of Zebedee (4:21; 10:2; 17:1); and (2) the Baptist (3:1–14; 4:12; 9:14; 11:1–19; 14:1–12; 16:4; 17:13; 21:25–26, 32).

of people using languages and categories they are familiar with, using medical language to communicate to physicians, sporting metaphor to athletes, and so on.

In the Four Gospels, the proclamation of God's kingdom was accompanied by a demonstration of God's power, like healings and exorcisms.[7] Various stories of healings are recorded throughout Matthew's Gospel: demoniacs (8:16, 28–34; 9:32–38; 12:22–24; 15:22–28); epileptics (17:15–18); a paralytic (8:6–13; 9:2–7). These miracles are clear evidences of God's presence with his people through Jesus (12:28).

5:1–16 BLESSINGS FOR PERSECUTED DISCIPLES AND THEIR ROLE IN THE WORLD

The Filipino word *masa* (or "the masses") plays a very important role especially during elections. Majority of the voters come from the *masa*, so candidates have to make sure they make promises to the *masa* hoping that it would encourage votes on election day. Whether they have the intention or ability to fulfill those promises is another story. In Matthew, the *masa* or the crowd has a somewhat different role; they are the spectators who marvel at Jesus' miracles, some of them receive Jesus' teachings and claims, they are Jesus' audience who can potentially become disciples, and they are the group who are not as hostile as the religious leaders but they do not have the faith of the disciples.[8]

After the "disciples" and the "crowds" were introduced in Matthew 4:17–25, they were now presented as Jesus' audience as he preached the Sermon on the Mount. Anyone who reads the Sermon must be able to identify either with the crowd or with the disciples. If one identifies with the crowd, one can ask, "After hearing what Jesus expected from his followers, am I willing to be his disciple and live accordingly?" And if one identifies himself as a disciple, one can ask, "After hearing what Jesus expected from his followers, am I living accordingly?"

5:1–12 The Beatitudes

Although Jesus pronounced blessings nine times, the way the last one is pronounced is clearly different from the first eight. The first eight blessings use

---

7. The crowd who heard Jesus' message were also beneficiaries of his healing (Joseph A. Comber, "The Verb *Therapeuō* in Matthew's Gospel," *JBL* 97, no. 3 [1978]: 433–434).
8. Warren Carter, "The Crowds in Matthew's Gospel," *CBQ* 55 (1993): 54–55, 64.

the third person, "Blessed are the . . ." (Matt 5:3–10), but the last one uses the second person, "Blessed are you" (5:11). Also, the first four groups that are blessed have names that begin with the Greek letter π (pi): poor (*ptōchoi*), mourners (*penthountes*), meek (*praeis*), and hungry (*peinōntes*).[9] Hence, in the Greek passage, it forms like two stanzas of a poem (two groups of four), and each stanza has thirty words and ends with the word *dikaiosūne* or "righteousness" (Matt 5:6, 10).[10] Thus the ninth line becomes a summary of either the eighth line or the eight lines.

The first part of Jesus' Sermon is often called the Beatitudes, which means pronouncement of blessings.[11] First, the poor in spirit possess the kingdom of heaven (5:3). The OT strongly emphasizes equal treatment for the rich and the poor. This is clear in the Lord's statement, "Do not pervert justice; do not show partiality to the poor or favoritism to the great, but judge your neighbor fairly" (Lev 19:15); but being poor and having righteousness is more desirable than having wealth with unrighteousness (19:22; 28:6). The poor are recipients of God's blessings mainly because they are often victims of oppression, and God's favor upon them is God's way of executing justice. Moreover, in many cases, being poor and helpless makes a person realize their need for God, like the prodigal son who realized his need of his father only when he lost everything he had (15:14–19). However, poverty in itself has no value. In Jesus' Sermon in Matthew, the recipients of God's blessings are not based on social classes. The "poor in spirit" are blessed. How can we understand this expression? Paul contrasts what happens "in spirit" from that which happens "in body" (1 Cor 7:34), between what can be seen externally, and what is "within" a person. This suggests that the phrase "in spirit" can refer to one's disposition, thoughts, perception, or feelings. When Matthew talks about the "poor in spirit," he could be referring to people who see themselves as those in need of God. In Matthew, the poor are recipients of the gospel (Matt 11:5) and of charity (19:21; 26:9). A person who considers himself "poor" allows himself to be recipients of these two things, and therefore has

---

9. Christine Michaelis, "Die Π-Alliteration der Subjektworte der ersten 4 Seligpreisungen in Mt v 3–6 und ihre Bedeutung für den Aufbau der Seligpreisungen bei Mt, Lk, und in Q," *NovT* 10 (1968): 148–161.
10. Mark Allan Powell, *God With Us: A Pastoral Theology of Matthew's Gospel* (Minneapolis: Augsburg Fortress, 1995), 120–122.
11. K. C. Hanson suggests that being "blessed" must be understood in terms of being "honored" ("How Honorable! How Shameful! A Cultural Analysis of Matthew's Makarisms and Reproaches," *Semeia* 68 [1994]: 87–93). See also Neyrey, *Honor and Shame*, 164–189.

no need to go "through the eye of a needle" to be part of the kingdom of heaven (19:23–24).

Second, those who mourn will be comforted (5:4). People mourn for two reasons: they are bereft because of the death of a loved one or because of misfortune. There are hints that Matthew's audience may have been going through grief caused by persecution (5:11–12), and the promise of comfort is implied (see comments for Matthew 3:1–12). Kōsuke Koyama aptly points out, "Comfort will come from God who is with us yet beyond us . . . The New Testament beatitudes point to the coming of the Reign of God."[12]

Third, the meek will inherit the earth (5:5). The Greek word for "meek" is *praus*, which is used only four times in the NT; three times in Matthew and once in 1 Peter 3:4. In two of those three occurrences in Matthew, the word describes the character of Jesus (Matt 11:29; 21:5). The passage that is most helpful in understanding Jesus' teaching about the meek inheriting the earth is Matthew 21:5, wherein Jesus enters Jerusalem as a gentle king. Unlike the typical conqueror-king who goes to another land ready to claim it with much confidence, Jesus arrives in Jerusalem as a meek king. In the story of Jesus' temptation, Matthew portrays him as God's heir (see comments on Matt 4:1–11);[13] and even as God's heir, Jesus did not come as a conqueror trying to acquire new territories for himself. Instead, God, the ruler of heaven and earth, grants everything to him. Jesus, the *gentle* king, did not show any sense of entitlement; and as the gentle *king*, those who follow him can also experience God's reign and presence (19:29: 25:34).

Fourth, those who are hungry and thirsty for righteousness will be satisfied (5:6). This statement is the last of the first group, and it stresses the importance of righteousness. In the OT, there are times when hunger and thirst are consequences of one's unrighteousness (Deut 28:48). The psalmists generally agree that God is able to satisfy both physical (Ps 107:4–9) and spiritual hunger and thirst (42:2; 63:1–6). Ancient Jews considered spiritual dryness as evidence of God's absence. This was implied in the question of the psalmist who was going through a time of spiritual thirst, "Where is your God?" (Ps 42:3). Conversely, they consider spiritual satisfaction as proof of God's presence. This is the same promise given to those who hunger and

---

12. Kōsuke Koyama, "Blessed are Those Who Mourn, for They Will Be Comforted," *CurTM* 20, no. 3 (1993): 206.
13. The "land" (*gē*) can sometimes refer to the "inhabited world" (Matt 24:14) or the territories under the rule of the Roman emperor (see Bertram L. Melbourne, "Acts 1:8 Re-examined: Is Acts 8 Its Fulfillment?" *JRT* 57, no. 2 [2001]: 4, n. 19).

thirst for righteousness.[14] Moreover, Jesus requires his followers to pursue righteousness that surpasses that of the scribes and the Pharisees (Matt 5:20), implying that these were not able to meet the righteousness he expected.

Fifth, the merciful will receive mercy (5:7). In the Philippines, the president has the authority to grant mercy ("presidential clemency") to criminals who have shown that their imprisonment had already transformed their character, thus additional time in prison is no longer necessary. In ancient times, as it is today, mercy was usually granted by those in authority to lawbreakers (27:15–26). For example, Matthew presents Jesus as "the Son of David" who has the authority to grant mercy particularly to those who have physical infirmities (9:27; 15:22; 17:15; 20:30–31); something that the ancient people would consider a punishment for sins, but a belief that Jesus had to correct (John 9:2). By commanding his followers to show mercy to others, Jesus redefines what mercy is and how it should be given. Mercy is no longer given only by one in authority to a subordinate; neither does granting mercy place the giver above the receiver. Each one can be a giver and a receiver of mercy (Matt 18:33); and Jesus' followers were expected to grant mercy to those who sinned against them, and this includes their persecutors (5:10–11). This is the quality that the Pharisees lacked (23:23; see also 9:13; 12:7).

Sixth, the pure in heart will see God (5:8). The OT acknowledges a human being's inability to be pure in heart before God, "Who can say, 'I have kept my heart pure; I am clean and without sin?'" (Prov 20:9). Confession is just the first step towards achieving this (Ps 51:10; Matt 3:6). The psalmist Asaph hints that the pure in heart finds favor before God (Ps 73:1), and this purity should be the character of one's thought, actions, and speech (73:2–12; Prov 20:11). The Jews considered purity of the heart as a necessity for worshipping God (Ps 24:4), and those who purify their hearts will not only receive God's blessings, but also his mercy (Matt 24:5). Once again, a pure heart is not a quality that describes the Pharisees (23:25–28).

Seventh, the peacemakers will be called sons (and daughters!) of God (5:9). Ancient Jews considered children a reward for the peaceable and barrenness a consequence of wickedness (Ps 37:37–38); blessings in the life to come also await those who pursue peace.[15] Peace is more than just an internal

---

14. William J. Dumbrell observes that the pronouncement of blessings in the Beatitudes is comparable to that in the Psalms ("The Logic of the Role of the Law in Matthew V 1–20," *NovT* 23, no. 1 [1981]:7).

15. In Psalm 37, a "man of peace" is considered righteous and blameless, and is set in contrast with "transgressors" (vv. 37–38). Jewish rabbis also teach the same principle (Mishnah *Pe'ah*

disposition; the state of one's heart is evident through one's words and actions; pursuing peace is equivalent to pursuing righteousness (34:13–15). The Pharisees' violent treatment of Jesus' followers clearly shows that their practice as contrary to what Jesus expected from his followers (Matt 23:33–35). Moreover, those who pursue peace are called "sons of God" (3:9), while the persecutors are "sons of those who murdered the prophets" (23:30).

Finally, those who are persecuted for righteousness' sake possess the kingdom of heaven (5:10). Pursuing righteousness does not guarantee a life free from suffering.[16] Matthew 5:10–12 may be a reflection of the believers' experience with their Jewish contemporaries. If we espouse a new set of values and beliefs, persecution will not be far behind. The kind of persecution they experienced was more than just being deprived of certain rights and privileges, or being slandered and ostracized, or of losing properties; many of them even suffered death. This is implied in the comparison between the persecuted believers and the prophets (5:12).

Jesus calls his disciples to count themselves blessed despite being persecuted (5:10–12; see also Jas 1:2–3) and not to retaliate but promote peace (Matt 5:9). Further he called them to acknowledge their own impurity and see God's mercy (5:8); by recognizing their own need for mercy they ought to show mercy even to their persecutors (5:7). He also shows his followers that although they may have mourned because of the sufferings they experienced, comfort is not far away (5:4), so they should desire to live according to Jesus' standard of righteousness like a hungry and thirsty person desires food and drink (5:6), and to follow Christ's example of meekness because there is no other way to acknowledge God's rule (5:5).

5:13–16 The Role of the Disciples in the World

The pronouncement of blessings shifts from a general third person (Matt 5:3–10) to a more specific second person declaration (5:11–12), which is followed by statements about the identity of the persecuted believers, namely, as the "salt of the earth" and "light of the world" (5:13–16).

In the OT, salt is associated with both healing and judgment. On the one hand, the prophet Elisha used salt to neutralize poisonous water making

---

1:1). John Lightfoot, *Commentary on the New Testament from the Talmud and Hebraica*, 4 vols. (Oxford: Oxford University Press, 1859), 2:99.

16. Many Jews may believe otherwise, but some earlier Jewish writings show that pursuing righteousness is no guarantee of an easy life. On the contrary, it may even invite persecution as in the case of Daniel (Dan 6), and the mother and her seven sons persecuted by Antiochus IV (2 Maccabees 7:1–23), to name a few.

it safe for drinking and useful for irrigation (2 Kgs 2:19–22). On the other hand, Abimelech sowed salt in a field after defeating Shechem which was a symbol that the city has been condemned for judgment.[17] Salt is also related to God's promise to his people. It is not only an essential ingredient of the various types of offerings (Lev 2:13; Num 18:19; Ezek 43:24), but also for incense to make the incense "pure and holy" (Exod 30:35). This symbolizes the permanent and unchangeable nature of God's promise to his people.[18] The use of salt as an image seems to have changed in the NT, which uses salt as a metaphor in relation to speech (Col 4:6; Jas 3:3–12, especially v. 12). If Jesus was using the metaphor in this way, it means that he was calling his followers to promote truthful and tactful speech; and this was particularly necessary for believers who were called to proclaim God's kingdom even to their persecutors.

Likewise, the relation between the metaphor of light and evangelism/mission is hard to ignore.[19] Light draws people to glorify God (Matt 5:16). In the OT, it is a metaphor for righteousness (Pss 37:6; 97:11; 112:4; Prov 4:18). Light is what the Gentiles saw when Jesus came (Matt 4:15–16; see also Isa 9:1–2; 60:1–3), and Israel, as "light to the Gentiles," was to proclaim God's kingship (Isa 49:5–6). Here, it is the function given the followers of Jesus (Matt 5:14–16).

To summarize, the Beatitudes seem to have a manifold purpose. First, they are a set of ethical standards to which the believers of Jesus were expected to adhere. Second, this standard inevitably defines them as a group distinct from the scribes, Pharisees, and Sadducees who fell short of God's expectations. Third, such ethical standards are to be practiced especially as they go through a period of persecution, and their sufferings were not to be used as an excuse for not meeting Jesus' standard of righteousness. Fourth, amidst the difficulties they had to undergo, God's blessings were pronounced for those who would endure. Finally, God's blessings include an affirmation of their task as missionaries, whose speech (salt) and action (light) would draw people to see God as the true king.

---

17. Arthur E. Cundall and Leon Morris, *Judges and Ruth*, TOTC (Leicester: InterVarsity, 1968), 134. See Deuteronomy 29:23; Psalm 107:34; Jeremiah 17:6.
18. William J. Dumbrell, "The Logic of the Role of the Law in Matthew V 1–20," *NovT* 23, no. 1 (1981): 12; Don B. Garlington, "'The Salt of the Earth' in Covenantal Perspective,'" *JETS* 54, no. 4 (2011): 716–717.
19. George Stuart Hendry, "Light of the World," *ThTo* 16, no. 4 (1960): 432; John W. Olley, "'You are the Light of the World': A Missiological Focus for the Sermon on the Mount in Matthew," *MiSt* 20, no. 1 (2003): 9–10.

5:17–48 RIGHTEOUSNESS FROM THE INSIDE OUT

The legend of the wise *sultan* (tribal chief from Southern Philippines) and the honest tax collector illustrates the value of integrity.[20] According to the legend, the *sultan* caught his tax administrator cheating and was forced to dismiss him. Several were appointed after him, but they also did the same and were also relieved from duty. As the position became vacant, and there were several applicants for the position, the *sultan* instructed them to pass through a dark room before meeting him. When they came out, a female dancer greeted them and invited them to dance. Only one danced with her, and the rest just stood still. The *sultan* spoke and appointed the one who danced as the new tax administrator. The other applicants could not believe what had happened, so the *sultan* explained his choice. It turned out that gold nuggets were scattered in the room that they went through. The other applicants pocketed some when they went through it and so they were afraid to dance for fear that the gold might fall out. The one who was not afraid to dance was the one who did not steal.

5:17–20 Jesus and the Law

Jesus also stressed the importance of integrity, and in the next part of his Sermon, he showed that a person's action may not necessarily indicate that Jesus' expectation for "righteousness" was met. What one does "in the dark" says something about one's character. In the Sermon, Jesus shows that righteousness refers to more than just the person's actions. It includes one's thoughts and intentions as well.

For ancient rabbis, the Law is fulfilled through one's practice and character.[21] In the OT, God's covenant with his people included pronouncements of blessings for obedience and curses for disobedience (Deut 27–28); in Matthew, blessings are pronounced for persecuted believers (Matt 5:3–12), and curses for the Pharisees (23:29–35). In the OT, direct commands and prohibitions are given (for instance, the Ten Commandments), including examples of righteous behaviors (Exod 21–23); in Matthew, Jesus went beyond external behaviors and actions to the internal motivations that result in certain deeds. Jesus' Sermon was the counterpart of the Jewish rabbis' *halakhah*. This word comes from the Hebrew word *halak*, which means "to

---

20. Based on the retelling of Johnny C. Young, *101 Popular Myths and Legends* (San Juan, Metro Manila: MG Reprographics, 1996), 372–375.
21. Str-B, 1:241–242.

walk," referring to the teachings of the Jewish rabbis on how to "*walk* the right path," take the right direction in life, and do the right things.[22]

Jesus' purpose was not to overturn the Law of Moses (Matt 5:17). The command, "do not think," suggests that his disciples should not even entertain the idea that Jesus came to do away with the Jewish Law. As far as the ethical requirements of the Law were concerned, Jesus came to fulfill them (see comments on Matthew 3:15 above on the meaning of "fulfill").

Jesus uses hyperbole (an exaggeration) to emphasize the importance of fulfilling the Law: that even the smallest stroke of letter must be fulfilled before "heaven and earth disappear" (5:18). Jewish rabbis also taught the importance of the smallest commandments. This idea is best summarized in these commands of the rabbis: "Run to the light as well as to the weighty commandments"; and "Be heedful of a light commandment as of a weighty one, for you do not know the recompense of reward of each commandment."[23] Jesus' statement in Matthew 5:18 affirms the validity of the Law, and at the same time announces its limitations.[24]

Jesus' affirmation of the Law is followed by a warning to his followers, which is also an indirect critique of those who were supposedly faithful adherents of the Law, namely, the scribes and the Pharisees (Matt 5:20). There is no question that righteousness includes external behavior and actions, but for Jesus, there is something more to righteousness than what other people see. This distinguishes the righteousness Jesus required and the righteousness displayed by the religious leaders (6:1–18; 23:1–36). Jesus' statement can also be understood as an assessment of the deficiency of the established religion of the Jews. His Sermon was not intended as a "blueprint for reforming the laws or institutions of earthly society,"[25] but as a way to make clear his ethical expectations from his followers.

---

22. For more discussions, see Philip Sigal, *The Halakhah of Jesus of Nazareth According to the Gospel of Matthew*, StBL 18 (Atlanta: Society of Biblical Literature, 2007); J. Daryl Charles, "The Greatest or Least in the Kingdom: The Disciple's Relationship to the Law (Matt 5:17-20)," *TJ* 13, no. 2 (1992): 142; Robert G. Hammerton-Kelly, "Attitudes to the Law in Matthew's Gospel: A Discussion of Matthew 5:18," *BR* 17 (1972): 31.
23. From the Mishnah *Avot* 2:1; 4:2. The command about bird's nest (Deut 22:6-7) provides a glimpse of the place of "smallness" in the divine economy (Charles, "Greatest or Least," 155).
24. Contrary to those who claim that the Law is eternal, Jesus said that the Law is valid only until a certain time. Hans Dieter Betz, "The Hermeneutical Principles of the Sermon on the Mount," *JTSA* 42 (1983): 23 n. 33.
25. Stephen Westerholm, "The Law in the Sermon on the Mount: Matt 5:17-48," *CTR* 6 (1992): 47.

In Asia in general, tradition remains highly valued. No wonder there is so much resistance when something new is being introduced. For instance, when Buddhism was first introduced in China, it was met with great opposition,[26] not only because Buddhism was foreign in origin, but also because it was a novelty at that time. Jesus was not against anything traditional, nor was he against tradition in itself, but he was specifically against the traditional interpretation of the Law that focused on the externals, hence limiting "righteousness" to mere actions. In his Sermon, Jesus challenged the tradition that was fixated only on external behavior, not internal transformation.

5:21–26 Anger and Murder

There are provisions in the Law that protects those who unintentionally kill another person. This shows that the Law takes into consideration the motive, and not just the visible acts (Num 35:11, 15; Josh 20:3, 9). The principle applies to the manslayer whether "they had unintentionally killed a neighbor without malice aforethought" (Deut 4:42; see also 19:4). It means that the Sixth Commandment is more than just a prohibition to kill (Exod 20:13; Deut 5:27; see also Exod 21:12–35); it is a command not to hate.

Hatred is not only expressed in taking another person's life, but also in disregarding the other person's dignity by using derogatory names (Matt 5:22). Jesus used two words from two languages as an example: the Aramaic word *rhaka* and the Greek word *mōre*, which basically mean the same thing.[27] Jesus considered the use of derogatory name unacceptable because it usually reflects one's hatred towards another. The goal is not simply to be politically correct or diplomatic in one's speech, but to have the right attitude towards other people reflected in the way we address them. Jesus' command does not only involve the one who is made angry, but also the one who makes another angry, who was instructed to take steps towards reconciliation (5:23–26).

5:27–32 Lust and Adultery

Decades ago, the expression *dalagang Pilipina* (Filipina lady) was still popular in the Philippines, and it was typified by the character of Maria Clara in José Rizal's novel *Noli Me Tangere*. She is the ideal Filipina who is modest and often portrayed as one who dresses in a manner that does not seduce men. Although this is the case, according to the novel, Padre Salvi was captivated

---

26. De Bary, *Sources of Chinese Tradition* (2nd), 1:422.
27. Roger D. Congdon, "Did Jesus Sustain the Law in Matt 5?" *BSac* 135 [178]: 119.

by her beauty. This story illustrates that although external factors can contribute to a person's sexual lust, it is more a reflection of one's heart.

The OT Law contains numerous commands against sexual misconduct, including rape, incest, bestiality, homosexuality, and adultery (Exod 22:16–19; Lev 18:6–18, 23; 20:10–21; Deut 22:22–30; 27:20–23). Jewish writings prior to the NT contain hints that there is more to sexual sins than one's improper behavior. In the OT, Job's vow not to look lustfully at a woman is considered part of proper sexual conduct (Job 31:1).[28] Two centuries before Christ, a Jewish scribe named Jesus ben Sirach also discouraged men to gaze at a woman because it is improper, and he also warned men not to have improper physical contact with another man's wife lest his heart be inclined to her and they commit adultery.[29] What this suggests is that for Jesus ben Sirach, adulterous relationship begins in one's heart and mind. The teaching of the Lord Jesus is no different. He strongly denounced a lustful gaze because it is the starting point of an adulterous relationship (Matt 5:27–28).

The gravity of such an offense is implied in the severity of its consequence. The exaggerated statement of Jesus that mutilation is to be preferred over continuous lust shows the seriousness of such act (5:29–30). Looking facilitates lusting; lust is what happens as a person processes in the mind what is seen, intensifying the desire for the other. Such thoughts are the starting point of an adulterous act, or any form of sexual sin (Rom 1:24); and following Jesus' command sets his disciples apart from the world that takes such offense lightly (1 Thess 4:5; 2 Pet 2:10).

Jesus' teaching about lust and adultery is immediately followed by a discussion on divorce and remarriage. There was no legislation in the OT concerning divorce; however, it can be assumed that this was practiced.[30] Divorced women are mentioned alongside widows, defiled women, and prostitutes as the kind of women Levitical priests should not marry (Lev 21:7, 14). It can be assumed that these women have had sexual relations with men already, and it is this factor that makes such union less than ideal (Ezek 44:21–22). Divorce was not always permitted. On the one hand, certain situations prohibit a man from divorcing his wife (for example, the marriage resulted from the man forcing the woman to have relations with him

---

28. For brief discussion on the links between adultery and lust from the writings of the rabbis, see M. D. Goulder, *Midrash and Lection in Matthew* (London: SPCK, 1974), 290.
29. See Sirach 9:5, 9.
30. Allen Verhey, "Divorce and the New Testament (1)," *RefJ* 26, no. 5 (1976): 17; "Divorce and the New Testament (2)," *RefJ* 26, no. 6 (1976): 28–31.

[Deut 22:28–29]). On the other hand, indecency can be grounds for divorce (24:1–4; see also Jer 3:1).

The debates among the rabbis with regard to the situations when divorce is allowable show the complexity and sensitivity of this question.[31] Jesus restricted divorce only for reasons of adultery; this echoes the provisions of Deuteronomy 24:1–4 concerning remarriage.

5:33–42 Fulfilling Vows or Not Making Vows

The primary principle concerning vows in the OT is perhaps best summarized in this statement: "When a man makes a vow to the LORD or takes an oath to obligate himself by a pledge, he must not break his word but must do everything he said" (Num 30:2; Lev 19:12). The OT considers it a "trap to dedicate something rashly and only later to consider one's vows" (Prov 20:25). This "rule," however, is followed by a list of situations when the breaking of vows is acceptable. These "exemptions" can be liberating because it allows a man (whether the husband or the father) some leeway regarding keeping a vow he did not make (Lev 30:3–16).

Ancient Jewish rabbis cited four types of vows that were not binding: (1) vows made after being provoked; (2) vows that are exaggerated; (3) vows made in error; and (4) vows broken under constraint. The rabbis also acknowledge that fulfilling or annulling a vow may be done for one's honor, the honor of one's parents or children; but in some instances, fulfilling or annulling a vow can also result in their dishonor.[32] Jesus understood the complexity of making vows, and highlighted the principle laid out in Deuteronomy 23:21–22, "If you make a vow to the LORD your God, do not be slow to pay it, for the LORD your God will surely demand it of you and you will be guilty of sin. But if you refrain from making vow, you will not be guilty." Thus Jesus instructed his followers not to make vows (Matt 5:33–37); the fact that God sees the real intent of a person and that he values the heart's intent as much as he values the person's actions make religious vows unnecessary.

---

31. There are at least three different rabbinic opinions when divorce is to be allowed: (1) Hillel allowed divorce for any reason; (2) Shammai restricted the reason to adultery; and (3) Akiba permitted a man to divorce his wife if she no longer find favor in the eyes of the man (Verhey, "Divorce [1]," 18).
32. The teachings of the rabbis concerning vows were preserved in the Mishnah, and one whole section (called a tractate) deals solely on vows, the *Nedarim* (see especially 3:1; 9:1, 9). These teachings likely reflect those of the Pharisees during Jesus' time. For more discussions on vows, see Bernd Kollman, "Erwägungen zur Reichweite des Schwurverbots Jesu (Mt 5,34)," *ZNW* 92, nos. 1–2 (2001): 20–32.

5:38–42 Justice and Retaliation

The statement "eye for eye, tooth for tooth" occur three times within the Law. First, within the section that deals primarily with executing justice for slaves (Exod 21:24; see also 21:12–36). There is an implied distinction between injuries done intentionally (21:14), unintentionally (21:22), and out of negligence (21:28–29). Injuries that result in death demand greater punishment than those that do not result in death (21:20–21). Second, within the section that shows that the Law applies to foreigners and natives living within Israel (Lev 24:10–23; especially v. 20). The death penalty applies to both blasphemy and murder (24:16–17), but personal injuries do not require as much to mete out justice (24:18–20). Third, within the section that deals with malicious witnesses who misuse the judicial system in order to harm another (Deut 19:16–21; especially v. 21).

These three laws show that although a distinction can be made between intentional and unintentional evil, the law of retaliation is supposed to promote justice and it applies to everyone; but it is a principle that can be abused. Moreover, as we can see in history, people groups that promote such a principle are more prone to be violent. The law of retaliation is more complex, and is thus very difficult to apply. Jesus offered a new principle which he set as the standard for righteousness.[33] Retaliation is the first step to create a cycle of violence. The establishment of the cities of refuge in the OT which protects the manslayer from the avenger in cases when the former unintentionally kills the latter's relative or friend is a clear proof that retaliation is not the basic purpose of the principle "eye for eye, tooth for tooth," but justice (Num 35:12, 19–27; Deut 19:4–6, 11–12; Josh 20:2–3, 5, 9). Jesus' principle addresses the root of this evil cycle (Matt 5:39–41; Rom 12:17); his teaching is not new but is a reiteration of the LORD's command to love neighbors by not taking revenge (Lev 19:18). The word *anthistēmi* (Matt 5:39) implies violent resistance. Thus, the issue is not whether to resist evil or not, but how one resists evil.[34]

5:43–48 Loving and Hating Others

Jesus' commands to turn the other cheek, to give both one's inner and outer garments, and to walk the extra mile relate to his final point: to love not only one's neighbors, but also one's enemies. This traditional teaching to "love

---

33. James F. Davis, *Lex Talionis in Early Judaism and the Exhortation of Jesus in Matthew 5.38–42*, JSNTSup 281 (London: T. & T. Clark, 2005), 149.
34. Carter, *Matthew and the Margins*, 151.

neighbors but hate enemies" is nowhere to be found in the Law. Although the OT acknowledges that hatred is naturally what one would feel towards an enemy (2 Sam 22:18, 41; Pss 18:17, 40; 21:8; 68:1; 83:2; 139:22; see also Dan 4:19), there is no command to do so.

Jesus statement, "You have heard that it was said" (Matt 5:43) reflects that hating one's enemies is socially acceptable, and therefore honorable, but he challenges this tradition by instructing his disciples to persevere in "imitating a shameless God" who shows goodness even to the undeserving,[35] and the disciples could do so by loving those who persecute them (5:44–45; see also 5:10–12). God's benevolence towards everyone is given as the motivation for doing the same. This can be illustrated using laws about loans. The Law contains prohibitions against taking the garment of borrowers as a pledge (Exod 22:25–27a), this comes with a guarantee that God is compassionate towards them (22:27b), and later a command to do good even to those who hate us (23:4–5). God's grace serves as the basis for the one who loans not to oppress the borrower by not taking from the latter's basic supplies to survive. Jesus broadened the scope of understanding this command by showing that one's response to evil is as important to God as the evil done. In short, God's concern was not just about the person taking someone else's garment, but also about the response of the one whose garment was taken.

The five challenges Jesus posed against traditional teachings of Judaism share the same principle, namely, external behavior is not the only thing that matters because these are mere results of one's internal dispositions. The same theme is emphasized in Jesus' discourse against hypocrisy in the next section.

6:1–18 RIGHTEOUSNESS AND THE PERCEPTION OF OTHERS

Legalism was valued in ancient China. Applying the same set of rules to everyone was considered the key to the success of some dynasties.[36] However, ancient Chinese sages understood the value, not only of the external practices,

---

35. Neyrey, *Honor and Shame*, 208–209.
36. James R. Ware, *The Sayings of Confucius*, Mentor Religious Classic (New York: Mentor Books, 1995), 14.

but also of the person's internal motivations. This is evident in some of their sayings:[37]

> *The gentleman understands what is right; the inferior man understands what is profitable.* (Confucian Analects 4:16)

> *The gentleman cherishes virtue, the inferior man cherishes possessions. The gentleman thinks of sanctions, the inferior man thinks of personal favors.* (Confucian Analects 4:11)

> *Refrain from exalting the worthy,*
> *So that the people will not scheme and contend;*
> *Refrain from prizing rare possessions,*
> *So that the people will not steal;*
> *Refrain from displaying objects of desire,*
> *So that the people's hearts will not be disturbed.* (Tao-te Ching 3)

The relationship between right actions and internal motivations was also at the core of the rift between Jesus and the Jewish religious leaders. In Matthew's account of Jesus' Sermon, another important aspect of righteousness comes to the fore, namely, people's perception. This is something that can be expected of a society that values personal honor highly.

Matthew 6:1 is the summary statement of Jesus' next three points in his Sermon: "Be careful not to practice your righteousness in front of others to be seen by them. If you do, you will have no reward from your Father in heaven." Three "acts of righteousness" are discussed: acts of mercy, prayer, and fasting.

6:1–4 Acts of Mercy

Both the ancient Jews and Christians considered almsgiving as evidence of piety (for example, Cornelius [Acts 10:2, 4, 31]). Giving to the poor was considered an act of righteousness (2 Cor 9:9). No wonder the early Christians regularly gave to those in need (Rom 15:25–28; 1 Cor 16:1–2; Gal 2:10).[38]

---

37. Based on Wm. Theodore de Bary's translations. Wm. Theodore de Bary, Wing-tsit Chan, and Burton Watson, *Sources of Chinese Tradition*, 1st ed., 2 vols. (New York: Columbia University Press, 1960), 1:31, 52.
38. Even a non-believer like Julian the Apostate acknowledged the Christians' compassion in helping the poor, although he did so with sarcasm (*Letter to Arsacius, Ep.* XXII. 430D). See R. Joseph Hoffmann, ed., *Julian's Against the Galileans* (Amherst, NY: Prometheus Books, 2004), 135 n. 439.

The OT Law contains provisions that foresee a society within which the needs of the poor people are supplied (Lev 19:9–10; 23:32; see also Ruth 2:1–23; Obad 5). The Jewish rabbis had also discussed and debated about how these commands regarding distributing the produce to the poor could be applied.[39]

Jesus' statement, "So when you give to the needy" (Matt 6:2), suggests that he was encouraging his followers to continue to do "acts of mercy" or almsgiving. However, he discouraged the sounding of the trumpet whenever alms were given. The sounding of trumpets is often construed metaphorically,[40] but there are reasons for us to think that this could be more than just a metaphor. In fact, Jesus' statement opens another window that allows us to see the religious and social dynamics relating to the practice of almsgiving in first century Jewish society. The discussion of the rabbis may reflect the kind of practice of many of Jesus' contemporaries. The rabbis mention the use of thirteen *shofar* chests for various types of offering. Elsewhere, they discuss about the offerings given to the poor, and how such offerings are to be brought to the "chamber of secret gifts." The sounding of the *shofar* may have accompanied the giving of the other type of offerings, which made it tempting for those who wanted recognition for their offerings to the poor, not to do so "in secret" but with the sounding of a trumpet.[41]

Aside from announcing it with "the trumpet," the practice of giving alms in the streets could be a way to invite others to glorify the almsgiver (Matt 6:2). The Jews believed that divine rewards await those who give alms (Acts 10:4, 31). Jesus did not challenge this idea, but clarified that those who seek to be glorified by others through acts of mercy already have their rewards; therefore, there is no longer any further rewards from God for them (Matt 6:2, 4). Hence, he instructed, "do not let your left hand know what your right hand is doing" (6:3). If those who brought their charity offerings did so "in secret," so that no one else knew what reward was due the giver except God, then there would be no one else to reward the giver except God.

---

39. Mishnah, *Pe'ah* 4:9–10; 5:1, 4–5; 6:1–2, 9–11; 7:8; 8:1–7. The rabbis' discussions also provide a glimpse on how certain traditions based on the Law expand and grow.
40. Robert A. Guelich, *The Sermon on the Mount: A Foundation for Understanding* (Waco, TX: Word, 1982), 287; Hans Dieter Betz, *The Sermon on the Mount: A Commentary on the Sermon on the Mount Including the Sermon on the Plain* (Minneapolis: Augsburg Fortress, 1995), 356.
41. Mishnah, *Sheqalim* 2:5; 5:6; 6:1, 5. Neil J. McEleney, "Does the Trumpet Sound or Resound: An Interpretation of Matthew 6.2." *ZNW* 76, nos. 1-2 (1985): 46.

6:5–15 Prayer

Like acts of mercy, prayer is a tangible and visible sign of piety in Judaism and Christianity. Prayer is not only part of their corporate worship; it is also part of the individual's spirituality. In Judaism, righteousness does not only involve moral actions, but the individual discipline of prayer is also integral to what they consider righteousness.[42] Luke leaves us no reason to doubt that the Christian discipline of prayer is inherited from Judaism (Acts 3:1).

The Law contains no explicit command to pray. Instead, it is exemplified by the faithful believers of the LORD. One form of prayer offered was the prayer of petition. Here, Jesus addressed one of the common misconceptions about it, namely, that the guarantee of answered prayer is proportional to the length of the prayer (Matt 6:7–8).[43] He pointed out that the "reward" of answered prayers will be given to those who do not use prayer as a means of showing off their spirituality (6:6). Moreover, Jesus assured his listeners that the "Father knows what you need before you ask him" (6:8). This suggests that prayer, for Jesus, is not a means for a person *to inform God* about the things he does not know; by implication, prayer is a means for believers *to know the Father* in ways they would not have known him without praying. Each line of the prayer highlights one particular character and deed of God.

The function of the prayer in Jesus' Sermon is worth focusing on. Jesus' statement in Matthew 6:8 makes it clear that his purpose was to assure the believers that their prayers would be heard and to address the misconception that longer prayers guarantee a more positive response from God. This seems to be rooted in another wrong assumption that prayer is a means to inform God of our needs as if he does not know them. Jesus corrected this false assumption by showing the opposite: *prayer is not a means for us to inform God something he does not know, but prayer is a means for us to know the one whom we would not know except when we pray and acknowledge him for who he really is*. No wonder Jesus shows us the various roles of God through each line of the prayer.

First, Jesus addressed God as the Father (6:9). It may not be a common practice among ancient Jews to address God simply as "Father" (see John 5:18), but the idea of God being a father is certainly found in the OT. His

---

42. George W. E. Nickelsburg and Michael E. Stone, *Early Judaism: Texts and Documents on Faith and Piety* (Minneapolis: Augsburg Fortress, 2009), 93.
43. The account of the confrontation between the prophets of Baal (or "lord"), who prayed from morning until noon (1 Kgs 18:26), and Elijah, who said a short prayer to the true LORD (18:36–37), provides a perfect illustration to Jesus' contrast.

fatherhood implies that he is the Creator (Deut 32:6). As a father, he provides for his children (see Matt 7:9–11; Jas 1:17). Like human fathers, God instructs his children (Deut 6:6–9; Ps 32:8; Prov 1:8; 3:1–2). God does not only have the qualities of a good father, in fact, he also has the qualities of a good mother (Isa 49:15). In the same way that human parents deserve respect from their children, the Father in heaven is also worthy of our reverence.

Second, Jesus acknowledged that the Father is Lord (6:10). As the Lord who reigns in heaven and on earth, he decides which of our prayers are consistent with his plans and which requests he cannot grant. Jesus' prayer in Gethsemane best illustrates this attitude of submission (26:39, 42). God's lordship is not based on his willingness to answer all our prayers affirmatively. On the contrary, his prerogative to say *Yes* or *No* to our prayers shows that he is Lord.

Third, Jesus confidently asked the Father for daily provisions (6:11). Jesus recognized human parents for their natural desire to provide for their children (7:7–11). This natural tendency is all the more seen in God. The OT provides numerous examples on how God provided for his people, whether through natural means (like land produce) and supernatural means (like the manna in the wilderness).

Fourth, Jesus presented God as the one who reconciles us to him and to others (6:12). Reconciliation is made possible only through forgiveness. The OT shows both God's justice and his compassion. Matthew also makes it clear that Jesus' death was necessary for humans to receive forgiveness (26:28).

Fifth, in the midst of temptation, God is the one who delivers from temptation those who trust him (6:13a). Jesus experienced temptation himself (4:1–11). It was the Spirit who led Jesus to the wilderness to be tempted (4:1), but he taught his disciples to ask God not lead them to temptation (6:13a). Paul instructed his readers to flee temptation (1 Cor 10:13; 2 Tim 2:22), and Jesus made it clear who it was who could deliver them.

Sixth, Jesus honored God as king (6:13b), to whom belongs all power and glory. The section closes with a command to forgive.[44] This further emphasizes Jesus' command to love one's enemies, even those who persecute us (Matt 5:10–12, 44–45).

---

44. The Lord's Prayer is distinct from the other portions of Jesus' exposition concerning hypocrisy as he referred to the audience using second person plural (Matt 6:9a) to third person plural (Matt 6:9b–13), and back to second person plural pronouns (6:14).

Jesus identified the various roles of God which can be seen in the kind of things he does for his children. These roles can be summarized using the acrostic P-R-A-Y-E-R.

Paternal role of God – Father	*Our Father in heaven, hallowed be your name.*
Rule of God on earth – Lord	*Your kingdom come, your will be done, on earth as it is in heaven.*
Allotments of God – Provider	*Give us this day our daily bread,*
Yearnings of God – Reconciler	*And forgive us our debts, as we also have forgiven our debtors.*
Empowerment of God – Rescuer	*And lead us not into temptation, but deliver us from evil.*
Reign of God eternal – King	*Yours is the kingdom, and the power, and the glory forever. Amen*[45]

6:16–18 Fasting

The third area Jesus addresses in relation to hypocrisy is fasting. Like prayer, there is no direct command in the Law instructing God's people to fast. However, there are numerous accounts of people fasting, whether individually or corporately, and for various reasons: (1) as part of religious rituals (Ezra 9:5; Isa 58:3–6; Jer 36:9; Joel 1:14; Zech 7:5; 8:19); (2) as part of the discipline of prayer (2 Sam 12:16, 21–24; 2 Chr 20:3; Ezra 8:21, 23; Neh 1:4; 9:1; Esth 4:16; Ps 35:13; Jer 14:12); and (3) as a sign of mourning (1 Sam 31:13; 2 Sam 1:12; 1 Kgs 21:27; 1 Chr 10:12; Esth 4:3; 9:31; Ps 69:10; Dan 6:18; 9:13; Joel 2:12, 15; Jon 3:5). Christians from the early centuries also practiced "social fasting" in order to save some resources through skipping meals and then using them for helping others in need.[46] The rabbis taught that God would satisfy in the world come the one who imposed hunger on himself for the sake of the Torah.[47]

The practice of fasting could also be used as a cover-up for an evil plot (1 Kgs 21:9–12); and like almsgiving and prayer, it could be used for

---

45. The Lord's Prayer is distinct from the other portions of Jesus' exposition concerning hypocrisy as he referred to the audience using second person plural (Matt 6:9a) to third person plural (Matt 6:9b–13), and back to second person plural pronouns (6:14).
46. Stephan Witetschek, "Going Hungry on Purpose: On *Gos. Thom.* 69.2 and a Neglected Parallel in Origen," *JSNT* 32, no. 4 (2010): 386–388.
47. See Babylonian Talmud, *Sanhedrin* 100a.

self-glorification. The students of Confucius recount the great sage's practice of fasting, "When Confucius observed sacrificial fasting, his clothing was spotlessly clean, his food was different from the ordinary, and in his dwelling his seat was changed to another place" (Confucian Analects 10:7).[48] Although Confucius did so, there is nothing in his students' recollection to suggest that Confucius was doing it only for religious display. The perceived sanctity of the religious ritual seems to be the reason behind Confucius' practice, in much the same way as those who go to church wearing "Sunday clothes." Jesus was not against those who uphold the sanctity of religious rituals, he was against drawing attention to oneself for self-glorification through religious rituals. He discouraged hypocritical fasting by using wordplay, "When you fast, do not look somber as the hypocrites do, for they disfigure (*aphanizō*) their faces to show (*phainō*) others that they are fasting. Truly I tell you, they have received their reward in full" (Matt 6:16). The Greek word *aphanizō* may mean to make someone/something unrecognizable, invisible, or dull in appearance, and *phainō* may mean to make someone/something recognizable, visible, or shine. In short, by fasting, hypocrites make themselves invisible, unrecognizable, and dull before other people in order to be visible, recognizable, and shine before the same people. In contrast, Jesus taught his disciples not to seek such recognition from other people, but from the Father.

In all three instances, Jesus emphasized one important principle: those who seek recognition from other people through religious disciplines such as almsgiving, prayer, and fasting will receive their rewards from them. However, what really counts is the reward that the Father guarantees to those who practice spirituality because it is right, even though such actions go unrecognized, because God is both the giver and a "safekeeper" of these rewards.[49]

6:19–7:6 LIST OF DON'TS

Matthew's account of Jesus' teaching concerning the "treasures in heaven" (Matt 6:19–20) provides a smooth transition to the series of "do's and don'ts" in the section that follows (6:19–7:6); first in the series of negative commands is Jesus' prohibition/command about storing one's wealth. Jesus' teachings

---

48. De Bary, *Sources of Chinese Tradition* (1st), 1:30.
49. See Nathan Eubank, "Storing Up Treasure with God in the Heavens: Celestial Investments in Matthew 6:1–21," *CBQ* 76, no. 1 (2014): 77. The contrast between the hypocrites' receiving the rewards from people (Matt 6:2, 5, 16) and the faithful ones' receiving the rewards from the Father (6:6, 18) makes it clear that God is not only a safekeeper but also the source of these rewards.

are, to some extent, comparable to the Law of Moses as both contain instructions on what to do and what not to do.

Matthew presents the first three of four instructions using similar sentence construction: "do-not-do-this . . . but-do-this-instead": (1) do not store treasures on earth . . . but store treasures in heaven (6:19, 20); (2) do not worry about your life . . . but seek his kingdom and his righteousness (6:25, 31, 33); and (3) do not judge . . . but remove the log in your eye (7:1, 5). The fourth prohibition is unique in its construction, but in all instances, the person's *eye* plays an important function in the process of obedience.

6:19–24 Don't Store Treasures on Earth . . . But Store Treasures in Heaven

The idea that the heavenly realm is a storehouse of treasures is not original to Matthew. In the Gospels, debt is used as a metaphor for sin (Matt 6:12; Luke 13:4),[50] and therefore some form of "payment" is necessary; for example, Christ's death as ransom (Mark 10:45; see also Matt 20:28). All humans are considered debtors.[51] In the same manner, good deeds are considered a form of investment and are means to reap rewards.[52] For Jesus, good deeds can be done both by the hypocrite and the one who is not, and both are guaranteed rewards. The difference is that the former does good to gain honor before other people, and they will get their rewards soon; the latter, in contrast, does so with different motivation, and must wait a while before they can get their reward from God. Moreover, the hypocrite's reward decays quickly (Matt 6:19), and the reward for the sincere is imperishable (6:20). Where one "invests" also determines one's commitment, as Jesus said, "For where your treasure is, there your heart will be also" (6:21).

His statement about the heart is followed by one concerning the eye, "The eye is the lamp of the body" (6:22), which many interpreters find somewhat perplexing. As can be expected, perplexing statements like this have drawn various kinds of interpretation throughout the centuries.[53] Scientifically, the

---

50. The Aramaic translation of the Hebrew Bible also renders "sin" as "debt" in some occasions (for example, *Targum Pseudo-Jonathan* on Deut 19:5); see Samuel Tobias Lachs, "On Matthew 6:12," *NovT* 17, no. 1 (1975): 6.
51. Mishnah *Avot* 3:17. The idea of forgiving debts is also seen in Leviticus 25 (Lachs, "On Matthew 6:12," 7).
52. Almsgiving is one of the means to acquire this (Tobit 4:5–11), and the LORD is the one who will repay one's good deeds (Prov 19:17; 2 Maccabees 12:45). This idea can be traced back to the Second Temple era; see also Eubank, "Storing Up Treasures," 79, n. 9.
53. Carl B. Bridges and Ronald E. Wheeler, "The Evil Eye in the Sermon on the Mount," *SCJ* 4 (2001): 69–76; Candida R. Moss, "Blurred Vision and Ethical Confusion: The Rhetorical

eye is an organ of the body through which an image or light "enters" the human brain. This is often called the "intromission" function of the eye. From this perspective, Jesus' statement makes no sense. However, more recent interpreters acknowledge the difference between ancient and modern understanding of the eye's function and propose what they call the eye's "extramission" function; this means the eye's function is not to absorb but to emanate light from within.[54] Solomon says "haughty eyes" show "a proud heart" (Prov 21:4). David claims that light was gone from his eyes because of sin (Ps 38:10). Some rabbis even suggest that the character of the bride or bride-to-be is evaluated through the woman's eyes.[55] In the OT, Leah was not chosen because she had "weak eyes" (Gen 29:17). Ancient Mediterranean people distinguished between healthy and evil eyes. They believe that a person with an evil eye has the power to cast spells on another, hence, they use incantations and amulets to protect themselves from the "evil eye."[56] This is comparable to the belief in the *mangkukulam* in the Philippines. The *mangkukulam* are believed to have the power to use evil spells and rituals to cause sickness, misfortune, and even death of another person, whether as an act of personal revenge or as a form of "service" to the ones who hired them. When Jesus used the expression "evil eye," he was using a language that could easily be understood by his contemporaries to refer to people whose evil intent comes out through their actions. In short, the eyes reflect what is in the heart of a person, whether good or evil. The healthy eye is characterized by singleness of focus (Eph 6:5; Col 3:22; see also Col 3:1); and the acts that come as a result of this is not for self-glorification.

Function of Matthew 6:22–23," *CBQ* 73, no. 4 (2011): 757, n. 3.

54. Several ancient writers discuss this. For example, Pythagoras called the human eyes the "portal of the sun" (Diogenes Laertius, *Lives of Eminent Philosophers* 8.129), and Plato believed that the eyes are bearers of light (*Timaeus* 45b–46a). Similar idea is implied in many Jewish writings (Ps 38:11; Prov 15:30; 29:13; see also Tobit 10:5; 11:14). Davies, *Matthew*, W. D. Davies and Dale C. Allison, *A Critical and Exegetical Commentary on the Gospel according to Saint Matthew*, 3 vols., ICC (Edinburgh: T. & T. Clark, 1988), 1:635–636; Dale C. Allison, Jr., "The Eye Is the Lamp of the Body," *NTS* 33 (1987): 67.

55. The Babylonian Talmud, *Ta'anit* 24a. Sinai Turan, "A Neglected Rabbinic Parallel to the Sermon on the Mount (Matthew 6:22–23; Luke 11:34–36)," *JBL* 127, no. 1 (2008): 81–93. See also Moss, "Blurred Vision," 762–763.

56. John Hall Elliott, "The Evil Eye and the Sermon on the Mount: Contours of a Pervasive Belief in Social Scientific Perspective," *BibInt* 2, no. 1 (1994): 53, 69.

6:25–34 Don't Worry about Your Life . . . But Seek God's Kingdom and His Righteousness

In the previous section, the rationale behind the command concerning the storing of treasures is explained at the end of the section (Matt 6:21); and this is introduced by the conjunction "for" (or "because"), followed by the proverbial statement, "The eye is the lamp of the body," and a short exposition of the statement (6:22–23). In this section, the proverbial statement, "No one can serve two masters," and its exposition is placed at the beginning (6:24). This is followed by the command not to worry (6:25). The command is introduced by the conjunction "therefore," suggesting that this is the practical implication of the proverb.

Jesus explains that the reason one cannot serve two masters is because "Either you will hate the one and love the other, or you will be devoted to the one and despise the other" (6:24). The statement about "loving" one master and "hating" the other recalls the LORD's command concerning the dividing of inheritance among children born within a bigamous (or even polygamous) marriage. The portion of the children of both the "loved" and the "hated" wives must be divided according to their birthright, and not the husband's preference (Deut 21:15–17). The explanatory statement, "he loves one and not the other," confirms that loving or hating one's master is not about one's emotion towards the master, but one's commitment.[57]

Some Chinese people believe in the *cái shén* (財神) or the "god of wealth," the god who "specializes" in the giving of wealth and one that can be called alongside other gods. Calling the gods may not necessarily be a sign of devotion to any of them, but just a means to tap on the available resources these gods can offer. Although ancient Jews do not have the same idea about the god of wealth, wealth is nonetheless set alongside God. Mammon, in this context is a personification of wealth, and is mentioned alongside God as a possible object of worship.[58] Therefore, devotion to wealth means a decreased devotion to the true God. In Jesus' Sermon, he implicitly reiterated the first of the Ten Commandments (Exod 20:3).

---

57. Christoffer H. Grundmann, "Mammon – Its Biblical Perception," *MiSt* 12, no. 2 (1995): 161.

58. The word *mamōnas* is very likely a transliteration of the Aramaic term for wealth/riches/money. It is often used in the Targum (Aramaic translation of the OT). The range of meaning of the word *māmôn* and *māmônāh* is discussed more thoroughly in Marcus Jastrow, *A Dictionary of the Targumim, The Talmud Babli and Yerushalmi, and the Midrashic Literature*, 2 vols. (New York: Pardes Publishing, 1950), 2:794.

The command not to worry suggests that worrying about one's earthly life is a manifestation of a person's eagerness to seek earthly enjoyment even if it endangers his commitment to the one true God. As in the previous section, Jesus highlights the role of the eyes by asking his listeners to look at how God cares for what may be considered less important than humans, like the lilies and the birds (Matt 6:25–30). Once again, Jesus refers to God as the Father in heaven which underscores his care for his people. Interestingly, the Hebrew expression *Yahweh Yireh*, which is often translated "the LORD provides" can be rendered "the LORD sees" (Gen 22:14). The disciples can *look* to the God who can *see* them.

Instead of worrying, his disciples are to seek God and his righteousness (6:33). The command is addressed primarily to his disciples, and not to the crowd.[59] This is one of the things that should distinguish them from the Gentiles who worried much about this life (6:32), and who thought that repetitious prayers always guarantee positive answers (6:7). The contrast between worrying and seeking God's kingdom and righteousness may suggest two things: (1) that worrying may lead to various forms of unrighteous acts, and (2) that worrying much about this life may be a reflection that one has *lost sight* of God's reign beyond this life.

7:1–5 Don't Judge Others . . . (But) Remove the Log in Your Eye

Jesus' prohibition against judging others is not given without qualification. Unlike his command concerning oaths in which he said, "Do not take an oath at all" (Matt 5:34),[60] which suggests absoluteness, Jesus said that the one who judges others will be judged by the same standard and that those who tried to remove the speck in another person's eye must remove the log from his own (7:5).

The principle of receiving the same treatment as one gives to another is found in various contexts in the Scriptures. For instance, according to Jewish wisdom, those who refuse to listen to the cries of the poor cannot expect God to listen to their cries when they need his help (Prov 21:13);

---

59. Craig L. Blomberg, "On Wealth and Worry: Matthew 6:19–34 – Meaning and Significance," *CTR* 6 (1992): 74; Richard J. Dillon, "Ravens, Lilies, and the Kingdom of God (Matthew 6:25–33; Luke 12:22–31)," *CBQ* 53, no. 4 (1991): 606–607.
60. The Greek adverb *holōs* ("completely") describes the verb *omosai* ("to take an oath"); thus the command may be rendered "Do not, under any circumstance, make an unnecessary vow to God" (Matt 5:34). In light of Jesus condemnation of the practices of the Pharisees (23:16–24), the vows to which Jesus referred have to do with gifts and offerings.

this proverb can perhaps be summarized thus, "God helps those who help others." Moreover, Jesus' "Golden Rule" stresses this idea (see discussion on Matthew 7:12 below). The same principle underlies Jesus statement on judging others (Matt 7:2).

Although the prohibition against judging others is clear, Jesus' command that the "log" in one's own eye should first be removed before the person can take the speck out from another person's eye suggests that correct judgments can be made by someone whose vision is cleared (7:5). A similar saying is used by the rabbis who talk about removing splinters in between one's teeth.[61] Once again, Jesus used an expression familiar to his contemporaries to discourage making unwarranted judgments against other people. The act of making judgments in itself is not Jesus' primary concern, but the person's attitude, whether the judgment was done for the purpose of condemnation or restoration, self-promotion or as an inevitable part of exhortation.

7:6 Don't Give Pearls to Pigs and What Is Holy to Dogs

The series of prohibitions closes with two proverbial statements about dogs and pigs being unworthy of receiving something good and pure. These two animals are characterized as unclean in the OT; dogs are unclean because of what they consume (Prov 26:11), and pigs are "unclean" making them inedible (Lev 11:7; Deut 14:8). No wonder they are used to represent evil people (Prov 26:17; Phil 3:2) and foolish ones (Prov 11:22). Here, dogs and pigs seem to refer to people who vehemently reject the good news and the disciples were called to discern carefully how they share the gospel.

This prohibition poses a twofold challenge to interpreters.[62] First, although the parallel between the two statements and the metaphorical languages are clear, what the dogs/pigs represent and to what the pearl/"the holy things" refer remain to be identified. Second, the connection between this prohibition and the previous three is unclear.

Similar proverbs are found in many rabbinic writings, some of which refer to the redemption of things dedicated to the Lord and the prohibition to redeem them for the purpose of feeding the dogs, "Holy things must not be

---

61. Babylonian Talmud *Arakhin* 16b; *Bava Batra* 15b. For an extended discussion, see George Brockwell King, "A Further Note on the Mote and the Beam (Matt 7:3–5; Luke 6:41–42)," *HTR* 26, no. 1 (1963): 73–74.
62. Huub van de Saandt, "'Do Not Give What Is Holy to the Dogs' (Did 9:5d and Matt 7:6a): The Eucharistic Food of the Didache in Its Jewish Purity Setting," *VC* 56, no. 3 (2002): 227 n. 11.

redeemed to be fed to dogs."⁶³ Once again, the similarity suggests that Jesus uses proverbial statements familiar to his Jewish audience. Some rabbis prohibited the teaching of the Law to the Gentiles because it was too precious to be given to "unclean people"; and they used pearl as a metaphor for this. The same idea is also seen in the works of non-Jewish writers.⁶⁴ Perhaps the best way to understand Jesus' statement is to look for hints within the Gospel. The disciples were told not to insist on teaching those who are unwilling to receive their teaching (Matt 10:14; Mark 6:11; Luke 9:5), not only because they are bold enough to reject the message (as though trampling underfoot the precious thing given to them), but because some would also not hesitate to attack the message bearer. Jesus was not teaching his disciples to make quick judgments in identifying the dogs and pigs, but Jesus calls for wisdom on the part of his disciples in their efforts to share the good news.

As for the connection between this fourth prohibition with the previous three, in the same way that the first two can be paired because both focus on earthly wealth/treasures, the final one can be paired with the third one because it "balances" the third prohibition ("Do not judge") by showing that there are occasions wherein right judgment is necessary as one identifies who are the dogs and the pigs. As one does so, it need not be done with "haughty eyes" (Prov 6:17; 21:4), but with "discerning eyes" (Prov 17:24; Isa 44:18).

The list of four prohibitions in Jesus' Sermon can be divided to two pairs. The first pair has to do with treasures in heaven; and they require healthy eyes that reflect the disposition of the heart (Matt 6:22–23) and ones that can see the provisions of the Father in heaven (6:26). The second pair has to do with proper discernment; and they require log-free eyes that reflect a heart that is willing to be corrected (7:3–5) and ones that are able to discern properly (7:6).

7:7–23 LIST OF DOS

Jesus' giving of instruction to his disciples, recalls Moses' giving of the Law to Israel (Exod 20:1–17). The event that was accompanied by "thunder and

---

63. Babylonian Talmud, *Bekhorot* 15a; see also Exod 22:31. For a list of other passages, see Van de Saandt, "Do Not Give," 230 n. 17.
64. Babylonian Talmud, *Hagiga* 3a; 13a; *Berakhot* 33b; *Yevamot* 94a. Sextus claims that godless people must not be taught about God (*Sentences* 81, 354, 365, 407, 451). See Craig A. Evans, *Matthew*, NCBC (Cambridge, NY: Cambridge University Press, 2012), 166.

lightning... the trumpet and... smoke" (Exod 20:18), all of which point to the glorious presence of the LORD.

Like Moses, Jesus did not just teach his followers what not to do, but he also instructed them what to do. Moreover, like the Law, Jesus' instructions to his disciples do not consist only a list of don'ts, but also a list of dos: (1) ask, seek, and knock; (2) enter the narrow gate; and (3) beware of false prophets.

7:7–12 Ask, Seek, Knock

This section may contain three commands, but they can be considered one command expressed in three ways. In this section, the Father is implicitly presented as the one who gives to those who ask (Matt 6:8), the one whose kingdom and righteousness is to be sought (6:33; see also 13:44–45), and the one who opens kingdom's door to those who knock (5:20; 7:21; 18:3; 19:23–24; 23:13).

Throughout the Sermon, God is consistently presented as the Father in heaven;[65] and one of his characteristics highlighted in the Sermon is his compassion and affection expressed through his provisions (7:9–11). The high mortality rate of children in ancient times was the reason many fathers refused to show affection to their children, although parental affection was still considered part of basic human instinct and responsibility.[66] This kind of compassion is a reflection of God's goodness which further assures the followers of Jesus that there is no need to worry about this life because he will provide (6:31–32), and that storing up treasures in heaven through sincere charity will not go unrewarded (6:1–4). Thus, the "Golden Rule" is an appropriate conclusion for his command to ask, seek, and knock.

It is noteworthy that both Jesus and Confucius set similar community ideals before their disciples, namely, the ideal of reciprocity. Jesus teaches that those who are merciful are the ones who can receive mercy (5:7), that those who give to the needy would receive a reward from God (6:2–3; 10:42; 25:34–46), that only those who are willing to forgive can expect forgiveness (6:12, 14–15; 18:32–35), and that one is judged in the same way he/she judges others (7:2).

---

65. Even outside the Sermon, God is referred to as the Father and becoming his children is an essential part of Christian discipleship (Henry Pattarumadathil, *Your Father in Heaven: Discipleship in Matthew as a Process of Becoming Children of God*, AnBib 172 [Rome: Editrice Pontifico Instituto Biblico, 2007], 203–209).

66. For example, Aristotle, *Nichomachean Ethics* 8.1.3; Epictetus, *Discourses* 1.23.3–5; 3.24.84–89; 4.7.35; Seneca, *De Benificiis* 3.11.1. Diane G. Chen, *God as Father in Luke-Acts*, StBibLit 92 (New York: Peter Lang, 2006), 28–29.

WHOSE GOLDEN RULE HAS MORE KARATS? CONFUCIUS' OR JESUS'?

There are many versions of the "Golden Rule,"[1] but discussions on the so-called "Golden Rule" of Jesus inevitably bring to mind the proverb attributed to Confucius. Confucius was once asked by one of his disciples Tzu Kung: "Is there any one word that can serve as a principle for the conduct of life?" To this question Confucius replied, "Perhaps the word 'reciprocity': Do not do to others what you would not want others to do to you'" (*Confucian Analect* 15:23).[2] His saying is sometimes compared to that of Jesus but construed negatively because of its negative and passive approach ("do not do . . .") compared to the positive and proactive character ("do . . .") of Jesus' "Golden Rule."[3] This comparison undermines the value of Confucius' teaching and it is often seen as inferior in value to that of Jesus. Although there is no question that Jesus is the savior, and Confucius is not "the way, the truth, and the life," pitting one against the other shows a misunderstanding of the essential purpose of their teachings. Both the positive and negative versions of the Golden Rule were results of a particular community issue being addressed. Such critique on Confucius' negative version is unnecessary, because the two sayings are essentially the same, even though they are phrased differently.[4]

Samson L. Uytanlet

---

1. For a list, see William Henry Paine Hatch, "A Syriac Parallel to the Golden Rule," *HTR* 14, no. 2 (1921): 193–194 n. 1; Gerd Theissen, "Die Goldene Regel (Matthäus 7:12//Lukas 6:31) über den Sitz im Leben Ihrer Positive und Negative Form," *BibInt* 11, nos. 3–4 (2003): 386–399.
2. De Bary, *Sources of Chinese Tradition* (1st), 1:25.
3. Bruce Chilton, "Jesus, the Golden Rule, and Its Application," in *The Golden Rule: The Ethics of Reciprocity in World Religions*, eds. Jacob Neusner and Bruce Chilton (London: Continuum, 2008), 77. The negative expression "do not do . . ." is also commonly used in ancient Palestine (Str-B, 1:459–460).
4. Theissen, "Die Goldene Regel," 399.

7:13–14 Enter the Narrow Gate

At first glance, the command to enter the narrow gate seems to have no connection to its immediate context. However, the implicit reference to God's rule in the previous commands (Matt 7:7–8) and the explicit warning against lip service in relation to it (7:21) suggests that the narrow gate is the entrance to the kingdom of heaven (5:20; 18:3; 19:23–24; 23:13).

A similar saying can be found in other writings.[67] The main point of Jesus' saying is that obedience may be difficult, but it is the way to "enter" God's kingdom. Of course, entering a narrow gate is still relatively easier compared to going through the eye of a needle. Nonetheless, it is clear that being a disciple of Jesus is accompanied by various forms of difficulties.[68]

7:15–23 Beware of False Prophets

False teachers can come from within the church (2 Pet 2:1) or from outside (2 John 10). Matthew 7:15–23 warns about this danger and exhorts the believers to be discerning in order for them not to fall prey to counterfeits.

Several agricultural metaphors are used to stress the warning and highlight the differences between the true and the false prophets. First, the false prophets may appear like sheep, but are really ravenous wolves (Matt 7:15). Ancient Jewish writers often compared the righteous to lambs and the wicked to wolves.[69] In the OT, sheep often symbolizes God's people (Pss 78:52; 79:13; Isa 40:11; Jer 13:17, 20; Ezek 34:17, 22; Mic 7:4). In Zephaniah 3:3, false prophets are compared to wolves, and this was also done by some NT writers (Matt 7:15; see also Acts 20:29). Wolves prey on weaker animals, no wonder wolves are used to describe people involved in violence and bloodshed,[70] and dishonest gain (Ezek 22:27). Although the metaphor of a wolf is associated with evil people and their activities, hope is offered for them as "sinners" who need to hear the gospel (Luke 10:3). The metaphor "ferocious wolves" in sheep's clothing accentuates Jesus' earlier teaching concerning the importance of the heart (Matt 5:20–48); the external and visible acts may not always be the best gauge of what is in a person's heart.

Second, the false prophets do not produce good fruit (7:16–18). The expression about bad trees not producing good fruits is expressed in variety of ways. For example, James says fig trees cannot produce olives, grapevines cannot produce figs, and salt ponds cannot produce fresh water (Jas 3:10–12).

---

67. Jesus ben Sirach taught, "The way of sinners is paved with smooth stones, but at its end is the pit of Hades" (Sirach 21:10, NRSV). This is part of a series of proverbs that stress the importance of righteousness and obedience. Libanius also talks about the "wide doors" that are open to sinners (*Oration* 9). See J. Duncan M. Derrett, "The Merits of the Narrow Gate," *JSNT* 15 (1982): 21.
68. G. Todd Wilson, "Conditions for Entering the Kingdom according to Matthew," *PRSt* 5, no. 1 (1978): 45–47; A. J. Mattill, Jr., "The Way of Tribulation," *JBL* 98, no. 4 (1979): 531–546.
69. This is best summarized in the word of Jesus ben Sirach, "What does a wolf have in common with a lamb? No more has a sinner with the devout" (Sirach 13:17, NRSV).
70. See 4 Esdras 5:18; John 10:22.

Similarly, wise and foolish speech and actions cannot come from the same source (3:13). Matthew talks about thorns not producing grapes, and thistles not producing figs (Matt 7:16); an illustration which he briefly summarizes, "A good tree cannot bear bad fruit, and a bad tree cannot bear good fruit" (7:18). This metaphor complements the previous one, because although the external and visible acts may not always be an indicator of what is in a person's heart, they can reflect the person's internal disposition.

The two agricultural metaphors "demonstrate that there is an irrefutable difference between the good and the bad tree and an inescapable connection between the character of the fruit tree and quality of the fruit produced."[71] The separation of the genuine and false also comes with a stern warning that it is not enough to do the right things (like calling God "Lord," performing services), because those who do not produce righteous fruit will be denied entry to God's kingdom (7:21–23).

Matthew presents God as the one who grants the kingdom to those who ask, seek, and knock (Matt 7:7). This implies that entry to the kingdom is a gift from the compassionate Father, who requires obedience nonetheless. The command to enter the narrow gate is a forewarning to the believers that sufferings and persecution may be part of their journey of obedience, which requires them to check both their external actions and internal dispositions.

---

71. Allison A. Trites, "The Blessings and Warnings of the Kingdom (Matt 5:3–12; 7:13–27)." *RevExp* 89, no. 2 (1992): 191.

FOLLOWING JESUS IN THE SERMON ON THE MOUNT

By and large, Asians are religious people. Taoists observe the first and fifteenth of the lunar month by burning joss paper and making offerings; and Muslims pray five times a day, especially on Fridays. However, these religious acts may have little to do with their ethical behavior. There are also those who do not adhere to any religion (atheists), yet they try to live good and moral lives by their own pragmatic standards.

In the Sermon on the Mount, Jesus sets his standards for his disciples, and the challenge is to "be perfect as your heavenly Father is perfect" (Matt 5:48). In these three chapters, Jesus weaves together worship, religious practices and ethics, thus showing that what we know and believe, our attitudes and our actions are all integral part of the Christian life.

While these are Jesus' unique teaching, they are firmly built on the Hebrew Scriptures or Old Testament, and are a fulfillment of the law. Many Christians today do not pay enough attention to the OT, thinking that it is old, difficult to understand, and irrelevant. Jesus' teaching here clearly shows that is not the case, in fact the OT is meaningful and relevant to understanding the person and message of Jesus. Furthermore, as we will see in this gospel, Matthew grounds the story of Jesus in the OT. Believers today must take time to learn the OT in order to be able to appreciate the New Testament in all its fullness and richness.

There is also a stark contrast between Jesus' Beatitudes (5:3–10) and the values of many cultures, thus his teachings pose a constant challenge to believers through all cultures and ages. The values here are so counter-cultural that they seem both impossible and unreal; though we also note that Thai culture values meekness, and peacemakers are appreciated in many troubled situations. The Beatitudes are constant reminders that Christian values are very different from that of the world, and by living out these values Christians are salt and light in their communities and societies.

The standards that Jesus gives here are not necessarily "higher" than those of other religions. For example, Jesus does not encourage loud and public prayers; instead, he taught his followers how to pray quietly and in secret. Prayer in other religions is transactional, seeking favors from the gods, but prayer for Christians is about seeking God's kingdom, forgiveness, and deliverance from evil. Prayer is therefore God-focused and not merely to demand that our needs be met. Prayer provides us a means to communicate with God to grow in intimacy with him. Thus, Christian prayer is not merely asking for our wants, for God already knows what we need and he will provide according to his sufficiency and our needs. Christian prayer is acknowledging God's sovereignty over us and the world, and

> seeking to align ourselves with him. This type of prayer is a stark contrast to other Asian religions.
>
> Jesus said to store treasures in heaven where moths and rust cannot reach; but such treasures cannot be seen on earth. This is different from people in society today who ostentatiously give large sums of money and seek to have monuments named after themselves or their families. Christian giving is discrete, not seeking human acknowledgment, but it is given in faith to a God who will reward us in his terms and in his ways. Therefore, those who are converted to Christianity should learn different ways of relating with God. Christian spirituality is also unique in its simplicity and thus can be a stark contrast to the other forms of spirituality around Asia.
>
> The Sermon on the Mount also shows the seamless integration between the religious and the ethical in a believer's life. Many Christians today lead a dichotomized life, where their worship of God on Sundays has little if anything to do with their work life on Monday or the way they spend their time or money. Pastors in Singapore lament that too often they see tempers flare in the church carpark right after the worship service.
>
> Jesus uses the analogy of good fruit (7:15–20) to illustrate how the good life of Christians can be seen. That good fruit must be a life not merely paying lip service to God's commands or using the Lord's name in vain, but in following Jesus in all aspects of life. When disciples live out the kingdom of heaven the way that Jesus commands, they are wise builders who build on solid rock who can weather whatever difficulties life gives them, and whose lives will have a long-lasting impact.
>
> **Kiem-Kiok Kwa**

7:24–27 THE PARABLE OF THE WISE BUILDER: CONCLUSION TO THE SERMON

The parable of the wise builder is an appropriate way to conclude Jesus' Sermon on the Mount. It poses a challenge to the disciples who heard Jesus' teachings to act accordingly. Even for the modern readers who are "eavesdropping" the message Jesus first addressed to his disciples (Matt 5:1–2), there is an implicit challenge to not be mere spectators "astonished" by Jesus' teachings (7:28), but to be listeners invited to obey what they hear.[72]

---

72. Mark Alan Powell, "Matthew's Beatitudes: Reversals and Rewards of the Kingdom," *CBQ* 58, no. 3 (1996): 479.

As a son of a carpenter (13:55; Mark 6:3), and very likely one himself, Jesus understood what is required to construct a building that can withstand storm. What makes a structure strong is not the visible portions (walls, roof), but the foundation and the place upon which the structure is built.[73] Real obedience is not just about what people see. In the same way that the unseen foundation of a building is essential to the structure, Jesus' teachings grounded in one's heart is critical to one's obedience. The parable provides a broader perspective about the relationship between correct actions and the heart. The image of the ravenous wolves shows that visible actions do not always reflect the person's internal disposition (7:15); the illustration of the good and bad tree implies that a person's internal disposition will be evident through one's actions (7:17–18); and the parable of the wise builder points to the necessity of actions that are grounded on a heart of obedience (7:24, 26; see also Jas 1:22–25).

Jones aptly summarizes the purpose and presentation of the parable of the wise builder thus: "the passion to persuade, the pastoral intent to protect, the desire to motivate and to invite change, and the willingness to warn prophetically by laying out a stark choice."[74] The parable of the two foundations is Jesus call to obedience that does not merely focus on external actions, but on a change, that begins from within.

7:28–29 THE AUTHORITY OF JESUS AND THE PRESENCE OF GOD

After observing the difference between Jesus and scribes, the listening crowd was astonished. The people in Jesus' hometown had the same reaction after they heard Jesus in their synagogue, wondering about the *source* of Jesus' authority to preach and perform miracles (Matt 13:54–55; see also 22:33). Matthew does not answer the question explicitly. In fact, there is no need to answer the crowd's question, because the answer should be obvious to Matthew's readers – God was with Jesus in his preaching and miracles. Likewise, the contrast between Jesus and the scribes is clear – God's presence with Jesus.

---

73. Rabbi Eleazar ben Azariah shared a similar story about a tree that is overturned and uprooted by the wind because it has few roots but abundant branches. Another teacher, Elisha ben Abuja, compared a house built upon stone with adobe underneath and one that has adobe on top of stones. See Mishnah *Avot* 3:8. Peter Rhea Jones, Sr., "On Rock or Sand? The Two Foundations (Matthew 7:24–27, Luke 6:46–49)," *RevExp* 109, no. 2 (2012): 235.
74. Jones, "On Rock or Sand," 240.

MATTHEW 8:1–9:34

The Healing Ministry of Jesus as Evidence of God's Presence

Healing was an essential part of Jesus' ministry. The truthfulness of the accounts of Jesus' miracles in the Gospel was generally accepted throughout the centuries until the eighteenth century. The "Enlightenment Period" seems to have dimmed the vision of many scholars to the reality of the supernatural.[1] Although some modern Asians are also beginning to doubt whether miracles can truly happen, generally speaking, Asians do not have difficulty accepting that miracles can still happen, whether through physical contact with something or someone who possesses or is possessed by divine power, or through other means. The belief that healing power can be transferred from one person or object to the sick in order to effect healing remains prevalent among many Polynesians, Africans, and Asians. The Polynesian term *mana* is often used to refer to this belief.[2] The stories of the hemorrhaging woman (Mark 5:25–34; Matt 9:20–22; Luke 8:43–48), Peter's shadow (Acts 5:15), and Paul's handkerchief (19:11–12) are evidences that such belief is also part of the worldview of many ancient Mediterranean people. In the Philippines, consulting the *arbolario* remains common in many regions. (An *arbolario* is a faith healer who uses various methods such as incantations, concoctions, or talisman for healing). Wiping the statue of the Black Nazarene in Quiapo Church in Manila using towels or handkerchiefs which are then used for healing is a practice, to say the least, tolerated by the Roman Catholic Church in the Philippines.

Despite some similarities between Jesus' healing (for example, healing through physical touch, necessity of faith) and these modern practices, there remains a fundamental difference between them, namely, in relation to their purpose. The healing stories show that Jesus is the Messiah and they teach some basic truths about discipleship (like the importance of faith and obedience). In many instances, the ones who were healed were also given another

---

1. Charles W. Hedrick, "Miracle Stories as Literary Composition: The Case of Jairus's Daughter," *PRSt* 20, no. 3 (1993): 217.
2. Donald H. Bromley, "The Healing of the Hemorrhaging Woman: Miracle or Magic?" *Proceedings* 25 [2005]: 23.

opportunity to join the society that despised and rejected them because of their sickness.³ It should be noted that Jesus did not heal just for the sake of healing; healing is an essential part of his proclamation of the kingdom of God. The threefold ministry of Jesus includes teaching, preaching, and healing, each one inseparable from the others.⁴

Health services are often included in the promise made by Filipino politicians during their campaigning and many of them present themselves as the ones who can provide the basic necessities for the well-being of the people. What Filipino politicians do today can be compared to what Roman emperors did during the time of Jesus. The emperors were considered as the one who could grant food, fertility, and health to the people.⁵ The prophet Isaiah envisioned something similar when God executes justice through his Messiah, which involves defeating the nations that were oppressing them, gathering of God's people, healing the sick, feeding the hungry, bringing an end to death and poverty, and the inclusion of people from all nations in God's plan (Isa 26:19; 29:18; 35:5–6; 42:7; 61:1). According to Isaiah, God's reign would be characterized by peace and righteousness (11:1–10) as the "shoot from the stump of Jesse" ruling over God's people (11:1; see also comments for Matthew 2:23); and as Matthew interpreted the vision, this ruler would be the evidence of God's presence with his people (1:23; see also Isa 7:14). God's presence is not only manifest in Jesus' birth and teaching, as seen in Matthew 1–7, but also in the miracles Jesus performed. What this means is that unless a nation acknowledges God as their true king, they can never experience the peace and well-being that only God can give.

Ancient writings contain numerous stories of miracles,⁶ and the way these stories are told shows that miracles are considered a normal part of life. Jesus is often compared with other ancient healers. Although there are similarities between the healings performed by Jesus and other healers, one

---

3. Warren Carter, "Jesus' Healing Stories: Imperial Critique and Eschatological Anticipations in Matthew's Gospel," *CurTM* 37, no. 6 (2010): 489.
4. Opoku Onyinah, "Matthew Speaks to Ghanian Healing Situations," *JPT* 10, no. 1 (2001): 141.
5. Carter, "Jesus' Healing Stories," 495.
6. There are accounts of healing gods like Hercules/Heracles (Eurepides, *Alcestis* 1136–1163), Asclepius (Greek Inscriptions 4.1.121–122), and Isis (Isidorus, *Hymn to Isis* 1.1–38; Diodorus Siculus, *Historical Libraries* 1.25.2-3). There are also accounts of healing heroes like Pythagoras (Porphyry, *Life of Pythagoras* 33), Empledocles (Diogenes, *Lives of Eminent Philosophers* 8.60-69), King Pyrrhus (Plutarch, *Pyrrhus* 3.4], Vespasian (Seutonius, *Vespasian* 7.2), and Apollonius [Philostratus, *Life of Apollonius* 3.39, 4.45, 6.43). Wendy Cotter, *Miracles in Greco-Roman Antiquity*, (New York: Routledge, 1999), 11–46.

must be careful not to allow these superficial similarities to blind us to the differences.[7] The origin of Jesus' power and his purpose for performing them clearly set him apart. As for the stories of miracles in Matthew, there seems to be a close relationship between God's supernatural work through Jesus and his call to discipleship. This is seen particularly in the accounts of Jesus' miracles alternating with the stories illustrating discipleship (Matt 8:1–10:42). This is summarized in Figure 7.[8]

Figure 7: Miracles and Discipleship

Miracles		Discipleship
The leper, the centurion's servant, and Peter's mother-in-law (8:1–17)	↘	
	↙	Would-be disciples (8:18–23)
The storm, the Gadarene demoniac, and the paralytic (8:28–9:8)	↘	
	↙	Calling of Matthew and the question of John's disciples (9:9–17)
Jairus' daughter, the bleeding woman, the two blind men, the mute demoniac (9:18–35)	↘	
		Sending out of the Twelve (9:36–10:42)

The stories of Jesus' healing and exorcism underscore the presence of God through Jesus. The same is manifested in the ministry of the disciples, which will be discussed in a separate section.

---

7. See Walter T. Wilson, *Healing in the Gospel of Matthew: Reflections on Method and Ministry* (Minneapolis: Fortress, 2014), 290–293.
8. For studies on the so-called "miracle section" of Matthew's Gospel, see Heinz Joachim Held, "Matthew as Interpreter of the Miracle Stories," in *Tradition and Interpretation in Matthew*, eds., Günther Bornkamm, Gerhard Barth, and Heinz Joachim Held, *NTL* (Philadelphia: Westminster Press, 1974), 165–299; Julius Schniewind, *Das Evangelium nach Matthäus*, NTD 2 (Göttingen: Vandenhoeck & Ruprecht, 1936), 37, 106.

Matthew

8:1–17 MIRACLES: PART 1

8:1–4 The Leprosy Patient

The first in this series of Jesus' miracles is the healing of the leprosy patient (see also Matt 4:23–24). In ancient times, even until now, a person with leprosy is rejected by the society because many fears that the disease is contagious. Although there are accounts of "hero lepers" in the OT (2 Kgs 7:1–20), leprosy is often considered God's judgment (Miriam [Num 12:10], Joab [2 Sam 3:29], Azariah/Uzziah [2 Kgs 15:3–5; 2 Chr 26:16–21], Gehazi [2 Kgs 5:26–27]).

Today, medical doctors refer to leprosy as Hansen's disease, which is already considered curable in many parts of the world. However, the term "leprosy" as it is used in the Bible may refer to various skin diseases that could be transmitted.[9] No wonder the OT Law required leprosy patients and those who showed signs of it to be quarantined (Lev 13:3, 4, 11, 21, 26, 31, 33). Added to the shame was the requirement for leprosy patients to shave their heads and shout "unclean, unclean" as a warning to the public so that any form of physical contact might be avoided (13:44–46).

Given the kind of humiliation that comes with having leprosy, the leper's initiative to approach Jesus publicly for healing was a bold step. He did not only open himself to the crowd's criticism, but there was also a possibility that the people might react violently and harm him physically.[10] His request, "Lord, if you will" (Matt 8:2), contrasts with statements like "Lord, it is your obligation to heal me!" or "I have the right to be healed!" He expresses humility. Jesus healed him by touching, which showed that the healing was more than just a restoration of physical health, but also included the breaking of social barriers, because the one who was once "untouchable" (Lev 5:2–3) could now be touched (Matt 8:3).[11]

Jesus instructed the man not to spread the news of his healing. He did not state the reason, but this may be understood in the light of Mark 1:45; the spreading of the news resulted in Jesus not being able to publicly enter a town to do ministry. Jesus may have had the same reason here. Moreover, his

---

9. Mary Ann McColl and Richard S. Ascough, "Jesus and People with Disabilities: Old Stories, New Approaches," *JPCC* 63, nos. 3–4 (2009): 3. Ancient Jewish rabbis also clarified how various types of skin diseases should be treated (Mishnah, *Nega'im* 1:1–14:13).
10. McColl, "People with Disabilities," 3.
11. John Paul Heil, "Significant Aspects of Healing Miracles in Matthew," *CBQ* 41, no. 2 (1979): 280.

instruction to the leper to offer the required sacrifices shows that he did not intend to break the Law; but as shown in his Sermon (Matt 5–7), he wanted his disciples to understand the basic principles of the commandments. Jesus also commanded the healed man to show himself to the priests "for a proof to them" (8:4). This statement was best understood as an invitation to the Jews to consider the evidence that God was present and at work through him, and to think seriously about God's offer of salvation to them.[12] In his Gospel, Luke mentions that there were many leprosy patients in Israel during the time of Elisha, but only Naaman was healed (Luke 4:27). It was this miracle that led a non-Israelite to confess that there was no God in all the earth except in Israel (2 Kgs 5:15). One of the reasons Jesus performed miracles in Luke is to reveal his identity, and the same is true in Matthew. Many Jews expected a Messiah who would be able to heal leprosy patients,[13] and this story clearly showed Jesus' identity as the Messiah (see also Matt 11:5).

8:5–13 The Centurion's Servant

Matthew identifies Jesus' ministry location as Capernaum. This was also the place where Jesus met a Roman centurion whose servant was sick. Josephus describes the city of Capernaum (or Caphernaum) as a beautiful city with fruitful soil that enabled locals to produce fruits the whole year. Trees that require cold (walnuts), warm (palm), and temperate (figs, olives) weather grow in Capernaum. Hence, Capernaum was called as the "ambition of nature." Fruits that were harvested during autumn were preserved for a while, and grapes and figs were available for ten months in a year. The land was watered by the streams and was called "the vein of the Nile."[14] Jesus ministered in a place where there were lots of agricultural products. No wonder Jesus used so many agricultural images in his teachings, like the parable of the sower, vineyard, and many others. Capernaum was also one of the places in Palestine where the Roman armies were stationed. The Romans divided their army into groups of a hundred soldiers and each group was led by a centurion. Matthew refers to the centurion using the Greek word *hekatonárchēs* or "ruler of a hundred" (Matt 8:5, 8, 13; 27:54), and Mark uses the transliteration of the Latin title *kenturiōn* (Mark 15:39, 44, 47).[15] Regardless

---

12. Jack Dean Kingsbury, "Miracle of the Cleansing of the Leper as an Approach to the Theology of Matthew," *CurTM* 4, no. 6 (1977): 346–347.
13. Heil, "Significant Aspects," 281; Wilhelm Michaelis, "Lepra, Lepros," *TDNT* 4:233–234.
14. See Josephus, *Jewish Wars* 3.10.8 §§ 516–521.
15. Thomas Nichol, "Centurion," *ISBE*, 1:629; Keener, *Matthew*, 264.

of how they were called, centurions were people in authority; and the one in this story recognized Jesus as a higher authority to whom he must submit. In this story, the centurion is reluctant to welcome Jesus to his house and preferred that his servant be healed from a distance. One possible reason is their strong cultural emphasis on reciprocity. If the centurion invited Jesus to his house, such hospitality might obligate Jesus to reciprocate by inviting him as well. This might place Jesus, the holy Jewish man, in a humiliating situation, whether he reciprocates and have an unholy Gentile come to his house, or not reciprocate and be accused of being unhospitable.[16] Whether this is the case, the story clearly shows that God's power at work through Jesus was not limited to the places where he was physically present. This should be a great encouragement for people today.

The information provided in the Gospel accounts is too little to know for certain the background and identity of the servant.[17] Perhaps the more important questions concern the centurion's hesitation to have Jesus visit the servant (Matt 8:8–9) and Jesus' amazement at the centurion's faith (8:10–13). The centurion was clearly a Gentile (8:10) and his relationship with Jesus was also complex. On the one hand, as a Gentile he was considered "inferior" to local Jews like Jesus. On the other hand, as the representative of the colonizing power, Rome, he was considered "superior" because the local Jews including Jesus had to submit to Roman authorities. The centurion's attitude suggested that he accepted his "inferior status" as Gentile despite the fact that Jesus belonged to their colonized nation.[18] More importantly, the importance of faith and submission regardless of one's status in the society is highlighted.

The healing of the centurion's servant demonstrates another aspect of God's presence: his presence is not limited to where Jesus is *physically*. Moreover, Jesus' acceptance of the centurion's faith attests to the universal scope of God's salvation, and that ethnicity is not a determinant for entrance to or exclusion from God's kingdom (8:11–12). Isaiah envisioned a future banquet prepared by the LORD for all nations, which highlighted the end of death and tears, and the removal of the reproach of Israel (Isa 25:6–9). Jesus may be alluding to this when he mentions the feast shared by Abraham, Isaac, and Jacob with those from the east and the west (Matt 8:11). The salvation of the nations (Isa 2:3; 9:1; 11:10; 18:7; 19:24–25; 42:6–7, 22; 56:3; 60:1;

---

16. J. Duncan M. Derrett, "Law in the New Testament: The Syro-Phoenician Woman and the Centurion of Capernaum," *NovT* 15, no. 3 (1973): 181.
17. Derrett, "Law in the New Testament," 179.
18. Keener, *Matthew*, 266–267.

8:14–17 Peter's Mother-in-Law

Peter and the other disciples followed Jesus after their earlier encounter with him (Matt 4:18–22). Now that they are back in their hometown in Capernaum (8:5; see also 4:13), Peter paid a visit to his ailing mother-in-law. As it is in Mark and Luke, the account in Matthew is brief and leads to the summary statement about Jesus' healing ministry in Galilee (Matt 8:14–17; see also Mark 1:29–34; Luke 4:38–41).

The OT contains healing stories that are more "dramatic" (for example, cleansing of leprosy patients, restoring sight to the blind) than healing fever. Luke seems to suggest that Peter's mother-in-law had suffered from something more than just an ordinary fever. He says that Jesus rebuked the fever (Luke 4:39), and two verses later, he rebuked the demons (4:41). This may be a hint that the fever of Peter's mother-in-law was a symptom of demonic activities; although this is difficult to ascertain. Matthew's story does not seem to include anything beyond the ordinary; but accounts of someone being healed of fever is not unique to the NT.[19] In modern times, at least in most parts of the world, healing fever seems trivial because it can easily be cured with paracetamol; this may not have been the case for ancient people. Nonetheless, we can still affirm that no sickness can be considered too trivial for Jesus to ignore.

Matthew concludes this story with a quotation from Isaiah. He explains that Jesus' healing is a fulfillment of the prophecy about the Suffering Servant (Isa 53:4; see also 1 Pet 2:24), who is also the Righteous Lamb (Isa 53:7, 11) and the Righteous Shepherd (1 Pet 2:25; Matt 9:36–38). This anticipates Jesus' sufferings on behalf of all sinners, as the guilt offering with which the LORD is pleased (Isa 53:10–12); and because he is the guilt offering accepted by God, forgiveness of sins is possible, and freedom from the consequences of sins like sicknesses become a reality.

---

19. Ancient rabbis recount a Jewish miracle worker named Hanina ben Dosa who healed the feverish son of Rabbi Gamaliel (Babylonian Talmud, *Berakhot* 34b). W. Barnes Tatum, "Did Jesus Heal Simon's Mother-in-Law of a Fever," *Dial* 27, no. 4 (1994): 155.

Matthew

8:18–23 DISCIPLESHIP: PART 1

After the first story of healing, Matthew moves to the first account that illustrates Jesus' expectation from his disciples. This is one of the episodes that only Matthew and Luke recorded (see also Luke 9:57–62). Both contrast the disciples who were eventually sent out as part of Jesus' mission (Matt 10:1–42; Luke 10:1–20), and those who were not willing to "pay the price" of discipleship (Matt 8:18–23; Luke 9:57–62). The word "disciple" can mean an apprentice, or a student.[20] Matthew highlights one of the characteristics of a disciple that Jesus expects, namely, commitment. In Matthew's story, Jesus encountered only two individuals who could have become Jesus' disciples, but whose attachments to certain things made them unwilling to follow Jesus wholeheartedly: the scribe and the man who needed to bury his father.

The first individual who almost became Jesus' disciple was a scribe. The scribes in Matthew were knowledgeable in the Scripture (Matt 2:4; 17:10). They were diligent in inviting people to become their students (23:15), except that they did not teach with authority like Jesus (7:19). They were guardians of tradition (15:1; 23:23); and like the Pharisees, they could not meet God's expectation of righteousness (5:20). They were called hypocrites who go through the religious rituals, but at the same time, actively oppress the people (23:13–14, 23, 25, 27, 29). They were Jesus' accusers (9:3), and they demanded signs from him (12:38). Despite witnessing Jesus' miracles, they rejected his claims of kingship. Together with the chief priests and elders, they were responsible for Jesus' death (16:21; 20:18; 21:15; 26:57; 27:41).

Many scribes and Pharisees during the ancient times were itinerant teachers (23:15). This was a common practice in ancient times. Some wandering teachers/philosophers, like the Sophists, did so to earn a living. They were known to give public lectures for money.[21] Jesus warned his disciples against this practice (10:8–10); and the same is implied in Jesus' reply to the scribe, "The foxes have holes and the birds of the air have nests, but the Son of Man has nowhere to lay His head" (8:20). This statement does not raise questions about God's ability and willingness to care for humans (6:25–26), but a response that presumably answers the unspoken concern of the scribe who expressed willingness to follow Jesus. Jesus was not a prophet who worked

---

20. For more detailed discussion on the definition of "disciple," see Michael J. Wilkins, *The Concept of Disciple in Matthew's Gospel: As Reflected in the Use of the Term* Μαθητής, NovTSup 59 (Leiden: Brill, 1988), 11–172.
21. Everett Ferguson, *Backgrounds of Early Christianity*, 3rd ed. (Grand Rapids: Eerdmans, 2003), 326.

for profit; and from a worldly viewpoint, becoming a disciple of Jesus was a profitless endeavor. This is perhaps the reason that nothing is said about the scribe anymore.

The second individual was a man who wanted to bury his father first before following Jesus. This may either suggest that his father recently had died and he wanted to pay his final respects, or his father was still alive and he wanted to fulfill his obligation as a son as long as his father was living. Either way, the man's desire was commendable. Giving older family members proper burial was an essential part of Jewish piety; and for this reason, Jesus' reply raises some problems. It is quite challenging to interpret Jesus' statement because it seems that he was promoting irreverence, or at the very least, irresponsibility. It is generally accepted that the statement "let the dead bury their dead" means "let the *spiritually* dead bury their *physically* dead relatives," although some considered this statement as a reference to the second burial known as the *ossilegium* or the practice of reburying the ancestor's bones.[22] What should be noted is how Jesus occasionally used exaggerated statements or hyperbole to stress his point. This was a practice common among ancient Jews. For example, Jesus talked about cutting off one's hands or plucking out one's eyes to stress the gravity of sin (Matt 5:29–30). Even Jesus' reply to the scribe about the Son of Man having "*nowhere* to lay his head" was an exaggerated statement (8:20, emphasis mine). Jesus' last statement, "let the dead bury their own dead," could also be considered as hyperbole – its purpose being to underscore the importance of following Jesus above other earthly concerns like showing respect to dead relatives; besides, it also draws attention to the urgency of the task that accompanies the disciples' decision to follow Jesus (10:1–42).

---

22. Byron R. McCane, "'Let the Dead Bury Their Own Dead': Secondary Burial and Matt 8:21–22," *HTR* 83, no. 1 (1990): 31, 34. For a brief review of the various interpretations of Matt 8:22/Luke 9:60 in the past, see Markus A. Bockmuehl, "'Let the Dead Bury Their Dead' (Matt 8:22/Luke 9:60): Jesus and the Halakhah," *JTS* 49, no. 2 (1998): 554–556.

FILIAL PIETY AND SOME ASIAN BURIAL PRACTICES

One of the ways the Jews practiced filial piety was by making sure their dead ancestors were given a decent burial.[1] The same thing can be said about the Chinese people. Filial piety is expressed by burying dead ancestors properly. This is an essential part of Confucius' teachings, who said, "While the parents live, serve them according to the rites. When they die, bury them according to the rites and make offerings to them according to the rites" (*Confucian Analect* 2:6).[2] For ancient Chinese, offering food to their dead ancestors continuously was a way to calm the hearts of those who remained alive because it meant that death did not cause them to forget their dead relatives. Of course, there is a fine line that separates superstition and idolatry in the form of ancestral worship from filial piety. Nonetheless, for Chinese people, burying dead ancestors properly is a way of paying respect to the dead ancestors.

In the OT, there are only two types of people who were not allowed by the Law to join even in a relative's burial: the high priests (Lev 21:11–12) and the nazirites (Num 6:6). Participation in these rituals made one ritually unclean, and priests and nazirites were to avoid them. Despite these provisions in the Law, the Jews showed flexibility in the practice of these requirements especially in cases wherein there was no one else who could perform such duty.[3] In the ancient rabbis' commentary on the book of Leviticus called the *Sifra* (Lev 21:11 §211), their commentary on the book of Numbers called the *Sifre* (Num 6:6 §26), even in the Babylonian Talmud (*Nazir* 47b) and the Mishnah (*Nazir* 6:5), there is a willingness to bend the rules a little bit just to make sure that the dignity of a human being is respected even if he is already dead by allowing their living relatives to give them a decent burial.

Samson L. Uytanlet

---

1. Martin Hengel, *The Charismatic Leader and His Followers* (Eugene, OR: Wipf and Stock, 2005), 8; Bockmuehl, "Let the Dead Bury Their Dead," 554. Ancient people consider it an expression of love to participate in burials (Str-B, 1:487), and giving dead people a decent burial, alongside the practice of justice, is also proof of one's faithfulness to God (4 Ezra 2:23).
2. De Bary, *Sources of Chinese Tradition* (2nd), 1:42.
3. Bockmuehl, "Let the Dead Bury Their Dead," 559.

Matthew 8:1–9:34

8:24–9:8 MIRACLES: PART 2

8:24–27 A Storm and the Disciples' (Lack of) Faith

The scribe and the man who needed to bury his father were part of the "crowd" who sought Jesus (Matt 8:20), and because of this they are distinguished from the "disciples" who followed Jesus to the boat (8:24). This episode serves as a good transition from an account about discipleship (8:18–23) to stories of Jesus' miracles (8:28–9:8), as it recounts a miracle performed amidst a storm and the disciples' response to Jesus. This story well illustrates that there is both danger and glory in being a disciple of Jesus.[23]

After the "interruption" in Matthew 8:18–22, Jesus and his disciples were able to push through with their plan to go "to the other side" of the lake (8:18), where they encountered some strong waves.[24] Even fishermen who were presumably familiar with the lake became desperate because of the force of nature they encountered (8:25).

One of the purposes of miracles in Matthew is to reveal Jesus as the divine presence among humans and to invite them to put their faith in God.[25] Despite the miracles performed previously in the presence of the disciples, they remained lacking in faith (8:26). Their address to Jesus as "Lord" shows a disconnect between what they say (expressing faith) and Jesus' assessment of their actions (expressing fear). The disciples' experience clearly broadened their understanding of Jesus' identity and works, and it provided additional reason for them to believe, especially as they would be sent out to do his work.[26]

8:28–34 The Gerasene Demoniac

In Matthew 8–9, Jesus was traveling throughout the region of Galilee. Matthew tells the stories of miracles as part of Jesus' travel. Upon their arrival

---

23. Günther Bornkamm, "The Stilling of the Storm in Matthew," in *Tradition and Interpretation in Matthew*, eds. Günther Bornkamm, Gerhard Barth, and Heinz Joachim Held, NTL (Philadelphia: Westminster Press, 1974), 57.
24. Interestingly, instead of the word *kuma* (or "waves of water") or *kludōn* (or "surge of water"), Matthew uses the word *seismos* (often translated as "storm"), which can be translated as "earthquake" (see Matt 24:7; 27:54; 28:2; Mark 13:8; Luke 21:11; Acts 16:26; Rev 6:12; 8:5; 11:13, 19; 16:18).
25. Paul F. Feiler, "The Stilling of the Storm in Matthew: A Response to Günther Bornkamm," *JETS* 26, no. 4 (1983): 401; Hubert Frankemölle, *Matthäus Kommentar*, 2 vols. (Düsseldorf: Patmos, 1994), 1:328–329.
26. The parallels between Matthew 8:23–27 and Jonah 1:3–16 also point to God's deliverance of his people (Feiler, "Stilling of the Storm," 404–405).

"on the other side" of the lake (8:18, 28), they were met by two demoniacs from the Gadarene village. There is no reason to doubt these stories of demon possession and dismiss these accounts as either fabrications or as accounts of people having a psychological disorder. On several occasions, I have witnessed people who were acting abnormally get well through prayer, and not through psychiatric treatment. The only logical conclusion was that these people were not suffering psychologically, but that there were spiritual elements involved in those situations.

The belief that the human world is the arena of spiritual confrontation between God and the demonic forces is common in the ancient Mediterranean.[27] This belief is shared by many Asians and Africans even in the modern era. Many interpreters find these miracle stories difficult to accept as accounts of real events, and stories of exorcism are even more difficult. Hence, focusing on the psychological dimension becomes the easiest way to explain such stories. Some speculated that the so-called demoniac was a potential draftee who was afraid of being summoned to join the Roman Legion or a soldier who was experiencing some post-traumatic stress disorder after witnessing a massacre. Others suggest that stories about evil spirits are means for ancient people to explain schizophrenia caused by oppression which in turn result in despising the powers that exploit them. Still others say that terms like "Satan" or "demons" are coded language used to personify evil or to refer to people through whom evil is seen, like the Roman Empire.[28] Thus, even the significance of the pigs in the story understood differently. Some say that the destruction of the swine points to the defeat of the evil powers through Jesus' resurrection and glorification, while others say that pig is a mascot of the Roman Legion stationed in Syria in AD 66–70 and suggests that the demoniac embodied Rome's "demonic rule," hence a defeat of the demons is also a defeat of Rome.[29] Matthew's accounts of healing (Matt 8:1–32) and his story of the resurrection (27:50–28:15) contain several parallels,[30] but this does not imply that these miracle stories are mere creations of a master writer.

---

27. John K. Ridgway, "A Correlation Between Healing and Peace in Matt 10:1–16," *Proceedings* 11 (1991): 105.
28. Carter, "Jesus' Healing Stories," 495; Norman A. Beck, *Anti-Roman Cryptograms in the New Testament: Symbolic Messages of Hope and Liberation*, WCLBS 1 (New York: Peter Lang, 1997), 5–6. For other examples, see John F. Craghan, "Gerasene Demoniac," *CBQ* 30, no. 4 (1968): 522–523, nn. 5–8.
29. John Bligh, "Gerasene Demoniac and the Resurrection of Christ," *CBQ* 31, no. 3 (1969): 388; Carter, "Jesus' Healing Stories," 495.
30. For details, see Bligh, "Gerasene Demoniac, 384–385; T. Milne, "St. Matthew's Parallel Narratives," *JTS* 5 (1904): 602–608.

There is a fine line that separates real demonic possession and psychological disorder, and although psychological disorders may be related to demonic activities, the former is insufficient to explain the latter. A worldview that embraces both and does not try to make light the truth about demonic activities allows the readers of Matthew to appreciate not only the literary beauty of the first Gospel, but also the practical implications of Jesus' ministry especially in regions like Asia where such activities remain evident.

Jesus' authority over the demonic powers is clear. His authority was recognized even by the demons (8:29), even though this was not always met with positive response by people (8:33–34).

9:1–8 The Paralytic

In the ancient Roman world, peace comprised every sphere of human life which included "domestic, social, military, economic, political, medical, and religious spiritual."[31] In the OT, human well-being was an integral part of God's offer of "peace." In the Gospels, health and healing are evidence of God's reign (Matt 4:17; 12:28); and like the healing of the centurion's paralyzed servant (8:6), this episode illustrates Jesus' ministry which Matthew summarized this way, "And he went throughout all Galilee, teaching in their synagogues and proclaiming the gospel of the kingdom and healing . . . paralytics" (4:23–24). This proclamation of the kingdom was done both verbally and through his actions.[32]

Although paralytics were not despised in the same way as the "unclean" leprosy patients and physical contact with other people remained possible, paralytics were considered cursed because of the ancient Jews' false assumption that physical disabilities were forms of divine judgment (see John 9:2–3). Even during the time of Martin Luther, many people still held on to this belief; and Luther was no exception.[33] Many Asians today have the same false assumption. Aside from being suspected for living a sinful life, people suffering from paralysis were considered unproductive members of the society, adding to their humiliation. It is worth noting that most of the people with disabilities in the Gospels are unnamed. "The blind" Bartimaeus is an exception (Mark 10:46). This observation may reflect the reality about

---

31. John K. Ridgway, *"Let Your Peace Come Upon It": Healing and Peace in Matthew 10:1–15*, StBibLit 2 (New York: Peter Lang, 1999), 208.
32. Frankemölle, *Matthäus*, 1:200.
33. Martin Luther, "'Take Your Bed and Go'. Sermon on Matthew 9:2–8," *WW* 16, no. 3 (1996): 282.

persons with disabilities (PWD) particularly the way they are accepted (or rejected) in societies. PWDs are often depersonalized, and referred to not by their names but by their disability.[34] We should note, however, that the stories of healing of the PWDs are not about the one who was healed, but about the one who healed them.

This story also illustrates the role of faith in healing (Matt 8:5; 9:2). In the two healing stories involving paralytics, the ones who exercised faith were *not* the paralytics themselves; or perhaps it is better to say, *not only* the paralytics. In both cases, the centurion's servant and the bed-ridden paralytic were not said to have believed in Jesus, although Matthew's silence does not necessarily mean they did not believe. The only thing clear was that the faith of the centurion and the "stretcher-bearers" was not to be considered a substitute for the faith of the two paralytics, but demonstrated confidence that translated to action, of seeking Jesus for help on behalf of the paralytics.[35]

Another important aspect of Jesus' identity shown in this story was his authority to forgive sins. Jesus' offer of forgiveness to the paralytic was opposed by the scribes, not because they did not believe that the paralytic needed forgiveness (indeed, the opposite is true), but because Jesus' claim meant he had authority that only belongs to God. This reflects the scribes' assumption that the task of forgiving was not delegated to Jesus.[36] His reply to his detractors' accusation of blasphemy is straightforward, "But that you may know that the Son of Man has authority on earth to forgive sins" (Matt 9:6). Three chapters later, Matthew shows that it is the Pharisees, and not Jesus, who are the real blasphemers (12:32–33). Jesus' actions (healing) only proved that his claim (authority to forgive sins) was true.

One of the challenges this episode presents is the conclusion drawn by the crowd that God had given authority "to men" to forgive sins (Matt 9:8). Several attempts have been made to identify who are the human recipients of God's authority. Some suggest that "the men" refer to the crowd, while others say it refers to the believing community who granted authority to pronounce forgiveness.[37] Often neglected is the fact that the Greek expression *tois anthrōpois* can be translated in many ways: one possibility is to translate it as "to humans," which would mean that human beings are given authority to forgive sins. But the expression can also be translated "for the sake of humans,"

---

34. McColl, "People with Disabilities," 7.
35. Onyinah, "Ghanian Healing Situations," 133.
36. Keener, *Matthew*, 290.
37. Wolfgang Schenk, "'Den Menschen' Mt 9:8," *ZNW* 54, nos. 3–4 (1963): 272–274.

which would mean that the authority was given to Jesus, but humans where the intended "beneficiaries" of this forgiveness.[38]

Although Jesus corrected the wrong assumption that *all* sicknesses were the result of sin (John 9:2–3), there is nothing in Jesus' reply to suggest that he denied the connection between sin and disease altogether. This connection remains clear in the Bible. Even the other ancient Jewish writings show this. This means if sin caused various forms of disease, restoration to health is possible only through receiving forgiveness and acknowledging God's rule. Many of Matthew's contemporaries anticipate health and healing as part of God's reign as king.[39] Each miracle story highlights a certain aspect of God's rule. For example, the exorcism of the Gadarene demoniacs demonstrates God's authority over evil spirits and the stilling of the storm shows his authority as Creator and ruler over his creation. The healing of the paralytic is evidence of God's authority to restore the health, both body (through physical healing) and the spirit (through forgiveness).

9:9–17 DISCIPLESHIP: PART 2

9:9–13 Matthew: Call and Banquet

The name Matthew could be a name given by Jesus to Levi the tax collector.[40] Like the four fishermen (Matt 4:18–22), Matthew willingly left his work in order to become his disciples (9:9). There is, however, a significant difference between the tax collector and the four fishermen in terms of their place in the society. The four fishermen did not belong to the rich class, and this made the rich tax collectors "more respectable" than them (see Luke 19:2). Nonetheless, since there was nothing morally unacceptable in being a fisherman, there was no reason for them to be despised like tax collectors. Tax collectors were considered despicable because: (1) they overtaxed the people, making the life of ordinary Jews more difficult (19:8); and (2) they collected taxes on behalf of the Roman colonizers, making them traitors. No wonder in this Gospel, tax

---

38. Schenk "Den Menschen," 275.
39. See Ezra 7:121-124; 8:52-54; 2 Baruch 29:5; 72:2-6; 73:1. Carter, "Jesus' Healing Stories," 496.
40. Rudolf Pesch, "Levi-Matthäus, Mc 2:14, Mt 9:9, 10:3: Ein Beitrag zur Lösung eines alten Problem," *ZNW* 59, nos. 1–2 (1968): 41–42.

collectors are listed alongside evil men (Matt 5:45–46), Gentiles (5:46–47; 18:17), sinners (9:11; 11:19), and prostitutes (21:31–32).[41]

Soon after Matthew left his tax booth, he dined with Jesus, his disciples, other tax collectors, and "sinners" (9:10). Although the NIV specifies "Matthew's house" (9:10), the Greek is actually vague and could refer to "Jesus' house." Either way, this gathering would have had some social implications. A student showing such hospitality to a teacher would have been commended by the rabbis,[42] and the same could be said of any teacher showing hospitality to students. However, a teacher having fellowship with sinners raised some question about his discernment. Instead of praising the disciple for honoring his teacher with a banquet, the Pharisees focused on Jesus' apparent lack of wisdom by not avoiding the "tax collectors and sinners" (9:11).

For ancient Jews, prudence could be shown by avoiding "bad company," but one did so *only* for the purpose of avoiding their influence (1 Cor 15:33),[43] and not out of a sense of superiority. The Pharisees in this episode exemplified the self-righteous and their judgmental attitude against which Jesus preached (Matt 7:1). The rabbis were open to the possibility of restoring sinners, even tax collectors,[44] but the Pharisees' attitude was the opposite in this episode. The quotation from Hosea 6:6 further justified Jesus' attitude towards the "tax collectors and sinners," drawing a sharper contrast between him and the Pharisees.[45]

9:14–17 Disciples of John the Baptist, of the Pharisees, and of Jesus

The contrast between Jesus and his religious contemporaries continues with the questions of John's disciples about the reason Jesus' disciples do not fast (Matt 9:14). Jesus' teaching about fasting and his statement "when you fast" suggest that fasting was already part of the disciples' religious activities (see 6:16–18). However, the question of John's disciples and Jesus' reply seem to suggest otherwise.

It is noteworthy that in Jesus' reply, he neither confirms nor denies his disciples' religious practice. In a wedding banquet, the guests *feast* rather than

---

41. Eric Ottenheijm, "The Shared Meal – A Therapeutic Device: The Function and Meaning of Hos 6:6 in Matt 9:10–13," *NovT* 53, no. 1 (2011): 7.
42. See Mishnah, *Avot* 1:4; Sirach 9:16. Ottenheijm, "The Shared Meal," 10.
43. See also Sirach 13:1; Mishnah, *Avot* 1:7.
44. Ottenheijm, "The Shared Meal," 8.
45. Mary Hinkle Edin, "Learning What Righteousness Means: Hosea 6:6 and the Ethics of Mercy in Matthew's Gospel," *WW* 18, no. 4 (1998): 362. See also discussion on Matthew 12:7.

fast. Jesus' question, "How can the guests of the bridegroom mourn while he is with them?" (9:15), suggests the impropriety of such conduct.[46] The bridegroom's departure, especially the violence he had to suffer before his departure, should be the cause for mourning.

Fasting can be an expression of mourning, which explains the connection between a "gloomy face" and fasting. However, the "gloomy face" had apparently become, not just a sign of grief, but also of religious fervor which inevitably led to hypocrisy (6:16–18). The question of John's disciples seems to have been more a question about the disciples' spiritual discipline, rather than the grief they would soon experience. Instead, Jesus shifted the discussion from fasting to mourning. This makes the question about fasting of secondary importance to Jesus' departure and his disciples' mourning.[47]

The illustrations of wine/wineskin and cloth/patch provide clues regarding the implication of the question of John's disciples (9:16–17). In both illustrations, the new objects (new wine, new/unshrunk patch) cause damage to the old ones (old wineskin, old cloth). The accusation of John's disciples about the religious practice of Jesus' disciples (or lack of it) implies that they had broken away from the good old spiritual discipline of fasting (Ezra 8:23; Neh 1:4; Isa 58:3–4; Jer 14:12; Zech 7:5), but Jesus' reply shows that this was not the case.

9:18–34 MIRACLES: PART 3

9:18–26 The Ruler's Daughter and the Hemorrhaging Woman

The final series of miracle stories presents Jesus, not only as healing the sick and exorcising demons, but even raising the dead. As in the first set of miracle accounts, Jesus' touch was essential for healing. The first episode is composed of two miracle stories combined together involving two unnamed females – a ruler's daughter and a hemorrhaging woman. Matthew begins his account with the girl already dead, and the interruption of the hemorrhaging woman creates some suspense in the story. The raising of the girl is important to show that Jesus was indeed the Messiah (Matt 11:2; see also Luke 7:19),[48]

---

46. Lanfranco M. Fedrigotti, *An Exegetical Study on the Nuptial Symbolism in Matthew 9:15* (Lewiston: Edwin Mellen Press, 2006), 89.
47. George C. Gianoulis, "Did Jesus' Disciples Fast?" *BSac* 168 (2011): 425.
48. Hedrick, "Miracles Stories as Literary Composition," 222, 229.

something which would continue to be talked about by his disciples as they proclaimed the kingdom of God (Matt 10:8). For ancient Jews, raising the dead was an act that only God could do (Ezek 37:5). However, this did not discard the possibility of God using human agent in the process.[49]

The ruler of the synagogue, identified as Jairus in the other two Gospels (Mark 5:22; Luke 8:41), came to Jesus *kneeling* as he petitioned Jesus to lay hands on his dead daughter (Matt 9:18). This suggests that the ruler believed that Jesus was able to raise the dead. This story is interrupted by the account of the hemorrhaging woman who came to Jesus with a false assumption that touching Jesus' garment would bring her health. Ancient writings contain accounts of people who received healing by touching statues of the gods. One example is the story of the blind man named Gaius who was instructed by Asclepius in a dream to touch the base of the god's statue with his hand and to use the same to touch his eyes. This act "saved" Gaius from blindness.[50] The similarities between the healing stories of Jesus and Asclepius were already observed even in the earlier centuries, and as a result, many wanted to preserve the practices of their old religion. Many Christians disagreed to the point that they even called Asclepius the "head of demons." Although there were obvious similarities between the two healers, Asclepius was a Greek god who was known to reject those who were impure and Jesus did the exact opposite.[51]

Like the leprosy patient, the hemorrhaging woman was also considered "unclean" and any form of physical contact with a bleeding woman, whatever the reason for bleeding (whether due to menstruation or hemorrhage), was believed to result in contamination (Lev 12:1–8; 15:19, 25; 20:18). This is very likely the reason the woman chose to stay *behind* Jesus, and to just touch the *fringe* of Jesus' garment (Matt 9:20). Openly announcing her condition would not only be scandalous, especially in a crowded place, it would also put her in a situation wherein she could be publicly humiliated and scorned. She would also open herself to possible rejection by Jesus. Jesus, however, did not do so, but he corrected her wrong assumption by showing her that it was not her *touch*, but her *faith*, that resulted in her healing (9:21–22).

---

49. Benjamin G. Wold, "Agency and Raising the Dead in *4QPseudo-Ezekiel* and 4Q521 2 ii," *ZNW* 103, no. 1 (2012): 8.
50. Patricia Cox Miller, *Dreams in Late Antiquity: Studies in the Imagination of a Culture* (Princeton, NJ: Princeton University Press, 1997), 115.
51. Emma J. Edelstein and Ludwig Edelstein, *Asclepius: Collection and Interpretation of Testimonies* (Baltimore: John Hopkins University Press, 1945), 332–335.

The story resumes with Jesus' visiting the dead girl. As it is with the other miracle stories, the element of physical touch is essential in raising the girl back to life.[52] Touching a corpse, according the Jewish Law, was like touching a patient with leprosy or a bleeding person; it could make a person ritually unclean (Lev 11:31–32; Num 5:2; 9:6–7, 10). In all three instances, Jesus went beyond what was socially and religiously acceptable, and assumed the role of the "representative of those helpless Israelites without a shepherd,"[53] showing that God's work cannot be bounded by social taboos.

9:27–31 The Two Blind Men

The news about Jesus raising a dead girl spread throughout the "district" (Matt 9:26). This explained why many people came to receive healing, including two blind men (9:27). Matthew does not explain how the blind men were able to *follow* him, whether they were just partially blind, or they had long been residents of that district so they were already familiar with the area, or whether they had another person guiding them. More essential to the story was the way they addressed Jesus as they asked for mercy, namely, as the healer, the Son of David.

The title "Son of David" used in reference to Jesus the healer recalls ancient Jewish belief that Solomon, the son of David, was a healer. The idea that Solomon was a healer/exorcist/ magician became accepted before the time of Jesus. The words of the two blind men are similar to the words of the old artisan in a story in the *Testament of Solomon*. The artisan appealed to Solomon for help because of his violent son, "King Solomon, Son of David, have mercy on me, an elderly man"; and in the same story, Solomon communicated with demons and exercised authority over them.[54] Although Solomon was considered a mortal like other humans, he was the recipient of special wisdom that included power over spirits and the knowledge to use herbs for healings, like the *arbolario* in the Philippines. Josephus also presents him as an exorcist.[55] All this explains why the blind man called Jesus the "Son of David" when they are asking for healing (see also Matt 9:27; 20:30).

---

52. Charles E. Powell, "The 'Passivity' of Jesus in Mark 5:25–34," *BSac* 162 (2005): 69.
53. Stuart L. Love, *Jesus and Marginal Women: The Gospel of Matthew in Social-Scientific Perspective*, Matrix 5 (Eugene, OR: Cascade, 2009), 135.
54. See Testament of Solomon 20:1, 6–21; Wisdom of Solomon 7:20.
55. See Josephus, *Jewish Antiquities* 8.2.5 §§44–47. Dennis C. Duling, "Solomon, Exorcism, and the Son of David," *HTR* 68, no. 3 (1975): 235–252.

As in the previous accounts, through Jesus' touch, the two blind men received healing (see 9:25), which confirmed he was the expected Messiah (11:5; 15:31). Faith is essential to receiving healing (9:29).

9:32–34 The Mute Demoniac

There are various manifestations of demon possession, which includes isolation in tombs (Matt 8:28; Mark 5:5) or the desert (Luke 8:29), fierceness (Matt 8:28; Mark 5:5), and extraordinary strength (Luke 8:29). It may also cause physical disabilities such as blindness (Matt 12:22) and muteness (9:22; 12:22; Luke 11:44), although others manifest possession with loud cries (4:33). In this story, demonic possession resulted in muteness (Matt 9:32). In the Gospel accounts, humans may be possessed by a single (Luke 4:35–36; 8:29) or by many demons (Mark 16:9; Luke 8:2, 20), and demons do not discriminate based on race and gender (Matt 15:22; Mark 7:16). Some have extraordinary power including the ability to foretell the future. Ancient Jews believed that demonic forces were in constant communication with God (Job 1:6–12; 2:1–7), a special "privilege" that allows them to know what God plans to do.[56] This belief system allows them to explain how some who are demon possessed become fortune tellers (Acts 16:16–19).

Mark describes the man delivered from demon possession as a person "in his right mind" (Mark 5:15), suggesting that demonic possession and psychological problems may have similar symptoms. No wonder some interpreters choose to explain demonic possession merely as a psychiatric disorder.[57] However, one must admit that other types of manifestation (like extraordinary strength, blindness, and fortune-telling) are difficult to explain using psychiatric reasons. Moreover, even if other stories are cases of psychiatric disorders rather than of demonic possession, for Jesus to heal without the use of modern medicine makes these miracles no less glorious than the others.

Based on the accounts in the Gospels, there were various means by which those who were demon possessed were healed. These accounts of exorcism show the power of God over these unclean elements. Three elements in this account recall Isaiah's record of God's promise (Isa 42:5–44:5). First, the deliverance of the mute demoniac and the healing of the blind men (Matt 9:27–35) recall God's promise of restoration of sight to the blind and freedom for those in prison (Isa 42:7; 43:8). Second, the crowd's reaction, "Never was anything like this seen in Israel" (Matt 9:33), recalls God's promise that

---

56. See Wisdom of Solomon 20:11–17.
57. Carter, "Jesus' Healing Stories," 494, n. 10.

he would do something new in Israel (Isa 42:9; 43:19). Third, the threefold ministry of Jesus (teaching in the synagogues, healing, and the proclamation of God's kingdom; see Matt 9:35) underscores the main thrust of the Lord's promise, namely, the people's acknowledgment that he is the Holy One, Creator, Redeemer, the Only God, and King (Isa 43:10–11, 15; 44:6).

As a result of all this activity, the conflict between Jesus and the Pharisees began to intensify. The people who experienced healing called Jesus "Lord" and acknowledged that he had more authority than the religious leaders (Matt 7:29; 8:1, 10). His actions that benefitted especially the weak made him the "model of the community," which challenged the Pharisees to show the same concern for the needy as well.[58] The Pharisees' comment that Jesus cast out demons by the power of demons (Matt 9:34) was a clear expression of their unbelief, an attitude that many of Jesus' Jewish contemporaries shared. This same attitude is addressed by Isaiah when he called Israel "blind" and "deaf" (Isa 42:18–19); and because of their "disabilities," they could not fulfill their role as the Lord's witnesses to the nations (43:8). This suggests that these healing and exorcism episodes were not just a retelling of incidents of Jesus' life. They revealed the identity of Jesus, and they highlighted the "blindness and possession of Israel which rejected its Messiah."[59]

Matthew's section on miracles (Matt 8:1–9:34) concludes with a summary of the threefold ministry of Jesus: (1) teaching in the synagogues; (2) preaching the good news of the kingdom; and (3) healing all diseases (9:35). All of this was evidence of God's presence with his people and the grace he made available for them.[60] Moreover, it set forth Jesus as the Messiah, the one through whom God's presence is made evident and his work made complete.

This section also includes stories that illustrate discipleship. Matthew does not cover up the disciples' lack of faith and their unimpressive background. Nonetheless, the story of the unwilling scribe and mourner implies the disciples' commitment to follow Jesus, many of whom Jesus appointed to continue his work. It is also noteworthy that Matthew concludes the series of healing stories with the account of the deliverance of a mute (not a deaf) demoniac prior to sending out the Twelve (9:35–10:1). This last account of

---

58. Evert-Jan Vledder, *Conflict in the Miracle Stories: A Socio-Exegetical Study of Matthew 8 and 9*, JSNTSup 152 (Sheffield: Sheffield Academic Press, 1997), 241.
59. William R. G. Loader, "Son of David, Possession, and Duality in Matthew," *CBQ* 44, no. 4 (1982): 585.
60. Blaine Charette, *Restoring Presence: The Spirit in Matthew's Gospel*, JPTSup 18 (Sheffield: Sheffield Academic Press, 2000), 96.

exorcism is the perfect transition because it shows that through Jesus, God's people can once again assume the role of God's witness to proclaim his kingship because Jesus has the ability to open one's mouth to proclaim this truth.

MATTHEW 9:35–10:42

The Disciples Sent Out to "Harvest"

From the late-1980s until early 2000s, members of a Bible-believing denomination in the Philippines have preached regularly near the public markets, buses, and even inside *jeepneys*.[1] Preachers from this group would also bring an offering bag with them and ask for offerings after they preached the gospel, and so they gained a reputation of being preachers for money. Some of their teachings are similar to those of the Evangelical churches, like the need to accept Christ and to turn from sin. For this reason, people who are not familiar with this group often confuse them with other local Evangelical groups. This practice of preaching/teaching for money is not something new. In ancient times, a group of philosophers known as the Sophists also received a bad reputation of being "philosophers for hire," traveling from one place to another to teach their philosophy for money. In contrast to these philosophers, Jesus instructed his disciples to preach, but not for money. Although he did not deny that the disciples had physical needs (Matt 10:11), he made sure that his disciples would not make their ministry as means for financial gain.

Missionary provision was one of the issues Jesus discussed as he sent twelve of his disciples out to preach the good news. As part of Jesus' threefold ministry of preaching, teaching, and healing, he commissioned the Twelve to do the same. The commissioning of the Twelve included Jesus' call to prayer, an identification of the participants in the mission (9:36–10:4), a list of prescriptions and prohibitions (10:5–8), instructions regarding their preparations and provisions (10:9–16), and some precautions and warnings about persecution (10:17–42).

9:35–10:4 THE TWELVE IDENTIFIED: THEIR PRAYER AND PARTICIPATION

Matthew 9:35 provides a brief summary of the threefold ministry of Jesus illustrated in Matthew 5:1–9:34: preaching and teaching (5:1–7:29), and

---

[1]. A *jeepney* is a locally assembled vehicle used for public transportation in the Philippines. Its design is followed after American military jeeps used during World War 2. It has a seating capacity that ranges from 8–16 passengers, and like buses, it has a particular route.

healing (8:1–9:34). Matthew provides a continuous story beginning from Jesus' ministry (5:1–9:34), followed by his commissioning of the twelve disciples (9:35–10:42), and the continuation of his travels around Galilee to do ministry (11:1–13:58). One thing is worth noting about the story of Jesus' commissioning of his disciples: it does not contain any details about what the disciples accomplished (contrast, for instance, Luke 9:6). Moreover, the following chapter begins with this statement. "After Jesus had finished instructing his twelve disciples, he went on from there to teach and preach in the towns of Galilee" (Matt 11:1). These two observations suggest that even the work assigned to the disciples was to be considered a portion of Jesus' overall task. In other words, the ministries of proclamation and healing were not the works of Jesus' disciples; they were Jesus' works through them.[2] This underscores the theme of God's presence because it focuses, not on the disciples doing the work of Christ, but on Jesus doing his work through his disciples.

Two agricultural images are used to describe the crowd on whom Jesus had compassion: (1) sheep without a shepherd; and (2) a harvest ready for the reaping. In ancient Israelite thought, the sheep (and cattle in general) and the harvest (inclusive of all types of crops) shared at least two common things: (1) they belong to God (Exod 22:29–30; Matt 21:34); and (2) they are used as images for people who sinned but whom God wanted to restore.

9:35–36 Sheep without a Shepherd

First, the crowd was likened to "sheep without a shepherd," and they are "harassed and helpless" (Matt 9:35). These two descriptions present an image of sheep that are being bothered, or perhaps being threatened, by a predator, but the sheep could not do anything about their situation. The image of the "sheep without a shepherd" is not unique in Matthew. It was used to refer to an army defeated in battle or without a leader.[3] A similar expression describes the confused army of King Ahab as they faced defeat against the Arameans (1 Kgs 22:17; 2 Chr 18:16), and the same expression was also used by Moses as he prayed to God to appoint a successor who would continue his work (Num 27:17; see also Isa 63:11).[4]

---

2. See also Dorothy Jean Weaver, *Matthew's Missionary Discourse: A Literary Critical Analysis*, JSNTSup 38 (Sheffield: Sheffield Academic Press, 1990), 125–126.
3. Francis Martin, "Image of Shepherd in the Gospel of Matthew," *ScEs* 27, no. 3 (1975): 275.
4. See also Judith 11:9; Mark 6:34. James L. Bailey, "Church as Embodiment of Jesus' Mission (Matthew 9:36–10:39)," *CiThM* 30, no. 3 (2003): 190, n. 4.

In the OT, God is ultimately the Shepherd who cares for his people (Pss 28:9; Isa 40:11). In contrast to the Good Divine Shepherd, Israel have had bad human shepherds (including both kings and prophets) who blindly led God's people to idolatry (Isa 56:11; Jer 2:8), caused God's flock to scatter (Jer 10:21; 23:1–2; 25:34–36; 50:6), and fed on the sheep instead of feeding them (Ezek 34:2). God is the Shepherd who would seek the lost sheep (34:10–22) and appoint a servant like David to rule and shepherd them (34:23–24), in order that the people may know him and experience his protection and presence (34:25–31). Ezekiel described this new experience in this way, "Then they will know that I, the LORD their God, am with them and that they, the Israelites, are my people, declares the Sovereign LORD. You are my sheep, the sheep of my pasture, and I am your God" (34:30–31a). This is part of God's promise to restore his people despite their sins.

9:37–38 Harvest Ready for Harvesting

Second, the crowd was likened to crops ready for reaping. In the OT, harvest is evidence of God's favor and blessings (Lev 26:3–5, 42; Deut 28:4, 11–12; 30:9–10), hence a joyous occasion (Ps 4:7; Isa 9:3); but it can also be a symbol of end-time promise (Amos 9:13–15) and judgment (Matt 13:37–43; Amos 8:2).[5] The story in Matthew 9:37–38 highlights the need of the crowd (being "harassed and helpless") and Jesus' response to meet this need (sending the Twelve to heal, preach, and teach). It also shows the readiness of the people (being ready to be reaped because the "harvest is plentiful") and Jesus' response to the situation (sending the Twelve to reap the harvest). Thus the image of harvest in this passage points not to God's coming judgment but to the readiness of the people to receive (through teaching and proclamation) and experience (through healings and exorcisms) the full extent of God's rule.[6]

The joy that came with Israel's salvation from their enemies was likened to the joy of the reapers (Isa 9:3). Isaiah also foretold that this salvation is something that the people from the land "beyond the Jordan" would experience (Matt 9:1). For Matthew, Isaiah's prophecy was fulfilled by Jesus' arrival to Capernaum in order to proclaim the kingdom of God (4:14–16), and we see it once again here as Jesus called his disciples to reap this harvest.

---

5. Blaine Charette, "A Harvest for the People: An Interpretation of Matthew 9:37f.," *JSNT* 38, no. 1 (1990): 29.
6. Francis Wright Beare, "Mission of the Disciples and the Mission Charge: Matthew 10 and Parallels," *JBL* 89, no. 1 (1970): 7.

It is also a prophecy that expects the coming of the one who would rule on God's behalf, whose name will be called "Wonderful Counselor, Mighty God, Everlasting Father, Prince of Peace" (Isa 9:6), and whose rule is evidence of God's presence (Matt 7:14).

There is no question that various forms of sufferings can make people receptive to the Gospel message, because sufferings or "harassments" make them realize that they are "helpless." This may be a reason why many Asian nations who have experienced some form of calamity are more open to turn to God; and the Jews of the first century who had been under cruel foreign powers and oppressive local rulers were also ready to be "harvested." Of course, not every Jew who heard Jesus' message turned to God, because ultimately, it is God who makes the people ready to accept the message of God's supreme rule and to be willing to live a life under him. There is also a necessity for the disciples to "[ask] the Lord of the harvest . . . to send out workers into his harvest field" (9:38).

10:1–4 The Twelve: Their Prayer and Participation

Jesus' instruction to the disciples to pray to the Lord of the harvest suggests that the work of reaping is ultimately the Lord's and that the Twelve are but God's recruits assigned to participate in his work. The Twelve is introduced for the first time here as a group. In Matthew, twelve is a number that sometimes represents full measure (12 years of sickness [9:20], 12 baskets of leftovers [14:20], 12 legions of angels [26:53]), and it is also the number of tribes of the original nation of Israel. Jesus' sending of the Twelve to seek the "lost sheep of Israel" (10:6) implies that the mission of the disciples begins with the nation that first rejected their God, and that their first task is to bring them the message that God wants to restore his relationship with them. The list of names of the Twelve is basic and does not include a list of their credentials. In fact, many incidents in the Gospel show that they are "unqualified."[7] This shows that although a person's achievement is important, that in itself is the determining factor whether one can participate in God's work.

In contrast with the crowd, the Twelve are empowered to serve.[8] Matthew summarizes the mission of the Twelve, "Jesus called the twelve disciples to him and gave them authority to drive out impure spirits and to heal every disease and every sickness" (10:1); the same acts were performed by Jesus in Matthew 8–9 as part of his proclamation of God's kingship. In the process,

---

7. Beverly Roberts Gaventa, "The Unqualified Twelve," *ChrCent* 110, no. 17 (1963): 549.
8. Bailey, "Church as Embodiment," 190.

God is shown to be the healer-shepherd of his people. In the OT, the promise of well-being is given to those under God's rule (Isa 9:6–7; 52:7; Ezek 37:25–28). The same can be said of Matthew, healings and exorcisms were considered the clearest manifestation of God's kingship.[9]

10:5–15 THE TWELVE INSTRUCTED: PRESCRIPTIONS, PROHIBITIONS, AND PROVISIONS

The account of Jesus sending out the Twelve is recorded in the three Synoptic Gospels (Matt 10:5–16; Mark 6:7–13; Luke 9:1–6). Matthew's account of this "mission orientation" provides the most detail. It includes specification of their target ethnic group (Matt 10:5–6), clear-cut job description and compensation (10:7–8), instructions about what and what not to bring (10:9–12), and a warning concerning the difficulties awaiting them and how to handle them (10:13–42). The first three will be discussed in this section and the last one in the next.

First, Jesus did not only specify the "target group" to whom the Twelve should preach, but he also prohibited them to go to certain groups (10:5–6). The Twelve were instructed to go, only to the "lost sheep of Israel." The metaphor of the lost sheep is often used to refer to God's people (Ps 119:176; Jer 50:6; Ezek 34), which includes the Jews living abroad (Ezek 28:25). This statement is difficult for two reasons: it clearly excludes those that are not "Israelites," and it raises a question about its implication for our mission today. Jesus clearly prohibited them to "go among the Gentiles" and to "enter the towns of the Samaritans" (Matt 10:6). This command seems unnecessary because the last thing that the disciples would do would be to preach to the Samaritans or Gentiles. John's description about the relationship between the Jews and Samaritans *before* the resurrection hints that the disciples would, at the very least, be reluctant to visit Samaritan towns for missionary trips like this (John 4:9). Even Luke's account of the early church's mission to the Gentiles *after* the resurrection suggests the same hesitation (Acts 11:1–18; esp. vv. 3, 12, 18). However, Jesus' command to go to all nations at the end of the Gospel makes it clear that their mission is not to be limited to the Jews only (Matt 28:16–20). Even in the earlier chapters of his gospel, Matthew

---

9. Giovanni Battista Bazzana, "Early Christian Missionaries as Physicians: Healing and Its Cultural Value in Greco-Roman Context," *NovT* 51, no. 3 (2009): 234.

hints that the mission of Jesus is broad in scope. The prohibition here seems to point to God's intent to first bring his message of forgiveness to Israel.

Jesus' instruction not to "go among the Gentiles" nor to "enter the towns of the Samaritans" (Matt 10:6) seems, at first glance, a command to make their mission exclusive to the Israelites. Some suggest that Jesus' statement shows that he was setting his own ministry (being limited to Israel) as the example for his disciples to follow, even though he wanted their mission to have a broader scope; some say that this is a sign of God's special favor for Israel. Several scholars offer varying explanations;[10] but what is clear is that an exclusive ministry to the Jews is not Jesus' intention. Matthew clearly shows that Jesus' mission is not limited only to Israel, but also to the Gentiles. This is seen in the quotation of Micah 5:2 (see Matt 2:6) and Isaiah 9:1–2 (see Matt 4:15–16). Micah foresaw the return of the Jews to their land so that they might be under God their Shepherd once again (Mic 5:4–5), and Isaiah envisioned a time when God's people would once again enjoy God's presence (Isa 9:3). The messages of these two prophets come with a promise that the Jews would experience freedom from their foreign oppressors; the same message that would definitely bring hope to the nation under Rome. Jesus' prohibition (Matt 10:6) seems to point to God's purpose of bringing his message of forgiveness to the Israelites, because they were the ones appointed to proclaim God's kingship to the nations (Exod 19:5–6; Isa 43:8–15). They were not able to do so in the OT, but the book of Acts shows that Jesus' disciples carried on this task. The command to focus on the lost sheep of Israel, therefore, must be seen as God's attempt to restore Israel and allow them to once again take the role as light to the nations.

The items that the Twelve are instructed not to bring with them are basic necessities for a longer trip, and this suggests that their mission is only short term. More importantly, the basic characteristic of the good news is emphasized through Jesus' remark: it costs nothing for its recipients. This recalls Isaiah's plea to Israel to seek God and his reminders of God's promise of salvation. He tells them that: (1) no payment is necessary to receive this offer of salvation (Isa 55:1–3); (2) "David," who is a symbol of the Messiah, was called to be God's witness to the nations (55:4–5); and (3) salvation is available for the Israelite who turn to God (55:6–7). Isaiah was expecting the day to come when both Israel and the other nations would acknowledge God

---

10. See Eric Baker, "Going Only to the Lost Sheep of the House of Israel: Matthew's Gospel Tradition," *Proceedings* 23 (2003): 85–88.

as ruler; and Matthew expected the same thing. This suggests that although the Twelve are sent only to the "lost sheep of Israel," this is only an initial step for the proclamation of the message of God's kingship to the nations.[11]

Second, the Twelve were instructed, "[as] you go, proclaim this message, 'The kingdom of heaven is near.' Heal the sick, raise the dead, cleanse those who have leprosy, drive out demons" (Matt 10:7–8a). This passage can also be translated this way: "Proclaim this message as you go, 'The kingdom of heaven is near,' and proclaim this message by healing the sick, by raising the dead, by cleansing the leprosy patients, and by driving out demons." Jesus' only command here is to "proclaim"; healing, raising, cleansing, and exorcising are actions that accompany their preaching. These are the same acts that accompany Jesus' proclamation of the kingdom; Matthew has records of Jesus healing the sick (8:5–15; 9:1–8, 18–22, 27–31), raising the dead (9:23–26), cleansing the leprosy patients (8:1–4), and casting out demons (8:16, 28–34; 9:32–34). In Luke, the Twelve gave reports on what they had accomplished (Luke 9:6, 10). After Jesus gave the instruction, the *disciples* went out to preach (Luke 9:6). However, in Matthew, after Jesus gave the instruction, *Jesus* went out to preach (Matt 11:1). Matthew does not say that the Twelve completed their mission, except that they were instructed to do as their Teacher did. This suggests that their ministry is but an extension of Jesus' ministry.

Third, Jesus gave a brief orientation to them about their compensation as workers. On the one hand, the Twelve are not to be preachers for hire. On the other hand, they are humans with physical needs like anyone else and therefore must be dependent on God's provisions through the hospitality of believers who freely accept the good news. Jesus stated the underlying principle for this instruction: "Freely you have received, freely give" (Matt 10:8b).

Jesus' instruction not to bring certain things could have various implications. First, this command distinguishes the Twelve from itinerant "philosophers for a fee" or "prophets for profit." Second, although the instruction does not make clear whether the Twelve really have gold, silver, copper, extra tunic, and staff to bring on their journey, what is clear is that by joining this mission they intentionally chose poverty, and this choice helped the disciples distinguish those who would receive the message (seen through their hospitality), and those who would refuse to receive the message (seen through

---

11. The earliest known writer to suggest that Jesus' prohibition was applicable only during the time of Jesus is Tertullian (*Flight in Persecution*, 6; *Prescription against Heretics*, 8).

being unhospitable). Third, the prohibition shows the urgency of the task, and that whatever is fulfilled within this short period is considered essential to God's greater purpose. Fourth, Jesus' statement echoes Isaiah's call to those who remained faithful to God that they should seek him because his salvation is free for those who desire to receive it (Isa 55:1–2, 6–7).

Healings and exorcisms are the outward manifestation of peace (Matt 10:8, 13; see Isa 57:18–19; Jer 16:1–5; 30:1–22); and like some philosophers, medical practitioners in the Greco-Roman world perform healings for a price. The Twelve are distinguished from them by performing these for free. Moreover, although healing in this context refers to deliverance from physical diseases and ailments, it need not be limited to it for it also includes the healing of the wounds of the nation brought about by foreign oppression, and this comes through an acknowledgment that there is only one true ruler, namely, God the king.

The disciples were instructed to look out for those who were "worthy" in the villages that they entered (Matt 10:11). The literary context suggests that "worth" here is based on nothing else but a person's willingness to receive the message by welcoming the messenger (10:11–14). This statement is comparable to Jesus' command neither to give what is holy to the dogs nor to throw pearls to swine (7:6). Those who show contempt for the messenger should not be forced to receive the message (10:14), but judgment awaits them (10:15). The severity of judgment is comparable to that of Sodom and Gomorrah (Gen 19:1–29).

10:16–42 THE TWELVE INFORMED: PRECAUTIONS AND PERSECUTIONS

The final section of Jesus' instruction to his disciples contains several warnings about the kind of danger they might face in the process. Matthew encouraged the persecuted believers by reminding them that while Jesus was still with them physically, he warned them of the dangers they would have to face because of what they believe. The same warnings could be given again and again even in different situations considering that the persecution of Christians remains widespread in many parts of Asia.

Jesus commanded his disciples to "be as shrewd as snakes and as innocent as doves" (Matt 10:16). The biblical story of the temptation of Adam and Eve explains why craftiness is associated with serpents in Jewish thought (Gen 3). Both Matthew 10:16 and the Greek version of Genesis 3:1 use the word *phronimos* or "clever." Wisdom or cleverness is not necessarily bad, in fact, it is desirable; clever people usually come up with good ideas that can make life easier. However, with increased cleverness also comes a greater ability to deceive; and this is illustrated in the story of the temptation of Adam and Eve with the serpent outwitting the first couple with its cleverness.

Innocence can mean purity of mind, and this purity of the doves makes it clear that the serpent's deceptiveness is unworthy of imitation. Nonetheless, Jesus' statement suggests that the serpent's wisdom *is* desirable as part of the needed skills as they face persecution while proclaiming God's kingdom.[12] This skill set was needed because, as Jesus explained, sending his missionaries to the world was like placing "sheep among wolves" (10:16a), where they would be in danger of being chased, harassed, wounded, killed, and even devoured. These wolves were their persecutors who might even be members of their own family, as the succeeding verses imply.

Jesus issued another imperative, "be on your guard" (10:17). The Greek can be literally translated "beware of men" (see comments for Matthew 9:8). This does not refer to people in general, but to the "wolves" among which the disciples are sent (10:16). Not everyone would be hostile to them, some would even welcome them and believe their message; but Jesus wanted them to be aware that there would be "wolves" ready to hinder their work and make their lives difficult. The same image of the wolves was used to refer to the false prophets who also confessed Jesus' lordship and did a lot of work similar to those of the apostles, but whose lives did not match their claims (Matt 7:15–23).

The kind of persecution they should expect includes unwarranted arrest, torture, interrogation (10:17–18), and betrayal even by family members (10:21–22). This warning comes with a promise of protection and divine deliverance. Even until today, Christians learn a particular way of talking, and the longer we are believers, the more we learn the appropriate language for certain situations. We learn certain kind of Christian rhetoric, and it could be that in some instances, we just know the right words to say even if it is not an expression of what we truly believe. Acknowledgment of divine assistance is a common part of ancient Christian rhetoric (Mark 13:9–11; Luke 12:11–12; 21:12–15; 1 Cor 2:1–5). Here, it is not just a matter of saying the right thing at the right time, but a matter of recognizing divine power; and God's

---

12. Simeon F. Kehinde, "Sheep among Wolves: A Quest for the Right Christian Response to Societal Ills," *OJT* 11 (2006): 16–17.

purpose is not fulfilled through "strategic defense," but through obedience to the Lord who send the disciples.[13] They acknowledge divine help because they believe that God is both willing and able to do so. The disciples are assured that one of the ways divine help can be experienced is through their impromptu speech when they are forced to appear before a court. This is necessary because the nature of the situation would make it difficult for them to prepare for their defense. Even during persecution, God's presence with them remains through the Spirit who would speak through them (Matt 10:20).

Although Jesus issued a warning about the kind of persecution that they might experience, the safety of Jesus' missionaries still mattered to him. Hence, he instructed them to leave the towns that would not welcome them (10:23; see also 10:14). The simplest explanation for such persecution is that Jesus, the Teacher, was persecuted (10:14–25); his persecution came in the form of mockery and false accusations, like his alleged association with Beelzebul.[14] Hence, the disciples could expect the same treatment (Matt 10:24–25).

Jesus' second statement, "you will not finish going through the towns of Israel before the Son of Man comes" (10:23), suggests that the work of evangelism is a continuous one. Although "you" clearly refers to the Twelve, in principle every follower of Jesus must also take responsibility for declaring God's rule. The number of scholarly opinions on this verse is clear evidence that it is hard to interpret. Many questions have also been raised, including: (1) whether the coming of the Son of Man refers to the Second Coming or the resurrection; (2) whether the "towns of Israel" are limited to those within Galilee or any place inhabited by Israelites; and (3) the meaning of the expression and the identity of the "Son of Man." Some even observe that the first and second halves of Matthew 10:23 seem to be unrelated, and that Jesus' view about the end times is unclear from his statement.[15] Despite the difficulties in understanding this passage, three things are clear from Jesus' instructions: (1) the task of proclamation is an urgent one; (2) those who belong to the nation of Israel still need to hear the Gospel, and this include those who are living within and outside the territories of Israel; and (3) since

---

13. Kenneth R. Chase, "Ethical Rhetoric and Divine Power: Reflections on Matthew 10:17–20 [and Parallels]," *BBR* 22, no. 4 (2012): 505, 509.
14. The most explicit statement about Beelzebul's identity is found in the Testament of Solomon 3:6, "I am Beelzebul, the prince of demons."
15. André Feuillet, "Les Origines et La Signification de Mt 10:23b," *CBQ* 23, no. 2 (1961): 182–198; Leopold Sabourin, "Matthieu 10:23 et 16:28 dans la perspective apocalyptique," *ScEs* 37, no. 3 (1985): 354–357.

the Twelve are addressed as representatives of the believers and could be considered co-participants in the work of Jesus, other disciples might also be involved in this work. This Mission is not just for the Twelve disciples, but it is for every disciple of Jesus throughout all generations, and throughout all the world. Having said this, it must also be clear, that although Jesus used Israel as an example of people who still need to hear the Gospel message, he did not exclude the Gentiles, whether they are Gentiles from Africa, North and South America, Antarctica, Asia, Australia, and Europe.

Persecution should not lead to fear resulting in discontinuation of their work of proclamation. Having the wisdom of a serpent (Matt 10:16) should enable the missionary to know when to leave a place for safety (10:23). The Twelve disciple-missionaries were instructed to continue the work without fear. First, so that the message that was once not openly proclaimed would be proclaimed to the people (10:26–27). Second, it is more prudent to be fearful of the one who could destroy both body and soul in hell than those who could simply kill the body (10:28). Matthew's understanding of the final judgment makes clear that the one who could destroy the body and soul in hell is a reference to God (3:12; 25:41). John Chrysostom interprets the statement "kill the body" as a reference to the persecution the believers would experience that include physical death, and that the expression "destroy both soul and body in hell" refers to eternal punishment (10:28). His interpretation remains accepted until today. The use of the word *psuchē* or "soul" in the Gospels is similar to the use of the word *nepesh* in Hebrew, which may refer to: (1) the vital life principle in man that requires food and can be killed (2:20; 6:25; 11:29; 20:20); (2) the seat of thought and emotions (12:18; 22:37; 26:38); and (3) the real self of man (16:25–26). Matthew does not deny the unity of a person, but expresses God's judgment using the ancient Greek idea of the body and soul.[16] For ancient Jews, only God could do so.[17]

The severity of God's judgment against their persecutors is matched by his grace of protection for his disciples; and this grace is expressed by comparing the believers with sparrows and hairs. These two objects that are not of much worth are used to emphasize God's care for Jesus' disciples. In the OT, the expression that not even a hair of a person would fall is an assurance of protection (1 Sam 14:45; 2 Sam 14:11; 1 Kgs 1:52; see also Dan 3:27; Luke 7:18). This exaggerated expression suggests that even the least significant

---

16. Pappas, "Exhortation to Fearless Confession," 242.
17. Str-B, 1:580–581.

portion of the human body such as a single hair strand will be protected. It is not normal for people to count their hairs, hence, "the hairs on my head" is an expression that refers to things too many to count, like the psalmist's enemies (Pss 40:12; 69:4). In the Gospels, however, it is used in the context of God's care. The point of the comparison is straightforward – what is normally considered as insignificant, such as human hairs and sparrows, are considered important by God, and he will care all the more for Jesus' disciples, for those willing to risk their lives for the sake of proclaiming the Gospel.

The final six verses (Matt 10:37–42) make clear that Jesus' instruction was not only for the Twelve, but also for all the believers who do the same work of proclamation. This is seen in the use of statements addressed to "anyone" (10:37). These basically sum up the instruction above. First, the believers' persecutors may even belong to their immediate families and they may be placed in a situation wherein they would have to choose between following God or their loved ones (10:37–38; see also 10:34–36). Second, the proclamation of the kingdom may endanger the believers' lives and put them in a situation wherein they would choose between being faithful which may result in death, and saving their lives by being unfaithful (10:39; see also 10:28). Third, hospitality towards missionaries is an expression of receiving the message of the kingdom and the reward is not only for the missionaries who do the work but also for those who show hospitality to them (10:40–42; see also 10:12–15).

MATTHEW 11:1–12:50

Stories Illustrating the Jews' Rejection of Jesus

Even in the modern period, there are numerous instances when people have come to a knowledge of Jesus through miracles. One example is the testimony of a Korean missionary who worked among the Kankana-ey tribe in northern Philippines and witnessed many people acknowledging Jesus as Lord because they had experienced miraculous healings.[1] This is one major difference between Western and Asian interpreters of Scripture. Western interpreters are generally more skeptical about miracles than their Asian counterparts.[2] Although supernatural occurrences can be counterfeit miracles of demonic origin, we must remember that counterfeits only presume the existence of real ones.

The proclamation of the kingdom is the primary reason why there are supernatural phenomena in the Scripture. Jesus performed miracles not for the sake of performing miracles, but because they were integral to his proclamation of God's rule. The restoration of health and life, and supernatural occurrences are, in many situations, clear signs of God's presence with the believers. Despite the miracles Jesus performed among the Jews, they still rejected him.

Matthew records only Jesus' instruction to the Twelve without any account that they went out to preach and perform miraculous acts. Although it may be assumed that they did so despite the lack of record. However, Matthew's statement, "After *Jesus* had finished instructing his twelve disciples, *he* went on from there to teach and preach in the towns of Galilee" (Matt 11:1, emphasis mine), focuses on Jesus alone as the active agent, even as he describes the disciples' work. This clearly highlights Matthew's understanding of the disciples' (and our) mission in relation to that of Jesus, namely, the disciples' mission is no more than a portion of Jesus' mission. His promise

---

1. Keener, *Miracles*, 1:268.
2. For a critique of Western skepticism on miracles, see Hwa Yung, *Mangoes or Bananas: The Quest for an Authentic Asian Christian Theology*, 2nd ed., ASMS 52 (Maryknoll, NY: Orbis, 2014), 1–8.

of his continuous presence with his disciples even after his ascension further accentuates this point (28:20b).

The proclamation and miracles of Jesus (4:17–9:35), together with his work assigned to his disciples (9:36–10:42), were done to invite people to put their faith in God. A significant part of faith is the recognition that Jesus is the Christ, through whom God's presence is manifested in physical form. The next two chapters of Matthew illustrate the opposite of what is expected. Instead of responding in faith, those who heard Jesus' message responded in unbelief. The question of John the Baptist about Jesus' identity and the negative response of the Pharisees on different occasions describe the various expressions of unbelief.

11:1–19 STORY OF UNBELIEF (1): JOHN THE BAPTIST

This is the third account in Matthew involving John the Baptist. The first account portrays John as the preacher who lived a simple life; he was a preacher of repentance and the baptizer, whose proclamation of the kingdom preceded and opened the way for Jesus' own ministry of proclamation (Matt 3:1–17). John's arrest was mentioned in passing not long after this account (4:12). In the second account, John's disciples came to Jesus to ask him about fasting (9:14–15). Although there is nothing in this story to suggests John's direct involvement in his disciples' interrogation of Jesus. In the third account, however, Matthew claims that while John was in prison, he sent his disciples to ask about Jesus' identity (11:2); and Matthew candidly describes John's doubts, just as he describes the disciples who remained doubtful of the risen Christ (28:17).

11:1–3 John's Doubt and His Question about Jesus' Identity

It seems that John's question is inconsistent with his attitude towards Jesus in the first account where he acknowledges Jesus as the one who is "more powerful than I, whose sandals I am not worthy to carry" (Matt 3:11). Matthew does not explain the reason for John's doubt.[3] Perhaps John was just being cautious because not everyone who does "the deeds of the Messiah" is the Messiah (11:2), as Jesus also warned about counterfeits (24:24); or perhaps John himself was beginning to doubt because he was not yet vindicated;

---

3. Donald Verseput, *The Rejection of the Humble Messianic King*, EuroUS 13/291 (Frankfurt: Peter Lang, 1986), 76.

or perhaps John was becoming impatient because his expectations of Jesus' reign was taking a while to be fulfilled. What is clear from John's question is that Jesus' works are those expected from the Messiah. Hence, they point to Jesus' identity as the Christ despite John's doubts (11:2). Jesus reminded John, "Blessed is anyone who does not stumble on account of me" (11:6),[4] to encourage John to believe and not doubt.

While John was in prison, he heard that Jesus performed the "deeds of the Messiah" or "the works of the Christ" (11:2). This suggests that the people had certain expectations of the coming Messiah, and that he was expected to do certain things to show that he was indeed the one expected to come. These "works" (11:5; see also 4:24; 15:30–31; 21:14) are exemplified in the ministry of Jesus: (1) recovery of sight for the blind (9:27–31; 12:22; 20:29–34); (2) restoration of strength for the lame/paralytic (8:5–13; 9:1–8); (3) cleansing of those with leprosy (8:1–4); (4) recovery of the hearing to deaf and speech to the mute (9:32–33; 12:22); (5) raising of the dead (9:18–26); and (6) proclamation of the good news to the poor (9:35). According to Isaiah, these are the works the Messiah would be doing (Isa 26:19; 29:18–19; 35:5–6; 42:7; 61:1).[5]

11:4–15 Jesus' Response about John's Identity and His Doubts

The account continues with Jesus' double-sided comment about John that includes both an affirmation of his identity and a critique of his doubts. First, Jesus acknowledged the prophetic ministry of John; he was not a "reed swayed by the wind," nor a "man dressed in fine clothes," but the "Elijah who was to come" (Matt 11:7–10, 14).

According to Jesus, John is not a "reed swayed by the wind" (11:7). In the OT, reed could be an image of tyranny, like the reed of Egypt that caused Israel's shoulders to break and their loins to shake (Ezek 29:6–7). The image of the "reed swaying in the water" points to God's judgment (1 Kgs 14:15; see also Isa 42:3; Matt 12:20), it is an image of the plant being shaken while it is being uprooted, and in the context of 2 Kings, it refers to the exile. In Matthew, the "reed" and the man in "fine clothes" could be an indirect

---

4. See comments for Matthew 18:1–10. Aristotle says that the best way to determine a person's identity is through his works (*Poetics* 1452a, 1454b–55a). Charles H. Talbert, "Matthew 11:2–24," *Int* 64, no. 4 (2010): 407.
5. Hanna Stettler, "Die Bedeutung der Täuferanfrage in Matthäus 11, 2–6 par Lk 7,18–23 für die Christologie," *Bib* 89, no. 2 (2008): 195–200.

reference to Herod Antipas. One of the type of coins used about the time of Jesus' ministry (ca. 19–27) contained an image of a reed with Antipas' name, and although he was not accorded the title "king" by Caesar, he assumed some kingly power (Matt 14:9; Mark 6:14), lived in a kingly home, wore "soft clothing," that was, royal robe.[6] Herod Antipas served as Caesar's messenger who made sure that the people within his jurisdiction continue to be loyal to the emperor.

In contrast to Herod Antipas, John was the LORD's messenger who made sure the hearts of the people were ready for the coming of his Messiah. John's fulfillment of OT prophecy identified him with the angel of the LORD sent to guide the people and to prepare the LORD's path (Exod 23:20–23; Mal 3:1), and with Elijah (4:5–6).[7]

The desert recalls John's simple lifestyle, abstaining from many of the luxuries this world can offer (11:7; see also 3:1–5). His prophetic ministry involved calling people (including their rulers) to repentance and a change of lifestyle; this eventually resulted in his imprisonment by Herod Antipas (14:3). Luke explains that John's imprisonment resulted from his confrontation with Herod Antipas about the latter's incestuous relationship. Antipas married the wife of his brother Philip (Luke 3:19–20); a sin that apparently ran in the family because Antipas' brother Archelaus also had the same relationship with Glaphyra, the wife of their half-brother Alexander.[8] The confrontation between John and Antipas recalled Elijah's confrontation with Ahab because he led Israel into idolatry (1 Kgs 16:29–17:1). This confirmed John's ministry as a true prophet. Knowing John's identity is important because it also confirmed the identity of Jesus; John as the forerunner of the Messiah and the one for whom the way was prepared (Matt 11:10).[9]

---

6. Herod Antipas lived in a kingly home (see Josephus, *Jewish Wars* 7.6.2–3 §§175, 178), wore the "soft clothing," that is, royal robe (*Jewish Antiquities* 14.9.4 §173; 16.7.3 §204; *Jewish Wars* 1.24.3 §480; 18.6.6–7 §§191–195; 19.8.2 §344; see also Acts 12:21). Matthew A. Bates, "Cryptic Codes and a Violent King: A New Proposal for Matthew 11:12 and Luke 16:16–18," *CBQ* 75 (2013): 81–82.
7. Marvin W. Meyer enumerates the importance of Elijah figure in connection to Jesus: (1) coming of Elijah is anticipated in Malachi 4:5; (2) some thought Jesus was the "Elijah who is to come" (Mark 6:15; 8:28; Matt 16:14; Luke 9:8, 19); (3) in the Transfiguration, Jesus was accompanied by Elijah and Moses, OT figures with unique manner of death; (4) the Seder meal during the Passover includes a special cup of wine for Elijah to celebrate hope for Israel ("Was John the Baptist Elijah? Interpreting the Gospel Evidence," *ReJJ* 32, no. 8 [1982]: 18–19).
8. See Josephus, *Jewish Antiquities* 17.13.1 §§3339–3341; *Jewish Wars* 2.7.4 §§114–116.
9. Talbert, "Matthew 11:2–24," 406.

Second, although John was considered "more than a prophet" and the greatest among humans, he was less than the "least in the kingdom of heaven" (11:9, 11). In the First Gospel, the distinction between the "least" and the "greatest" in the kingdom is made three times: (1) in the Sermon on the Mount, the least do not teach and practice righteousness, while the great does the opposite (5:19–20); (2) in this saying of Jesus about John (11:11); and (3) in Jesus' reply to the disciples who are discussing as to who is the greatest among them, those with a child-like faith are considered "greatest" (18:1–3).[10] In Matthew, John is portrayed as one who practiced and taught righteousness, but his question about Jesus' identity demonstrates his doubts. Hence, Jesus' comments about him being the "least in the kingdom of heaven" despite being the greatest "among those born of women" (11:11), but worse than John's doubts were the people's unbelief.

11:16–19 Violent Men, Children in the Marketplaces

Although Matthew has no qualms in relating John's doubts, Jesus and his disciples are not portrayed as a rival faction of John's group. On the contrary, Matthew presents both Jesus and John as messengers of God's kingdom who suffered rejection from those who refuse to believe. There are two main reasons why Jesus and John, and their disciples are sometimes considered as rival groups. First, Josephus did not mention John's "Great Successor" in his comments about John;[11] and second, John's disciples remain a group distinct from the Christians even decades after Jesus' ministry (Acts 19:1–5). For some, these two factors suggest that the real John and the real Jesus may not have crossed paths, and that the disciples of John were really hindrance to the growth of Christianity. Consequently, the Gospel writers had to invent stories about the encounters between Jesus and John in order to silence their Jewish critics by showing John had prepared the way for Jesus.[12] Such reconstruction requires more warrant. The disciples of John who were not aware of Jesus' works and the Holy Spirit are those residing in Ephesus when Paul arrived there (19:1–2). When and how did they get to Ephesus remains unknown, and Luke did not say how they encountered the Baptist or how they had been exposed to John's teachings; the only thing we know is that they

---

10. The distinction between great and less in this world and in the next is common even in the rabbinic writings, like in their commentary on Ruth (Ruth Rabbah 13, on Ruth 1:17) and in the Babylonian Talmud (*Bava Metz'ia* 85b). Benedict Viviano, "The Least in the Kingdom: Matthew 11:11, Its Parallel in Luke 7:28 (Q), and Daniel 4:14," *CBQ* 62, no. 1 (2000): 49.
11. Josephus, *Jewish Antiquities* 18.5.2 §§116–119.
12. Morton S. Enslin, "John and Jesus," *ZNW* 66, nos. 1–2 (1975): 4–11.

were unaware of the things that happened in Galilee and Judea more than a decade earlier, such as the ministry of Jesus and the giving of the Spirit.

In this account, two images are used to present the people's unbelief: the violent men who forcefully seize the kingdom and the children in the marketplaces who are impossible to please. First, "violent men" reject the message of the kingdom (Matt 11:12–15). The kingship of God is the essential message of "the Prophets and the Law," and of John the Baptist (3:2). This message is intrinsically political, because if God is king, this makes earthly rulers like Herod and Caesar no more than usurpers of power. The violence perpetrated by the Herodians on anyone who might pose a threat to their power was one of the hindrances to the proclamation of God's kingdom (2:1–16; 14:1–12).

The "violence" which the kingdom of heaven experienced is typically interpreted as a destructive form of violence, although a few interpreters take this as positive force in the sense that people are experiencing the benefits of the new era, hence, people are "forcing their way in" (11:12).[13] The problem is that the word *biastēs* ("violent person") is never used in a positive sense. Some take "violence" as a form of false teaching and "violent men" as false teachers based on the use of the expressions *hamas* ("violent") in the Qumran writing to refer to apostasy.[14]

It should be noted that this "violence" occurred from "the days of John the Baptist until now" (11:12). The time frame was given that started with John's public ministry. Matthew recounts the violence which Herod had done on John (14:1–12). The Herodians, particularly Antipas and his people, could be the "violent men" that Jesus referred to. Decades later, the violent death of Herod's army was interpreted as a vindication of John.[15] The prophecy of Malachi could provide some information in understanding this. The coming of the messenger does not only prepare the way for the LORD's coming as the ruler of his people (Mal 3:1); it marks the day of separation between those who serve God and belong to him from those who do not serve him (3:17–18); and the coming of the figure of Elijah signals both God's coming judgment (4:15) and restoration/call to obedience (4:14, 16). The core of John's message is this – God is king; and those who claim to be kings are counterfeit rulers including Herod Antipas, the "reed swayed by the

---

13. Rod Doyle, "Matthew 11:12: A Challenge to the Evangelist's Community," *Colloq* 18, no. 1 (1985): 22, nn. 8–23; Bates, "Cryptic Codes," 77–80.
14. Doyle, "Matthew 11:12," 24; Barbara Elizabeth Thiering, "Are the 'Violent Men' False Teachers?" *NovT* 21, no. 4 (1979): 293–295.
15. See Josephus, *Jewish Wars* 18.5.1 §119.

wind" and the "man dressed in fine clothes," whose "violent men" had been subjecting the kingdom of heaven "to violence, and . . . have been raiding it" (Matt 11:12).

Second, the "children sitting in the marketplaces" also reject the message (11:16–19).[16] The reason for these children's criticism of John and Jesus seems arbitrary, and they listen only as long as they are pleased with the preachers (very much like many church goers today). These children's accusation against Jesus being "a glutton and a drunkard, a friend of tax collectors and sinners" (11:19) hints that these "children" were the religious leaders (9:10–11). The charge against the Baptist of having a demon (11:18) is the same as the accusation that Jesus exorcised by the power of Beelzebul (10:25; 12:24). Matthew recounts the religious leaders' rejection of John and Jesus (21:23–26), except that their rejection of John was not very blatant because of their fear of the people who regarded John as a prophet. This illustration of the children in the marketplaces anticipated more stories of rejection (Matt 12), especially by the Pharisees and other religious leaders who were not only "hard-to-please" because of their unbelief, but were actively finding ways to discredit Jesus.

The Herodians and the Pharisees were collaborators in the death of Jesus (22:15–16; see also Mark 3:6; 8:15; 12:13);[17] and the two images ("violent men" and "children sitting in the marketplaces") were clearly references to them.

11:20–30 STORY OF UNBELIEF (2): UNBELIEVING CITIES AND THE OFFER OF SABBATH

John's doubt cannot be compared to the unbelief of the Herodians and the Pharisees. The stories of unbelief continue with Jesus denouncing the cities that were the primary beneficiaries of his miracles. Matthew states that the reason for Jesus' reprimand is "because they did not repent" (Matt 11:20). This shows that the main purpose of Jesus' miracles is to bring the witnesses and beneficiaries of the miracles to a point of repentance.

---

16. Epictetus mentions about children who say 'I won't play any longer' when the game no longer pleases them (*Discourses* 24.20). Talbert calls this the "parable of arbitrary rejection" ("Matt 12:2–24," 407).
17. Pierson Parker, "Jesus, John the Baptist, and the Herods," *PRSt* 8, no. 1 (1981): 11.

11:20–24 Unbelieving Cities Denounced

Matthew shows the extent of the people's unbelief and severity of the corresponding punishments by comparing them with people known for their wickedness (see comments for Matthew 10:15). Sodom and Gomorrah are mentioned only in association with wickedness and God's judgment (e.g. Isa 1:9–10; Amos 4:11; Zeph 2:9). Tyre and Sidon were cities known for idolatry (1 Kgs 11:1, 5, 33; 16:31; 2 Kgs 23:13). They had been good friends with Israel at some points (2 Sam 5:11; 1 Kgs 5:1; 9:11, 12), and at other points their oppressors (Judg 10:12; Isa 23:7). Punishments were declared because of their sins (e.g. Jer 25:22; 27:3; 47:4; Ezek 26:1–28:26), but they were two of the nations that were expected to be part of the community that worship the God of Israel (Pss 45:12; 87:4). Accounts of miracles in Tyre and Sidon are also recorded (for example, exorcism of the Canaanite woman's daughter [Matt 15:21–28; Mark 7:24–31], the miracle in Zarepath [Luke 4:26; see also 1 Kgs 17:9]), and the receptiveness of the people is attested by the Gospel writers (Mark 3:8; Luke 6:17–19).

Three cities are mentioned to represent those that reject Jesus: Chorazin, Bethsaida, and Capernaum. Chorazin is never mentioned except here (Matt 11:21; see also Luke 10:13), but presumably is included among the unnamed cities in which Jesus preached and performed miracles (Matt 9:35; 11:1). Bethsaida, another Galilean city from where Peter, Andrew, and Philip originated (John 1:44; 12:21), was a city that witnessed the healing of a blind man (Mark 8:22–26; see also 6:45, 56) and the feeding of the multitude (Luke 9:10–17). Capernaum was the city where Jesus initially ministered (Matt 4:13), healed the centurion's servant (8:5–13) and Peter's mother-in-law (8:14–16). In response to Nazareth's rejection, Jesus' also mentioned the miracles performed in Capernaum, "Surely you will quote this proverb to me: 'Physician, heal yourself!' And you will tell me, 'Do here in your hometown what we heard that you did in Capernaum'" (Luke 4:23).

The difficulty in understanding this passage arises because Tyre and Sidon also witnessed some miracles, and many people from Bethsaida and Capernaum had been responsive to the Gospel as well. It seems best to understand Jesus' statement as a generalized statement to emphasize that *miracles are performed to lead people to repentance, and receptiveness and rejection have corresponding consequences.*

11:25–30 The Real Sabbath

Gentleness and humility are two of the virtues taught by Confucius, and these two qualities are important especially for those who govern. He once told a story about Ch'en Kang who asked Tuan-mu Tz'u whether their master, upon arriving at a certain place, would demand information about its administration or would the information just be given to him. Tuan-mu Tz'u said, "Our master gets it through his gentleness, his superiority, his humility, his restraint, and his complacency. How differently from others does our Master seek his information?" In another instance, Tuan-mu Tz'u once asked about the "Great Man," to which he received this reply: "First he sets the good example, then he invites others to follow it."[18] In this last section, Matthew shows Jesus to be the gentle king who invites people to be under his rule by setting an example of humility.

The theme of God's kingship and faith continues in Matthew's account of Jesus' discourse about the true Sabbath. God's sovereignty and kingship is expressed in many ways. First, it is expressed in Jesus' address to God as the "Father, Lord of heaven and earth" (Matt 11:25a).[19] The declaration of God's universal kingship anticipates the proclamation of God's kingship throughout the world (28:16–20).

Second, it is seen in Jesus' declaration that the knowledge of God's rule does not result from human wisdom and intelligence but from divine revelation (11:25b). Matthew does not decry such wisdom and intelligence as barriers to understanding the kingship of God (take for instance, the magi from the east [2:2]). He clarifies, however, that revelation, not human insights, is the means to receive such understanding. This idea is shared by other NT writers (1 Cor 1:17, 26–27; 2:1–13).

Third, it is seen in the Father's giving his authority to the Son (11:27). In short, just as the Father is "Lord of heaven and earth," the Son now shares his authority as "Lord of heaven and earth." This statement had political implications because Roman emperors also claimed the same authority. No wonder Jesus warned his disciples about the possibility of being brought before kings to be interrogated (10:18), so they need to be prepared. Jesus never incited his followers to rebel against earthly kings, but he called people to acknowledge the real "Lord of heaven and earth."

---

18. Ware, *Sayings of Confucius*, 22–23, 27.
19. Ovid claims Jupiter's sovereignty and the Roman emperor's rule on his behalf, "Jupiter controls the heights of heaven and the kingdoms of the triformed universe; but the earth is under Augustus' sway. Each is both sire and ruler" (*Metamorphoses* 15.858–859).

Fourth, it is presented as an invitation to bear the yoke of Jesus (Matt 11:28). This is an invitation particularly to those who are not yet his disciples.[20] In the OT, the "yoke" is often used as an image of being under one's rule, particularly in relation to foreign rulers (e.g. Lev 26:13; Isa 9:4; Jer 27:8, 11–12). Similar use of the image is found in other ancient Jewish writings.[21] The same can be said about the image of a "burden" (Isa 9:3; 14:25; 10:27). It is often observed that ancient Palestinian farmers used a pair of oxen in farming, and so the yokes they use were designed to be used by two animals. The image of the believer being yoked together with Jesus is a beautiful one, with Jesus walking alongside us as we journey this life; but Jesus did not say, "be yoked together with me." Instead, he said, "Take my yoke upon you" (Matt 11:29). In short, Jesus is not the other ox plowing alongside the believer, but the farmer driving the animals as they work. The reason being under Jesus' yoke can be an enjoyable one is because the yoke driver is "gentle and humble in heart," and those who obey will not be burdened but can "find rest" for their souls, because his yoke is easy and his burden is light (11:29–30). Jesus' invitation is an invitation to be under his kingship, a rule characterized by gentleness and not tyranny, and thus, unlike the oppressive rule of the Romans. This invitation also comes with a promise of rest (or Sabbath).[22] And how can Jesus give them Sabbath? Because he is the Lord of the Sabbath! And this invitation provides a smooth transition to the stories of confrontation between Jesus and the Pharisees who refused Jesus' offer of rest.

12:1–8 STORY OF UNBELIEF (3): THE PHARISEES ON HARVESTING ON SABBATH

Rejecting Jesus' offer of his yoke is a rejection of his kingship and passing by the opportunity to experience the rest he is offering. One of the ways this rejection is expressed is the disapproval of the hard-to-please "children sitting in the marketplaces" (Matt 11:16–19), with which Matthew concretely illustrates using the various stories of the Pharisees' rejection of Jesus.

The story is set on a Sabbath in a certain grain field, the owner of which is not identified. Jesus and his disciples were hungry and began plucking

---

20. Verseput, *Rejection*, 146.
21. The yoke is sometimes used in relation to the Law or to "Wisdom" (Sirach 51:25–26; 2 Enoch 34:1–2). Celia Deutsch, *Hidden Wisdom and the Easy Yoke: Wisdom, Torah, and Discipleship in Matthew 11.25–30*, JSNTSup 18 (Sheffield: JSOT Press, 1987), 127.
22. The Hebrew word for "rest" is *shabbat*.

some grain to eat. It is not clear whether the Pharisees followed Jesus' group wherever they went or whether they just happened to be there at that time. Matthew only recounts the confrontation, and that the Pharisees used the issue to discredit Jesus. In another similar story, the Pharisees raised the issue of eating with unwashed hands (15:2–20; see also Mark 7:1–23), but here, the issue was about picking grains on a Sabbath.

It is common in the Philippines to see children pick fruits like *macopa* (wax apple), *duhat* (black palm), *santol* (cotton fruit), *bayabas* (guava), *kaimito* (star apple), and *mangga* (mango) from branches of trees that extend beyond a property to the streets. There seems to be an unspoken rule that passersby can pick some fruit to eat as long as they do not enter the property. Some provisions in the Law suggest that ancient Jews had a similar practice.

The last of the Ten Commandments is about covetousness: "You shall not covet your neighbor's house . . . or anything that belongs to your neighbor" (Exod 20:17). The word "anything" makes the statement all inclusive, and presumably it includes fruits from your neighbor's tree and crops from your neighbor's land. However, even in the OT, there is a provision that allows a person to eat the fruits growing within another person's property, except that they are not allowed to harvest and take the fruits home (Deut 23:24–25). The rabbis acknowledged this principle as well, although according to some rabbis, reaping is one of the works prohibited during the Sabbath, and may have been interpreted as harvesting.[23] The legalistic tendency of the Pharisees is evident in this episode in particular. The Pharisees did not accuse the disciples of stealing,[24] because there was really nothing immoral or illegal in what the disciples did. It is a culturally acceptable practice. The Pharisees, however, were able to raise questions about the legality of their action, implying that their hunger was not enough justification for them to pluck grains to eat because it was a Sabbath. Jesus' drew an analogy between the disciples and David's fighting men who ate the consecrated loaves which were reserved only for the priests (Matt 11:3–4; see also 1 Sam 21:1–6).[25] Some provisions

---

23. Picking fruits, eating them in the field, and not taking them home is a principle allowed by the rabbis (Mishnah, *Bava Metzi'a* 92a). The problem is that according to some rabbis, reaping is one of the works prohibited during the Sabbath, and their action may have been interpreted as harvesting (see Jubilees 2:29). This way of looking at it is seen both in the Mishnah (*Shabbat* 7:2) and the Babylonian Talmud (*Shabbat* 19a). Boaz Cohen, "The Rabbinic Law Presupposed by Matt xii.1 and Luke vi.1," *HTR* 23 (1930): 91–92; John Mark Hicks, "The Sabbath Controversy in Matthew: An Exegesis of Matthew 12:1–14," *ResQ* 27, no. 2 (1984): 80.
24. Hicks, "Sabbath Controversy," 80.
25. Early church fathers interpreted this passage in connection with the Eucharist (Joseph A. Grassi, "The Five Loaves of the High Priest (Mt xii, 1–8; Mk ii, 23–28; Lk vi, 1–5; 1 Sam xxi,

of the Law allowed only the priests to eat certain foods (Lev 6:26, 29; 7:6, 14, 31; 22:10–16; 23:20). Punishment for desecrating the loaves by eating them unlawfully is mentioned in the Law (Lev 22:16), but the extremely difficult situation of David and his men led the priests to be flexible in meeting the requirements of the Law. The disciples' situation, however, was by no means similar to that of David and his army. Nonetheless, Jesus declared the disciples "guiltless" (Matt 12:7b); and his quotation of Hosea 6:6 the second time shows that the Pharisees and not the disciples are the ones who are guilty (Hosea 6:6 is only quoted by Matthew, and he does so twice; see comments for Matthew 9:12–13). His indictment against the Pharisees points to their inability to truly understand the Scriptures (Matt 12:7a). All this shows the real purpose of this episode, namely, Jesus is the real authoritative interpreter of the Law's requirement, and not the Pharisees.

Jesus' argument that the priests were breaking the Law on the Sabbath may be alluding to the temple services which they had to perform even on the Sabbath (Num 28:9–10). This shows that temple services are considered more important than the Sabbath; and as could be expected, some rabbis considered human life as more important than the Sabbath rules. The point is this: if the priests are breaking the law of the Sabbath because of temple services, the disciples are no more obliged to keep the Sabbath because they are with the one greater than the temple.[26] There is no unanimity among Jewish rabbis as to how much work could be done during the Sabbath; but temple services were considered acceptable.[27] Jewish rabbis would discuss cases wherein the Law did not clearly specify which command should be given priority; like in the cases where the day for a boy's circumcision is a Sabbath; should the boy be circumcised and thereby work be done, or should the Sabbath be observed and the law of circumcision ignored? Unlike the rabbis, Jesus did not point to specific laws and discuss which law should be given priority. Instead, he pointed to himself in comparison with the temple. The temple symbolized the divine presence with his people, an idea best summarized by Ezekiel's description of Jerusalem where the temple used to stand, "And the name of the city from that time on shall be: 'THE LORD IS THERE'" (Ezek 48:35). Jesus became the clearest evidence of God's presence with his

---

1–6)," *NovT* 7, no. 2 [1962]: 122).
26. An example of this principle is found in the Tosefta (*Shabbat* 15:16). Keener, *Matthew*, 356; Yong-Eui Yang, *Jesus and the Sabbath in Matthew's Gospel*, JSNTSup 139 (Sheffield: Sheffield Academic Press, 1997), 306.
27. The details of the debates among the rabbis are recorded in the Mishnah (*Eruvin* 10:10–15).

people, and he is also the one who could make the final decision as to what is lawful and unlawful.

The theme of justice and compassion resonates with the quotation of Hosea 6:6. The prophet Hosea had to deal with various forms of injustice in their society, including "swearing, lying, murder, stealing, and committing adultery" (Hos 4:2). The lack of mercy and justice in the society was a result of God's people breaking their covenant with God (6:7). The same issues continued during the time of Jesus. The quotation from Hosea did not only provide a glimpse of the social problems the Jews faced during the time of Jesus and the kind of burden the religious leaders imposed on the people (Matt 23:1–12; see also Hos 10:13). It also highlighted both God's desire to restore his people (2:19) and his requirement of repentance. Hosea summarizes it thus, "But you must return to your God; maintain love and justice, and wait for your God always" (Hos 12:6). Jesus is calling the people to do the same, and the invitation to be under his "yoke" (or lordship) remains (Matt 11:28–30). This is what the people needed in order to be released from the burdens imposed by the Pharisees (23:1–12).

Hosea's call for repentance echoes in Jesus' words. But what is repentance? Considering how various ancient and modern languages express the same idea allows us to see this concept more broadly. Biblical languages express repentance in different ways. In Hebrew, for example, the expression *shuv* (or "turn") is used. The expression draws the image of a person who is going in the wrong direction who needs to turn around to the right path. No wonder, the OT has another related expression: "stiff-necked" (Deut 10:16; 2 Kgs 17:14; Neh 9:29; Jer 7:26). In the same way that those who are stiff-necked cannot turn their heads, the unrepentant refuse to turn their heads and return to where they should be. This metaphor was used even by Greek-speaking Jews and they used the Greek word *sklērotrachēlos* (Acts 7:51). The Greeks have the word *metanoeō* ("to change one's mind"), the very same word used in the NT. The implication is that a change of mind should result in a change of action.

Chinese Christians use the expression *huǐ gǎi* (悔改). The two characters can be taken separately: *huǐ* (悔) can mean "regret" and *gǎi* (改) means "to change"; together they mean "to repent," suggesting that repentance requires having regrets for the wrong that was done and necessitates a change in behavior. In Tagalog, the word *sisi* is the root word for *manisi* ("to blame") and *magsisi* ("to repent"). This implies that repentance requires an admission of one's fault or willingness to take the blame. As we can see, no one language can capture the richness of what repentance is, and therefore needs to be supplemented using other words or ideas. Nonetheless, they show various elements necessary to make right our relationship with God: a need for a change of mind and heart, turning away from wrong and back to the right path, willingness to admit sin and take the blame, and a change in one's actions.

12:9–21 STORY OF UNBELIEF (4): THE PHARISEES ON HEALING ON THE SABBATH

In the previous encounter, the Pharisees raised an issue about the disciples' gathering food on a Sabbath; in this second incident, they questioned the legality of Jesus' healing on this sacred day. The Jews were by no means inflexible in their observance of the Sabbath, especially when a person's life was at stake. The practice of one's profession on Sabbath was prohibited by the rabbis; this includes the practice of medicine. There is no hint, however, that Jesus was considered a professional physician.

The Pharisees' sensitivity to those in need of rescue is actually implied in Jesus' question (Matt 12:11). The Pharisees' real concern was not Jesus' ministry of compassion, which many of them shared but Jesus' claim that he is the Lord of the Sabbath and what this claim entails. The value of a person's life and health over religious observances is clearly an important theme in this story. This is implied in Jesus' statement, "How much more valuable is a person than a sheep! Therefore, it is lawful to do good on the Sabbath" (12:12). However, the identity of Jesus as the source of a person's life and health is even more significant. Matthew shows this through Jesus' healing of the man with a withered hand and the divine declaration that he is God's servant (12:13–21).

Jesus' healing was much more than just proof that he was a miracle worker or divine healer. The quotation from Isaiah 42 underscored God's kingship once again (Matt 12:17–21). The prophet Isaiah declared God as the King of Jacob (Isa 41:21) and the only one true God (41:29). He sent his messenger to announce this (41:22–23, 27–28), and this is essentially what Jesus and John did; they proclaimed the kingdom of God. Israel was the servant (41:8; 44:1, 21; 45:4; 49:3) who was tasked to proclaim God's universal and sole kingship (42:8). What Israel failed to do, Jesus would do as God's servant: promote justice (42:2–4), project the light of righteousness (42:6), and proclaim freedom for the oppressed (42:7). This came, not only with a promise of forgiveness (49:6), but also a challenge to loyalty to the one true

God which had a high price tag (such as losing some social privileges). The Pharisees' response of plotting to kill Jesus suggests they had understood this (Matt 12:14), but were unwilling to respond to God's Messiah.

12:22–37 STORY OF UNBELIEF (5): THE PHARISEES ON JESUS' EXORCISM

Matthew further illustrates the Pharisees' unbelief by recounting their accusation of Jesus as a demonic exorcist. The accusation is both theoretically and practically possible. In the Philippines, for instance, even in these days, there are *arbolario* who are known to be *mambabarang* or *mangkukulam*. The *mangkukulam* or *mambabarang* are persons who are believed to have the capacity to use demonic powers to pronounce curses on a person causing various forms of sicknesses or sometimes death. As explained in the comments for Matthew 8:1–9:34 above, the *arbolario* are herbal healers, and they claim to have the ability to reverse the curse of the *mangkukulam* or *mambabarang* through the use of herbs and incantation. One may also consider the malicious statement of the Pharisees' as evidence that they considered such scenario as a likely explanation. Unfortunately, there are virtually no documented accounts of Jewish exorcists who were themselves involved in demonic activities other than these hints from the Gospels. Jesus did not deny this possibility; he simply denied that this was true in his case because he healed by the Spirit of God and his healing was an integral part of God's rule (Matt 12:28).

Like the paralytic (9:1–8), this demon-possessed man received healing because some unidentified persons brought him to Jesus (12:22). Matthew's accounts of demonic possession show that demonic activities are manifested in various ways, such as fierceness (8:28), muteness (9:32–33; 12:22), and blindness (12:22). The other Gospel writers record demonic activities resulting in abnormal behaviors (Mark 5:15; Luke 6:27, 35; John 10:20), violence (Luke 4:23), and extraordinary strength (8:29). The symptoms of demonic possession were "healed" (Matt 12:22),[28] and so the man was no longer blind and mute. The reaction of the Pharisees shows that Jesus did not just deal with the symptom, but he dealt with the root of the problem (12:24), which is, the demonic influence.

---

28. Matthew used the Greek word *therapeuō* or "to heal." The idea of "healing" a demon-possessed person is common in the Gospels (Matt 4:24; 17:18; Luke 8:2, 36; 9:42); a more common expression is the "casting out of demons" (Mark 1:34; Matt 10:8).

The crowd's response shows that they were no different from the Pharisees, because their amazement was one of unbelief (12:23).[29] Their expectation of a "healer" Son of David was also evident in their question (see comments on Matthew 9:27–31). There is an implied contrast between the crowd and the Pharisees. The crowd's doubt is seen in their question, but this is still incomparable with the Pharisees' affront against Jesus, "It is only by Beelzebul, the prince of demons, that this man casts out demons" (12:24).

In his response, Jesus stated an important principle about unity – that a kingdom divided against itself cannot stand (Matt 12:25). His statement implies that if he cast out demons by Beelzebul, his very action would already be causing Satan's "kingdom" to crumble (12:26). While this would not be a bad thing, it was clearly not the case. Jesus' statement reflects the assumption that there is a conflict between two powerful kingdoms, even though they are unequal in power. It was also clear from his reply which kingdom he represented and with a hint of sarcasm he turned to the Pharisees to ask, "And if I drive out demons by Beelzebul, by whom do your people drive them out? So then, they will be your judges" (12:27). Jesus was God's representative, and his exorcism was evidence of God's reign for he did not only rule over humans but also over the spiritual powers.[30] Jesus illustrates God's victory over the powers of darkness through the image of the strong man being bound and his house being plundered.

The Pharisees' accusation shows that they were not on Jesus' side (12:30), but more serious was Jesus' assessment that their accusation was equivalent to blasphemy of the Holy Spirit (12:31). This statement has been construed in multiple ways throughout the centuries. The context, however, suggests that this form of blasphemy is a specific type of blasphemy, namely, calling the Spirit of God "Beelzebul," and hence, attributing his work to the devil. These words not only reflect the unbelief of the Pharisees (Matt 12:33–35), they will also be the basis of God's judgment against them (12:36).

---

29. Their question (Matt 12:23), "Could this be the Son of David?" can perhaps be translated more accurately, "This one is not the Son of David, is he?" In Greek, the word *mēti* is typically used in questions that expect a negative answer, implying that Jesus is *not* the Son of David, although he shows signs that he is.

30. Craig A. Evans, "Inaugurating the Kingdom of God and Defeating the Kingdom of Satan," *BBR* 15, no. 1 (2005): 67.

THE "BLASPHEMY AGAINST THE HOLY SPIRIT" AND CESSATIONISM

Some early Christians understood "blasphemy against the Holy Spirit" as speaking against the word of the Lord spoken through his prophets (Didache 11), while others say it is a believer turning away from the faith (Origen). Others say it happens when a person calls the power of the Spirit the power of the devil (Ambrose), or when one denies the deity of the Holy Spirit (Basil). Still others say that calling Christ Beelzebul (Athanasius, Augustine, Jerome) is this kind of blasphemy, and some relate it to impenitence (Lombard) or impenitence with failure to believe in forgiveness (Luther, Calvin).[1] Some explain the difficulty of Jesus' statement by saying that while this story was being handed down as a tradition, there must have been some details in the story that were added, or lost, or incorrectly transmitted.[2] This last one is somewhat speculative.

Although the Gospels do not provide us with a dictionary definition of "blasphemy against the Holy Spirit," the details of the story, provide some clues as to what it might be. Jesus performed miracles, and he did so with the power of the Spirit (see Matt 12:18). However, after a few verses he was accused of performing the miracles by Beelzebul, to which he responded that those who say this was committing blasphemy against the Holy Spirit. What this means is that blasphemy against the Holy Spirit happens when a person says that the work of the Spirit is the work of the devil, and in the process, calls the Holy Spirit "Beelzebul." This seems to be one of the difficulties cessationists must face. (A cessationist is someone who claims that miracles no longer exist after the Twelve Apostles). The reason is that, if there are no longer real miracles in the modern times, then every supernatural occurrence can only be attributed to the devil and are counterfeit miracles; but if one claims that this is so, whether implicitly or explicitly, even those that are genuinely the work of God are attributed to the devil, and this act is what Jesus called "blasphemy against the Holy Spirit."

Samson L. Uytanlet

---

1. Nicholas Lammé, "The Blasphemy against the Holy Spirit: The Unpardonable Sin in Matthew 12:22–32," *MAJT* 23 (2012): 19–26.
2. Burton Scott Easton, "The Beelzebul Sections," *JBL* 32 (1913): 73; M. Eugene Boring, "The Unforgivable Sin Logion Mark iii.28–29/Matt xii.31–32/Luke xii.10: Formal Analysis and History of the Tradition," *NovT* 18, no. 4 (1976): 258, 277–279; J. C. O'Neill, "The Unforgivable Sin," *JSNT* 19 (1983): 37–39.

12:38–48 STORY OF UNBELIEF (6): THE PHARISEES ON SIGNS

In the account that follows, the Pharisees came with scribes to Jesus "the Teacher" to ask him to perform miracles. Their request seems to suggest that Jesus' miracles were prerequisites for their faith. However, the story makes it clear that they asked for signs, not because they wanted to believe and they needed some basis to do so, but because they already refused to believe. At this point in the Gospel, Jesus had already performed numerous miracles (Matt 8–9), their demand for more signs was simply uncalled for; and this is not the last time the Pharisees would make such a demand (16:1).

Jesus' description of the scribes and the Pharisees as a "wicked and adulterous generation" underscores the unbelief/unfaithfulness that motivated them to demand for a sign (12:39). In the OT, adultery does not refer only to an extramarital relationship, it is also associated with other forms of wickedness (Jer 7:9; 23:10, 14; Ezek 23:37; Hos 4:2), and more particularly, to unbelief and idolatry (Jer 3:8–9; Ezek 6:9). In Matthew, the metaphor of adultery is used to symbolize faithlessness or unbelief. Jeremiah's statement about Israel's sin also illustrates this, "Have you seen what faithless Israel has done? She has gone up on every high hill and under every spreading tree and has committed adultery there" (Jer 3:8). God's people was considered his "bride," for them to turn away from God to other gods was comparable to a wife abandoning her husband to commit adultery. Jesus pointed out the religious leaders' unbelief further by contrasting them with the Ninevites and the queen of Sheba who responded in faith to Jonah and Solomon.

First, Jesus told the religious leaders that the only sign that would be given them is the sign of Jonah who survived three days and three nights in the belly of a sea monster. Divine judgment for unbelief and deliverance of the faithful ones are implied in this analogy. Moreover, the Ninevites' positive response to an extraordinary occurrence is a stark contrast with the Pharisees' rejection of Jesus, so the consequences of their responses would also be different (Matt 12:41; see also 11:21–24).

Even during the first few centuries, Christian interpreters already understood this as a prophecy about Jesus resurrection.[31] Although there is no doubt that the story of Jonah does have relationship with the resurrection, it is more than just a prophecy about Jesus being raised from the dead. There are three similar themes in Jonah's story and that of Jesus: (1) divine judgment;

---

31. A. K. M. Adam, "The Sign of Jonah: A Fish-eye View," *Semeia* 51 (1990): 182–184.

(2) the prayer of God's messenger; and (3) divine deliverance. God's judgment was declared against the Ninevites (Jon 1:2), in the same way that it was announced against the Pharisees (Matt 12:30–37). Jonah prayed while in the belly of the sea creature (Jon 2:1–10), and Jesus prayed in Gethsemane for deliverance (Matt 26:36–44). Both Jonah and Jesus were delivered by God. Thus, the resurrection was not just a sign that the Pharisees can observe, but it was evidence of God's deliverance of Jesus from death, just like Jonah was saved from the belly of the fish.[32]

Jesus also claims that "something greater than Jonah is here" (12:41). It is not very clear from the context in what sense Jesus sees himself as "greater" than Jonah. One may suggest, perhaps, that Jonah was God's prophet-messenger to Nineveh, but Jesus was more than just God's prophet-messenger. Jesus' presence with the Jews is equivalent to God's presence with them, and if the messenger received a positive response from the Gentiles from Nineveh who repented of their sins (12:41), a more favorable response should be expected from Israel. Moreover, Jonah's deliverance from the sea monster resulted in the repentance of the Ninevites; but Jesus' resurrection points both to the hope of forgiveness for Israel (Ezek 37) and hope of a new life for all the believers (Rom 6:4).

Second, the queen of Sheba responded proactively, and this was also commendable, especially for someone who came from a distant place to hear "Solomon's wisdom" (Matt 12:42; see also comments for Matthew 9:27–31). Some of Jesus' contemporaries believed that Solomon had extraordinary power over demons, and that his knowledge included the use of herbs and incantation. Jesus healed without the use of these means, and in this sense, he was "greater than Solomon."[33] Jesus' extended discourse regarding the behavior of the evil spirits further affirmed the comparison between Jesus and Solomon in terms of their ability to exorcise (12:43–46).[34] This truth is particularly important especially for Asian countries where there are people who rely on faith healers for healing.

---

32. John Woodhouse, "Jesus and Jonah," *RTR* 43, no. 2 (1984): 36–40.
33. See Wisdom of Solomon 7:20. Larry Perkins, "Greater than Solomon (Matt 12:42)," *TJ* 19, no. 2 (1998): 213.
34. In Josephus, Solomon produced incantations (*Jewish Antiquities* 8.2.5 §§45, 47); Eleazar even appealed to the name of Solomon to exorcise demons in the presence of Vespasian (*Jewish Antiquities* 8.2.5 §§46–48). His name is also adjured in incantations in the Greek Magical Papyri, and Aramaic incantation texts contains similar materials (Perkins, "Greater than Solomon," 208–209, 212–213).

The OT characters used for comparison with Jesus shared similar opportunity of ministering to Gentiles who responded positively to them and to their messages: Jonah the preacher/prophet called the Ninevites to repentance and Solomon the healer/exorcist/king whose wisdom was sought by the queen of Sheba. Jesus' proclamation of the kingdom to Israel also included a call to repentance accompanied by healings and exorcism; yet he received a response that was the opposite of what Jonah and Solomon received.

12:46–50 STORY OF UNBELIEF (7): JESUS' FAMILY

The series of stories of unbelief closes with Jesus' biological mother and brothers as examples. There are hints, especially in the Fourth Gospel, that Jesus' brothers remained unbelieving (John 7:2–5); and Jesus anticipated something similar for his disciples (Matt 10:35–37).

Jesus' ministry and claims about his identity brought both shame and danger to his family. His claim to be the Messiah (which implies his kingship) was seditious because it challenged the incumbent ruler. Moreover, his actions resulted in the people asking, "Isn't this the carpenter's son? Isn't his mother's name Mary, and aren't his brothers James, Joseph, Simon, and Judas? Aren't all his sisters with us?" (13:55–56). This situation clearly brought embarrassment to his family. These may have been the reason behind his brothers' action;[35] and in this case, embarrassment and fear are expressions of unbelief. This explains Jesus' warning against being ashamed of him and his words (see Luke 9:26). Jesus replied to the crowd saying that his mother and brothers were those who do the will of God, and they were his true disciples (Matt 12:39–40). This story redefines kinship for Jesus' followers.

The miracles of Jesus recorded in Matt 8–9 were concrete evidence of the presence of God who was at work in the ministry of Jesus and his people were the direct beneficiaries of these miracles. Jesus' miracles were an integral part of his proclamation of God's kingship and these were performed to elicit faith in the person of Jesus.

In this section, unbelief is expressed in various ways, but they all have one common denominator, namely, an unwillingness to acknowledge what Jesus' teachings and miracles revealed about his identity. Several things about Jesus'

---

35. In some extreme cases, family members may even be willing to hand over their relatives for execution (see also DeSilva, *Honor, Patronage, Kinship and Purity*, 194). This is still true in many Asian countries, especially those that are predominantly Muslim.

identity are worth noting. First, Jesus is the Christ, whose miracles demonstrate both God's presence and his beneficent rule over his people. Therefore, miracles must result in faith on the one true God (Matt 11:20–24). Second, as the Christ, he is God's co-ruler. His invitation to be under his yoke is an invitation to be under his rule, and he alone can offer a non-oppressive type of reign, a kingship characterized by rest (Sabbath) because he is the Lord of the Sabbath (11:28–30; 12:8). Third, he is the authoritative interpreter of the Scripture, because he alone understood the mind of God (12:3–7; see also 11:25–27). Fourth, he is greater than the temple because he is the clearest proof that God is present with him. Fifth, he is greater than Jonah. The ultimate sign of God's work in Jesus is the resurrection which implies both the restoration of God's people and the hope of a new life for the believers. Sixth, Jesus is greater than Solomon, because he healed without the use of herbs and incantations (12:42–45). The primary demarcation between Jesus' disciples and those who are "outside" is faith, and this is illustrated in the story of Jesus being sought by his mother and brothers (12:46–50).

MATTHEW 13:1–58

Jesus Uses Parables to Teach about God's Kingdom

In cultures that value honor and shame, the use of parables in confrontations can be a less aggressive alternative to direct confrontation; this is done in order to "save the face" of the one being confronted. It allows the person to change certain actions or mend broken relationships without being *openly* shamed.

Aside from indirect confrontations, parables are also used for teaching purposes, such as what we see in Matthew 13. This was a common practice in ancient Israel, and Jewish rabbis also used parables to illustrate ethical principles.[1] Six of the seven parables in Matthew 13 explicitly mention the "kingdom of heaven," thus providing Matthew's readers glimpses of the nature of God's reign. The placing of these seven parables between two stories of rejection is worth noting (Matt 12:46–50; 13:54–58), because the two stories of rejection, first by his family (12:46–50), and then by his "fatherland" (Greek, *patris*, in this context, "hometown"; 13:54–58) function like two "bookends" for the parables. The story of Jesus' rejection by his kinsmen shows what it truly means to have a relationship with God, and it also opened opportunities for Jesus' mission elsewhere,[2] because this section follows the accounts of Jesus' commission to the Twelve (10:1–42) and stories of unbelief (11:1–12:50). With the disciples as the primary audience of the parables and their interpretation (see Figure 8), these parables can be considered as a part of Jesus' "mission orientation" for the disciples regarding the nature of the kingdom that they were to proclaim, the possible responses they would encounter as they do the work, and the Lord's expectations from his disciple-missionaries.

---

1. Eniola Nihinlola, "'The Weeds among the Wheat': Hermeneutical Investigation into a Kingdom," *OJT* 12 (2007): 88; Elizabeth Waller, "The Parable of the Leaven: A Sectarian Teaching and the Inclusion of Women," *UTSQR* 35, nos. 1–2 (1979–80): 99.
2. Céline Rohmer, "Aux frontiers du discourse en paraboles (Mt 13,1–53)," *Bib* 92, no. 4 (2011): 608–609.

Figure 8: Listeners of Jesus' Parables and Their Interpretations

Parable	Presented to		Interpretation given to	
	Disciples	Crowd	Disciples	Crowd
Sower	13:1–3	13:1–3, 34	13:10	13:1–3, 10
Tare and wheat	13:24	13:24, 34	13:36	
Mustard seed	13:31	13:31, 34		
Leaven	13:33	13:33, 34		
Treasure	13:36			
Pearl	13:36			
Dragnet	13:36			

USE OF PARABLES AND CONFRONTATIONS IN A SHAME-BASED CULTURE

European and American interpreters explain the purpose of Jesus' parables in the following ways: (1) as essentially moral stories teaching universal truths (Adolf Jülicher); (2) as a way of discussing about the imminent end (Albert Schweizer); (3) as a way of discussing God's present rule (C. H. Dodd); and (4) as a way of discussing God's rule both at present and in the future (Joachim Jeremias).[1] Others suggest that parables provide the disciples a glimpse of God's rule, or a means for Jesus to reveal himself in a veiled way to those who already have spiritual insight, yet at the same time there is an implied invitation to everyone to become Jesus' disciples. They are neither the remedy nor the cause of spiritual blindness, but they reveal the condition of blindness of which the crowd is unaware. Later interpreters have focused on the literary features of parables and move away from the idea that every parable has only one meaning.[2] Often ignored is the use of parables in the Bible in stories of confrontations. In a shame-based culture, the use of parables can be a discreet way of confronting a sin. The effectiveness and propriety of this approach in all cultures is not the purpose of this discussion. The purpose of this section is simply to describe how things are done in cultures wherein shame is a huge factor to consider in confrontations. When stories are used to address a problem, there is no guarantee that others who hear and know of the situation would not understand what is going on, therefore shaming the person who sinned is not totally avoided; but confronting discreetly in some cultures remains more acceptable than doing it openly. Hence, it is not surprising to hear something like, "I have a friend who has an uncle whose officemate has a cousin that owns flocks and herds. He has a neighbor who only had one ewe lamb, but when a visitor came, he took his neighbor's lamb and slaughtered it to serve his guest" (see 2 Sam 12:1–4). The one being confronted is expected to already know that the confronter is talking about him, and the conversation should not reach the point when the confronter would have to say, "You are the man!" (12:7).

Similar dynamics can be observed in some of Jesus' confrontation of the chief priests and the Pharisees (Matt 21:42–45). Matthew describes their response thus, "When the chief priests and the Pharisees heard Jesus' *parables*, they knew he was *talking about them*" (Matt 21:45, emphasis mine). There were times when Jesus would openly reprimand the religious leaders with the crowd present, calling them, for instance, a "brood of vipers" (12:34; 23:33). Yet more often, the reprimand comes in a subtler form like the use of parables.

In reality, the one being reprimanded is also shamed, and the one who confronts can do it with ill motives even if the confrontation is done indirectly. Nonetheless, in some cultures, indirect confrontation is more acceptable than shaming openly. Grace as a motivation for confrontation is most commendable. This can be illustrated in Jesus' confrontation with the religious leaders in the story of the woman caught in adultery (John 7:53–8:11). Jesus stooped down to write on the ground when asked to decide about this matter. There seems to be no way to know what he wrote on the ground, but the action can be understood based on some information about their culture. Had Jesus gazed at them while saying, "Let any one of you who is without sin be the first to throw a stone at her" (8:7), the gaze could bring as much embarrassment to the religious leaders as it did to Hazael when Elisha looked at him (2 Kgs 8:11). Embarrassing the Jewish leaders could have resulted in hardening of their hearts, and possibly cost the woman her life. With Jesus stooping down to write, the religious leaders had the opportunity to quietly disperse (John 8:9), having understood that none of them was without sin. So, perhaps the correct question to ask is not *What did Jesus write on the ground?* but *Why did Jesus stoop down to write on the ground?* The answer: Jesus' reply to the Jews is embarrassing enough to silence them (8:7); by stooping down he allows those who were condemning the woman an opportunity to exit gracefully. This shows that Jesus' aim was not simply to shame them, but to teach them about grace by setting an example. He clearly did not condone the sin of the woman, but he showed grace even in addressing the woman's sin.

Jesus' manner of confrontation can be explained by looking at what is culturally acceptable, but he did not just follow the cultural norm. Instead, he

> challenged it by introducing a new norm for those who follow him, namely, through loving confrontations (see discussion on Matthew 18:15–20).
>
> **Samson L. Uytanlet**

> 1. John Dominic Crossan, "Seed Parables of Jesus," *JBL* 92, no. 2 (1973): 264.
> 2. Robert H. Albers, "Perspectives on the Parables – Glimpses of the Kingdom of God," *WW* 4, no. 4 (1984): 453; Songer, "Jesus' Use of Parables," 493, 500; Mark Bailey, "The Kingdom in the Parables of Matthew 13 [Part 1]: Guidelines for Interpreting Jesus' Parables," *BSac* 155 (1998): 29.

13:1–23 THE SOWER: THE PARABLE AND ITS INTERPRETATION

Matthew 12 tells us how Jesus moved from the grain fields (Matt 12:1), to one of the synagogues (12:9), to an unspecified location where encountered the Pharisees and scribes (12:15), to a house of an unidentified person (12:46). There is nothing in the story that suggests that these are chronological accounts. However, these stories share something in common – they all emphasize the theme of unbelief. Before Matthew 13:36, the crowd is still with Jesus (13:1–35); but in the following section, they are no longer present (13:36–50). The crowd was still with him when he told the parable of the sower and its explanation, and the first three parables of the kingdom (tares and wheat, mustard seed, and leaven). But with the exception of the parable of the sower, the crowd was only overhearing what Jesus was telling his disciples (13:10–11). Jesus left the crowd in 13:36, went to the house, and began talking *only* with the disciples. They were no longer present when Jesus interpreted the parables of the tares and wheat, and the last three parables of the kingdom (treasure, pearl, and dragnet).

Parables were already used in the previous chapters (for example, 11:16–19), but this is the first time Matthew mentions Jesus teaching in parables. Although the parable of the sower is not explicitly called a "parable of the kingdom," it can be considered as an introduction to these kingdom parables.[3] As an agricultural society, the use of agricultural images was common

---

3. Stanley D. Toussaint, "Introductory and Concluding Parables of Matthew Thirteen," *BSac* 121 (1964): 351.

in ancient Jewish writings (Ezek 17:1–24; 20:46–49). Jesus' interpretation describes the four types of soil in which the seed was sown (Matt 13:18–23). This is the reason why the focus of most interpretations of the parable has often been on the various types of responses to God's word. However, when Jesus interpreted this parable, he refers to the parable as the "parable of the sower" (13:18; 13:3), and not the "parable of the soils." In other words, according to Jesus, *the parable is primarily about the one who spreads the word, and not the one who hears it.* Moreover, the primary addressees of this parable are the disciples, the ones commissioned to proclaim the kingdom of God (10:1; 11:1). Even in Jesus' interpretation of the parable, he addressed the disciples, "You, therefore, listen to the parable of the sower . . ." (13:18). The crowd in Matthew 13 are merely eavesdroppers who could respond to the message in four possible ways.[4] Jesus' message is addressed to the ones who proclaim the word, *and they should expect to encounter various types of responses, because not everyone would respond positively* (Ezek 2:1–10; 3:6–7). Nonetheless, to the ones who hear, they must be like the good soil. The crowd should understand the importance of responding in faith, because openness of one's heart leads to greater perception of God's truth.

First, there were seeds that fell on the roadside and were eaten by the birds (Matt 13:3–4);[5] the birds represent the evil one who snatches the word from those who refuse to believe (13:19). The reality of spiritual battle is clear here. The image of the sower is often used for God in Jewish writings,[6] but in this Gospel, the task of sowing is partly delegated to the disciples also.

Second, there were seeds that fell on shallow ground and did not live long but were scorched by the sun (13:5–6). These refer to hearers who received the word, but did not remain faithful after being scorched by persecution (13:20–21). New Testament writers often speak of spiritual maturity in terms of growth like that of a plant (1 Cor 3:6–7; 2 Cor 9:10). The seed planted in this second type of soil only grew in one direction – there is upward growth without being rooted downward. Hence, it is important to "take root below and bear fruit above" (2 Kgs 19:30; see also Isa 37:31). This is the ideal process of growth.

---

[4]. The dynamics of indirect confrontation is also evident in this. As the people hear about the four types of responses, they are expected to understand that their response should be like the fourth type of soil.

[5]. Parables may have allegorical elements such as this one. Philip L. Culbertson, "Reclaiming the Matthean Vineyard Parables," *Enc* 49, no. 4 (1988): 260.

[6]. For example, 2 Esdras 4:26–32. See Mark Bailey, "The Kingdom in the Parables of Matthew 13 (Part 2): The Parable of the Sower and the Soils," *BSac* 155 (1998):179.

Third, there were seeds that fell among thorns and produce shoots that did not live long because they were choked (Matt 13:7); and these refer to those who received the word also, but did not remain faithful because they are choked by the worries of life and the "deceitfulness of wealth" (13:22). The proverb used by Matthew, "Do people pick grapes from thornbushes, or figs from thistles?" (7:16; see also Luke 6:44), illustrates the use of thorns and thistles as metaphors for evil. In the OT, they are unwanted elements that can hamper worship (Hos 10:8; Isa 34:13; see also Heb 6:8); they are part of the consequences of sin (Gen 3:18); and a symbol for hardship (Ezek 2:6). In this parable, thorns refer to anything that draws a person's attention away from God's word and in the process, prevents a person from truly benefitting from it.

Fourth, there were seeds that fell in good soil that produced crops (Matt 13:8, 23); and these are the ideal listeners. The image of fruit-bearing may relate to a person living according to God's purposes as shown in various forms of good deeds (Col 1:6, 10); and Matthew consistently used this image to refer to one's actions that show a person's internal disposition (Matt 3:8, 10; 7:16, 17, 18, 19, 20; 12:33; 21:9).

Jesus concludes the parable with the statement, "Whoever has ears, let him hear" (Matt 13:9), addressing the eavesdropping crowd, allowing them a chance to respond positively to the Gospel message. The statement echoes Ezekiel's words to the audience that he knew would not heed his message (Ezek 3:27; see also Rev 13:9).

The use of parables here may be considered part of God's judgment against those who refused to believe,[7] as seen in Jesus' explanation for his use of parables (Matt 13:10–17). He drew a sharp distinction between the disciples and the crowd, "to you . . . to them" (13:11); the disciples receive the "knowledge of the secrets of the kingdom" while the crowd does not. In Jewish thought, a mystery is knowledge that would remain unknown unless communicated through divine revelation (Dan 4:9; Rev 1:20; 10:7; 17:5, 7). This does not only underscore God's discretion and initiative, it also highlights the privileges and special favor the early Christians claim to have.[8]

Furthermore, the quotation from Isaiah 6:9–10 drives the wedge further between the disciples and the crowd; the former listens with understanding while the latter does not. The quotation recalls the time when King Uzziah

---

7. Bailey, "The Kingdom in the Parables (Part 2)," 172, n. 3.
8. Marius Nel, "The Mysteries of the Kingdom of Heaven according to Matthew 13:10–17," *Neot* 43, no. 2 (2009): 279, 283–284.

had just died and there was no human king in his place yet (Isa 6:1). The Assyrians were rising to power and threatening to conquer Jerusalem; but God reminded the prophet that he remained king (6:5), and the kingdom of heaven continued despite the possible "end" of the kingdom of Judah. Isaiah must proclaim the kingdom of heaven even though many will not listen to his declaration (6:8). It is noteworthy that in Matthew, the quotation was *about* the crowd and addressed *to* the disciples; in the same way that the statement in Isaiah was *about* Israel and addressed *to* the prophet Isaiah. Parables do not make people become disciples, but as disciples, they have the privilege of receiving the interpretation of the parables.[9] This may suggest that in the same way Isaiah was sent (6:8), the disciples were now commissioned as apostles ("one sent") to preach to a different generation of the same people group, but the anticipated response would not be different. The prophet was commissioned to preach with clarity, but the people's already-hardened heart would become even harder, leading to judgment.

13:24–43 THE PARABLES OF THE KINGDOM: PART 1

After the parable of the sower, six parables were presented in two sets-of-three. The first set of parables was introduced by the statement, "Jesus told them another parable" (Matt 13:24, 31, 33); the second set with, "(Again) the kingdom of heaven is like" (13:44, 45, 47). The use of images related to agriculture continues with the first set of parables.

13:24–30 The Wheat and Tares: The Parable

The parable of the wheat and tares can also be called the parable of the two sowers, the man who sows good seed and the enemy who sows bad seeds. This parable is only found in Matthew, which hints that one of the issues the early believers were facing was the presence of non-believers within the believing community.[10] Like the previous parable, this one was addressed to the disciples and related to their evangelistic efforts. The parable underscores not only Jesus' teaching that God's rule is *already* present, and therefore it must be proclaimed, but also the reality that the believing community could also be a mixture of good and evil, and the ultimate separation of the two groups

---

9. Douglas S. McComiskey, "Exile and the Purpose of Jesus' Parables (Mark 4:10–12; Matt 13:10–17; Luke 8:9–10)," *JETS* 51, no. 1 (2008): 77.
10. Interestingly, the Greek word *zizania* sounds like the Hebrew *zānah*, which means fornication (Nihinlola, "The Weeds among the Wheat," 92, n. 15).

will take place only in the *future*. This means that the gospel must not only be preached outside the believing community, but even within the churches.[11]

Jesus' interpretation that the "field is the world" where the "people of the kingdom" and the "people of the evil one" exist together (Matt 13:38) implies that the world is the battleground of God and Satan; and because the "enemy" is a trespasser (13:25), he is neither the owner of the field nor someone who belongs to or is related to the owner. Theologically, this implies that the world belongs to God, and the kingdom of God is already universal in its extent, except that God is not universally acknowledged as king. The delay in the collection of tares is not seen as the delay of judgment, but as a prolonged protection for the wheat, lest it be damaged together with the tares (13:29; see also 2 Pet 3:9). Nonetheless, the sower of good seeds made sure that the separation will happen during the harvest (Matt 13:30).

Weeds are sometimes used as fuel, and so are thorns (Ecc 7:6). However, the burning of the weeds does not imply its usefulness as fuel, but the judgment against those who cause others to sin and those who break the law (Matt 13:41). Farming analogies, such as the separation of the wheat and chaff, are also used in John the Baptist's preaching (3:12),[12] and points to God's judgment in the end. Fire, on both occasions, is the medium of judgment (3:12; 13:40–42; see also 25:41).

The interpretation of the parable was given only to the disciples (13:36). This may imply that the proclamation of God's reign is not about scaring people with the reality of divine judgment, as real as it may be, but simply inviting people to acknowledge the kingship of God. The reality of judgment, nonetheless, should be the motivation of the disciples to proclaim God's rule. The interpretation concludes with the statement, "Then the righteous will shine like the sun in the kingdom of their Father" (13:43a), echoing the vision of Daniel 12:3 of God's eternal reign. Similar expressions are found in Judges 5:31 that distinguish between the enemies of the Lord and those who love him; and in 2 Samuel 23:3–4, the last words of David that foresee the rule of the Messiah who will rule with righteousness and shine like the sun. The similarities between Jesus' interpretation of the parable of the two sowers and Daniel's vision of God's rule are hard to ignore. Both passages: (1) foresee

---

11. Robert K. McIver, "The Parable of the Weeds among the Wheat (Matt 13:24–30, 36–43) and the Relationship Between the Kingdom and the Church as Portrayed in the Gospel of Matthew," *JBL* 114, no. 4 (2012): 644, 658–659.
12. The same image is also used in rabbinic writings like their commentaries on Genesis (Genesis Rabbah 61:6; 83:5). Bailey, "The Kingdom in the Parables (Part 3)," 267.

the end of time (Matt 13:39; Dan 12:2, 4); (2) discuss the separation of the righteous from the wicked (Matt 13:40–42; Dan 12:1–2); (3) point to the judgment against the wicked (Matt 13:40; Dan 12:2b); and (4) look forward to the righteous shining forth (Matt 13:43; Dan 12:3).

13:31–35 The Parables of the Mustard Seed and the Leaven

The parables of the mustard seed and the leaven are two distinct parables that complement each other;[13] both underscore the great potential of a universal *recognition* of God's kingship. God's universal rule is already a given fact in this Gospel (Matt 5:34–35; 11:25). Hence, the growth process that these two parables illustrate is not about the growth (or "expansion") of God's kingdom but the growing recognition of God's kingship. God's rule is universal in scope, and for this reason, even those who refuse to acknowledge his rule are already under his jurisdiction, and thus he has the rightful authority to pass judgment. The growth of the mustard seed to a huge tree is not as realistic as the leavening process,[14] but both clearly emphasize growth.

Traditionally, a mustard seed is an image of what is small.[15] The description may be a bit exaggerated; nevertheless, the picture of unimaginable growth is clear. The growth of the seed is such that it can become bigger than many garden plants and eventually become a tree (Matt 13:32). The parable closes with a quotation from Daniel 4:12 (see also Ezek 17:22–24) about birds coming under the shade provided by the "mustard tree." In the OT, the idiom "to be under one's shade" means "to be under one's rule"; see for example, Jotham's statement about Abimelech's rule over Shechem (Judg 9:15), Ezekiel's comment about the rule of Assyria (Ezek 31:3–18; esp. vv. 6, 12, 17), and Daniel's remark about the empire of Babylon (Dan 4:12–15). Shade is also used as an image of protection (Ps 121:5; Songs 2:3). As the

---

13. Waller summarizes the two major views on the relationship between the two parables: (1) the two parables provide contrasting images (J. Jeremias); and (2) two parables are distinct (C. H. Dodd) ("The Parable of the Leaven," 99–100).

14. The use of hyperbolic language is common in ancient Jewish setting, which is very similar to many African cultures (Plutarco Bonilla, "Jesus, What an Exaggerator!" *JLAT* 8, no. 2 [2013]: 79; David Seccombe, "Incongruity in the Gospel Parables," *TynBul* 62, no. 2 [2011]: 163).

15. Ryan S. Schellenberg correctly observes that the use of the image is not uniform enough to achieve a "proverbial" status ("Kingdom as Contaminant? The Role of Repertoire in the Parables of the Mustard Seed and the Leaven," *CBQ* 71, no. 3 [2009]: 528–532, 543). See Mark Bailey, "The Kingdom in the Parables of Matthew 13 (Part 4): The Parable of the Mustard Seed," *BSac* 156 (1999): 453 n. 21.

small mustard seed grows to be a great tree under which the birds find shade,[16] the kingship of God will also be *recognized* to a great extent.

Likewise, the parable of the leaven also paints an image of growth. The image of leaven is often seen as an image of moral corruption (1 Cor 12:6–8; Gal 5:9; see also Exod 34:24; Lev 2:11); but like the mustard seed, the image of leaven is used in various ways. It is used positively to refer to perfection, and negatively to anger, corruption, sensual pleasure, and evil impulse.[17] In Matthew, the only other occasion this image is used is in 16:6, 11–12 (see also Mark 8:15; Luke 12:1), referring to the "teaching" of the Pharisees and Sadducees. If Matthew is using the metaphor of leaven in the same way here, then the parable of the leaven points to the transformative power of the Christian message. The word of God can transform lives (Heb 4:12). In the same way that a whole batch of dough rises with a little leaven, and the teachings of the Pharisees and Sadducees can mold one's character towards their ways (hence the disciples should beware of them), so the Christian message has the capacity to change the lives of individuals and communities. Moreover, the image of leaven "hidden" within sixty pounds of flour (Matt 13:33) may depict a community of believers that was not officially recognized by the Roman authorities. The expression "mixed into about sixty pounds of flour" can be more accurately translated as "hidden into about sixty pounds of flour" (13:33). Yet this "underground movement," according to Jesus, had the potential to quietly infect and transform the dough within which it is placed.[18]

The growth experienced by the mustard seed and caused by the leaven is the opposite of that experienced by the seed thrown on the rocky ground (13:5–6, 20–21). Persecution should not prevent the growth of Christianity. With these parables, Jesus assured those who recognized God's rule that growth will happen, whether visible or less obvious (1 Cor 3:6).

13:36–43 The Wheat and Tares: Its Interpretation
(See comments for Matthew 13:24–30 on pages 144-146.)

---

16. Birds of the air are sometimes used as symbol of gentile mission (Ezek 17:23; 31:5–6; Dan 4:12, 21; see also 4 Enoch 90:33, 37) (Bailey, "The Kingdom in the Parables of Matthew 13 [Part 4]," 455).
17. For references, see Schellenberg, "Kingdom as Contaminant," 527, 538–540.
18. George Wesley Buchanan, *The Gospel of Matthew*, MBC 1, 22 vols. (Lewiston: Mellen Biblical Press, 1996), 1:608

THE "EXPANSION" OF GOD'S KINGDOM: DOES GOD'S KINGDOM REALLY NEED TO EXPAND?

The expression "expansion of God's kingdom" is one that is commonly used in relation to evangelism. Evangelization, especially of people groups that have little or no Christian witness, is seen as taking new "territories" for God. This image presents the process of evangelism as if the evangelists are members of the armies of the conqueror God who are ready to take new lands for him. There is no question that the OT refers to God as a warrior and conqueror (Num 32:4), and the NT undoubtedly refers to Christians as his soldiers (2 Tim 2:3–4), but the Bible, especially the Gospels, do not talk about evangelism in terms of conquest. The image of the divine conqueror is associated with divine judgment (Rev 19:11–16), not about expansion or enlargement of his domain.

The language of expanding God's kingdom has a colonial overtone, wherein taking new lands for the human king was the main goal of colonization, and the "Christianization of the heathen" and taking new territories for the divine king was an essential part of the process. However, the problem is not so much because the expression is associated with the colonial missionaries. *The greater problem is that the idea is inconsistent with what the Gospels teach.*

In the OT, some people considered the gods as divine rulers of certain territories. This is seen, for instance, during the war between Israel and Aram. Some officials of the Aramean king assumed that the God of Israel is one of the "gods of the hills" (1 Kgs 20:23), so they advised him to lure the Israelite army to the plains with the assumption that they would be victorious with the help of their gods. After Naaman was healed of leprosy, he acknowledged that he was healed by Israel's God, "Now I know that there is no God in all the world except in Israel" (2 Kgs 5:15). Again, this suggests that the territory of the healer God is limited to the land of Israel. However, God's rule over *all* nations was proclaimed in the psalms (Pss 9:17–20; 10:16; 59:5; 67:2–4; 72:11, 17; 96:3, 10; 108:3; 117:1; especially 22:27–28; 47:8; 113:4). Even during the time of exile, God rebuked the lying prophets for giving the Jews false hopes of peace but at the same time he assured the Jews that his presence will still be with them even while they were in exile. Thus, he said to them, "'Am I only a God nearby,' declares the Lord, 'and not a God far away? . . . Do not I fill heaven and earth?' declares the Lord" (Jer 23:23–24), implying that his domain is not limited to the Promised Land only, but reached even the land of their Babylonian conquerors.

The same idea is expressed in the NT. Jesus' prayer, "your kingdom come, your will be done, on earth as it is in heaven" (Matt 6:10), points to God's reign not just in the heavenly realm, but also in the earthly. Again, Jesus refers to God as the "Lord of heaven and earth" (Matt 11:25; see also Luke 10:21; Acts 17:24). Jesus also invites people to take his yoke, or to put it another way, to be under his yoke (see comments for Matthew 11:29), or be under his rule. Although Jesus talks about the kingdom like a tree that grows and all the birds come for shades under it (see comments for Matthew 13:31–35), what grows is not the extent of his rule, but the extent to which his rule is acknowledged and recognized by the people. Many people are not aware of God's reign, and therefore the good news must be spread. No wonder Matthew also talks about the proclamation of the kingdom (Matt 4:23; 9:35), *and not its expansion*. God is the heavenly ruler over all creation (Isa 6:1; 66:1), and his rule is made known through its proclamation (40:3, 10). His kingship is not something that needs to be established, neither is there a need for his kingdom to be expanded nor enlarged. The Bible does not anticipate the time when God would *become* king, he *already* is! What is anticipated, therefore, is the time when God would be recognized for who he really is. This can happen only through the proclamation of the kingdom. The extent of his kingdom is vast, and it does not require any "expansion" at all. God is not in the business of taking new "territories" that do not belong to him in order to "expand" his domain. What, then, is evangelism? It is declaring to the trespassers of God's rule and the trespassers in God's domain, that they are subjects of the one true king and by acknowledging his rule, they will be considered children/heirs of the one Father in heaven. The only reasonable way to compare evangelism and conquest is to see that Jesus' ultimate "conquest of nations" is not accomplished with sword, but through teaching and baptizing.[1]

So, what can we do now? It seems to me that it is time to rethink our perspectives about evangelism and mission. Perhaps it would also be good to stop using the expression "expanding God's kingdom." Christians are called, not to expand God's kingdom, but simply to proclaim it!

Samson L. Uytanlet

---

1. Kenton L. Sparks, "Gospel as Conquest: Mosaic Typology in Matthew 28:16–20," *CBQ* 68 (2006): 661.

13:44–52 THE PARABLES OF THE KINGDOM: PART 2

Like the previous set of three parables, the second set includes two shorter parables that are complementary (treasure and pearl), and a longer one that underscores the separation of the righteous and wicked on the day of judgment, except that the arrangement is reversed.

13:44–46 The Treasure Finder and the Merchant

The parables of the hidden treasure and the pearl point to the exceeding great value of the kingdom that worldly wealth is worth giving up in exchange for it. The story of the man who found a hidden treasure does not contain much detail. Readers of the Gospel are neither informed how the treasure finder was related to the original owner of the field, nor what he was doing in the field.[19] Matthew does not explain the moral problem raised by the man's action either. The man's willingness to abandon all he has for something more valuable is clearly the main point of the story.

The parable of the merchant shares the same emphasis. Like the treasure finder, the merchant was willing to give up what he owns to possess the valuable pearl (Matt 13:45–46), which recalls Jesus' disciples who left everything to follow him (4:20–22; 19:27; see also Mark 10:28; Luke 5:11, 28). The expectation of voluntary poverty is also implied in Jesus' instruction to the disciples sent to proclaim the kingdom (Matt 10:9–10).

The actions of the treasure finder and the merchant are also contrary to the description of the thorny ground in the parable of the sower (13:7, 22). With these two parables, Jesus indirectly presented his expectations from his disciples regarding their handling of worldly wealth.

13:47–52 The Parable of the Dragnet and the Illustration of the Householder

Like the parable of the wheat and tares, the parable of the dragnet highlights the "harvest" and the segregation that will happen on the day of judgment. God's angels will reap and separate the wheat and tares into two groups (Matt 13:39–40). Similarly, the angels will gather the fish and segregate the good from the bad ones (13:49–50).

---

19. J. Duncan M. Derrett lists the possible relationship between owner of the field and finder of the treasure: day laborer, servant-tenant, lessee, independent contractor, contractor's servant, trespasser ("Law in the New Testament: The Treasure in the Field [Mt. xiii, 44]," *ZNW* 54, nos. 1–2 [1963]: 37–40).

The metaphor of fishing was something that many of Jesus' disciples could identify with, since they were formerly fishermen themselves (4:18–19; Mark 1:16–17; Luke 5:1–11; John 21:1–11). At times, two boats were required to gather large numbers of fish (Luke 5:6–7, 9–10),[20] in the same way, partnerships in mission is often necessary for a greater harvest.

The parables of the kingdom conclude with the householder throwing out old and new treasures (Matt 13:52).[21] The householder is someone who is supposed to protect and secure the property and the owner of the vineyard or perhaps chief among the slaves (13:27; 20:1, 11; 21:33; 24:43). Instead of keeping the treasures, he is disposing them, suggesting that sacrificial disposal of some earthly possessions may at times be necessary.

Scribes are people expected to seek ancient wisdom, be concerned with prophecies, preserve sayings, understand parables, seek hidden meaning of proverbs, travel to foreign land to learn what is good and evil, set their hearts on knowing God, and be diligent in prayer, and if God is willing, be filled with spiritual understanding and knowledge of mysteries.[22] Jesus' revelation given exclusively to the disciples suggests that the scribes mentioned in Matthew 13:52 refer to the disciples who were recipient of divine mysteries (13:11).

---

20. Mark Bailey, "The Kingdom in the Parables of Matthew 13 (Part 7): The Parables of the Dragnet and the Householder," *BSac* 156 (1999): 283.
21. A more accurate translation of the Greek word *ekballō* should be "throw out" or "dispose," not "bring out" (Peter Phillips, "Casting Out the Treasure: A New Reading of Matthew 13.52," *JSNT* 31, no. 1 [2008]: 8, 17–19).
22. See Sirach 39:1–8.

LIVING OUT THE KINGDOM

Jesus came and proclaimed the kingdom of heaven which he explained using parables. These pictures of the kingdom give us both the inspiration and the vision to live today. By using parables, Jesus shows that the kingdom is broad and that being a Christian is not about having a passport to heaven, but it is about allowing the good news of Christ to permeate all our personal, corporate, and social lives.

The parable that the kingdom of heaven is like a mustard seed is particularly encouraging since the number of Christians in many Asian countries is very small. The promise is that though it is small and insignificant, it can grow exponentially. That growth is organic. This is clearly demonstrated in China when all Christian missionaries were expelled in 1951 and yet the church grew strongly in the next decades until now when it is estimated that about one third of the population of China are Christians.

Another parable that is of special encouragement is that the kingdom is a mix of weeds and wheat, and bad fish caught up with the good fish (13:47–50). For the time being, in the world and even within the church today, there is sin and evil and wrong doing. Every now and then scandals hit the press, such as when church pastors commit crimes. At other times, there are disagreements that lead to divisions in the church. These are common problems that Christians and the church face everywhere. In his ultimate wisdom, the King allows that. But despite this mix, Christians have the hope that one day the righteous and the holy King who sets up this kingdom will come to judge (chs. 22, 25) and the terms of that final judgment may take some people by surprise (22:11–13; 25:37, 44).

Judgment gives us hope. No matter what difficult situation we face – whether it is chronic illness or persecution, we know that there will come a time when Jesus will return. Then, not only will there be an end to suffering and pain, but Jesus will also judge and separate the good and bad fish, the wheat and the weeds. There will be an end to those who are not of the kingdom, and rewards for those who are in God's kingdom.

The character of the king determines to a large extent the nature of the kingdom. Only a few countries today have kings, notably Japan and Thailand. While these modern-day kings have merely ceremonial roles, yet their presence provides some stability in their countries. Jesus as the king of the kingdom of heaven plays a much more significant and active role in his kingdom. He welcomes sinners and the lost into the kingdom (18:13) and is a generous paymaster, giving those who worked for one hour the same as those who worked for the day (20:15). He values the qualities that children bring into the community (18:2–4).

> As citizens of the kingdom then, Christians live out the qualities and characteristics of the King and seek to build his kingdom on earth (6:10). Those qualities of open hospitality, generosity to others and child-like innocence, trust and faith should be hallmarks of Christians and the Church everywhere. Furthermore, in today's fast-paced world in which we face the threats of terrorism, living out these qualities of the kingdom of heaven will be a powerful witness. Where there is fear and mistrust of strangers and people of other faiths, Christian hospitality and generosity can help to build bridges. For example, under a state sponsored initiative to build inter-religious understanding in Singapore, some pastors have the opportunity to invite leaders of other religious faiths into their churches. On these occasions, when they present clearly the gospel message, pastors can correct misunderstandings and misconceptions about Christianity, the church and the gospel. Furthermore, non-Christians can meet and interact with Christians in an open and honest way and that is surely positive. These are some of the many opportunities for living out the kingdom in the various spheres of life.
>
> **Kiem-Kiok Kwa**

13:53–58 REJECTION AT NAZARETH

The reason for Jesus' redefinition of kinship (Matt 12:48–50) is hinted at in the story of the Nazarenes' rejection of Jesus (13:53–58). The action of Jesus' mother and brothers can be interpreted in terms of them saying to him, "You are embarrassing us! We too have to live in this town!" Especially with the people murmuring (13:55–56), "Isn't this the carpenter's son? Isn't his mother's name Mary, and aren't his brothers James, Joseph, Simon, and Judas? Aren't all his sisters with us?" The ancient Jews' idea of honor is comparable to the Filipino concept of *dangal*. People's actions can bring disgrace not just to themselves, but to the whole family as well.[23] Aside from the embarrassment that Jesus' actions may have brought to the family, the volatile political conditions at that time meant that any claim to kingship could be interpreted as political uprising.[24]

---

23. For a fuller discussion, see Narry F. Santos, *Turning Our Shame into Honor: Transformation of the Filipino HIYA in the Light Mark's Gospel* (Quezon City: LifeChange Publishing, 2003), 49–59.
24. Jesus' claim to kingship is implied in the parables (Mark Bailey, "The Kingdom in the Parables of Matthew 13 [Part 8]: The Doctrine of the Kingdom in Matthew 13," *BSac* 156 [1999]: 449).

The wisdom and power of Jesus were seen clearly and readily acknowledged by those who attended the synagogue (13:54), but they remained in a state of unbelief (13:58). Jesus' deeds only resulted in the people's astonishment, not faith. By calling himself a prophet, Jesus placed himself alongside God's messengers who spoke beforehand the things God planned to accomplish and those who were rejected and persecuted by the people for being offended by God's message.

Jesus spoke in parables *because of* – not *to cause* – people's unbelief.[25] Like the Sermon on the Mount, Jesus' parables may have been spoken on different occasions, collected and arranged by the Evangelist to form a literary masterpiece (see summary in Figure 9). Aside from the implicit call to follow Jesus, there is a clear invitation in the parables to the readers to self-examination.[26] Yet a more dominant theme is the unbelief of the people. These themes appear in Matthew 8–9 (Jesus' miracles), and continue in Matthew 10 (the disciples' commission), and on into Matthew 11–12 (the various expressions of unbelief). The disciples were appointed to continue Jesus' mission. Just as Jesus was persecuted, the disciples could expect rejections and persecutions; and the mission required sacrificially giving up worldly wealth for that which is far more valuable. As they continued in the mission that Jesus' gave them, they would be like the scribes who throw out both old and new treasures.

---

25. Dan Otto Via, Jr., "Matthew on the Understandability of the Parables," *JBL* 84, no. 4 (1965): 430, n. 2.
26. Harold S. Songer, "Jesus' Use of Parables: Matthew 13," *RevExp* 59, no. 4 (1962): 500.

Figure 9: Overview of Jesus' Parables in Matthew 13

Parable	Opening Statement	Main Point
Sower	"He told them many things in parables . . ." (13:3)	The disciple-missionaries are to expect various types of responses as they proclaim the kingship of God; not everyone will respond positively.
Two Sowers (Wheat and Tares)	"Another parable he presented to them . . ." (13:23)	Judgment against those who reject God's kingship. There will be a period when those who acknowledge God's rule and those who do not co-exist. (Remember the first type of soil.)
Mustard Seed	(13:31)	Growth of Christianity despite persecutions. (Remember the second type of soil.)
Leaven	(13:33)	
Treasure Finder (Treasure)	"(Again) the kingdom of heaven is like . . ." (13:44)	Sacrifice for something more valuable. Cost of discipleship despite the reality of the worries of life and deceitfulness of wealth. (Remember the third type of soil.)
Merchant (Pearl)	(13:45)	
Fishermen (Dragnet)	(13:47)	Judgment against those who reject God's kingship. There will be a period when those who acknowledge God's rule and those who do not co-exist. (Remember the first type of soil.)

MATTHEW 14:1–16:20

Discovering Who Jesus Is and His Lessons on Discipleship

Tseng Ts'an, a Confucian scholar, once said, "Daily I examine myself on three points: Have I failed to be loyal in my work for others? Have I been false with my friends? Have I failed to pass on that which I was taught?"[1] A person's action is not the only thing that matters, a person's internal disposition or the "heart" is as important as one's deeds. This is also one of the highlights of Jesus' teachings and is seen particularly during his confrontation with the Jewish religious leaders about the "tradition of the elders" (Matt 15:2, 18–20).

After the section on Jesus' teachings using parables, Matthew records several stories of miracles and confrontations with the Pharisees and scribes that lead to Peter's confession that Jesus is the Christ (16:16). As it was in the previous accounts of miracles (Matt 8–9), these supernatural deeds of Jesus were the means by which his identity was revealed.

14:1–12 THE DEATH OF JOHN THE BAPTIST

At first glance, the account of John's death seems out of place in this series of episodes that climaxes with Peter's confession. Matthew's stories are by no means chronologically arranged. Herod's concern about Jesus' miracles clearly came after John died (Matt 14:2); but the feeding of the five thousand may have occurred after the news about John's death reached Jesus and he went to a secluded place where the crowd followed him and he fed them (14:13). However, it is clear that questions about Jesus' identity were raised even by secular rulers because of the miracles he had performed.

Herod Antipas' belief about Jesus' miracles based on the news he heard was a mixture of truth and false assumption: that miracles performed by Jesus were true, but the assumption that he was able to do so because he was John the Baptist who was raised was false (14:2). In Matthew, Antipas is the second Herodian mentioned and his political tenure was being threatened because of Jesus. The political situation was volatile. The Jews also wanted to

---

1. Ware, *Sayings of Confucius*, 21.

make Jesus king because of the miracles he had performed (John 6:15). If this happened, however, there could be civil unrest that could prove Antipas' inability to promote peace and might result in the emperor appointing another person to replace him. His grandfather, Herod the Great, also saw Jesus as a threat to his rule (Matt 2:2–3). In both cases, the political implications of Jesus' claim to be the Christ/"king of the Jews" and the potential trouble that might result from this is implied.[2]

Both Matthew and Luke comment that the confrontation between John the Baptist and Herod Antipas about his incestuous affair with his sister-in-law resulted in John's imprisonment (14:3–4; see also Luke 3:19–20). Matthew refers to Herodias as "his (Antipas') brother Philip's wife" (Matt 14:3), suggesting that Philip remained the legitimate husband of Herodias despite her relationship with Antipas. Hence, the relationship is both immoral and illegal. Matthew also made the critical remark that John was imprisoned "because of Herodias" (or "for the sake of Herodias"; 14:3), suggesting that she was the reason behind the Baptist's imprisonment. Although Antipas was responsible for the act,[3] Herodias was the motive for the plan, although Herod was afraid to kill John because "he was afraid of the people, because they considered John a prophet" (14:5).[4]

The story recalls Jezebel's plot against Elijah after he confronted Ahab for leading the nation to idolatry because of his wife's influence (1 Kgs 16:31–17:1; 19:1–2). This strengthens the association between John the Baptist and Elijah,[5] and by extension, the analogy between Jesus and Elisha. The Gospels explicitly mention that John is Elijah, but there is no reference to Jesus being Elisha. Nonetheless, their association cannot be ignored. Although it seems impossible that early believers would ascribe to Jesus the "relatively inferior" role of an "Elisha" in relation to John as the "Elijah," one must take into consideration the fact that Elisha was given a "double

---

2. In Josephus' account, John the Baptist was considered a potential troublemaker, and Herod Antipas' fear of losing his power in Galilee is the reason for putting John to death (*Jewish Antiquities* 18.5.2 §§116–119). Antipas' popularity and security comes at the expense of John's life (Regina Janes, "Why the Daughter of Herodias Must Dance [Mark 6:14–29]," *JSNT* 28, no. 4 [2006]: 455).
3. Take note that Herod is the subject of the verbs "arrested" and "bound" (Matt 14:3); and Herodias was his motivation.
4. For a more thorough discussion on the similarities between John and the prophets during the Second Temple Period, and how this influenced John's contemporaries with regard to their expectations of a prophet, see Robert L. Webb, "Juan el Bautista: Un Profeta de su Tiempo," Gabriel Ramirez Rios, trans.; *Kairós* 16 (1995): 23–38.
5. Janes, "Daughter of Herodias," 433.

portion" of Elijah's spirit and he performed twice as many miracles as Elijah. Moreover, although there was no expectation of Elisha's return, his association with John should have made this obvious. Elisha was an itinerant miracle worker whose primary area of ministry was in Northern Israel, just like Jesus; and this was recognized by later writers.[6] The similarities between Elisha's miracles and those of Jesus are also noteworthy. Although Elisha performed a number of miracles that Jesus did not perform (floating axe head, purifying of contaminated water), and Jesus did miracles that Elisha did not do (exorcisms, healing of blind, paralytic), a number of their miracles are similar: healing of leprosy patients (Mark 1:40–45; Matt 11:4–5; Luke 7:21–22; 17:11–19; see also Luke 4:27); multiplying loaves (2 Kgs 4:42–44; John 6:1–15); bringing the dead to life (1 Kgs 17:17–24; 2 Kgs 4:18–37; Mark 7:24–30; John 4:46–54); ability to see/hear from a distance (2 Kgs 5:26; 6:12, 32; John 1:48–49; Mark 11:2; 14:13–14; Luke 22:10–11). Even the sequence of Elisha's story and Jesus' story in Mark is comparable.[7]

The connection between Jesus and Elisha is shown further in the feeding of the five thousand (Matt 14:13–21; 2 Kgs 4:42–44). First, the amount of food was limited: twenty loaves with some ears of grain in the one case (2 Kgs 4:42a) and fives loaves with two fishes in the other (Matt 4:17). Second, the food was given to "the man of God": Elisha (2 Kgs 4:42) and Jesus (Matt 4:18). Third, there were instructions to feed the people (2 Kgs 4:42b; Matt 4:16). Fourth, the question was raised by Elisha's attendant who brought food for a hundred people (2 Kgs 4:43) and the disciples who distributed the food to five thousand men and their families (Matt 4:17). Fifth, they were instructed to distribute food (2 Kgs 4:43; Matt 4:19). Sixth, there were leftovers (2 Kgs 4:43–44; Matt 4:20). One of the highlights of Elisha's ministry was the healing of the Aramean officer, Naaman the leprosy patient, who, after his restoration to health confessed, "Now I know that there is no God in all the world except in Israel" (2 Kgs 5:15). Likewise, Jesus' ministry opened the way for the "God of Israel" to be known even among the Gentiles (Matt 15:31).[8] Moreover, not long after the account of the miraculous feeding by Elisha (2 Kgs 4:42–44), he performed a miracle by causing an axe head float

---

6. For example, Sirach 48:12–14; Josephus, *Jewish Antiquities* 9.8.6 §§182.
7. Raymond E. Brown, "Jesus and Elisha" *Perspective* 12, no. 1 (1971): 87–88, 95.
8. See comments on the second account of feeding (Matt 15:32–39).

(6:1–7). Likewise, after the account of the miraculous feeding by Jesus (Matt 14:13–21), he performed a miracle by walking on water (14:22–29).[9]

Like Jezebel, Herodias was her husband's greatest influence. She was able to influence Antipas to arrest and imprison John, and although Herod's fear of losing popular support kept him from putting the Baptist to death for a time (14:5), Herodias' plan was brought to fruition through her daughter (Mark 6:21–29; see also Matt 4:6–11). In both accounts, the daughter danced during Herod's banquet. Her dancing pleased him and he promised to grant her any request, and being "prompted by her mother" (14:8), she asked for John's head on a platter. In an honor-shame culture where one's promise is considered of highest value, Herod's impulsiveness proved to be disastrous. He had to choose between maintaining his popular image by not keeping his promise and sparing John's life and losing his face among his elite guests. John's life was given in exchange for Antipas' image as a ruler with a word of honor; and John's death anticipated that of Jesus (17:12).[10]

It is clear from this episode that although Jesus "did not do many miracles" (13:58), the few were enough to cause the Jews, including their rulers, to raise questions about his identity, and confuse him with John. No wonder when Jesus asked his disciples, "'Who do people say that the Son of Man is?' They replied, 'Some say John the Baptist'" (16:13–14).

14:13–21 A STORY OF JESUS FEEDING THE MULTITUDE: THE FIVE THOUSAND

The news about John's death reached Jesus through John's disciples (Matt 14:12). After hearing this, Jesus withdrew to a secluded place, very likely, to grieve for John (14:13). Jesus' journey transitions from the story of the Baptist's death to the account of the feeding of the crowd. Although still grieving, Jesus' pastoral heart did not allow his grief to prevent him from ministering to the multitude.

Prior to this incident, crowds had been following Jesus (8:1, 18; 9:36; 13:2), either to listen to him teach or to receive healing. As in the previous accounts, Jesus ministered to the crowd out of compassion (14:14), which motivated him to: (1) send out the Twelve (9:36); (2) feed the 5,000 (14:14);

---

9. For similarities between Moses and Jesus, see Dane Ortlund, "The Old Testament Background and Eschatological Significance of Jesus Walking on the Sea (Mark 6:45–52)," *Neot* 46, no. 2 (2012): 320–325.
10. Fiedler, *Das Matthäus-evangelium*, 272.

(3) feed the 4,000 (15:32); and (4) heal the blind man (20:34). Details from other Gospel accounts provide useful information in understanding Matthew's account of the feeding. First, the disciples' estimate that the amount of money needed to buy food for crowd would be two hundred denarii (Mark 6:37; John 6:7) or the equivalent of eight months' salary of a daily wage earner.[11] This explains the disciples' suggestion to Jesus that he should send them to the villages to buy food for themselves (Matt 14:15). Second, Jesus' intention in not sending them away is explained in the Fourth Gospel. He already planned to feed the crowd, but wanted to test the disciples (John 6:6; Matt 14:16).

As it is in the other Gospel accounts, fives loaves and two fishes amounted to all the food available, and Jesus used what was available to feed the crowd. Fives loaves and two fishes are often interpreted in relation to the Communion;[12] and this is because the fourfold act of Jesus (taking the bread, giving thanks for it, breaking it, and distributing the pieces) are very similar to what Jesus did at the Last Supper (14:19; 26:26–29).[13]

Matthew records that Jesus ordered the crowd to sit down on the grass (14:19). It sounds unusual for grass to be found in the desert. As Origen observes,[14] yet it seems that the more important question here is the possible significance of this detail. The crowd being asked to sit on grass has drawn an image similar to that of Psalm 23 wherein the sheep was made to lie down in green pastures (Matt 23:2), provisions prepared for them (23:5), with their cups overflowing (23:5), and the assurance of God's presence (23:6). Like the account of feeding by Elisha, there were leftovers after Jesus fed the crowd (2 Kgs 4:43–44; Matt 4:20). The leftovers could easily be misunderstood as extravagance or waste, but in the cases of these two stories of feeding, it is evidence of ample provision from the God. Once again, God's presence is experienced through Jesus' miracles.

---

11. In Matthew 20:2, the workers in the vineyard agreed to work the whole day for a denarius. This may hint that during Matthew's day, this is the typical amount paid to workers for a whole day's work. Hence, not counting the Sabbath, 200 denarii is equivalent to 200 working days or almost eight month's wages.
12. Richard H., Hiers and Charles A. Kennedy, "Bread and Fish in the Gospels and Early Christian Art," *PRSt* 3, no. 1 (1976): 46.
13. Terrence Cuneo, "Protesting Evil," *ThTo* 70, no. 4 (2013): 435.
14. Peter J. Scaer, "The Lord's Supper as Symposium in the Gospel of Mark," *CTQ* 72, no. 2 (2008): 124.

Matthew 14:1–16:20

14:22–36 JESUS WALKED ON WATER

In the previous episode, Jesus ministered to the crowd even though he desired to be alone after hearing of John's death. However, he did not allow his own need of solitude to prevent him from ministering to others (Matt 14:13–14). Yet at the same time, he did not allow the ministry to keep him from spending time alone with God. This is something worth reflecting upon especially for those of us involved in pastoral ministry. Jesus' willingness to minister to the people even during his time of grief shows that he did not consider his ministry a 40-hour-per-week job but a 24/7 ministry that requires regular time to recharge and be refreshed.

After ministering to the crowd, he immediately called his disciples to embark by boat (14:22–23). So, having sent the disciples (14:22) and the crowd (14:23) away, Jesus was left alone, and he went up the mountain to pray. In Matthew, the "mountain" is a location of spiritual battle/temptation (4:8), it is where Jesus preached his Sermon (5:1; 8:1), a place of revelation (17:1, 9; 24:3; 26:30), and the place from where Jesus ascended to heaven (28:16). Jesus' activities on or near mountains are comparable to those of Moses; and for Moses the mountain was a meeting place with the LORD (Exod 19:1, 20), a place for receiving revelation (20:1–18; 32:15; 34:4, 29; Lev 25:1) and giving instructions (24:7), and it is also the last place where he went before he was taken away by God (Deut 34:1–6). Ancient Jews believed that heaven is where God resides (Ps 115:3; Ecc 5:12).[15] Hence, going up the mountain can be a symbolic practice of approaching or moving near the presence of God.

After a time of prayer, Jesus went to meet his disciples who were on their way to the other side of the sea by boat (14:24–26). In Matthew, near the "sea" is where Jesus called his first disciples (4:18), it is where he preached the parables (13:1), performed miracles of healing (15:29), and it is also a chaotic place which Jesus calmed (8:24–26). In contrast to mountains, ancient Jews associated seas with evil and chaos;[16] nonetheless, the sea is a place of salvation amidst turmoil (Exod 14:13–31; 15:1–22; Job 26:12; Pss 65:7; 89:9; 93:4). Matthew's description, "the boat was already a considerable distance from land" (14:24),[17] may suggest that the disciples were nowhere near their

---

15. "Heaven," in OT, is where God resides (Gen 24:3, 7; 2 Chr 36:33; Ezra 1:2; 5:11, 12; 6:9, 10; 7:12, 21, 23; Neh 1:4, 5; 2:20; Pss 14:2; 53:2; 57:3; 80:14; 136:26; Dan 2:18, 19, 37, 44; 5:23; Jonah 1:9).
16. J. G. S. S. Thomson, "Sea," in *New Bible Dictionary*, 2nd ed. (Leicester: IVP, 1982), 1080–1181.
17. In the Greek, Matthew used the word *stadious* (plural; sometimes translated "stadia," a distance of about 600 feet) without specifying the magnitude; the distance may be unknown, but it is a long one.

destination, and yet too far from their origin to go back. In other words, they were trapped in the middle of the sea with waves making it difficult for them to reach the shore. It was at this time when Jesus came to them walking on water.

The account of Jesus walking on the water finds some parallels in Buddhist traditions. Jesus walking on water depicts him as the one who conquers chaos.[18] Some consider this story as too fantastic to be true, and many have questioned its historicity.[19] However, it is hard to imagine that such story would be created without any historical basis at all.[20] Perhaps more significant is that the story climaxed with the disciples' declaration of Jesus as the Son of God (Matt 14:33). This comes after Peter's prayer for salvation (14:30), which echoes the psalmist's cry for help as he drowns in the "mire" of dishonor (Ps 69:2; especially vv. 5–8, 30–33).[21] For the first time in Matthew's Gospel, the disciples bowed down before him (Matt 14:33). Prior to this account, the magi (2:2, 8, 11), the leper (8:2), and the synagogue officials (9:18) bowed before Jesus. It is becoming clearer that Jesus is one having divine status.

15:1–20 THE TRADITION OF THE ELDERS: WASHING OF HANDS AND THE *QORBAN*

The account of Jesus walking on water points to Jesus' divine identity. In the following story, Jesus' identity as the authoritative interpreter of Scripture is underscored. Three chapters earlier, Jesus also had a similar encounter with the Pharisees regarding the "unlawful" practice of his disciples who plucked grain on a Sabbath to eat (Matt 12:1–8), except this time, it was about the disciples not washing their hands before eating (Matt 15:1–20). Proper hygiene is part of the LORD's requirements from the Israelites. He required the washing of items owned by leprosy patients (Lev 13:53–59). There are provisions in the Law about waste management and sanitation such as covering of excrement using spades (Deut 23:13), presumably to avoid spread of disease

---

18. Andrew Angel, "Crucifixus Vincens: The 'Son of God' as Divine Warrior in Matthew," *CBQ* 73, no. 2 (2011): 307.
19. For examples of these works, see Pieter F. Craffert and Pieter J. J. Botha, "Why Jesus Could Walk on the Sea but He Could Not Read and Write: Reflections on Historicity and Interpretation in Historical Jesus Research," *Neot* 39, no. 1 (2005): 10–14.
20. J. Duncan M. Derrett, "Why and How Jesus Walked on the Sea," *NovT* 23, no. 4 (1981): 330. See also Rachel Nicholls, *Walking on Water: Reading Mt. 14:22–23 in Light of Its Wirkungsgeschichte* (Leiden: Brill, 2008), 200.
21. Angel, "Crucifixus Vincens," 308.

caused by an unclean environment. There are also commands regarding the washing of cooking utensils (Lev 6:28). Some of God's requirements about washing are ceremonial. For example, priests wash hands before performing priestly duties (Exod 30:18–21; 40:11–14, 30–32), cleansing of leprosy patients (Lev 14:5–18), those who discharge bodily fluid or had contact with people who had such discharge (15:1–33), and those who ate animals that had not been slaughtered properly (17:15–16). Jesus was not against any of these laws. He even commanded one with leprosy whom he healed to present himself to the priest (Matt 8:4), who would presumably require him to wash his clothes as part of the cleansing process (Lev 13:6). There was no indication that Jesus was opposed to this practice.

The ceremonial washing of hands was part of the religious rituals of the Pharisees.[22] The issue was more than just proper hygiene, but a disregard of a body of commands they considered sacred. Matthew makes it clear in the remark of the Pharisees and scribes that the disciples' violation was not a neglect or disobedience of a scriptural command, but the breaking of the "tradition of the elders" (Matt 15:2). Likewise, Jesus' reply to the religious leaders shows that he was not against every form of tradition, but only those that invalidated the laws of God by giving more importance to human traditions (15:3, 6).

Jesus was not against being ritually clean; his concern was the pursuit of ritual cleanliness at the expense of mercy (9:13; 12:7; 23:23), especially towards one's family members. Jesus challenged the Pharisees' practice of ritual purity by pointing out the practice of neglecting the needs of one's (elderly) parents using the guise of religious devotion. This was done through the vow called the *qorban*, a vow to abstain from something, like eating dried figs, by declaring it as a sacred offering.[23] This form of abstinence could be good and noble, except when it was in violation of the Torah, especially if people abstained from helping their parents who were in need.

Moving back to the question of ritual purity, Jesus explained to his disciples, "What goes into someone's mouth does not defile them, but what comes

---

22. The Mishnah provides glimpses of the kind of conversations the ancient rabbis had about when to wash hands. Rabbi Shammai, for instance, advised that the washing of hands must be done *before* one prepares the wine for dinner, and *after* sweeping the floor; Rabbi Hillel, in contrast, taught that the washing of hands must be done *after* one prepares the wine for dinner, and *before* sweeping the floor (*Berakhot* 8:2, 4). Ritual washing of hands was also done by some priests in order to eat unconsecrated food in cases when the Pentecost falls on a Friday (*Hagiga* 2:4–5).
23. See Mishnah, *Nazir* 2:1. For the various views about the *qorban*, see discussion in George Wesley Buchanan, "Some Vow and Oath Formulas in the New Testament," *HTR* 58, no. 3 (1965): 319; Bailey, "Vowing Away the Fifth Commandment," 201.

out of their mouth, that is what defiles them" (Matt 15:11). Records show that the Jewish rabbis also emphasize the importance of the heart.[24] Clearly, many rabbis would agree that what comes out of the mouth can make a person unclean. However, there are provisions in the law that show external factors can also make a person unclean. Aside from the OT classifications of animals as clean or unclean for human consumption (Lev 11:2–47), foods that touch anything unclean were also considered unclean (Lev 7:19–20). Even the place where consecrated food is eaten must be clean (Lev 10:14);[25] the person must also be ceremonially clean (Lev 7:21; 22:4–7), and cleansing for unclean persons could be done so that they could participate in meals (17:5; see also 22:8). Discussions about situations not explicitly mentioned in the Torah were done by the rabbis; for instance, opinions on whether a person should be considered unclean if he is not allowed to eat heave offerings but accidentally does so.[26] Jesus' challenge to the Pharisees who claim that eating "unclean" food can make a person unclean makes clear his own view about the matter (Matt 15:11). The description of the Pharisees as blind guides who led people astray also sets Jesus apart as the one who truly understands the essence of God's command (15:14–15).

The main issue in Matthew's discussion is not about food, but about the heart, the source of sin expressed in various ways such as murder, adultery, sexual immorality, theft, false witness, and slander (15:18–20; see also Exod 20:13–17). By citing the sixth to tenth commandments, it is clear that Jesus did not nullify the Law (see also Hos 4:2; Jer 7:9),[27] but explains that there is something more than just the outward act of obedience.

---

24. The Mishnah records the thoughts of the rabbis concerning the relationship between the heart and the mouth, and the importance of the heart in what one does. Some of them taught that one cannot make vows unless the heart and mouth agrees (*Terumot* 3:8). Also, reciting the Shema just to fulfill a religious obligation and not out of the heart is considered useless (*Berakhot* 2:1); conversely, the prayer of those riding on a donkey but cannot dismount during prayer time can be acceptable if they directed their heart to God (*Berakhot* 4:5–5:1), and even the leaven inside the house during Passover can be "nullified in the heart" (*Pesahim* 3:7). The also taught intention to kill or harm is more offensive than the act itself (*Sanhedrin* 9:2).
25. See also Mishnah, *Kelim* 8:10–11.
26. Mishnah, *Terumot* 8:2.
27. See also 3 Baruch 4:17. Christian Stetler, "Purity of Heart in Jesus' Teaching: Mark 7:14–23 par. As an Expression of Jesus' *basileia* Ethics," trans. Kathryn Williams, *JTS* 55, no. 2 (2004): 478.

FILIAL RESPECT AND THE *QORBAN*

One of the core values of the Chinese people is filial respect. In fact, many have taken this to the extreme, resulting in the practice of ancestral worship. Although the practice of ancestral worship is clearly unbiblical, filial respect is not. The OT contains numerous commands related to filial respect. Aside from the command to honor one's parents (Matt 19:19; Exod 20:12; Deut 5:16; Eph 6:2), a curse was pronounced against those who dishonor them (Deut 27:16) and death was the penalty for those who spoke evil against their parents (Exod 21:17; Lev 20:9; Prov 20:20). There are also commands against striking one's parents (Exod 21:15; Prov 19:26), humiliating them by exposing their nakedness (Lev 18:17; 20:19), and rebellion which is penalized by death (Deut 21:18, 19).

The Pharisees also upheld the value of filial respect and would have condemned the practice of neglecting one's parents.[1] Yet there were those who neglected their parents' needs using the *qorban* as an excuse. Instances like this are documented in the Mishnah (*Nedarim* 5:6; 8:7; 9:1; *Bava Qamma* 9:10). It is important to note, however, that the Jewish rabbis also taught that in some instance, vows could be nullified in order to practice filial respect (*Nedarim* 9:1).[2] Two archaeological discoveries in the last century demonstrate that such a practice existed during the time of Jesus: the fragment of a stone vessel has been found bearing the inscription *qorban* with two bird-like figures similar to the sacrifices required in Leviticus 12:8, and also an ossuary lid with an inscription that says, "Everything that a man will find to his profit in this ossuary (is) an offering to God from the one within it."[3] Even among the rabbis, there were disagreements whether coins placed in a vessel marked as "offering" should be considered consecrated. Rabbi Hillel accepted as a second tithe anything placed in a container marked as "tithe," but Rabbi Shammai insisted that it also be taken into consideration whether the container was made of clay (the offering is consecrated) or metal (the offering is unconsecrated) (see Mishnah, *Ma'aser Sheni* 4:9–10).

Fulfilling one's vows is important and necessary;[4] however, this could be done by depriving some people, including relatives, of certain reasonable benefits. The prophet Malachi denounces the practice of robbing God through one's tithes and offerings (Mal 3:8–9). In the same way, those who rob their parents were also denounced (Prov 28:24). Even in the NT, filial respect in the form of providing for parents in need was commanded (1 Tim 5:3–8). Jesus complains about this type of misguided religious zeal (Matt 15:4–6), which he followed with a quotation from Isaiah 29:13 (see also Matt 15:7–9). By doing so, Jesus imitated the prophet Isaiah who decried the people whose reverence to God was based on a "tradition learned by rote" (Isa 29:13, NASB), rather than a genuine devotion to God. Jesus was not minimizing the importance

> of fulfilling one's religious vows (Matt 23:23), but he was emphasizing the importance of doing so with a correct disposition of the heart. The main point of Jesus' view about the religious vows, filial respect, and ritual purity is the same, namely, they are essentially heart issues.
>
> **Samson L. Uytanlet**
>
> ---
>
> 1. The Pharisees are presented as those who neglect their parents for the sake of their religious vows. For a discussion on possible reasons for such stereotyped portrayal, see E. P. Sanders, *Jewish Law from Jesus to the Mishnah* (Philadelphia: Trinity Press International, 1990), 55–57.
> 2. Jon Nelson Bailey, "Vowing Away the Fifth Commandment: Matthew 15:3–6// Mark 7:9–13," *ResQ* 42, no. 4 (2000): 204–205.
> 3. Bailey, "Vowing Away the Fifth Commandment," 199; Joseph A. Fitzmyer, "The Aramaic Qorbān Inscription from Jebel Ḥallet Eṭ-Ṭûri and Mark 7.11/Matt 15.5," *JBL* 78, no. 1 (1959): 60–65.
> 4. Fulfillment of vows was necessary (Mal 1:14; Eccl 5:4–5; see also Sirach 18:22–23; Damascus Document 9:1; 16:6; Philo, *Special Laws* 1.247–254). Various oath formulas were also used in declaring their oaths and vows (Buchanan, "Some Vows and Oath Formulas," 326).

15:21–28 THE FAITH OF THE CANAANITE WOMAN

The account of John's death clears the confusion about Jesus' identity because it shows that Jesus is *not* John the Baptist who was raised from the dead (Matt 16:14). The divine identity of Jesus is underscored in the accounts of the feeding of the five thousand and his walking on water. His role as the authoritative interpreter of the Scripture is once again seen in his encounter with the Pharisees and scribes; and one of the issues raised in this encounter was the Jewish purity rituals that segregated the Jews from Gentiles, a concern further probed in the story of Jesus' encounter with the Syro-Phoenician woman.[28]

The account begins with Jesus withdrawing to the regions of Tyre and Sidon (Matt 15:21). Prior to this incident, Jesus "withdrew" from the crowd

---

28. Much studies have been done on this story. Melanie S. Baffes, "Jesus and the Canaanite Woman: A Story of Reversal," *JTAK* 35, no. 2 (2011): 17–18; Musa W. Dube, "Readings of Semoya: Batswana Women's Interpretations of Matt 15:21–28," *Semeia* 73 (1996): 111–129; Leticia A. Guardiola-Sáenz, "Borderless Woman and Borderless Texts: A Cultural Reading of Matthew 15:21–28," *Semeia* 78 (1987): 70–72; Roy A. Harrisville, "The Woman of Canaan: A Chapter in the History of Exegesis," *Int* 20, no. 3 (1966): 278 n. 20; Nancy Klancher, *The Taming of the Canaanite Woman: Constructions of Christian Identity in the Afterlife of Matthew 15:21–28*, SBR 1 (Berlin: De Gruyter, 2013).

twice in order to get away from them (Matt 12:15; 14:13). A visit to gentile territory could be a good way to avoid a Jewish crowd, but in this case, Jesus' reason for travel is not so much an avoidance of one group, but an attempt to include the other (see also John 4:4). His withdrawal from the crowd resulted in his ministry to the "outsiders." This did not happen without a controversy because of Jesus' derogatory and discriminating remark against the Canaanite woman.

The social background of the woman is unclear from Matthew's story. Some say she was a poor peasant because of the typical condition of people in the area, while others suggest that she may have belonged to the upper class of the society because instead of using a mattress, the woman's daughter slept on a bed.[29] The only thing that is clear is her ethnic background; as a Canaanite she was an enemy of Israel.[30] Although Jesus had previously commended the receptiveness of Tyre and Sidon when compared to Chorazin and Bethsaida (Matt 11:21–22), in the OT, they are condemned (Isa 23; Joel 3:4; Ezek 26–28; Zech. 9:1–4). The animosity between the Jews and the Tyreans and Sidonians is clear.[31] Matthew's use of the description "Canaanite" (Matt 15:22), instead of "Syro-Phoenician" (Mark 7:26), may be understood as his way of pointing to the huge ethnic and religious divide between the woman and Jesus. As a "Canaanite," she was not only a Gentile, she was also an enemy. Through Jesus' commendation of the woman, he acknowledged the huge social, ethnic, and cultural barrier between them,[32] yet these barriers did not exclude her from participating in God's blessing of salvation. The inclusion of Rahab and Tamar in Jesus' genealogy already anticipates the inclusion of the Canaanites among God's people. This, of course, provides hope for most of the people in the world, as most of us, like the Canaanite woman, is Gentiles.

---

29. Daniel S. Schipani, "Transformation of Borderlands: A Study of Matthew 15:21–28," *Vision* 2, no. 2 (2001): 15–16; Perkinson, "Canaanitic Word," 67; Gerd Theissen, *The Gospels in Context: Social and Political History in the Synoptic Tradition*, trans. Linda M. Maloney (Edinburgh: T. & T. Clark, 1992), 72–75.

30. Glenna S. Jackson, "A Source for Matthew's Story of the Canaanite Woman," *Proceedings* 14 (1994): 49. A few interpreters from earlier centuries think she was an Israelite. For example, Apollinaris of Laodicea, Fragment 81 (see Joseph Reuss, *Matthäus-Kommentare aus der griechischen Kirche*, TUGAL 61 (Berlin: Akademie-Verlag, [1957], 25); Roy A. Harrisville, "The Woman of Canaan: A Chapter in the History of Exegesis," *Int* 20, no. 3 (1966): 278.

31. James W. Perkinson, "A Canaanitic Word in the Logos of Christ; or The Difference the Syro-Phoenician Woman Makes to Jesus," *Semeia* 75 (1996): 67–68.

32. Schipani, "Transformation of Borderlands," 15–16; Glenna Jackson, *'Have Mercy on Me': The Story of the Canaanite Woman in Matt 15.21–28*, JSNTSup 228 (Sheffield: Sheffield Academic Press, 2002), 70–82.

The challenge in understanding the story is that Jesus' initial response to the woman seems to suggest that salvation is only for Israel. When the Canaanite woman came out crying to the "Son of David" to heal her demon-possessed daughter (see also comments on Matthew 9:27–31). Jesus' initial response was to ignore her (Matt 15:23a). This is unacceptable in any culture, but easily justifiable for those who consider themselves superior. Jesus' indifference was coupled with the disciples' suggestion to send her away because she had been shouting at them (15:23b; Acts 16:17–18). Hence, the start of the conversation between Jesus and the woman was rather unpromising.

First, Jesus replied by saying he was only sent "to the lost sheep of Israel" (Matt 15:24; see also comments on Matthew 5:15–20). This statement shows God's promise of forgiveness for his people, but does not limit salvation to Israel alone. Second, with the Canaanite woman's insistence, Jesus replied using "dog" as a metaphor to describe, not just the mother of a demon-possessed girl, but also the ethnic group to which she belonged (15:26). Although Matthew uses the word *kunarion* ("little dog" or "puppy"), instead of *kuōn* ("dog," a full grown one), calling her "little dog" was actually no less derogatory. Why did Jesus do so? Considering how Jews accept Gentiles who wanted to convert to Judaism may help us understand the dynamics in the story.

Discouragement was used by ancient Jews to test the sincerity of proselyte candidates.[33] If she was a Gentile who was willing to put her faith in the God of Israel (15:31), Jesus' challenge could be considered part of the test. No wonder Jesus praised her, "Woman, you have great faith!" The miracle is not the main point of the story; the woman's faith is. Her "great faith" contrasts with the disciples' "little faith" (6:30; 8:26; 14:31; 16:8; see also Luke 12:28).[34] He granted her request (15:28); and like the centurion's servant (8:5–13), the daughter of the Canaanite woman was also healed from a distance; and the mother's response serves as a reminder that God's reign is not limited to certain people groups only.[35]

---

33. An example of this is found in their commentary on Ruth (Ruth Rabbah 2:6). See also Jackson, "Matthew's Story of the Canaanite Woman," 51–52; see also Paul Ehrman Scherer, "Gauntlet with a Gift in It: From Text to Sermon on Matthew 15:21–28 and Mark 7:24–30," *Int* 20, no. 4 (1966): 387–399.
34. Baffes, "Jesus and the Canaanite Woman," 16; Scott, "Test Case for Jesus' Manners," 41.
35. Schipani, "Transformation of Borderlands," 17–18; see also his other work, "Matteo 15:21–28: Como Narrativa Paradigmática para el Cuidado Interconfesional," *Kairós* 46 (2010): 85–99.

In a society that values male Jews, there are two reasons she would be despised: she was a woman and she was a Canaanite. Ironically, Matthew demonstrates that the woman was the one who truly understood God's plan of salvation. She could demonstrate her faith, not by defending her people from the insult of being called dogs, but by acknowledging that the gentile-puppies and the Jewish-sheep have the same master.[36] The story clearly foresees the salvation of the nations. Melanie Baffes aptly summarizes the main thrust of this story: "God is present for all who are faithful, regardless of class, race, ethnicity, gender, age, or any other culturally or socially-imposed distinctions."[37] She could benefit from this because she believed.

15:29–39 ANOTHER STORY OF JESUS FEEDING THE MULTITUDE: THE FOUR THOUSAND

After Jesus' encounter with the gentile woman, Jesus had another encounter with a crowd, who were likely Gentiles as well. The account begins with a summary statement of Jesus' ministry (Matt 15:29–31). Three types of summary statements are found in Matthew: (1) descriptions of Jesus' preaching/teaching ministry (4:23; 9:35; 11:1); (2) his passion predictions (16:21; 17:22–23; 20:17–19); and (3) other middle section summaries (12:15–21; 14:34–36; 15:29–31).[38] These statements are very important in understanding Jesus identity and earthly task, which is to proclaim God's kingship through his teachings and miracles. He would be rejected resulting in his death, yet despite his impending sufferings and repeated rejection, he continued his ministry.

Jesus went to the mountain again, presumably to spend some time in prayer (14:23), when the crowd came to him for healing. Four types of people who came are specified: the lame, the crippled, the blind, and the mute (15:30). Their healing was part of God's promise of salvation (Isa 35:4–6). After experiencing God's presence through Jesus' healing, the crowd began to glorify the "God of Israel" (Matt 15:31).

Jesus' expressed motive for healing the crowd was his compassion towards them (15:32). This is reminiscent of the previous story of feeding (14:14).

---

36. Amy-Jill Levine, *The Social and Ethnic Dimensions of the Matthean Salvation History*, SBEC 14 (Lewiston, NY: Edwin Mellen Press, 1988), 152.
37. Baffes, "Jesus and the Canaanite Woman," 20.
38. Thomas J. Ryan, "Matthew 15:29–31: An Overlooked Summary," *Hor* 5, no. 1 (1978): 31–32.

Nothing was said about the food the crowd consumed during the first two days they were with Jesus (whether they brought food enough for two days or they had other sources). We are also not informed whether most of them did not stay through this period. What is clear is that another miracle of feeding was about to happen but this time with another group of people who were likely Gentiles.[39] There is not enough information within the text to confirm this, but if this assumption is correct, it becomes clearer that Jesus' ministry extended beyond ethnic boundaries.

Figure 10: Two Accounts of Feeding in Matthew

14:13–21	15:32–39
Aftermath of Jesus' withdrawal to a secluded place (14:13)	Aftermath of Jesus' withdrawal to a secluded place (15:29)
Set along the sea shore (14:14)	Set along the sea shore (15:29)
Healing of a large crowd (14:14)	Healing of a large crowd (15:30–31)
Jesus' compassion (14:14)	Jesus' compassion (15:32)
Jesus ordered the disciples to give them food (14:16)	Jesus told the disciples he wanted to give them food (15:32)
Disciples' question: Where do we get food for all of them? (14:15)	Disciples' question: Where do we get food for all of them? (15:33)
Jesus asked for what is available (14:18)	Jesus asked for what is available (15:34)
5 loaves, 2 fish (14:17)	*7 loaves, 2 fish* (15:34)
Jesus ordered the crowd to sit on the grass (14:19)	Jesus ordered the crowd to sit on the ground (15:35)
Jesus took the bread, gave thanks, broke them, disciples distribute (14:19)	Jesus took the bread, gave thanks, broke them, disciples distribute (15:36)
All were satisfied (14:20)	All were satisfied (15:37)
12 baskets of leftovers (14:20)	*7 baskets* of leftovers (15:37)
5,000 men plus women and children (14:21)	*4,000 men* plus women and children (15:38)
Jesus sent the crowd away after they were fed (14:22)	Jesus left the crowd after they were fed (15:39)

---

39. Hilary of Poitiers' commentary on Matthew is the earliest known work to identify the four thousand as Gentiles (J. R. C. Cousland, "The Feeding of the Four Thousand Gentiles in Matthew? Matthew 15:29–39 as a Test Case," *NovT* 41, no. 1 [1999]:1–2).

A comparison between the two accounts of feeding shows the similarities between the two accounts and the second story seems like a replay of the first one with a few numerical variations (see Figure 10). The numerical differences show that these accounts refer to two distinct and separate events. The repetition highlights both Jesus' manner of teaching, and the disciples' deficiency in learning. This story prepares for Jesus' assessment about his disciples, "You of little faith . . . Do you still not understand? Don't you remember the five loaves for the five thousand, and how many basketfuls you gathered? Or, the seven loaves for the four thousand, and how many basketfuls you gathered?" (16:8–10).

There are numerous instances in Mathew wherein God is presented as one who provides food to the people. He provides "daily bread" for his disciples (6:11), and so his children are not supposed to worry about what they should eat (6:25–34). God also promised to provide for those who ask for their needs, including food (7:7–11). When the disciples were sent to preach the kingdom, God used the people who hear the gospel to provide for the disciples' daily needs (10:9–15). The two accounts of feeding also highlight God's character as the Creator-Father in heaven who provides not only for the believers but even for those who do not believe.[40]

16:1–12 REQUESTING SIGNS FROM HEAVEN

After the feeding of the four thousand, Jesus traveled to the "vicinity of Magadan" (Matt 15:39). This region is often identified with Magdala, the place of origin of Mary Magdalene (or Mary of Magdala). It is located on the west shore of the Sea of Galilee, in between Capernaum (to its south) and Tiberias (to its north).[41] It is the last place where Jesus and his disciples stayed before traveling northward to Caesarea Philippi where Peter confessed Jesus as the Christ.

Jesus had another confrontation with the "Pharisees and Sadducees" who asked him to give them a "sign from heaven" (Matt 16:1). The religious leaders initiated this in order to test Jesus (16:1) and question his authority (see also 19:3; 22:18, 35). In their more recent encounters with Jesus, the Pharisees were with the scribes (12:38; 15:1). The last time the "Pharisees

---

40. James P. Grimshaw, *The Matthean Community and the World: An Analysis of Matthew's Food Exchange*, StBibLit 111 (New York: Peter Lang, 2008), 188–189.
41. S. S. Smalley, "Magdala, Mary," in *New Bible Dictionary*, 2nd ed., (Leicester: IVP, 1982), 722.

and Sadducees" were together was when some of them came to John to be baptized (3:7). The two groups did not have much in common. In fact, at some points in history they were against each other, but they were willing to work together against their common enemy. As demonstrated in politics throughout history, "my enemy's enemy can be my friend."

At first glance, the religious leaders' demand for signs was legitimate and may suggest that they had doubts similar to that of Thomas (John 20:24–29). Matthew's portrayal of them, however, and Jesus' response show that their demand for a sign from heaven was not evidence of sincere doubt, but of defiance and unbelief.

Jesus responded by calling the Pharisees and Sadducees a "wicked and adulterous generation" (Matt 16:4), which echoes his earlier assessment of the Pharisees and the scribes (12:39). Moreover, he reiterated that no other sign would be given them except the "sign of Jonah" (12:39–40; 16:4). This suggests that this story can be understood in connection with the earlier story with the Pharisees and scribes demanding for a sign.[42]

Figure 11: Demands for Sign

	12:38–45	**16:1–4**
People involved	scribes and Pharisees (12:38)	Pharisees and Sadducees (16:1)
Demand	sign (12:38)	sign from heaven (16:1)
Jesus' assessment	evil and adulterous generation (12:39)	evil and adulterous generation (16:4)
Available sign	sign of Jonah; 3 days and 3 nights in the belly of sea monster (12:39–40)	color of sky (16:2–3); sign of Jonah (16:4)
Sign to be expected	Son of Man: 3 days and 3 nights in the heart of the earth (12:40)	Son of Man: coming in the clouds (see also 24:30)
Significance	Death and resurrection	Ascension and return

---

42. See Elian Cuvillier correctly notes that without 12:2–3, Jesus' reply is clearly an invitation to interpret 16:1–12 in light of 12:38–45 ("Discerner les signa temporum ou la 'contemporanéité' évangélique: Mt 16, 1–4 et Mt 24–25," *Théoph* 18, no. 1 [2013]: 12–14).

This episode is comparable to the previous one involving the Pharisees and scribes (Matt 12:38–45) as shown in Figure 11. These two episodes show two things. First, Jesus did not perform "miracles on demand." His miracles were done, not only to benefit those who needed them, but also to elicit faith; and miracles are not necessary for those who refuse to believe from the very start. Second, these stories highlight the significant events of Jesus' passion and return. The ultimate signs that Jesus is who he claimed to be are: the "sign" of his death and resurrection (12:38, 40), and the "sign from heaven," which is his ascension and return (16:1; 24:30).[43]

After leaving the Pharisees and Sadducees, Jesus warned the disciples against the "yeast of the Pharisees" (16:6). Unlike many countries in eastern Asia wherein rice is the staple food, bread is the main element of the ancient Jewish diet. No wonder Jesus' statement was misunderstood by the disciples as referring to an ingredient of the food that they ate regularly. Even after seeing two feeding miracles, the disciples were still clueless as to what Jesus' could do (16:9–10). His assessment of the disciples as men "of little faith" (16:8) shows that they were, in essence, not very different from the Pharisees and Sadducees; but unlike the religious leaders, they were not defiant.

The leaven of the Pharisees and Sadducees referred to their teachings (16:8; see also comments for Matthew 13:31–35). The term "unleavened" is an expression that metaphorically referred to sincerity or purity (1 Cor 5:8). No wonder in the OT, the Israelites were instructed to remove the leaven from their house whenever they celebrated the Passover (Exod 12:15). In Luke 12:1, he specifies that the leaven of Pharisees refer particularly to one kind of sin, namely, hypocrisy. Leaven is an agent of fermentation, and just as a little amount of leaven can affect the whole dough, their teachings could affect people; they could lead a person either to believe or reject Jesus.[44]

---

43. Cuvillier, "Discerner les signa," 14; James Swetnam, "No Sign of Jonah," *Bib* 66, no. 1 (1985): 126.
44. David P. Moessner, "The 'Leaven of the Pharisees' and 'This Generation': Israel's Rejection of Jesus according to Luke," *JSNT* 34 (1988): 42.

WELCOMING PEOPLE IN THE CHURCH

The word "church" appears only in Matthew's Gospel and not in any of the other gospels. Jesus himself is the one who established the church who will be his bride (Rev 9:7, 21:1–10). Today, the word "church" can refer to a magnificent building with many resources, or to a small group of worshippers meeting in a home under constant fear. In many parts of Asia, the Christian community remains a minority. No matter what the church looks like on the outside, all churches stand on the theological truth that Peter proclaimed, Jesus Christ, the Son of the living God.

The church is the one body where people from every tongue, tribe and nation can gather together as family, sisters, and brothers through the blood of Jesus Christ. Jesus welcomed the Canaanite woman to take the crumbs from the table of Jews (15:21–28). Although from a different culture, since she acknowledged Jesus as Lord and healer and so demonstrated great faith, Jesus welcomed her. In the same way, we should also be quick to welcome different people into our Christian faith communities: those who come from different racial backgrounds, or socioeconomic class. In evangelism, it is sometimes easier to reach out to people who are like us. But the success and ease of this approach should not preclude us from reaching out to those who are different from us.

The cultural diversity of Asia is reflected in the churches. For example, some denominations in Asia are divided along linguistic lines: the Methodist Church in Malaysia has English-speaking, Chinese-speaking, Tamil-speaking, and indigenous annual conferences under its General Conference. This diversity reflects the color and richness of the country, though building unity can be challenging. Thus, the national language (Bahasa Melayu or Malay language) or English is then the working language in the church; though it is not necessarily the heart language of all the believers there.

One place where a great diversity of people can be seen is in the city. Due to globalization and migration, cities today attract professionals in transnational companies, students, and skilled migrant workers who offer the work of their hands. All these people can be seen on the streets of a globalized city like Shanghai or Singapore. Hence churches in cities have a unique opportunity to reach out to and share the gospel with a broad range of people. In healing the Canaanite woman's daughter, Jesus welcomed one who was culturally different to the table. Today, as it is in Jesus' day, culture and social classes separate different groups. While many of our societies are divided along these lines, the church can be a marvelous witness for the truth that the gospel is for everyone and that it is at the cross where each one finds forgiveness and grace.

> What binds Christians together through space and time, and despite cultural and socioeconomic differences is that the church stands on the theological truth that Peter proclaimed, "You are the Christ, the Son of the living God" (16:16). Thus, it is not so much what the church looks like on the outside, but what she is ontologically, in her essence, that makes the church who she is. While some of the largest churches in the world by attendance are in South Korea, other Asian churches are generally small, meeting in homes and wherever they can find space. The differences in physical buildings do not diminish the fact that both are the "church" as long as they stand on that same proclamation that Peter made.
>
> From the context of this passage, the church thus stands on the totality of who Jesus is: the one who predicts his own suffering and death and the one who is transfigured in the next scene. That is why the churches which only preach blessings are wrong because they are not giving the whole picture of who Jesus is. Thus, there can be diversity in culture, language and class, because there is unity in belief.
>
> **Kiem-Kiok Kwa**

16:13–20 JESUS' IDENTITY REVEALED; PETER'S CONFESSION

After seven episodes, several aspects of Jesus' identity have been presented (see Figure 12 for summary); and these are climaxed with the account of Peter's confession.

Jesus and his disciples moved nearly fifty kilometers northward to Caesarea Philippi after his last encounter with the religious leaders at Magadan (Matt 15:39; 16:13). Caesarea Philippi is located southwest of Mt. Hermon, near the territory of ancient Dan, presently called Banyas near the border between Israel and Lebanon.[45] The region of Caesarea, Philippi has a long history as a sacred territory. One of the earliest cultic activities recorded is that of Micah at Dan (Judg 17–18). The shrine of Jeroboam I, which remained even until the time of Amos, was rebuilt by Ahab (1 Kgs 12:26–31; see also Amos 8:14). A bilingual Aramaic and Greek inscription with a statue of Aphrodite was uncovered by archaeologists. The *Paneion*, a sacred grotto dedicated to the god Pan, was built during the Hellenistic period. Herod erected a temple in honor of Augustus. Even until the third century AD, the place continued to

---

45. David J. Zucker, "Jesus and Jeremiah in the Matthean Tradition," *JES* 27, no. 2 (1990): 294.

have religious significance.[46] During the time of Jesus, the shrine of *Paneion* remained there, and pagan worship, or to use Paul's language, demon-worship (1 Cor 10:19–21), was practiced. In this environment, Jesus asked his disciples about his identity (Matt 16:13, 15).

Figure 12: Jesus' Identity Revealed

Story	Jesus Revealed
John the Baptist beheaded (14:1–12)	Jesus is not John the Baptist
Five thousand men, plus many women and children, fed (14:13–21)	Divine identity
Jesus walked on water (14:22–36)	Son of God, divine identity
The Pharisees and scribes, and their questions about the tradition of the elders (15:1–20)	Authoritative interpreter of Scriptures
The Canaanite woman as recipient of blessing for the "lost sheep of Israel" (15:21–28)	Authoritative teacher testing potential converts
Four thousand men, plus many women and children, fed (15:29–39)	Representative of the God of Israel to the nations
The Pharisees and Sadducees, and their demand for signs from heaven (16:1–12)	Son of Man who is soon to come

Jesus' first question concerned the popular opinion about him (16:13). As it still is today, there was confusion about Jesus' identity.[47] Jesus' miracles were considered an indicator that he was a prophet (Luke 7:16; see also John 6:14). Although not all prophets were miracle-workers, for ancient Jews, miracles were clear evidence of one's prophetic ministry. This is why the people mistook him as one of the prophets who came back to life (Matt 16:14). First, Jesus was mistaken for John the Baptist. Matthew traces the origin of this confusion to Herod Antipas (14:1–12). Although there is no record in Matthew that John performed miracles comparable to those of Jesus, they share the same message of repentance and the kingdom. Second, some thought he was Elijah. The prophecy about the coming of Elijah created this expectation (Mal 4:5), and the miracles Jesus performed made him a likely candidate. Third, he was mistaken as Jeremiah whose reappearance was

---

46. George W. E. Nickelsburg, "Enoch, Levi, and Peter: Recipients of Revelation in Upper Galilee," *JBL* 100, no. 4 (1981): 583, nn. 24–32.
47. For a brief discussion on the various images of Jesus in different times and locations, see Cham Kaur-Mann, "Who Do You Say I Am? Images of Jesus," *BlTh* 2, no. 1 (2004): 19–44.

expected prior to the NT era.[48] The similarity between Jesus and Jeremiah is also alluded to by other evangelists (Jer 5:21; see also Mark 8:18). The expectation of the reappearance of Jeremiah may be the reason some people mistook Jesus for the weeping prophet.

Jesus' second question had to do with his disciples' own understanding of his identity. The popular opinion was not less important for Jesus because they too ought to know him, but his main concern, at least in this instance, was to make sure his disciples know who he really was. Peter took the initiative to reply to Jesus' question, "You are the Messiah, the Son of the living God" (Matt 16:16). That Jesus is a divine figure is clear in Peter's acknowledgment that Jesus is the "Son of the living God." His identity as the Messiah is not based on a political office, but on his relationship with God.[49]

In response to Peter's confession, Jesus blessed him and announced his role in the kingdom (16:16–19).[50] Several elements in Jesus' reply are worth noting. First, Jesus addressed Peter as "Simon Bar-Jonah" (16:16a), an Aramaic expression that means "Simon son of Jonah." The importance of the expression "Bar-Jonah" lies not in identifying the biological father of Simon, but in the role Simon Peter had to assume as the "son of a prophet." The expression "son of a prophet" refers to a prophet's apprentice (1 Kgs 13:27; 20:35; 2 Kgs 2:9, 15; Amos 7:14), thus highlighting Peter's emerging role as prophet who would minister both as a preacher (Acts 2:14–36; 3:11–26) and a miracle worker (3:1–10; 5:15–16) like Jesus.[51] Just as Jonah was appointed a preacher to the "nation" of Nineveh (Jonah 1:2), Simon's assignment was also to preach to "all nations" (Matt 28:19), both Jews and Gentiles. The expression also recalls the "sign of Jonah," which not only provides a smooth

---

48. See for example 2 Maccabees 15:13–15; 2 Esdras 2:18. Zucker, "Jesus and Jeremiah," 302–304; Bruce T. Dahlberg, "Typological Use of Jeremiah 1:4–19 in Matthew 16:13–23," *JBL* 94, no. 1 (1975): 73.
49. Justin, *Dialogue with Trypho* 76; Irenaeus, *Against Heresies* 21.7; Theodoret of Cyrus, *Commentary on the Visions of the Prophet Daniel* 2.34–35. See Tucker S. Ferda, "The Seventy Faces of Peter's Confession: Matt 16:16–17 in the History of Interpretation," *BibInt* 20, no. 4 (2012): 423.
50. This passage is one of the clearest dividing line between Roman Catholicism and Protestantism. As Joseph A. Burgess writes, "Tell me your exegesis of Mt. 16:17-19, and I will tell you your exegesis of the rest of the Gospels" (*History of the Exegesis of Matthew 16:17–19 From 1781 to 1965* [Ann Arbor, MI: Edwards Brothers, 1976], 1). Even interpreters from the early centuries do not share common interpretation of this passages (Tomas Aquinas, *Catena Aurea: Commentary on the Four Gospels,* ed. John Henry Newman, 4 vols., [Boonville, NY: Preserving Christian Publication, 2009], 1:584–586).
51. Henry A. Corcoran, "Viewing Biblical Narratives Through a Literary Lens: Practicing Narrative Analysis on Matthew 16:16-20," *ChrEJ* 3, ser. 7, no. 2 (2010): 308.

transition to Jesus' passion predictions in the succeeding episodes, but also directs Simon's attention to the importance of Jesus' death.

Second, Jesus reminded Simon that his knowledge was not possible without divine revelation (16:16b). "Flesh and blood," an expression that means "people," are unable to access this truth without divine aid. Jesus' declaration to Peter recalls his earlier statement about the favorable position of the disciples as recipients of divine revelation (11:27; 13:16–17), further distinguishing them from the crowd.[52]

Third, Jesus renamed Peter, and declared his plan to establish his Church (16:18a). The giving of new names, in the OT, signified important turning points, not only in the life of the person whose name was changed, but also in history. For example, Abram's name was changed to Abraham and Sarai's to Sarah in anticipation of the birth of Isaac through whom Abraham would become the "father of many nations" and Sarah the "mother of kings" (Gen 17:5, 15–16). Jacob's name was changed to Israel; as a man who used to struggle against humans (25:22–26), but was transformed into a man who wrestled with God and was blessed (32:28). There is no question that Peter would play a significant role in the early church as seen in the Acts of the Apostles. In fact, legends about Peter that developed during the early centuries show the significant role Peter played in the establishment of the Church.[53] However, Jesus' remark that "I (that is, Jesus) will build" and his claim that what would be established is "my (that is, Jesus') Church" makes clear the limited role of Peter in the establishment of the Church (Matt 16:18).

Fourth, Jesus promised the Church that the "gates of Hades will not overcome it" (16:18b). The image used here is comparable to Jesus' illustration about binding the strong man and entering his house to plunder it (12:29). The "gates of hell" cannot be interpreted independently from the expression "keys of the kingdom of heaven" (16:19a). Opening the gates of heaven with their keys also opens the gates of hell, and even in the territories where evil reigned, God will be proclaimed as king.

Fifth, Peter was given authority to "bind and loose" (16:19b).[54] Binding and loosing are terms commonly used by Jewish rabbis to refer to their

---

52. Parackel K. Mathew, "Authority and Discipline (Matt 16:17-19; 18:15-18) and the Exercise of Authority and Discipline in the Matthean Community," *CV* 28, no. 3 (1985): Mathew, "Authority and Discipline," 120–121.
53. Jesse Sell, "Simon Peter's 'Confession' and the Acts of Peter and the Twelve Apostles," *NovT* 21, no. 4 (1979): 354–356.
54. For the various interpretations of these expressions, see Richard H. Hiers, "'Binding' and 'Loosing': The Matthean Authorizations," *JBL* 104, no. 2 [1985]: 233–235; Joel Marcus, "The

authority to declare what is lawful and what is not, or for priests to declare what is clean and what is unclean. If this is how Matthew uses these expressions, it suggests that Peter (and presumably the other apostles) carry on Jesus' role as the authoritative interpreter of the Scriptures. The disciples' authority is not the authority to withhold forgiveness, but the authority to declare what is sinful and what is not.[55]

The Tagalog expression *kapit* can mean "to hold on," but it can also refer to "connections" and is used especially in situations wherein people have good social or political connections. This is often used with negative connotations. Having the right *kapit* works in the world, and this is true both at present and during ancient times, but Jesus wants to change the disciples' mindset about this. This whole section closes with Jesus prohibiting the disciples (not just Peter) to speak about Jesus' identity openly, "Then he ordered his disciples not to tell anyone that he was the Messiah" (Matt 16:20). This prohibition can be considered a lesson on discipleship. Having had Jesus disclose himself to the disciples, they ought to have known the identity and authority of Jesus who also informed them of the authority they would assume; but having such authority was not about being aligned with recognizable human powers, whether political or religious.[56] It was not about their *kapit*, but it is about experiencing God's presence and power, and acknowledging and proclaiming God's rule.

Gates of Hades and the Keys of the Kingdom (Matt 16:18–19)," *CBQ* 50, no. 3 (1988): 443.
55. Mark Allan Powell, "Binding and Loosing: A Paradigm for Ethical Discernment from the Gospel of Matthew," *CurTM* 30, no. 6 (2003): 439.
56. Kathleen Anne McManus, "Who Do You Say that I Am?" *WW* 29, no. 2 (2009): 138; M. Jack Suggs, "Matthew 16:13–20," *Int* 39, no. 3 (1985): 138.

MATTHEW 16:21–22:14

Jesus' Prediction of His Death: Lessons on Discipleship

After several stories that reveal Jesus' identity, Matthew begins recounting Jesus' prediction of his own death with the statement, "From that time on Jesus began to explain to his disciples that he must go to Jerusalem and suffer many things at the hands of the elders, chief priests and the teachers of the law" (Matt 16:21). Prior to this, Jesus only hinted about his sufferings (8:17; 12:39–40; 16:4), but from this time on, Jesus was more upfront about his impending death. Jesus had earlier informed his disciples that they would be persecuted (5:10–12, 44–48; 10:17–20, 38–39). This time it is clearer that their sufferings were the results of Jesus' sufferings.

In Matthew 16:21–23:39, Jesus prophesied about his death three times, and each one is followed by accounts that highlight Jesus' various expectations from disciples, such as faith and faithfulness (16:21–17:20), humility and forgiveness (17:22–20:16), and submission and authority (20:17–23:39).

16:21–17:20 JESUS' FIRST PREDICTION: LESSONS ON FAITH AND FAITHFULNESS

Jesus explained to his disciples the details of his death for the first time: the location would be in Jerusalem, the people who would be actively involved are the chief priests and the teachers of the law, and he would certainly be raised again on the third day after his death (Matt 16:21). This prediction is followed by a series of stories that illustrate the first lesson on discipleship, namely, faith/faithfulness.

16:21–28 Peter Rebukes Jesus and Jesus' Explanation of the Cost of Discipleship

The first story that illustrates the demand of faith/faithfulness is the account of Peter rebuking Jesus. Jesus disclosed that "he must go to Jerusalem and suffer" (Matt 16:21). Ancient Greeks use the word *dei* ("it is necessary") to express necessity, and in Matthew, the word is used only in these four instances: (1) Elijah's return (17:10); (2) certain things to happen before the end (24:6);

(3) fulfilling the Scripture through the manner of Jesus' arrest (26:54); and (4) Jesus' sufferings at the hands of the religious leaders (16:21a). Jesus' resurrection and his sufferings are inseparable, "he must be killed and on the third day be raised to life" (16:21b). Jesus anticipated his resurrection, but this could only happen after his death. Jesus showed faithfulness and by doing so, he set an example for those who would become his disciples.

Jesus identified "the elders, the chief priests and the teachers of the law" as the people behind his sufferings (16:21). This was an official legal rejection by the religious leaders.[1] In Matthew, the chief priests and elders were the ones who questioned Jesus' authority after he drove out the merchants from the temple (21:21). Together with the high priest Caiaphas, they plotted to kill Jesus (26:3; 27:1), and together with the teachers of the Law, they presented false witnesses during his trial before the high priest (26:57–61). The elders and chief priests were the ones who sent soldiers to arrest Jesus (26:47) and paid Judas to betray Jesus (27:3). They brought accusations against Jesus before Pilate (27:12), and when Pilate was trying to find ways to set Jesus free, they convinced the crowd to request for Barabbas' freedom instead of Jesus in order to make sure Jesus was executed (27:20). The chief priests and the elders, together with the scribes mocked Jesus during his trial before Pilate (27:41). They also bribed the guard stationed at Jesus' tomb to report that the disciples came to steal the body of Jesus in order to deny Jesus' resurrection (28:11–12).

When Peter heard Jesus' prediction about his death, he took Jesus aside before rebuking him (16:22). This must be seen as an appropriate act in a shame-based culture because he avoided humiliating Jesus publicly. Interestingly, at this point, Peter, known as Simon Bar Jonah, had forgotten about the sign of Jonah (12:39–40; 16:4, 16). Despite the assurance of the resurrection, Peter refused to accept that *it was necessary* for Jesus to suffer this way.

There are three possible reasons for Peter's response, all of which are addressed in Jesus' reply. First, for reasons of friendship. No one would desire to see friend go through such sufferings, but as Jesus said, Peter was not responding as a friend but as an enemy. Jesus' initial response was, "Get behind me, Satan! You are a stumbling block to me" (16:23).[2] "Satan" is a word

---

[1]. Paul A. Tanner, "The Cost of Discipleship: Losing One's Life for Jesus' Sake," *JETS* 56, no. 1 (2013): 45.
[2]. Jesus' reply can be interpreted in three ways: (1) as a strong rebuke, "get out of my sight/way"; (2) as a gentle reprimand, "get behind me"; or (3) as a challenge, "follow me from

transliterated from the Hebrew which means "enemy." In Matthew, it is used as a proper name for the devil (4:1, 5, 8, 10). He is the tempter (4:3) and he is also referred to by the name Beelzebul (12:26–27). Peter was an enemy, not a friend, because he was hindering Jesus from completing his divinely appointed task.

Second, it is beyond Peter's expectation for Jesus to suffer this way. First century Jews, expected a Messiah to liberate them from the Romans and restore the kingdom to Israel (Acts 1:6). A messiah who would be sentenced to death was the last thing they expected. However, as Jesus said, Peter was not thinking like God but like humans (Matt 16:23), considering only what was convenient and practical, and not seeing God's larger plan of saving humanity.

Third, if their master suffered, it is very likely that they would, too. So, Jesus made clear his expectations from his disciples, "Whoever wants to be my disciple must deny themselves, take up their cross and follow me" (16:24). Convicted criminals during the first century were required to carry their own cross before they reached the place of execution, and anyone carrying his/her own cross was as good as dead.[3] Dead people no longer push their own agenda but submit to God's purposes. They are willing to say to God, "thy will be done," instead of "my will be done." This attitude is exemplified by Paul (Phil 3:7–14).

Jesus then turned to the other disciples, and using metaphors of investment he clarified the reasons for denying oneself and taking up one's cross remains the best option (Matt 16:25–27): (1) those who try to save their life eventually lose it, and conversely, those who are willing to lose their life gains it (16:25); (2) the world can offer nothing more important than a person's life (16:26); and (3) Jesus will one day reward each person according to what they have done (16:27). There is no point in distinguishing the physical life and the spiritual/eternal life here because ancient Jews did not make such a clear distinction. Moreover, the English word "life" is actually translated from the Greek word *psuchē* or soul, which refers to the total person including the spirit and the body. When people refuse to make an absolute commitment to be Jesus' followers, whether because of the various forms of sufferings or persecutions they must endure or because of the various opportunities they would miss out on, they are in the process of trying to "save their life." Those

---

behind." Regardless of how one interprets this, there is a clear demand for unconditional obedience. Dennis C. Stoutenburg, "'Out of Sight!', 'Get Behind Me!', or 'Follow After Me!': There Is No Choice in God's Kingdom," *JETS* 36, no. 2 (1993): 173-178.
3. Tanner, "The Cost of Discipleship," 49.

who think they are gaining by saving their life are missing out on the opportunity to live their lives in the presence of God. Jesus' final reason is a quotation from Psalm 62:12. David, the writer of this psalm, acknowledges God as the savior and invites people to find "rest in God" (Ps 62:1–2, 5). Despite various forms of sufferings like physical assault or verbal slander (62:3–4), David affirms that his "salvation and . . . honor depend on God" (62:7). In response to God's salvation, David calls everyone to be honest in their business dealings as he acknowledges the power and mercy of God (62:10). Jesus also used metaphors of investment in issuing a call to be his disciples, and he used the conclusion of this psalm to explain why his disciples should make the "right investments" to be his disciple (Matt 16:27).

Jesus concludes his challenge by informing the disciples that some of them "will not taste death" before they see Jesus come in his kingdom (16:28).[4] For the disciples who first heard Jesus' statement and who knew that his demand for discipleship might mean sufferings and persecutions, or even death, Jesus' conclusion provides an assurance that he can indeed "reward each person according to what they have done" (16:27).[5]

17:1–13 Jesus' Physical Form Changed before the Disciples

The belief that divine beings can become human is not unique to Christianity. Some of the major religions that originated from Asia like Hinduism also believe in the concept of incarnation. The belief in the resurrection is what sets Christianity apart from others, and the disciples were given a preview of Jesus' bodily transformation in the story often called the "Transfiguration" wherein Jesus' physical form changed.

This story recalls the experience of Moses at Mount Sinai not long after the Law was given to him (Exod 20). In Matthew, the event occurred *six days* after Jesus first informed his disciples about his death (Matt 17:1); likewise, *six days* after God's covenant with Israel was confirmed, he called Moses to communicate with him personally (Exod 24:16). Jesus and Moses did not

---

4. Some follow Ambrose's suggestion that death here refers to spiritual death, not a physical one. For example, J. Edward Dallas, "Matthew 16:28: The Promise of Not Tasting Spiritual Death before the Parousia," *TJ* 30, no. 1 (2009): 85.
5. These last two verses are typically seen as a reference to the Second Coming (Matt 16:27–28), but the Greek word *erchomai* can either mean "come" or "go," so it is possible to interpret Jesus statement as a reference instead to his ascension. This story is followed by the story of Jesus' Transfiguration (17:1–13), which is a preview of his ascension; and it is followed by the story of exorcism wherein Jesus asked to his faithless disciples, "how long shall I stay with you?" and he is clearly talking about his departure/ascension (17:17). Indeed, some of them witnessed his ascension.

bring many companions with them; only Peter, James, and John were with Jesus (Matt 17:1), and only Joshua was with Moses (Exod 24:13). The meeting place between God and his messengers was *high mountain* (Matt 17:1; Exod 24:15). The disciples saw Jesus' face shining like the sun and clothes as white as light (Matt 17:2); and the Israelites saw the glory of God like fire on mountaintop (Exod 24:17); subsequently, when Moses came down his face shone (34:29–31). One important detail in the story of Moses that is missing in the Gospel – Moses took the blood of young bulls and sprinkled it on the people saying, "This is the blood of the covenant that the Lord has made with you in accordance to these words" (24:8). Moses sacrificed an animal and sprinkle its blood to seal God's covenant with his people, but at this point in the Gospel, no blood was sprinkled because it was yet to be shed (Matt 26:28), and Jesus would offer nothing other than himself.

Aside from the change in physical appearance (shining face and clothes white as light), the transformation of Jesus also allowed him to communicate with people long gone, like Moses and Elijah. What is the significance of Moses and Elijah? Some say they represent "the Law and the Prophets." Others point to the unique deaths of these two OT figures, but Enoch also had a "unique death," and he is not included. There is a third thing that Moses and Elijah have in common, which best fits the story of Jesus' Transfiguration; both are examples of those who suffer because of their faithfulness to God.[6] Like Moses and Elijah, Jesus was about to go through much suffering and the glorious appearance of the two OT giants is an assurance to Jesus that glory awaits him after his sufferings.

When Peter saw Jesus with Moses and Elijah,[7] he offered to make three tents for each of them (Matt 17:4). It is unclear why Peter offered to do this. Regardless of Peter's reason for his offer, the tent recalls the "tent of meeting" where Moses would go to inquire of the Lord (Exod 33:7–11). The tent is not only a place where God is present, it is also a place of God's revelation.[8] Moses received God's revelation in this tent (see also Ezek 37:24–28). Peter

---

6. Morna D. Hooker, "'What Doest Thou Here, Elijah?' A Look at St. Mark's Account of the Transfiguration," in *The Glory of Christ in the New Testament*, ed. L. D. Hurst and N. T. Wright (Oxford: Clarendon Press, 1987), 61.
7. Interpreters from the early centuries say that the vision was not only given to the disciples, but also to Moses and Elijah who saw a vision of Jesus (Bogdan G. Bucur, "Matthew 17:1–9 as a Vision: Neglected Strand in the Patristic Reception of the Transfiguration Account," *Neot* 44, no. 1 [2010]: 15–16).
8. Sigfred Pedersen, "Die Proklamation Jesu als des eschatologischen Offensbarungsträgers (Mt 17:1–13)," *NovT* 17, no. 4 (1975): 257.

was not finished speaking when God declared, "This is my Son, whom I love; with whom I am well pleased. Listen to him!" (Matt 17:5). God's second declaration that Jesus is his Son (Ps 2:7) was followed by a command, "Listen to him." These words were first spoken about the prophet like Moses whom God promised to raise up after him (Deut 18:15). This is a clear lesson on discipleship; knowing Jesus' identity ultimately requires obedience.[9] Jesus do not need a tent to be made for him, because he is Immanuel, the presence of God in human form. He is the prophet like Moses through whom God is revealed.

If Jesus is the prophet like Moses, what was the role of Elijah together with them? The account of Jesus' Transfiguration also associates Elijah with John the Baptist who had been killed by Herod Antipas, as recorded earlier in this Gospel (Matt 14:1–12). Like Jesus, Moses, and Elijah, John the Baptist is also an example of one who suffered because of his faithfulness to God's work. Jesus describes John's death this way, "Elijah has already come, and they did not recognize him, but have done to him everything they wished," to which he also concludes, "In the same way the Son of Man is going to suffer at their hands" (17:12). The story of Jesus' Transfiguration points to his future glory, that is, his glory when he comes back again; it also shows his glory as God raised him again from the dead and he ascended to heaven; but the Transfiguration is also a clear reminder that his glory comes only after his suffering. This has an implication on Christian discipleship and worship, as Albert C. Winn says, "The transfiguration reminds us that Christian worship is on the way to the cross."[10]

17:14–20 The Disciples Could Not Perform Exorcism and Lessons on Faith

This is the third and final story in a series after Jesus' first prediction of his death (Matt 16:21). In the first account, Jesus taught his followers that faithfulness is the most essential element in becoming his disciple (16:24-26); and, confronted as they were by the one who set an example of faithfulness despite persecutions and sufferings, the disciples had no choice but to "Listen to him" (17:5). This final account underscores the importance of faith.

---

9. James A. Penner, "Revelation and Discipleship in Matthew's Transfiguration Account," *BSac* 152 (1995): 208.
10. Albert C. Winn, "Worship as a Healing Experience: An Exposition of Matthew 17:1–9," *Int* 29, no. 1 (1975): 72.

Jesus, together with his three disciples went back to join the crowd when a man came up to him and knelt before him (17:14). Kneeling is more than just a physical action; it is a posture that reflects one's attitude. It can be a posture of worship before God or gods, or a sign of helplessness as someone surrendering to a conqueror after being defeated in war.[11] In some cases, it can be a posture of mockery like the soldiers who knelt before Jesus pretending they were his loyal subjects (27:29); but it can also be a posture of desperation – that is, of someone asking for mercy (Mark 1:40).

The father of the demon-possessed epileptic was desperately seeking help. His words, "have mercy," recall the requests of the two blind men (Matt 9:27; see also 20:30–31) and the Canaanite woman (15:27). In all these instances, the request for mercy was a request for healing. His son is said to have had seizures like an epileptic (17:15). The word *selēniazomai* (or "moonstruck," which is used only in Matthew 4:24; 17:15) was translated "lunatic" in earlier English versions (like the KJV) because of the popular belief that the moon could affect a person's sanity. The description of the boy's condition (17:15) favors the more recent translations. Also, the use of the word *selēniazomai* together with paralytics (4:24) may suggest that this was a physical, rather than a mental or psychological disorder. However, regardless of his real condition, it caused him much suffering, putting him in danger of being burned or drowned (17:15). Jesus' response shows that his suffering was caused by demonic activities (17:18).

The father explained that while Jesus was away, he brought the boy to the disciples, but they could not heal him (17:16). Presumably, the disciples who tried to heal the boy were the nine others who were not with Jesus on the mountain (17:1). Jesus replied with a forceful remark, "You unbelieving and perverse generation" (17:17). This statement is clearly addressed *only* to his disciples because: (1) nowhere in the Gospels did Jesus rebuke anyone for seeking his mercy; (2) the disciples were given authority earlier to perform such task (10:1–4), and so by this time they have been able to heal the boy; and (3) Jesus authorized them to perform the task in view of his departure, and their inability to do so showed that they were not ready for Jesus' departure.

Jesus used different statements to rebuke the Pharisees and his disciples. To the Pharisees, he said, "A wicked and adulterous generation" (12:39;

---

11. The word *gonupeteō* or "kneel" is rarely used in the NT (Matt 17:14; 27:21; Mark 1:40; 10:17). It is the posture of a worshiper (Polybius, *Histories* 15.29) or someone who is surrendering after being defeated in war (Appian, *Illyrian Wars* 3.2.9).

16:4); but to the disciples, he said, "You unbelieving and perverse generation" (17:17). On the one hand, there is an essential similarity between these two remarks. On the other hand, there is a clear distinction between the Pharisees who were *actively defiant* as they looked for signs and the disciples who were *passively deficient* in faith.

When the disciples asked Jesus privately why they could not drive out the demon, Jesus pointed to their "little faith," "if you have faith as small as a mustard seed, you can say to this mountain, 'Move from here to there,' and it will move. Nothing will be impossible to you" (17:20). Earlier interpreters like Hilary of Poitiers interpreted Jesus' metaphor of the mountain as a reference to the devil.[12] In the same way that it is humanly impossible to move mountains by mere words, it is also humanly impossible to command the devil to come out of a person. The metaphor, however, could refer to anything that hinders the work of God in one's life. The small size of the mustard seed is usually the focus of interpreting Jesus' statement about the faith like the mustard seed. However, we may ask, *If small faith is enough, why did Jesus rebuke the disciples for having "little faith"?* Jesus' assurance of answered prayers may shed some light to this question, "if you have faith *and not doubt . . . you can say to this mountain, 'Go, throw yourself into the sea,' and it will be done*" (21:21; italics mine). The similarity of Jesus' words in Matthew 17:20 and 21:21 invites us to understand the one in light of the other. Faith like a mustard seed is not a small amount of faith, but it is faith that is not mixed with doubt.[13]

Matthew recounts three stories after Jesus predicted his death for the first time, and in all of them, Jesus taught his disciples lessons of faith and faithfulness. In the first account, Jesus rebuked Peter for trying to obstruct God's plan, of which Jesus' suffering is a part. Jesus then laid out his expectations from his disciples, that is, they must be willing to suffer as well. In the second account where Jesus was transfigured, he set an example of faithfulness, as one who is willing to suffer even to the point of death. In the final episode, Jesus taught his disciples the necessity of faith in order to do God's work. He requires the kind of faith that is unmixed with doubt.

---

12. Hilary of Poitiers, *Comm. Matt.* 17§7. Based on Hilary of Poitiers, *Commentary on Matthew*, FC 125, trans. D. H. Williams (Washington, DC: Catholic University of America Press, 2012), 188.
13. James W. Scott, "The Misunderstood Mustard Seed Matt 17:20b; Luke 17:6," *TJ* 36 (2015): 45.

Matthew

17:22–20:16 JESUS' SECOND PREDICTION: LESSONS ON HUMILITY AND FORGIVENESS

The first series of stories after Jesus predicted his death shares a common theme, namely, faith and faithfulness. Jesus pronounced his death a second time, and although this contains less detail, Jesus once again assured his disciples that his death would be followed by his resurrection (Matt 17:22). Unlike the previous series of stories following Jesus' prediction, the second set of stories illustrates Jesus' teaching about discipleship, focusing particularly on humility and forgiveness. These stories include Jesus' dialogues with Peter and the other disciples, the Pharisees, and the rich man.

17:22–27 Jesus Paid the Temple Tax

One of the most memorable events in Philippine history towards the end of the Spanish Era (1521–1898) is the "Cry of Pugad Lawin" (August 1896), during which Andres Bonifacio led the *Katipuneros* in tearing their *cédula*. The *cédula* is the certificate of registration signifying that a person was part of the Spanish government, and tearing this certificate means that they no longer recognized themselves as part of Spain's regime. The Romans during Jesus' era required their subjects to be registered as well (Luke 2:2), and part of the people's obligation was to pay taxes to their colonizers. During the time of Jesus, aside from taxes paid to the Romans, Jews also paid temple taxes.

In this story, the collectors of the temple tax asked Peter whether Jesus was paying temple tax, and Peter confirmed that Jesus was fulfilling his obligation (Matt 17:24–25). Even before the temple was built,[14] the Jews were already required to pay "atonement money" of half a shekel for every male twenty years old and above (Exod 30:11–16), and the amount was the same regardless of one's social condition. When the tabernacle was being built, voluntary offerings were given for "the work on the tent of meeting" (35:20–21); and after the temple was constructed, collections were made annually for the work of the temple (see 2 Chr 24:4–14; Neh 10:32–34). During the reign of the Persians, funds were taken from the royal treasury of Persia for the work of the temple (Ezra 6:8–10; 7:18–24); and during the time of the Greeks, monies were also provided by the Seleucids for its maintenance.[15] During

---

14. For a more comprehensive discussion of the history of the temple tax, see Simon Légasse, "Jésus et l'impôt du Temple (Matthieu 17, 24-27)," *ScEs* 24 (1972): 362–365; Sara Mandell, "Who Paid the Temple Tax When the Jews were under Roman Rule," *HTR* 77, no. 2 (1984): 223–232.
15. See 1 Maccabees 10:39–44; 2 Maccabees 3:3.

the time of Jesus, the payment of the temple tax continued using another currency; instead of half a shekel, every person paid two drachmas (Matt 17:24, 27).

After Peter's conversation with the temple tax collectors, he went back to the house and even before he told Jesus about his conversation with them, Jesus asked him, "From whom do the kings of the earth collect duty and taxes – from their own children or from others?" (Matt 17:25). The incident recalls Ahijah's encounter with the wife of King Jeroboam II when her son got ill. She disguised herself to ask about her son's condition and when she came to the prophet's house, even before she spoke a word, Ahijah began telling her what would happen to the prince (1 Kgs 14:1–20). The story also recalls Elisha's confrontation with his servant Gehazi. After Naaman was healed of his leprosy, Gehazi sought to extort money from Naaman, pretending to be sent by Elisha. When Gehazi came to see Elisha, even before he spoke a word, the prophet told him that he was aware of what his servant had done (2 Kgs 5:19–27). Jesus' ability to know even the things happening where he was not physically present puts him alongside these OT prophets.

Jesus' question specified the recipients of the temple taxes, namely, the "kings of the earth" (Matt 17:25). The expression is always used in both the OT and NT to refer to secular rulers and not to the priests who receive the temple taxes (e.g. 1 Kgs 4:34; Rev 6:5), and this makes the passage difficult to understand. It was not until the temple was destroyed in AD 70 when the Romans would take the two drachmas (the same amount that was paid for the temple tax) for the temple of Jupiter.[16] During the time of Jesus, although the Jews had to pay taxes to Rome, they remained in control of the taxes paid to the temple. In other words, during the time of Jesus, "the kings of the earth" did not receive the temple tax.

This story may be considered an example of recounting history in order to address a contemporary situation. The question was not whether Jesus and Peter had a conversation about paying the temple taxes, nor whether they ever discussed about the taxes given to the "kings of the earth." Matthew recalls the incident to address an issue that Matthew's readers were facing, namely, whether to continue paying the temple taxes even though it did not go to the work of the Jerusalem temple. Jesus' words answered the question clearly, "But so that we may not cause offense," they ought to continue to pay these taxes (Matt 17:27).

---

16. Josephus, *Jewish Wars* 7.6.6 §218.

Jesus distinguished the "children" of "the kings of the earth" (an expression that refers to their citizens) from the "others" (17:25–26). Despite belonging to another domain, the "others" were not exempt from the taxes imposed by the "kings of the earth," and therefore they must pay it. This is a lesson in humility. Even though they knew who the true king was, they were being taught to acknowledge earthly rulers, for submission to them was not always equivalent to defying divine authority. On the contrary, it was consistent with godly principles. The disciples' loyalty to God did not usually require disobedience to earthly authorities.

What prompted the temple tax collectors to ask Peter whether Jesus was paying taxes was explained in the final verse (17:27). During their conversation, Jesus and Peter had not paid their taxes yet. So Jesus instructed Peter to go fishing, and assured him that he would catch a fish with the money inside its mouth to pay for their taxes. God's hand was clearly in this matter because it is not common to catch a fish to find precious items in its mouth or belly.[17]

18:1–35 Jesus' Reply to the Disciples' Question on Greatness and Peter's Question on Forgiveness

There is a traditional Chinese saying, "Children have ears, but no mouth." Children are considered insignificant in many cultures. They are considered unimportant because they do not contribute much to the society, even in places where there are child laborers, their contributions are not acknowledged. Ancient Mediterranean people treated children the same way. However, in the teachings of Jesus, they were seen as examples of humility (a quality that every disciple of Jesus must have) and are objects of the disciples' care and protection.

This is second in the series of dialogues after Jesus predicted his death the second time. Matthew 17 concludes with the story of Jesus paying taxes to the "kings of the earth" (Matt 17:25).[18] This account suggests the idea that there are two (unequal) kingdoms, one ruled by the "kings of the earth" to whom even Jesus paid taxes and one in which God rules. Earthly rulers are

---

17. A similar story was recorded by Herodotus. After Polycrates' victory against the Lacedaemonians, he feared that the gods might be jealous of his successes and cause a reversal of fortune. So he disposed of his emerald and golden seal, but found them again inside the belly of the fish given to him by a fisherman as a gift. He concluded that "the hand of heaven was in this matter" (Herodotus, *Histories* 3.42.4; see also 3.40.1–43.2).
18. Jerome suggests that when the disciples saw Jesus paying his and Peter's taxes perceived that Jesus preferred Peter over the others leading them to ask the question who is the greatest among them (Aquinas, *Catena Aurea*, 1:621).

distinguished by ranks, and this may have prompted the disciples to ask who is the greatest in the kingdom of heaven; more so at this point when they already knew that Jesus was about to depart, they begun to think about his possible successor. This question may have been in the thoughts of the disciples since they heard of Jesus' comments about John. Jesus praised John the Baptist for being the greatest "among those born of women," yet he is less than the "least in the kingdom of heaven" (11:11). The idea that John was out of the "race" as to being the greatest raised perhaps the question as to who among the "great ones" in the kingdom was the greatest. They had clearly misunderstood Jesus' comment about John, for he referred to the Baptist's doubts about his identity (see comments for Matthew 11:4–15), and not about rank in the kingdom.

With this wrong idea of greatness, the disciples asked Jesus, "Who, then is the greatest in the kingdom of heaven?" (18:1). Jesus' statement is sweeping, "Unless you change and become like little children, you will never enter the kingdom of heaven" (18:3). What this implies is that instead of thinking about who among them was "the greatest in the kingdom," they ought rather to first make sure that they had already entered the kingdom. Jesus required his disciples to "change and become like little children" (18:3). In the Greek, this command is followed by three statements introduced by a relative pronoun: (1) whoever humbles himself/herself (17:4); (2) whoever welcomes a child (17:5); and (3) whoever causes them to stumble (17:6). These statements are not hypothetical remarks, but are comments that contain implied commands. How could the disciples of Jesus "change and become like little children" (18:3)?

First, they ought to be characterized by humility. Jesus explained, "Therefore, whoever takes the lowly position of this child is the greatest in the kingdom of heaven" (18:4). This clarifies Jesus' point in using children as examples of those who enter the kingdom, namely, they are characterized by humility. Humility is required to enter the kingdom, and the same quality is necessary for one to forget about the question of greatness. When the desire for greatness no longer consumes them, that will be the mark of true greatness. One may not (and need not) totally agree with Hilary's description of children given below, but it contains *some* truth about children that explain why Jesus have used them as examples of humility:

> [Children] believe everyone because they trust what they hear. They follow their father, they love their mother, they do not know how to wish evil on their neighbor, they are indifferent

to the desire for riches, they are not arrogant, they do not hate, they do not lie, they believe what is said to them, and they accept as true what they hear.[19]

Second, disciples are expected to welcome children (18:5). This statement about welcoming children (being members of the insignificant people of the society) suggests that Jesus was not only referring to anyone who may be considered unimportant. Daniel Patte summarizes well, "Being like a child is also being able to receive a child, because if one perceives oneself as lacking something important, one can welcome those who are in the same situation."[20] Jesus explains that welcoming children is equivalent to welcoming him (18:5; see also 25:34–46). Hospitality is a virtue that the disciples must have. In the same way that they expect people to welcome them as they preach the kingdom of heaven (10:12–15), so they must welcome even those whom the world normally rejects.

Third, the disciples should not be the cause for the "little ones" to sin (18:6). The Greek word *skandalizō* may mean "to cause another to sin."[21] The seriousness of Jesus' command is once again expressed by use of exaggerated language such as the gouging of one's eye or the cutting off of one's hands or feet (18:8–9; see also 5:29–30). Jesus used another comparison saying that it is better for one to have a millstone tied to one's neck and be drowned in the depths of the sea rather for one to cause the "little ones" to sin (18:6). Jesus' illustration may have been based on the story of Augustus who was said to have ordered that heavy weights be tied around the necks of the tutor and servants of his son Gaius because they took advantage of their master's sickness, and acted arrogantly and greedily in their province.[22] Even in the OT and NT, millstones were used as weapons of divine judgment (Judg 9:53; 2 Sam 11:21; Rev 18:21).

Jesus' gave his final command, "See that you do not despise one of these little ones," adding that their angels are always in the presence of the Father (Matt 18:10). The OT is clear that God sends his angels to protect people. His angel was with Israel as they traveled (Exod 23:20), in the same way as the angel Michael aided Daniel in his time of struggle (Dan 10:13; 12:1).

---

19. Hilary, *Comm. Matt.* 18§1 (FC 125:193).
20. Daniel Patte, "Jesus' Pronouncement about Entering the Kingdom Like a Child: A Structural Exegesis," *Semeia* 29 (1983): 40.
21. In particular, it is to cause others to commit the sin of unbelief (Matt 13:21, 57; 15:12; 17:27; 24:10; 26:31; see also Psalms of Solomon 16:7).
22. See Suetonius, *Augustus* 67.

Angels are ministering spirits who help God's people in their time of need (Heb 1:7, 14).[23]

Jesus continued with an illustration of the shepherd looking for the lost sheep. His question, "What do you think?" makes it clear that he was citing a hypothetical scenario about a man who had one hundred sheep and one of them wandered away (Matt 18:12). He asked whether a shepherd would not abandon the ninety-nine sheep in order to look for the one that is missing. In a real situation, it is unlikely that a shepherd would do so; but Jesus' question expects an affirmative answer. What situation would cause a shepherd to abandon ninety-nine in order to search for the missing one? Paul J. Achtemeier reasons that there are two scenarios that would make him do so: (1) the sheep that went astray must be extremely valuable to the shepherd that he is willing to take such a risk to recover it; or (2) in comparison with the typical shepherd, this shepherd must have so much concern for the lost sheep.[24] On several occasions, Jesus used exaggerated and impractical illustrations to deliver his point. Not only would it be impractical to abandon ninety-nine for one, but Jesus also compared the joy of finding the one lost sheep with the joy of having the ninety-nine that never went astray (18:13–14). However, the main point of his story is not to lead people to think that saving one is worth the risk of losing the ninety-nine. The point of this parable is to stress the extreme value of the lost sheep that the shepherd is even willing to take great risk just to recover it. By doing so, the shepherd does not only demonstrate the value of the sheep, but also reveals his own character.

The disciples asked Jesus who was the greatest in the kingdom, and this was not just a question of the Twelve, but a question that many Christians are still asking today, though perhaps not as loudly. Jesus addressed the disciples' question, but his answer was clearly not only for them but for all his disciples. The essence of his reply is clear – that instead of striving to be the greatest among their peers, they should aim to be like a humble child because this is the mark of true greatness.

Jesus' reply to the disciples' question about greatness did not end with his commands about having a child-like humility and the need to protect

---

23. Jerome's theory that every person is assigned a guardian angel the moment they are born lacks a more solid scriptural basis (see John J. Collins, "The Gospel for the Feast of the Guardian Angels [Mt. 18:1–10]," *CBQ* 6 [1944]: 433). Nonetheless, we can affirm the angels' role as ministers of God's people.
24. Paul J. Achtemeier, "It's the Little Things that Count (Mark 14:17–21; Luke 4:1–13; Matthew 18:10–14)," *BA* 46, no. 1 (1983): 30–31.

these "little ones" (18:1–10). His discussion continued with an illustration of God's desire to restore those who sinned and a command on how the community of disciples could do so (18:12–20). In other words, the disciples are not only supposed to avoid causing the "little ones" to sin, they are supposed to restore those among them who did. Jesus' command concerning church discipline cannot be interpreted separately from the disciples' question about greatness.[25] Unless the one who disciplines learns child-like humility (see also Gal 6:1–10), church discipline would be no more than fault-finding; and unless the one being disciplined learns child-like humility, there will be limitless excuses not to listen to godly counsel.

This parable serves as a good transition from Jesus' discussion about the value of the "little ones" whom the disciples should care for and not cause to sin (18:3–10), to his discussion about the brother (or sister) who sinned within the community of disciples (18:15–20). Jesus had laid out his moral and ethical standard for his followers in his Sermon (Matt 5–7), and two of the qualities he expected from his disciples were humility (5:5) and forgiveness (5:38–48). Here he set the practical guidelines on how to go about restoring the lost sheep. This set of guidelines applies not only for personal offense, but also for offenses against the community.[26]

Jesus commanded his followers to confront the sinning brother or sister privately (18:15). This is the first step. Confronting a person publicly places the offender in a shameful situation, and shaming an offender may only result in the person's unwillingness to listen. The OT also advises not to be hasty in bringing a matter to court (Prov 25:7–8).[27] Jesus gave this command in hope that the private confrontation would lead the offender to realize his fault. Moreover, Jesus used language of kinship in discussing about forgiveness and restoration. Humans are naturally more inclined to forgive family members than other people,[28] and by reminding the disciples that the person who sinned is a "brother/sister," Jesus was stressing the bond that the disciples

---

25. Jeffrey A. Gibbs and Jeffrey Kloha, "'Following' Matthew 18: Interpreting Matthew 18:15-20 in Its Context," *Vision* 2, no. 2 (2001): 18.
26. Interestingly, the phrase "against you" (Matt 18:15) is not found in all manuscripts.
27. Similar advice was given in Sirach 19:13–17; 20:2–3; *Testament of Gad* 6; *Sifra* on Leviticus 19:17. In Plutarch's *Morals*, he advises that one must be frank in confronting a person who did wrong, but not to shame the offender publicly because the person will only be inclined to protect his honor by not being open to change. He also warns that confrontation can be motivated by arrogance and a desire to find fault (*How to Distinguish a Flatterer from a Friend*, 25–27).
28. Rikard Roitto, "Reintegrative Shaming and a Prayer Ritual of Reintegration in Matthew 18:15–20," *SEÅ* 79 (2014): 106.

have with one another. Being children of the same Father, they have more reason to forgive.

The second step suggests that not all offenders will realize their wrongdoing, even if the confrontation was done in a way that avoids publicly shaming them. Hence, Jesus advised the one doing the confrontation to bring two to three witnesses (Matt 18:17; Deut 17:6). The witnesses that the OT Law requires are persons who saw the crime being committed, and not those who are dependent on hearsay. Moreover, the role of these two witnesses was simply to ensure that no innocent person would be penalized by death. Problems arise in situations wherein there are no firsthand witnesses who saw the offense committed by the church member. In the OT, the priests are given the responsibility to decide on difficult cases (17:7–9). However, Jesus' commands presume that the confrontation is done for the purpose of forgiveness and restoration, not for fault-finding and condemnation. Thus, other church members who know and understand the situation may be required to stand in place of a "witness" whose only goal is to see the restoration of a sinning brother or sister.[29]

Two attempts to restore the "straying sheep" may not always be enough. Hence Jesus added a third step in the process, and that to bring the matter to the church (18:17). The application of this command in Asian churches varies. Even among the churches in the Philippines, the command seems too idealistic to be practiced. Generally speaking, local Filipino churches are more open in applying this principle by having a member who sinned make a public confession. Chinese-Filipino churches are less open to such a practice. Both agree, however, that restoration of the person who sinned is the sole goal of church discipline. Bringing the matter to the church does not guarantee repentance, and this is clear in Jesus' statement, "if they still refuse to listen"; but when all steps are exhausted, then Jesus advised, "treat them as you would a pagan or a tax collector" (18:17). This seems to contradict Jesus' own teaching about loving the unlovable. Yet this expression should be understood in the light of Jesus' other comments about pagans and tax collectors, namely, they are people whose life principles and manner of living are inconsistent with the standard he set for his disciples (5:46–47; 6:7), but they are nonetheless people to whom God's grace may extend (9:10–11; 11:19; 21:31–32). The church is given authority to "bind" and "loose," that

---

29. William G. Thompson, *Matthew's Advice to a Divided Community: Mt. 17,22–18,35*, AnBib 44 (Rome: Biblical Institute Press, 1970), 183.

is, to decide what is to be considered right or wrong (18:18; see comments for Matthew 16:18).

As the members of the church attempt to restore a sinning brother/sister, God promised them his presence as well (18:19–20). The numbers "two or three" disciples together experiencing God's presence points back to the number of witnesses required for church discipline to progress. This does not, in any way, suggest that a Christian who is alone cannot experience the presence of God. The numbers "two or three" have to do with process of discipline, because in the same way that only two or three witnesses are necessary in order for such discipline to be conducted.[30] Moreover, the assurance that "it will be done for them by my Father in heaven" (18:19) must be understood in connection with the church discipline. As the disciples take seriously and use carefully the authority given by Jesus to restore a sinning brother, the Father will certainly work among them. The presence of God should not only be a deterrent so that Christians will not abuse such authority, but it is also an assurance that such activity has divine approval.[31]

Peter raised a follow-up question in response to Jesus' command whether there is limit to the number of times a person could be forgiven (18:21). The question logically follows Jesus' three-step plan to restoration, because these steps assume that the offender only sinned once, which may not necessarily be the case. Hence, Peter's question is a valid one. Jesus replied by telling the parable of the unmerciful servant.

The question of Peter whether they should forgive up to seven times (18:21) shows that he already expected Jesus to tell them that restoring a brother or sister who sinned required the church to show compassion more than once. The number seven is symbolic of completion, hence, Peter was essentially asking whether they should attempt to restore a sinning brother as often as they needed. By forgiving a brother or sister "seven times," from a human point of view, is already doing more than enough; but God's compassion is beyond what humans can offer. This is suggested in Jesus' reply that "seven times" is not enough, but that they should forgive "seventy-seven times" (18:21). This recalls Lamech's words, "If Cain is avenged seven times, then Lamech seventy-seven" (Gen 4:24), suggesting the unlimited extent of vengeance. In short, Peter was essentially asking whether they should forgive

---

30. The rabbis believed that God is present when there are two or three gathered together to read and study the Torah (Mishnah, *Avot* 3:2).
31. David D. Kupp, *Matthew's Emmanuel: Divine Presence and God's People in the First Gospel*, SNTSMS 90 (Cambridge, NY: Cambridge University Press, 1996), 198–200.

a brother or sister as often as they needed, but Jesus said they should do more than what the brother or sister needed.

The parable begins with the statement, "the kingdom of heaven is like" (Matt 18:22). In relation to the authority given to the disciples to conduct church discipline, this statement serves as a reminder that this authority must be within the boundaries of God's moral and ethical principles. Moreover, it points to God as the merciful king who serves as the example of mercy and forgiveness. In this parable, the king wanted to settle an account with his servants to whom he had lent money (18:24–25). The language of "debt" has already been used as an image for sin (6:12; 18:12). The first debtor owed the king "ten thousand bags of gold" (18:24). The Greek expression is *muriōn talantōn* ("myriads of talents") or "ten thousand talents," which is equivalent to what a regular worker could earn for working daily for more than twenty-seven thousand years.[32] The point of the huge amount is simple – there is no way that the worker could ever pay his debt all his life. Thousands of generations of his descendants after him would still be in debt. Hence, selling the servant's wife and children as slaves would be a meager start for paying this endless debt (18:25). The portrayal of the king who required the servants to be imprisoned should be seen as the people's idea of an earthly king, not Matthew's portrayal of God's character.[33] The servant asked for patience, promising that he would pay back everything he owed (18:26), but the king did not just give him an extension for him to pay his debt, but cancelled his debt and set him free (18:27). This detail illustrates what Jesus was saying to Peter, namely, that forgiveness must not only be seven times but seventy-seven times. The king did not just give a grace period for the payment of the debt; he did more than what was necessary by cancelling the debt. The king's action also provides us with a clear definition of what forgiveness is, namely, it is refusing to seek payment even if one has the right to do so.

The parable continues with this servant meeting a fellow servant who owed him "a hundred silver coins" (18:28). The Greek expression is "one hundred denarii" which is worth one hundred days or about three months of work. The first servant choked the second one while demanding payment (18:28), something the king did not do to him; and like the first servant, the

---

[32]. The amount of ten thousand talents is equivalent to ten million denarii. A denarius (plural, denarii) is equivalent to the daily wage of a worker, which means ten thousand talents is equivalent to the worker's salary for ten million days (or more than 27,378 years) of work.
[33]. Arland J. Hultgren, *The Parable of Jesus: A Commentary* (Grand Rapids: Eerdmans, 2002), 25.

second one asked for a period of extension to pay what he owed. The contrast between ten thousand talents and one hundred denarii is clear. The first servant owed much more to the king than the second servant owed the first. Paying a debt equivalent to three-month salary is much easier than paying a debt equivalent to wages for twenty-seven thousand years. Yet the first servant had the second one put in prison for his debt (18:30).

The other servants told the king what the first did to the second. It is normal for people to show sympathy towards someone with the same kind of work, and this explains why the other workers informed the king about the matter.[34] When the king heard what the first servant did, he reminded him that he cancelled his enormous debt (18:32–33), and remarked, "Shouldn't you have had mercy on your fellow servant just as I had on you?" (18:33). Hence, the master imprisoned him just as he did to the second servant, and in addition, the merciless servant was handed to the guards to be tortured (18:34). The image of the torturer points to the severity of the sin of not forgiving a brother or sister, knowing that we all need God's forgiveness as well. In some ways, the one who refuses to forgive is tortured by his or her lack of forgiveness. There are details in the story that were not mentioned, like how did the first servant incur such a huge amount of debt or was the second servant set free from prison when the king learned what happened to him. The point of the parable remains clear: God is the compassionate king who cancels our debts of sin, and with that same compassion Jesus' disciples must show forgiveness to the brother or sister who sinned, whether it is an offense against an individual or against the community (18:15).

19:1–15 Jesus' Reply to the Pharisees' Question on Divorce and the Disciples' Question on Celibacy

This is the third in the series of three dialogues between Jesus and the other characters in Matthew after Jesus predicted his death the second time. At first glance, the question of divorce does not have any connection with Jesus' teaching on church discipline and forgiveness. Hence, one considers that divorce could be avoided through forgiveness, Jesus' discussion on divorce flows smoothly from the previous discussion on forgiving a "brother or sister from your heart" (18:35).

---

34. J. Duncan M. Derrett calls this "professional solidarity" (*Law in the New Testament* [London: Darton, Longman & Todd, 1970], 41).

The last location mentioned in Matthew's narrative was in Capernaum (17:24), and here, the story is set in Judea "to the other side of the Jordan River" (19:1). People followed Jesus to seek healing (19:2). The crowd was presumably still with Jesus when Pharisees came to ask him whether it was lawful for a man to divorce his wife "for any or every reason" (19:3). The Law in the OT allows a man to divorce his wife if she "becomes displeasing to him" (Deut 24:1). It became a subject of discussion among the Jewish teachers as to what kind of displeasure is included in this provision. Many have observed that the phrase "for any or every reason" is only found in Matthew's account (see Mark 10:2), and suggest that Matthew had taken into consideration the ongoing debate even among the Pharisees concerning the grounds for divorce. Two influential Jewish teachers had opposing views on this matter. Shammai claims that sexual immorality is the only ground for divorce, while Hillel claims the grounds for divorce could be as simple as a wife spoiling her husband's food.[35] In this story, Matthew makes it clear that the Pharisees asked the question for the purpose of testing him (19:3).

Jesus replied by pointing back to the creation story as he discussed God's purpose for marriage (see Gen 2:24): (1) marriage from the beginning is between a man and a woman (Matt 19:4); (2) marriage makes the male and the female one separate unit from their respective parents (19:5); and (3) marriage is a bond made by God and therefore must not be destroyed by humans (19:6). The point is that God himself designed how marriage should be by creating a man and a woman, joining the two together to become one, and therefore divorce is not according to God's design for marriage. To this the Pharisees also appealed to the Scripture, pointing to the provision that allows a man to divorce his wife (Deut 24:1). This provision allows divorce if the man finds "something indecent about her." The word "indecent" (Hebrew, *ervah*) means "nakedness" or "bare." It can refer to the "undefended parts" of a city (Gen 42:9, 12) or an "exposed part" of a human body (Exod 20:26; 28:42). The word may also refer to illicit sexual behavior including incest (Gen 9:22; Lev 18:6–18; 20:11, 17, 19–21), homosexual relations (Gen 9:22), or harlotry (Ezek 16:36–37; 23:28–29). Other types of sexual misconduct mentioned in the Law include premarital sex (Deut 22:13–21), extramarital affair (22:22), and rape (22:23–29). What this suggests is that the

---

35. See the Mishnah, *Gittin* 9:10. There are numerous discussions in the tractate *Gittin* about the grounds for divorce and procedures for filing one, which may suggest that divorce was rampant among the Jews during the time of Jesus as much as it is today in many parts of the world.

provision in Deuteronomy 24:1 allows divorce only on the grounds of illicit sexual behavior, and not "for any or every reason" (Matt 19:3).

Jesus explained that though this provision was "permitted," it was not a given "command," by Moses (19:7–8). With his statement, Jesus' judgment about the issue is made clear. There is a huge difference between what is commanded and what is permitted; a person who gives a command expresses his will, and a person who gives permission concedes to what others want even though it may be inconsistent with his or her will. Moses "permitted," and Jesus' reply implies that it was not what he wanted; and he did so because "your hearts were hard" (19:8). There is a similar expression in Tagalog, *pusong bato* or "heart of stone," which refers to someone who has no compassion; but in the Greek OT, *sklērokardia* or "hard heart" (the same expression used in Matthew 19:8) is used to refer to someone who is disobedient (Deut 10:16; Jer 4:4). His statement suggests that although God's original design is for marriage to be an inseparable bond between a male and a female (Gen 2:24), the people continued to disobey, and therefore Moses permitted divorce. The point is that one cannot use this provision to justify divorce.[36]

Jesus also added, "anyone who divorces his wife, except for sexual immorality, and marries another woman commits adultery" (Matt 19:9). This verse poses two difficulties for interpreters: (1) the meaning of sexual immorality (or the Greek word *porneia*), and (2) whether the exception is applicable only for divorce or for both divorce and remarriage. First, what is the meaning of *porneia*? The NT uses the word without specifying what type of illicit act is being referred to, but the Greek OT uses the word specifically for prostitution (Gen 38:24), or adultery and extramarital affairs (Hos 1:2). Many of these passages use the word metaphorically to refer to Israel's (the bride) unfaithfulness to God (the husband). Adultery or extramarital relationship best fit the context of Matthew 19, although the scope of *porneia* need not be limited to this.[37]

Second, is the exception applicable only for divorce or for both divorce and remarriage?[38] If it applies only for divorce, it means that divorcing on the

---

36. Gary D. Collier, "Rethinking Jesus on Divorce," *ResQ* 37, no. 2 (1995): 96.
37. There is another Greek word, *moicheia*, which means adultery. Perhaps in order to avoid redundancy, *porneia* is used, or else Jesus would say, "anyone who divorces his wife, except for *adultery*, and marries another woman commits *adultery*."
38. Allison suggests that Matthew includes Jesus' statement about adultery and abstinence to explain Joseph's decision to divorce Mary quietly and abstain from any relations with her until Jesus was born (Dale C. Allison Jr., "Divorce, Celibacy and Joseph [Matthew 1.18–25 and 19:1–12]," *JSNT* 49 [1993]: 4–6).

grounds of the spouses' adulterous affair is allowed, but remarriage is not. If it applies both to divorce and remarriage, it means that divorcing and remarrying are only allowed if the spouse has committed adultery. Related to this question is whether the Greek expression *mē epi*, which is often translated as "except," is correctly translated or whether it should be translated, "not even inclusive of." This suggests that even adultery is not a sufficient ground for divorce. The traditional Protestant view allows the remarriage of the offended party.[39]

The disciples followed-up on this by commenting that it was better to remain unmarried rather than go through the difficulty of divorce (Matt 19:10). Jesus used the example of the eunuchs, but clarified, "Not everyone can accept this word, but only to those to whom it has been given" (19:11–12).[40] Paul's interpretation of Jesus' teaching sheds light on this question. His statement, "To the married I give this command (not I, but the Lord)" (1 Cor 7:10), shows that he was aware of Jesus' teaching about divorce and remarriage. According to Paul, the Lord taught that the wife must not divorce her husband (or a husband his wife), but in case divorce is unavoidable, then the woman (or the man) must remain unmarried (7:10–11). Although it appears that in Jesus' teaching, the wife is presumably the one had been unfaithful and in Paul's example, it was the husband, the principle is the same. Divorce is not the first option, but if it is unavoidable, then they must remain unmarried. Jesus and Paul do not only share the same principle about divorce and remarriage, they also share the same principle about celibacy. Paul addresses the singles and widows to remain unmarried, but if they cannot control themselves, then marriage is a better option (7:8–9).

It is noteworthy that the passage on divorce follows Jesus' discussion on humility (18:1–10), addressing sin (18:12–20), and forgiveness (18:21–35). This suggests that there is a better option than divorce even in cases when adultery has been committed, and that is forgiveness and restoration. In addition to this, considering that the consequences of divorce affect the children the most, Matthew reminds us of the value of children in the eyes of Jesus in the passage immediately after that on divorce (19:13–15). Matthew simply says, "People brought little children to Jesus" (19:13). The Greek reads,

---

39. Some Evangelicals do not agree with this view. For example, William A. Heth, "Another Look at the Erasmian View of Divorce and Remarriage," *JETS* 25, no. 3 (1982): 263–272.
40. Some suggest that eunuchs are those who went through divorce but could not marry without committing adultery. See Quentin Quesnell, "'Made Themselves Eunuchs for the Kingdom of Heaven' (Mt 19,12)," *CBQ* 30 (1968): 335, n. 1.

"children were brought to Jesus," without identifying who brought the children to Jesus; it could be their parents or someone else. We do not know how many of those children Jesus blessed had parents who were divorced but we may infer from this that Jesus came, not only to heal those who are sick physically, but even the children who come from broken families.

Children were brought to Jesus in order for him to lay his hands on them and pray for them (19:13), and when the disciples rebuked the people for bringing children to Jesus, he made it clear that the kingdom belonged to them. Children are important in Matthew's Gospel. Entrance to the kingdom requires becoming like a child (18:3), and the children are the ones who would later welcome Jesus shouting "Hosanna to the Son of David" (21:15–16). Children, prayer, and the kingdom are three things that go together in Matthew's Gospel.[41] Jesus taught his disciples that when they pray, they should approach God as his children who pray that his rule be experienced on earth as it is in heaven (6:9–10). This principle applies to children, to the disciples, and even to those parents or couples contemplating divorce.

19:16–20:16 Jesus' Reply to a Rich Man's Question on Eternal Life and Peter's Question on Possessions

This is the fourth and last story in the series of dialogues after Jesus' second prediction of his coming sufferings and death. It begins with a certain man asking Jesus what "good thing" he must do to receive eternal life (Matt 19:16). This man is young, pious (19:20), and rich (19:22). Addressing Jesus as "Teacher" was a typical way to show respect. At times, it was done sincerely, like the scribe who could have been a disciple of Jesus (8:19); sometimes, it was with hidden motives, like the Pharisees wanted to test Jesus (12:38). The rich man's question revealed his initial assumption on how a person could receive eternal life, namely, a "good thing" must be done first before one could receive it. Jesus did not immediately correct this assumption; actually, his reply is rather vague, and could be translated, "only one is good" (19:17a). The one that is good can refer to the keeping of the commandments (19:17b), or if interpreted in the light of Mark's account where Jesus said, "no one is good – except God alone" (Mark 10:18; see also Ps 16:2). This makes God the only standard of goodness.

---

41. Karl-Heinrich Ostmeyer, "Jesu annahme der Kinder in Matthäus 19:13–15," *NovT* 46, no. 1 (2004): 7.

Jesus continued by saying that the rich man could enter life by keeping the commandments (Matt 19:17). Evangelicals have emphasized, and rightly so, that salvation can never be earned by good works. Thus, Jesus' reply can be puzzling. When the rich man asked Jesus to clarify which commands he ought to keep, Jesus enumerated five of the commandments he ought to obey (19:18–19). To this, the man replied that he had carefully obeyed the commandments Jesus mentioned (19:20). What is noteworthy is that when Jesus listed the commandments that the rich man ought to keep, he mentioned only the 5th to the 9th commandment; the prohibitions against murder, adultery, theft, and false testimony, and the command to honor one's parents. Jesus did not mention the tenth commandment, namely, the command not to covet (Exod 20:12–17; especially v. 17; see also Deut 5:16–20). This is not a simple oversight. Had Jesus included, "you shall not covet," in his list, the rich man may not have been able to say with honesty, "All this I have kept" (Matt 19:20). Jesus could have simply told the rich man that what he needed was to obey the tenth commandment, but that would immediately have embarrassed the man. Hence, Jesus affirmed first what the rich man had done before showing him what else still needed to be done.

When the rich man asked Jesus what he still lacked, Jesus replied, "If you want to be perfect, go sell your possessions and give to the poor and you will have treasure in heaven. Then come, follow me" (19:21). Some explain that Jesus demanded the rich man to sell his possessions because God is against class distinctions, and others say he did so because the rich man placed his security on his wealth. Some also suggest that it was Jesus' evangelistic strategy to show the rich man that there is no way to meet God's standard, and others say that it was to expose the rich man's sin.[42] Earlier, Jesus commanded his disciples to store treasures in heaven (6:19–21), although he did not specify how to do so. In this story, Jesus gave specific instructions on how to have "treasure in heaven" (19:21). The basic reason for this requirement, as Jesus explained, was that "where your treasure is, there your heart will be also" (6:21). Jesus' command may have prompted the early church to sell their possessions and share the proceeds with one another (Acts 2:45; 4:32–35), although some did so with dubious motives like Ananias and Sapphira (5:1–11). Matthew explains that the rich man's wealth had been keeping him from storing treasure in heaven, and thus he went away sad after hearing

---

42. Steve Barr, "The Eye of the Needle – Power and Money in the New Community: A Look at Mark 10:17–31," *ANR* 3, no. 1 (1992): 35.

Jesus' demands (Matt 19:22). His grief may suggest his sincerity in seeking Jesus, and the struggle he had having to choose between the good that he could enjoy on earth and the prospect of future wealth in heaven.[43]

This story also challenges the typical method we use today in evangelism. Receiving eternal life is more than just praying a sinner's prayer. Jesus' command to the rich man to "go" and sell his possessions if he really wanted to receive eternal life and to "come" and follow him suggests that receiving eternal life and lifelong discipleship are inseparable. In fact, *salvation and becoming a disciple cannot be clearly distinguished in the Gospel of Matthew.* The rich man's response led to Jesus' comment, "it is hard for someone who is rich to enter the kingdom of God" (19:23). Jesus said it was "hard," he did not say it was "impossible"; but he then compared a rich person entering the kingdom with a camel going through the eye of a needle (something that is impossible), and concluded that the latter was even "easier." In essence, Jesus was saying that it is "impossible" for the rich to enter the kingdom. Nonetheless, he assured his disciples that even if something was humanly impossible, God could make it possible (19:26).

After Jesus spoke, the disciples asked, "Who then can be saved?" (19:26). This question reflects their wrong idea about the priority by which humans are saved. The rich man was not the only one who thought that some "good things" needed to be done in order to receive salvation; the disciples' question shows that they, too, shared this misconception. The OT teaches that poverty results from laziness (Prov 6:9–11; 20:13; 23:20–21) and riches are blessings (Prov 10:22; Gen 24:35; Deut 15:4). Riches are also the reward for righteousness, faithfulness, and generosity (Prov 13:22; 22:9; 28:20, 27). The financial security of descendants is the responsibility of the older generation, and this can be summarized by this proverb, "A good person leaves an inheritance for their children's children, but a sinner's wealth is stored up for the righteous" (Prov 13:22). This can be interpreted in this way – that wealth is a clear sign of God's blessing upon a person. No wonder, then, that the disciples asked Jesus this follow-up question, "Who then can be saved?" (19:26). If the pious (someone who pleases God) and rich (one with whom God is

---

43. There is no reason to assume that the rich man ultimately rejected Jesus because the text did not say so. See discussion of Andrew D. Clarke, "'Do Not Judge Who Is Worthy and Unworthy': Clement's Warning Not to Speculate about the Rich Young Man's Response (Mark 10.17–31)," *JSNT* 31, no. 4 (2009): 447–448.

pleased) cannot receive eternal life, then who can?[44] Jesus assured them that what is impossible from a human standpoint is possible with God.

Jesus also assured the disciples that they did not make a wrong decision in giving up what they had to follow Jesus, and at the same time reminded them not to be presumptuous about their place in the kingdom because of their sacrifices (19:28–30). There is no question that the disciples sincerely needed assurance from Jesus that their giving up of their earthly treasures would result in something good for them (see 4:18–22; 9:9). One should not ignore the comparison between the rich man (one who refused to exchange earthly for heavenly treasure) and the disciples (those who gave up earthly treasure). Whatever the disciples had abandoned – relationships and possessions – they had received back as they were incorporated into a new "family" who shared possessions and took care of each other's needs (for example, Acts 2:45; 4:32–35). In short, they had stored up "treasure in heaven" which they already partially enjoyed while they were still on earth. Moreover, the disciples were also promised that they would be rewarded with authority in the coming kingdom (Matt 19:28).[45] Jesus' statement, "But many who are first will be last, and many who are last will be first" (19:30), can be taken both as an encouragement and a warning. It is an encouragement because even though they are "last" in this world because of the things they gave up, they can also be "first" in the one to come; and it is a warning also not to be too presumptuous because those who think they are "first" in the one to come could be the "last."

To illustrate what he was saying, Jesus told the parable of the workers in the vineyard (20:1–16). In this parable, the landowner went to the marketplace five times throughout the day to hire people to work in his vineyard, in the early morning (20:2), in the middle of the morning (20:3), at noon (20:5a), in the middle of the afternoon (20:5b), and in the late afternoon (20:6).[46] On each occasion, he promised to give the workers a denarius (a typical day's wage during Jesus' days). In the evening, when the workers were

---

44. Barr, "The Eye of the Needle," 36.
45. The NIV translates the Greek *palingenesia* as "renewal of all things." Literally, it means "rebirth," but in this context, it can mean resurrection (J. Duncan M. Derrett, "Palingenesia (Matthew 19:28)," *JSNT* 20 [1984]: 51–58). Paul also talks about the resurrection like being born from the womb of death. He refers to Jesus as the "firstborn from among the dead" in talking about his resurrection (Col 1:18).
46. One major interpretation of these five different hours is that it refers to five periods of history (J. M. Trevel, "The Labourers in the Vineyard: The Exegesis of Matthew 20:1–7 in the Early Church," *VC* 46, no. 4 [1992]: 362). As appealing as this may be, nothing in the text to require such interpretation.

called to receive their salary, those who came in the late afternoon were called first and were given a denarius.⁴⁷ Those who came earlier naturally expected to receive more, but the landowner gave them the same amount, reasoning that they agreed to receive that amount only for the whole day's work. There is clearly inequity, but Jesus was not advocating unfair treatment of workers. The parable is not about fairness; it is about the generosity of the landowner (20:13–15). The parable does not set aside the idea of rewards for one's sacrifice,⁴⁸ but it is an invitation to a humble dependence on the One who is good and generous.

Matthew recounts a series of four dialogues that teach lessons on humility and forgiveness after he predicted his death the second time. In the first dialogue between Jesus and Peter about temple taxes, Jesus set an example of humility by willfully subjecting himself to earthly rulers and paying the temple tax. This is followed by the second dialogue in which the disciples asked who is the greatest among them, and to which Jesus set a child as an example of humility saying that eternal life is available only to those who become like children. Humility is also seen in how one treats those considered "insignificant" in their community, not causing them to sin and forgiving those who do. The discussion on forgiveness is implied in the third dialogue between Jesus and the Pharisees about divorce, wherein Jesus made clear that divorce is not part of God's design for marriage, implying that forgiveness is a better option than divorce even in cases wherein one party has been unfaithful. The fourth and final dialogue in the series recounts the conversation between the rich man and Jesus about eternal life and heavenly treasure, and Jesus' assurance to his disciples about their rewards coupled with a warning not to be too presumptuous about this.

---

47. Although the information we have is that daily wage earners receive one denarius a day, there is no way to be sure whether this is sufficient for the worker and his family to live a decent life (William R. Herzog II, *Parables as Subversive Speech: Jesus as Pedagogue of the Oppressed* [Louisville, KY: WJKP, 1994], 89–90).

48. Nathan Eubank, "What Does Matthew Say about Divine Recompense? On the Misuse of the Parable of the Workers in the Vineyard (20:1–16)," *JSNT* 35, no. 3 (2013): 244.

SELLING ONE'S POSSESSION TO RECEIVE ETERNAL LIFE: A THEOLOGICAL REFLECTION ON EVANGELISM

Asia has adopted many evangelism tools from the West, and many of these materials generally are a "one-size-fits-all" type of material. However, it does not take long before we realize that many of these materials are not suitable for use, at the very least, in some Asian contexts. To cite one example, one tool introduces the Gospel with the question whether a person knows where he or she would go after dying. For Chinese people, especially the older generations, it is offensive to talk about dying, especially to talk to them about their impending death. The result of using this "one-size-fits-all" tool is that it immediately shuts the ears of a potential hearer of the Gospel. The same question can be asked by rephrasing it, "Where do you think you will be after one hundred years?" Older persons will know that you are already talking about their death without specifically mentioning it.

What can we learn from Jesus' method of evangelism? He did not use a "one-size-fits-all" method but adjusted his method to the needs of the hearers. Take for example, when he talked with Nicodemus, he required this Pharisee to be "born again" (John 3:3). One chapter later, when he talked with the Samaritan woman about this same salvation, he did not require the woman to be "born again," but to drink the living water that leads to eternal life (4:14). Nicodemus was a Jew, a biological descendant of Abraham, and therefore a recipient of God's promise of blessings. Thus, when Jesus told Nicodemus that he must be born again to see the kingdom of God, he was in essence saying that it was not enough for Nicodemus to be *born a descendant of Abraham*, he must be "born again." This is not something the Samaritan woman could claim. Her situation was different. Her having had five husbands shows her thirst for love and acceptance (4:17–18). No wonder, then, that Jesus, instead of asking her to be "born again," offered her a drink that would satisfy her, not only on earth, but even for eternity. In the case of the crowd whom he fed and that wanted to make him king by force, Jesus said to them that eternal life is reserved for those who eat his flesh and drink his blood (6:51–58). Jesus made it clear that the reason he required them to do so was that though they had their fill (6:26), their purpose should not only be to have food for their stomachs, but for their spirits also (6:27).

In the story of the rich young ruler, we have another unique case. The one who sought eternal life may have been a pious person like Nicodemus, but his possessions had become a hindrance to him experiencing the life that Jesus was offering. Jesus did not ask him to be born again or to drink of the living water, but to sell his possessions and give the proceeds to the poor! How Jesus offered eternal life in these four instances should make us rethink the assumption that there can be a "one-size-fits-all" approach in evangelism.

Samson L. Uytanlet

20:17–22:14 JESUS' THIRD PREDICTION: LESSONS ON AUTHORITY AND SUBMISSION

20:17–19 Jesus' Third Prediction

This section is the third series of stories after Jesus predicted his death. Jesus gave more details about his death (Matt 20:17–19): it would be in Jerusalem; the chief priests and teachers of the law would orchestrate his death; Gentiles would mock, torture, and crucify him; and he would be raised to life again. Matthew focuses on the authority of Jesus and the necessity to submit to him. He presents Jesus as the Son of David who entered Jerusalem as the king who carried out God's rule, requiring his people to "bear fruit" and accommodating the Gentiles under his kingship. The section also includes a series of three parables that emphasize lessons on obedience to God the king.

Actually, Jesus needed to predict his death only once for the disciples to know the certainty of his death. For Jesus to do so thrice stresses the certainty that this will happen soon. This explains why the disciples had been pondering as to who among them could succeed Jesus once the leadership post becomes vacant (20:20–28). Moreover, having mentioned the involvement of the chief priests and teachers of the law in his death, this only underscores the responsibility of the religious leaders and the gravity of their sin against the Messiah.

20:20–28 The Request of the "Mother of the Sons of Zebedee"

Mencius, one of the most influential Confucian sages, once taught, "[In the constitution of the state] the people rank the highest, the spirit of the land and grain comes next, the ruler ranks the least."[49] Jesus was not the only one who taught about servant leadership, yet he was one of the few who exemplified it through his life (Matt 20:28), and he was the *only one* whose sacrifice provided benefits for his followers even after their life on earth.

Jesus promised his twelve disciples seats of authority (19:28). The two sons of Zebedee may have thought that this promise was about rankings within the kingdom and may have informed their mother about it. Even in Matthew 18:1–3, the disciples had already shown signs of struggle among themselves as to who was the greatest among them. Peter, James, and John had been the more prominent ones among the twelve during the time Jesus

---

49. In *Selections from Mencius* VII B:14. De Bary, *Sources of Chinese Tradition* (1st), 1:96.

was on earth with them; and with Peter around, there was no guarantee that the two brothers would be numbers 2 and 3 behind Jesus. In this story, the "mother of the sons of Zebedee" played the role of the traditional mother who would walk an extra mile to ensure the welfare of her sons (see also comments on Matthew 26:37). This was just like Sarah who pressured Abraham to send Ishmael away to make sure Abraham's inheritance would go to Isaac (Gen 21:8–13), Rebekah who masterminded a plan to deceive her own husband and took away the blessing of her elder son Esau in order to make sure it went to her favorite son Jacob (27:5–17), and Bathsheba who lobbied for Solomon to make sure he became king in place of David (1 Kgs 1:15–37).[50] Like Bathsheba, the "mother of the sons of Zebedee" also wanted to ensure the political welfare of her sons, and requested that they would be "seated" closest to Jesus (Matt 20:21). In the OT, the angels are said to be standing on the right and on the left sides of God (1 Kgs 22:19; 2 Chr 18:18), and the throne of the queen mother at the right of Solomon (2 Kgs 2:19). Even in the NT, Jesus is portrayed as one seated at was located the right hand (or "right hand side") of God (Mark 16:19). The seats to the "right" or the "right and left" sides of the ruler are seats of authority; an authority lower only than that of the king.

In human politics, climbing up the political ladder requires lobbying, knowing the right people, and having the right connections; and glory can be attained by being shrewd. The mother of James and John was clearly thinking in this way as well. Jesus used this opportunity to clarify, first, that his throne is not a human but a divine throne; and second, that glory is not to be achieved by human politics, but through sufferings (Matt 20:22–23). Jesus asked, "Can you drink the cup I am going to drink?" (20:22) which was another way of asking whether they were willing to go through the same suffering that he would go through. In both the OT and NT, the "cup" is used as a metaphor for what God has allotted to a person, whether blessings (Ps 16:5; 23:5), judgments (11:6; 75:8), or sufferings (Matt 20:22–23; 26:39). James and John were with their mother in this but were silent throughout until Jesus asked them the question. When they told Jesus they were willing to suffer, he told them that they would indeed suffer for his sake (Matt 20:23). James was killed by Herod Agrippa I (Acts 12:1–2), and John was exiled in Patmos (Rev 1:9).

---

50. Emily Cheney, "The Mother of the Sons of Zebedee (Matthew 27:56)," *JSNT* 68 (1997): 16.

The other ten disciples heard what the mother and her two sons did and were indignant (Matt 20:24). Their reaction suggests that they would have done the same if given the opportunity, except that the two "got ahead" of them and asked first. Jesus called them all and taught them about authority, "You know that the rulers of the Gentiles lord it over them and their high officials exercise authority over them. Not so with you" (20:25–26a). He acknowledged that the disciples would be given authority, but this authority was not to be exercised in the way that the rulers of the Gentiles used their authority. Jesus said that the disciples were not to "lord it over" (Greek, *katakurieuō*) the others. Aside from this passage, the word is only used three times in the rest of the NT (Mark 10:42; Acts 19:16; 1 Pet 5:3); and except for Acts 19:16, the other passages do not shed much light on what the word means. The way it is used in the Greek OT, however, may provide some ideas on what it means to "lord it over" someone. It is used to refer to: (1) one nation *conquering* another (Num 32:22, 29; Ps 10:5; Dan 11:39); (2) the Messiah *subduing* all his enemies (Ps 110:2); (3) a lion *catching* his prey before devouring it (Ps 10:9); (4) sin *having dominion* over humans (Ps 119:13; see also 19:13); (5) death *overpowering* humans (Ps 49:11); and (6) God *exercising authority* over a wayward son so he is unable to continue in his wrong ways (Jer 3:14). In the NT, it refers to a demon-possessed man *overpowering* other humans (Acts 19:16). What do all these have in common? The subject "lords it over" the object by rendering the latter powerless. The authority Jesus gave his disciples did not give them the right to render others powerless, but as he exemplified it, he exercised his authority by making himself powerless through death, in order to empower others to serve (Matt 20:28).[51] Moreover, by giving the disciples authority to do what he did, he empowered them to be servants of God.

20:29–21:11 Jesus Heals Two Blind Men before Entering Jerusalem as King

There are two accounts of Jesus healing two blind men (Matt 9:27–31; 20:29–34). The first account happened in "his (Jesus') own town" (9:1), and the healing of the blind men occurred in the house where he was staying (9:27–28). The second account, according to Matthew, happened when Jesus and his disciples were on their way out of Jericho (20:29). The different

---

51. For a discussion on how the early interpreters explain this passage in light of what Paul said about Jesus death and glory (Phil 2:6–8), see J. Christopher Edwards, "Pre-Nicene Receptions of Mark 10:45//Matt 20:28 with Phil 2:6–8," *JTS* 61, no. 1 (2010): 194–199.

locations for the two stories hint that Matthew is describing two similar events, and not just one told twice over. This raises the question as to why Matthew had to relate two similar stories.

John tells us that he did not record everything Jesus said and did, but carefully chose some stories for a certain purpose (John 21:25). The same can be assumed about Matthew. Considering the two seemingly identical stories, one may conclude that Matthew is using them to illustrate two different things. The first is part of a series of stories of Jesus' miracles (Matt 8:1–9:35). These stories of healing illustrate God's presence with Jesus as he empowered him to heal, exorcise, and perform miracles. They also illustrate God's presence with the people, and how his presence can bring peace and well-being in the lives of those who believe in him; and this promise of blessing comes with a clear demand for discipleship (for details, see comments for Matthew 8:1–9:35). Matthew tells the second story of healing of two blind men together with others that highlight Jesus' authority as king (20:29–34). This may also be the reason that there is an emphasis on the fact that the blind men's address Jesus as "Lord." In the first account, the two blind men called out to Jesus, "Have mercy on us, Son of David" (9:27), and then addressed Jesus as "Lord" in response to Jesus' question (9:28). In the second account, the blind men called out to Jesus twice and said, "*Lord, Son of David*, have mercy on us" (20:30–31; emphasis mine), an expression first used by the Canaanite woman (15:22).

In contrast to the crowd who showed no concern for the blind men and even rebuked them for seeking Jesus (20:31), Jesus stopped to ask how he could serve them (20:32; see also 20:28). Moreover, he showed compassion on them and touched their eyes so that they could be healed (20:33–34). This story of healing points to Jesus as the compassionate servant-king who is about to openly declare his true identity (as king) and to ultimately accomplish his greatest act of service (his death).

After healing the blind men in Jericho, Jesus traveled a distance close to 10 kilometers and stopped at Bethphage before entering Jerusalem (21:1), which is another three kilometers. Jesus sent two of his disciples to bring a donkey with her colt to him (21:1–2). The challenging part in understanding Matthew's story is determining why he asked for two animals.[52] From a practical standpoint, it would be difficult to separate the donkey from her

---

52. For a brief discussion on the previous works, see Wayne Coppins, "Sitting on Two Asses?: Second Thoughts on the Two-Animal Interpretation of Mathew 21:7," *TynBul* 63, no. 2 (2012): 276–281.

colt,[53] but more important than practicality is the fulfillment of Zechariah's prophecy.[54]

Zechariah prophesied about God's salvation of his people. The promise of the LORD's presence and peace (Zech 8:1–3) would be manifested in these ways: (1) old people and young children would enjoy peaceful community in the streets (8:4–5); (2) people would do business without fear (8:9–10); (3) fruitful land (8:12); and (4) religious celebration would be joyful (8:19). Moreover, Zechariah anticipated not only the salvation of the Jews from foreign powers and judgment of Israel's enemies (8:8; 9:1–8), but also the salvation of other nations (8:20–23; 9:12–17). This is not going to be accomplished through weapons of war (9:10), but through the coming of the shepherd (9:16–17), who would come "righteous and victorious, lowly and riding on a donkey, on a colt, the foal of a donkey" (9:9–10). Zechariah also hints at the death of the shepherd-king when he talks about freedom for the prisoners through "the blood of my covenant" (9:11).

There are only a few recorded instances wherein donkeys are used by rulers (Judg 10:4; 2 Sam 16:2), but Jesus riding on a donkey and Matthew's quotation of Zechariah 9:9–10 highlight Jesus' entry to Jerusalem as the legitimate yet humble king (see also Gen 49:10–11).[55] The crowd welcomed him as they would a dignitary (Matt 21:8) and acknowledged him as the king (21:9). The declaration of acceptance, which is also a quotation from Psalm 118:25–26, is significant especially during the time when the Jews were under Roman rule. Psalm 118 is a psalm of praise to God (118:1–4). For a people under foreign rule, which the Jews understood as a consequence of their sins, this psalm provided hope of freedom as it expressed trust in what God could do even though they were surrounded by human enemies (118:5–10), taking hold of God's promise of salvation from their enemies (118:11–17). The psalm also welcomed the one who would bring about this salvation (118:19–21, 25–26), and anticipated his rejection as well (118:22–24).

The crowd did not only acknowledge Jesus as the savior anticipated in Psalm 118 (see also Matt 21:9), but they also recognized him as the "prophet from Nazareth in Galilee" (21:11). Messianic pretenders like Judas the Galilean had come from Galilee (Acts 5:37; see also John 7:52), but it was

---

53. Albrecht Frenz, "Mt XXI 5.7," *NovT* 13, no. 4 (1971): 259.
54. Coppins, "Sitting on Two Asses," 287; David Instone-Brewer, "The Two Asses of Zechariah 9:9 in Matthew 21," *TynBul* 54, no. 1 (2003): 95.
55. Clay Alan Ham, *The Coming King and the Rejected Shepherd: Matthew's Reading of Zechariah's Messianic Hope* (Sheffield: Sheffield Phoenix Press, 2005), 40–44.

also the place of origin of the real Messiah (see comments for Matthew 2:23). His role as a prophet here did not highlight his preaching ministry as much as it did in his suffering (see comments for Matthew 21:35; 23:29–39).

21:12–17 Jesus Overturns the Vendors' Tables in the Temple Courts

When Jesus entered Jerusalem, the crowd acknowledged him as king (Matt 21:9–10), and when he entered the temple, the people, particularly the children, declared him as the "Son of David" (21:15). This happened after Jesus overturned the tables of the vendors and money changers in the temple.

The temple was first planned by David (2 Sam 7:1–17; 1 Chr 28:1–29:9) and eventually was built by Solomon (1 Kgs 5:1–6:38; 2 Chr 3:1–7:22). It became the center of politics/religion in Judea. A century and half later, it was repaired by Joash (2 Chr 24:1–14), but was destroyed by the Babylonians after another two and half centuries (2 Kgs 25:8–12; 2 Chr 35:15–19). Zerubbabel rebuilt the temple after the Jews returned from exile (Ezra 4:1–6:18). Four centuries later, when Herod the Great became king of Judea, he rebuilt/renovated the old structure and made a larger and more elaborate building. Josephus describes this temple structure as having an innermost section that only the priests could enter. Men could enter the court leading to the area restricted for priests, and women were allowed only in the area outside the men's area. Foreigners were only allowed outside the women's court. Josephus recalled that outside the gate into the women's court, there was a warning sign that pronounced death on any foreigner who tried to go beyond the area reserved for foreigners and anyone who was "impure."[56] It is very likely that the vendors set up shop in the area reserved for non-Israelites, making the area crowded so that it became more like a bazaar, thus preventing the foreigners from worship.

Jesus came in to this court, overturned the tables,[57] and rebuked the vendors by quoting from Isaiah 56:7 and Jeremiah 7:11 (Matt 21:14). In Isaiah, God calls his people to do justice and righteousness, and keep the Sabbath (Isa 56:1–2). He also addresses the Jews' problem of idolatry (57:3–13), and raised accusations against Israel's leaders (their shepherds and

---

56. Josephus, *Jewish Antiquities* 15.11.5 §§ 417–419.
57. The cleansing of the temple is an act that addresses the sins of the people, particularly the religious leaders. Eduardo dela Serna, "Los Idolos, Causantes del Asesinato de Jesús de Nazaret," *CdT* 16, no. 1 (1997): 120–122. Even in Greco-Roman writings, the act of overturning tables in temples symbolize a restoration of religious purity (Marc Huys, "Turning the Tables: Jesus' Temple Cleansing and the Story of Lycaon," *ETL* 86, no. 1 [2010]: 161).

blind watchmen) who do not protect the people and who lack understanding (56:9–57:2). Part of the problem was the exclusion of foreigners in worship (56:3–8), and God declared that "my house will be called a house of prayer *for all nations*" (56:7; emphasis mine). A similar message is emphasized in Jeremiah. God calls his people to do justice, and not to oppress foreigners, orphans, and widows (Jer 7:1–8). He addresses the sins of the people particularly idolatry, adultery, murder, falsehood, and theft (7:9–11). Using Shiloh as an example, God warns that disobedience can lead to the destruction of the city (7:12–15) and that judgment awaits Jerusalem (7:16–20).

Jesus' overturning the vendors' table symbolized the impending destruction of Jerusalem and its temple. It was also a call to the religious leaders to ensure that justice and righteousness be practiced, and that foreigners were not excluded from worship. The coming of the blind and the lame to Jesus at the temple for healing (Matt 21:14) was more than just Matthew's recounting of what happened, but was his way of saying that the people who were typically excluded from worship were now included and enjoying the privileges of being under Jesus' rule. Moreover, the chief priests and teachers of the law did not question Jesus for creating such chaos by overturning the tables. Jesus is not the first one to do such an act; Nehemiah also threw out Tobiah's household goods from the room which was supposed to be used as storeroom for grain offering, incense, and temple articles (Neh 13:4–9). There may have been other similar instances like this as well. It seems that what troubled the religious leaders was not Jesus' action, but the children's pronouncement. Hence they asked one another, "Do you hear what the children are saying?" (Matt 21:16). The religious leaders should have served as "watchmen" who saw the coming destruction, and as "shepherds" who cared for God's people (Isa 56:10–11) and led them in acknowledging God's rule. Instead, they hindered the people from acknowledging Jesus as Messiah. In contrast, the children were the ones who were bold in proclaiming Jesus as king (Matt 21:15–16).

21:18–22 Jesus Curses the Fruitless Fig Tree

After Jesus' confrontation with the priests and teachers of the Law, he and his disciples went to Bethany and stayed there overnight. Jesus had friends living in Bethany, like Lazarus and his sisters (John 11–12), and Simon the Leper (Matt 26:6); and they may have provided Jesus and his disciples with or helped them find a place to stay. The next day, on their way back to Jerusalem, Jesus saw a fig tree, and hoping to find fruits, he was disappointed because there was none. Jesus then said, "May you never bear fruit again," and the tree withered immediately (21:19).

In the OT, fruitful fig trees were evidence of a fruitful land (Num 13:23; 20:5; Deut 8:8), and the enjoyment of figs was a sign of safety and security (1 Kgs 4:25; 2 Kgs 18:31; Isa 36:16; Mic 4:4; Zech 3:10); both were considered blessings from God. Moreover, the destruction of figs (Jer 5:17; Amos 4:9) and fruitless fig trees (Hab 3:17) were symbols of misery; both were considered as symbols of God's judgment. The fig tree was also one of the OT symbols for the nation of Israel (Hos 9:10), and at times God lamented as he compared the nation to a fruitless fig tree (Mic 7:1).[58] Micah describes Israel's "fruitlessness" in relation to the sins of the people like bloodshed (7:2), bribery (7:3), marital unfaithfulness (7:5), and dishonoring of parents (7:6). While he pronounced God's judgment against the people (7:4), he announced hope of salvation (7:7). The same image is used in the Gospels when John the Baptist said to the Pharisees and Sadducees, "Produce fruit in keeping with repentance" (Matt 3:8). Like God, who was disappointed because of the fruitlessness of Israel (Mic 7:1), Jesus was also disappointed to see the fruitless Israel of his day (Matt 21:19).

When the disciples saw the tree withered after Jesus cursed it, they asked him how it happened (21:20). Jesus replied by telling them about the importance of prayer (21:21–22). His statement, "If you believe, you will receive whatever you ask for in prayer" (21:22), is broad and may suggest that it is not only the drying up of the living fig tree that is possible; – even the fruit bearing of a barren fig tree was just as possible. In other words, prayer is an essential part in being fruitful.[59]

21:23–27 The Chief Priests and the Elders Question Jesus' Authority

In the earlier chapters of Matthew, the location of Jesus' ministry is primarily in Galilee (Matt 4:12–20:16). After his third and last prediction of his death (20:17–19), the location shifted to Jerusalem. It is unclear from the Gospels as to how much time he spent preaching in the Jerusalem temple during the day and spending the evenings in Bethany (21:17–18; see also Luke 21:37), but it was long enough for him to say, "Every day I sat in the temple courts teaching" (Matt 26:55).

---

58. David E. Holwerda, "Perplexing Texts: Figs, Demons, and Swine," *Reff* 29, no. 9 (1979): 8.
59. Mark Moulton, "Jesus' Goal for the Temple and Tree: A Thematic Revisit of Matt 21:12–22," *JETS* 41, no. 4 (1998): 571.

While Jesus was teaching in the temple, the chief priests and elders came to him to question his authority for "doing these things" (21:23). "These things" presumably refer to his teaching and preaching ministry in the temple, and his acceptance of the kingly honor (21:9, 15–16). The people had acknowledged him as the "prophet from Nazareth in Galilee" (21:11), in the same way that they acknowledged John as a prophet (21:26). Thus, when Jesus asked them about John's authority, they could not say what they really thought because they were afraid of the people (21:24–27). The priests' question ultimately focused on whether Jesus' authority came from God. The religious leaders' question about his authority led Jesus to use three parables to elaborate his divine given authority.

21:28–32 The Parable of the Two Sons

Three parables follow, and the first is about two sons who were instructed by their father to work in the vineyard. The first son refused to obey initially, but later changed his mind and went to do what his father instructed him to do (Matt 21:28–29). The second son agreed to work at first, but later changed his mind and did not do what his father instructed him to do (21:30).[60] Jesus asked the priests and elders, "What do you think? . . . Which of the two did what his father wanted?" (21:28, 31).

Both sons are not without guilt. The commands in the OT are clear about showing reverence to one's parents (Lev 19:3), which does not only include commands against mocking and cursing them (Exod 21:17; Lev 20:9; Prov 20:20; 30:11, 17), but also the requirement to follow their instructions (23:22–25). Obedience need not be limited to those instructions that pertain to one's morals, but they also include commands about daily tasks (15:19–20). The first son's initial refusal is nothing less than disrespect, and the second son's agreeing to work and later not doing it is no different, in fact, worse. Even the religious leaders agree that the first son is the one who is truly obedient (Matt 21:31).

From Jesus' explanation of the parable, it is clear that the first son represents the "tax collectors and prostitutes," or "sinners," in general, who may have initially said *No* to God, but when John came preaching the kingdom of God, they were the ones who responded positively to him (3:5–6; Luke

---

60. Some manuscripts have the two sons interchanged. For a discussion on this and how interpreters tried to solve the difficulty, see Wendell E. Langley, "The Parable of the Two Sons (Matthew 21:28-32) Against Its Semitic and Rabbinic Backdrop," *CBQ* 58, no. 2 (1996): 228-243.

3:10–14). Hence Jesus said they are "entering the kingdom" before the religious leaders (Matt 21:31). The religious leaders, however, in an attempt to give an impression to the people that they had responded to John even though they refused to recognize his authority (21:25–26), said *Yes*, but actually refused to obey (3:7–10). By their earlier question to Jesus, it is also clear that they refused to acknowledge his authority (21:23).

21:33–46 The Parable of Wicked Tenants

In response to the question about his authority (Matt 21:23–27), Jesus told them another parable about the landowner who planted a vineyard and rented it to some farmers while he went on a trip (21:33–34).[61] Towards the harvest season, he sent his servants to collect his share of the harvest, but the tenants beat one, killed another, and stoned the third one. This was then repeated until he decided to send his son, whom the wicked servants killed (21:35–39). The landowner then took the land and rented it to other tenants who gave him his share of the harvest (21:40–41).

The distinction Jesus made is not between Israel and the Gentiles, but between fruitless and fruitful people (21:43). The fruitless ones refer to the Pharisees (21:45) who also reject the Stone (21:42), while the fruitful ones refer to those who do the opposite, whether Israelites or the Gentiles who come from the east or the west (8:11).

The prophet Isaiah also tells of a similar parable. Like the landowner in Jesus' parable, the one in Isaiah also planted a vineyard with a wall, winepress and watchtower (Isa 5:1–2, 5; see also Matt 21:33). Instead of producing good grapes, the vineyard produced bad ones (Isa 5:2–4). Isaiah explains that the vineyard represents the people of Israel and Judah, many of whom continue in their injustice and bloodshed (5:7), and acquire land through unrighteous means (5:8). The result of their sin is the desolation of their land (5:5–6). Moving back to the parable of Jesus, it is not difficult to see that the landowner in the story represents God who is entitled to receive his "share of the crop" (see also Matt 21:21) and the son is Jesus.[62] The description of the servants who were sent to collect the owner's share fits the prophets who were sent before Jesus; some of whom were beaten like Jeremiah (Jer 37:15), some were killed like Elijah's contemporaries (1 Kgs 18:13; 19:1, 10, 14),

---

61. Absentee landlords are common during the time of Jesus (for example, see Pliny the Younger, *Epistles* 10.8).
62. The allegorical element of this parable cannot be ignored. Derrett, *Law in the New Testament*, 30.

and others stoned to death like Zechariah (2 Chr 24:20–21). Several prophets were persecuted for delivering God's message to his people. The way the Jewish leaders treated Jesus would be the same as the way they treated the earlier prophets (Matt 23:34, 37; Luke 11:47–49; 13:34; Acts 7:52).

The wicked tenants clearly refer to the religious leaders, and they understood that Jesus was talking about them (Matt 21:46). Interestingly, the priests during the time of Jesus were the few in Israel who owned lands, some of them having added "house to house" and joined "field to field" (Isa 5:8), yet in this parable they were the tenants. Justice would require that the wicked tenants be punished, and death is a reasonable consequence for their action. Yet the landowner did not seek justice in this way, but rather acted to "bring those wretches to their wretched end" (Matt 21:40–41) and rent the land to "a people" who could produce fruit (21:43). The "wretches" who refuse to give the owner the fruits of the land and the "people" producing fruit are distinguished by their willingness to acknowledge the authority of the land owner, by giving him his due.[63]

Jesus quoted again from Psalm 118, and this time, he referred to the Stone rejected by the builders (118:22–23; Matt 21:42). Unlike the crowd who received Jesus as king (Matt 21:9; see also Psalm 118:25–26), the priests and elders rejected him as king. The political implication of Jesus' claim could not be ignored. Either he was one of the messianic pretenders during his era, or he was the real king, and Caesar and the governor he appointed in Judea were the royal pretenders. Jesus' claim could potentially create chaos in the city, and this was *partly* the reason the religious leaders tried to suppress Jesus, but the greater reason was explained by Matthew. They understood that they were the wicked tenants who refused to give the landowner his share of the harvest and the builders who rejected the Stone (21:44–45), so they started to plan how to get him arrested. However, they could not do anything drastic, and once again, it was because they were afraid of the people (21:46).

---

63. Interpreters do not agree about the identity of this "people" who produce fruit (Matt 21:43). Some suggest it refers neither to Jews nor Gentiles, but a community of believers (Graham N. Stanton, "Revisiting Matthew's Communities," in *SBL 1994 Seminar Papers*, ed. Eugene H. Lovering, Jr. [Atlanta: Scholars Press, 1994], 9–23). Others say it distinguishes between believing Jews and non-believing Jews (Anthony J. Saldarini, *Matthew's Christian-Jewish Community* [Chicago: University of Chicago Press, 1994], 30). Still others view it as Israel including the believing Gentiles (Dennis C. Duling, *A Marginal Scribe: Studies in the Gospel of Matthew in a Social-Scientific Perspective*, Matrix 7 [Eugene, OR: Cascade Books, 2012], 325–326). Despite the differences, they all share something in common, there is a distinction between those who believe in Jesus and those who do not.

CONFRONTATION IN HIERARCHICAL AND SHAME-BASED CULTURES

Confronting another person is difficult and awkward, and Asians in particular find it hard to speak directly to another person. Asians value indirect speech and direct speech is considered rude; although some would view indirect speech as not telling the truth. If that person is older or is in a position of authority, confrontation is much more difficult. Thus, to avoid confrontation, Christians would suffer in silence or gossip. Such behavior does not build healthy communities and instead could actually harm the community.

This cultural quagmire needs to be dealt with sensitively as we study the example of Jesus. The aim for Christians, as much as possible is to live harmoniously with those around them as well as to speak the truth in love (Eph 4:25, 29). Also, Christians seek to build up the life of, and relationships within, the community. Jesus also lived in a culture of honor and shame and so we can learn from how he dealt with those who challenged him.

Throughout his public ministry, Jesus was challenged by the established Jewish leadership. They asked him difficult questions about faith and life, as they tried to trap and discredit him (Matt 21:45-46; 22:22, 46). Jesus responded to them directly, such as in answering the Sadducees about the question of marriage at the resurrection; or indirectly such as telling parables like that of the workers in the vineyard (Matt 20:1-16). There is a place for speaking directly on matters of faith and doctrine. Today Christians can do so with the authority of Scripture and so attempt to win over those who have different views.

Sometimes Jesus chose to tell stories (Matt 22:1-14). These stories gave his opponents something to think about. Such an indirect way works well in the Asian context as both sides can save face. It is often also not appropriate especially for younger persons to challenge their elders; or for Christians to directly challenge the more powerful in society. Telling stories, whether orally or through other media, can be a subversive and gentle way of dealing with opposition.

Confrontation could also include the task of apologetics, which is giving reasons for our faith. Sometimes this means that we need to have a much better grasp of Christian doctrine, faith and belief in order to be able to present it convincingly to others. At other times apologetics involves us studying the other religions and worldviews so that we can speak about how the Christian faith is different from them. Jesus knew that the Sadducees were being inconsistent (22:33) and so could challenge their views.

We know that the words spoken in confrontation are just one aspect of confronting another person; our own posture and tone also play an important part. It is difficult to tell what tone Jesus' spoke with when he confronted his

> opponents, but knowing his character we can guess that he could be both firm and yet polite; and so we must be. Whether we disagree with those within the church, or trying to convince others about the truth claims of the gospel, we always need to be gentle in our speech and humble in our posture. We must not be in the situation where we win the argument but lose the friendship and respect of the other person because of our arrogance or combativeness. One way we can demonstrate humility is to listen to the other, and to understand not just their words but also their unspoken emotions and concerns behind their words. Such listening will take time and patience. When disagreements are in the context of relationships in a faith community, then other and every day actions and behavior will also be part of how we relate with those whom we disagree with.
>
> Investing in that process will go a long way not just to give a reply to the question or issue, but to build up relationships within the body of Christ. Then even when we disagree with others, we will not cause division in the church but rather build and strengthen it.
>
> **Kiem-Kiok Kwa**

22:1–14 The Parable of the Wedding Banquet

This is the third parable Jesus told in response to the question of the priests and the elders about his authority (21:23–27). Jesus likened God's rule to a king who prepared a wedding banquet for his son, but the invited guests refused to attend the wedding (22:1–3). A second group of servants were sent to inform the invited guests that choice food had been prepared, but one ignored the servants, another went to do their business, and the rest killed the servants (22:4–6). This enraged the king who sent his army to destroy the city (22:7), and he sent some servants to go to the streets and gather anyone they could find, good and bad alike until the banquet hall was filled with guests (22:8–10). When the king saw a guest not wearing wedding clothes, he asked why he was not wearing the proper attire, and when he could not answer, he was bound and thrown out to a place where he was tortured (22:11–13).

As in the previous parable, it is not difficult to see who are being represented by the characters in the parable. Interpreters throughout the centuries generally agree that the king represents God. In Jewish writings, the image of the wedding banquet is typically associated with God's future judgment (Isa 25:6–10; Luke 14:15; Rev 19:7–9). Celebration of the feast is enjoyed by those who were part of the banquet and judgment is for those who are not part of it.

In this parable, those who were invited first spurned the king's invitation (22:3). Attendance is an expression of allegiance to the king.[64] In any culture, rejecting the king's invitation without a valid reason is a sign of disrespect and disloyalty. To make matters worse, even after the king sent another group of servants to call them again – hence giving them another chance to respond, they continued to ignore the invitation and some even went on to kill the servants sent to them (22:4–6). Luke recounts the same parable but has included other excuses given by those invited to the banquet; one just bought a field and wanted to see it, one bought five yoke of oxen and wanted to try it, and one just got married (Luke 14:18–20). These reasons were considered valid for not joining Israel's army according to Moses; the fainthearted (Deut 20:4), the one who just bought a field (20:5), the one who just planted a vineyard (20:6), and the one who was pledged to be married (20:7) or recently married (24:5). In this parable, however, they were considered invalid excuses to ignore the king's call.[65] Jesus also mentioned those who passively ignored the invitation and actively got involved in violence killing the king's servants (Matt 22:6). This detail recalled the previous parable in which the landowner's servants, who were sent to receive the king's share of the harvest were killed by the original tenants (21:35–36). Yet unlike the landowner, the king in this parable sent his army to destroy the murderers and burn their city (22:7).[66] With Jesus' discussion about the destruction of Jerusalem (Matt 24), it is clear that the parable also depicts the coming judgment on Jerusalem, particularly their leaders who were responsible for the death of the prophets sent to them (23:33–39).

In this parable, the king had originally excluded those in the streets (22:10), something that the rich people such as the religious authorities in Jerusalem would have done; and going to the streets to invite people to a wedding banquet was not normal. Yet the king invited those who are not originally invited, and now the situation is reversed – that is, those who should

---

64. See also Exodus Rabbah 18:10. Richard Bauckham, "The Parable of the Royal Wedding Feast (Matthew 22:1–14) and the Parable of the Lame Man and the Blind Man (Apocryphon of Ezekiel)," *JBL* 115, no. 3 (1996): 484.
65. Humphrey Palmer, "Just Married, Cannot Come," *NovT* 28, no. 4 (1976): 241–242.
66. Matthew is the only Gospel writer to call the religious leaders "murderers" or "sons of murderers" (Sjef van Tilborg, *The Jewish Leaders in Matthew* [Leiden: Brill, 1972], 46). This indirect depiction of the religious leaders as "murderers" (Matt 22:7) will be made explicit later (23:31, 35).

have been part of the banquet were now those on the "outside," while those who should have been outside were now enjoying the feast. The previous parables provide the explanation for this, namely, that the people who were considered "unworthy" by the religious leaders would be given the chance to enjoy the benefits of being part of God's rule (21:31).

The point of inviting other guests is not because food would be wasted, but because the wedding could not be cancelled (22:4).[67] When the king saw a man among the guests not wearing appropriate wedding attire, he questioned the man for not wearing one, and when the man could not answer he was punished (22:11–13). The king addressed the man, "Friend" (Greek, *hetairos*; 22:12). In Matthew, the address "Friend" is not really a friendly address (20:13; 26:50).[68] The harsh response of the king is difficult to interpret. One must consider that in some of Jesus' parables, the person that represents God may have a character that does not accurately portray God, like the judge in the parable of the persistent widow (Luke 18:1–8). The point of the king's judgment, however, is not about the king's bad temper, but the passive defiance of the man for not wearing wedding attire. In ancient Jewish custom, and it may be said of most cultures even today, those who attend banquets are expected to show up in proper attire.[69] There is no reason to think that the people in the street do not have any dress for such occasions, or that they had no time to borrow.[70] The point of this parable, however, is that showing up at the wedding banquet of the king's son ill-dressed is as contemptuous as actively dismissing the king's invitation. This explains the harsh judgment.

Jesus closes the parable with the statement, "For many are invited, but few are chosen" (22:14). The Greek word translated as "invited" is *klētos*, related to the word *kaleō*, or "to call." The statement can be rendered, "many are called, but few are chosen." Both expressions are essentially the same and both are used for Israel (Isa 43:1; 44:5; 45:3–4; 48:12). There is actually a play on words, many are *klētoi*, but few are *eklektoi*, puns are used as mnemonic device in an oral/aural culture. In this context, it simply points to the fact that not everyone invited/called to share the king's celebration would respond to the king's invitation.

---

67. Bauckham, "Royal Wedding Feast," 485.
68. Herzog, *Subversive Speech*, 92; Carter Lester, "Matthew 22:1–24," *Int* 62, no. 3 (2008): 309.
69. An example of such discussion is found in the Babylonian Talmud, *Shabbat* 153a.
70. Bauckham, "Royal Wedding Feast," 485.

Matthew presents a series of stories after Jesus predicted his death for the third time, and as in the two previous series, one particular lesson on discipleship is emphasized. In this series, it is the lesson on authority and submission. In response to the internal conflict among his disciples regarding the issue of greatness, Jesus taught lessons on humility particularly in the exercise of authority. It is clear that Jesus was setting himself as the prime example, that authority must be exercised through sacrifice, and his death is the best example of this. Having presented Jesus as the example for the disciples Matthew then presented him as the compassionate king who cares for the needs of the lowly like the blind and the lame. He entered Jerusalem being recognized as king by the crowd. He is the king who desires to see people from all nations able to worship God; hence, he drove out the vendors in the temple courts. He is also the king who expects to see good fruits from his people; hence, he cursed the unfruitful fig tree. His authority is questioned by the religious leaders, and he responded with three parables: the two sons, the wicked tenants, and the wedding banquet. The three parables have essentially the same message,[71] God's people, to whom he first offered salvation, have constantly rejected him and his messengers. Thus, judgment would come upon them for their rejection, but there would be hope for those who will respond to him, and this offer was not only for the Jews but also for the nations.

---

71. Rowland Onyenali, *The Trilogy of Parables in Mt 21:28–22:14*, AfTS 3 (Frankfurt: Peter Lang, 2013), 259–261.

MATTHEW 22:15–46

The Attempts of the Pharisees and Sadducees to Discredit Jesus

Matthew has consistently presented Jesus as the Messiah/king for whom the Jews had been waiting through the stories related to his birth, the prophecies he fulfilled, the stories of miracles he performed, and the messages he preached. His predictions about his death made clear that he would attain the glory of kingship only through sufferings, and his entrance to Jerusalem was the initial step towards this goal. Hence, after his third and last prediction, he publicly entered Jerusalem as king. The crowd received him, the children declared his praise, but the religious leaders rejected him, and the judgment he pronounced against them produced greater conflict between them. Consequently, the chief priests and the Pharisees tried to find ways to arrest him but could not, because the crowd esteemed him as prophet (Matt 21:45–46).

Jesus had been preaching in Jerusalem regularly during this period (26:55; Luke 19:47; 22:53), and people had been coming to him (Matt 21:14). Arresting him publicly without sufficient grounds was not only illegal, but it might also potentially create disorder. For sure, the religious leaders could not find anything immoral or illegal in Jesus' deeds. At this point, the best strategy the chief priests and the Pharisees had was to discredit him by showing his teachings to be erroneous. Thus, the Pharisees "laid plans to trap him in his words" (22:15). The Sadducees came to question Jesus as well. In this section, Matthew records three accounts wherein Jesus was asked difficult and controversial questions that were aimed at discrediting him. He silenced his interrogators by answering all the questions and by asking one that they could not answer.[1]

---

1. David Daube points out that these four incidents may not necessarily happened in sequence, but Matthew placed them together because these four questions represent four types of questions distinguished by the early Jewish rabbis. The Talmud reports about some Alexandrians who came to interrogate Rabbi Joshua ben Hananiah (late first or early second century) with four sets of three questions. The first set includes legal questions, the second historical, the third is plainly vulgar intended for ridicule, and the fourth concerns principles on moral and successful life. Each of the questions in Matthew's record correspond to these categories: question on legality of taxes paid to Caesar; historical question about the David's relation with

22:15–22 QUESTION #1: TAXES

The first question was asked by the Pharisees and it concerned the legality of paying taxes to Caesar. Matthew clearly states the reason they came to Jesus to ask this question, "to trap him in his words" (Matt 22:15). In this story, Jesus also sensed their "evil intent" (22:18). His entry to Jerusalem and the people's recognition of his kingship could easily be interpreted as inciting rebellion. The way to test his loyalty to their earthly rulers would be his view on paying taxes.

The Pharisees sent not only their disciples, but also some Herodians to question Jesus (22:16). They approached Jesus by addressing him as "Teacher," followed by the statement, "we know that you are a man of integrity and that you teach the way of God in accordance to the truth. You aren't swayed by others, because you pay no attention to who they are" (22:16). At first, this may sound like a compliment; but considering the whole story, it was more of flattery.[2] The statement may have been true about Jesus, but the intention was questionable (22:18).

Then they asked whether it was right to pay taxes to Caesar (22:17). This was a controversial question that various Jewish groups may have answered differently. An indefinite answer would raise questions about his authority as a teacher, but a definite answer, whether *Yes* or *No* would only invite critics from various political/religious groups. If Jesus said they should not pay taxes, some pious Jews would have disagreed with him on account of the OT teachings to obey the king (Prov 24:21; Ecc 8:2). Moreover, refusal to do so would be considered rebellion. The presence of the Herodians may also have been a tactic to force Jesus to say that they should pay taxes to Caesar, but if he did so, it would nullify his claims to be king because he was subjecting himself to Rome. It would potentially invite the Jewish revolutionaries, those who zealously eliminated Jews who showed loyalty to Rome, to plot Jesus' death and in the process help the religious leaders with their plan.[3]

---

the Messiah; the ridiculous question about woman with seven husbands; and the question concerning the greatest commandment relates to moral principles (*The New Testament and Rabbinic Judaism* [Salem, NH: Ayers Publishers, 1984], 158–160).

2. Ancient rhetoricians like Themistius (4th century AD) differentiate friendship from flattery and hypocrisy. Both flattery and hypocrisy are displayed as friendship (David Konstan, "Friendship, Frankness and Flattery," in *Friendship, Flattery, & Frankness of Speech: Studies on Friendship in the New Testament World*, ed. John T. Fitzgerald, NovTSup 82 [Leiden: Brill, 1996], 17). No wonder Jesus called the Pharisees in this story (Matt 22:18).

3. Josephus recounts how Judas the Galilean persuaded the Jews not to pay taxes to the Romans and how the sicarii treated those willing to pay taxes like enemies and how they plundered

Jesus knew that it was a trap (22:18), and so he asked for a coin used to pay these taxes and said, "Whose image is this? And whose inscription?" (22:19–20). Some modern coins still have the face of monarchs, like those used in Thailand or the United Kingdom. Ancient coins bearing the image of Caesar, like the modern counterparts, function as visual aids to remind the people of the emperor's earthly authority and the status of Rome as the "favored of the gods."[4] When the people responded to Jesus' question and acknowledged it was Caesar's image, Jesus replied, "So give back to Caesar what is Caesar's and to God what is God's" (22:21). Submission to human authorities is not inconsistent with submission to God. On the contrary, submitting to human government is considered submitting to God, who installs human rulers. Jesus taught what other Asian religious teachers would teach as well.[5] On the one hand, Jesus indirectly answered *Yes* to their question, because in order to give to Caesar what belongs to him, they had to pay their taxes. Therefore, no one could accuse him of inciting rebellion. On the other hand, Jesus' reply ought to have pacified those whose zeal led them to rebellion because Jesus proclaimed that there were those that belonged to God, and these should be given to him. Acknowledging the authority of earthly rulers is *not necessarily* equivalent to defiance against God's authority. Submission to divine authority requires submission to human authorities, and even human rulers are all under God's rule, whether they acknowledge it or not.

---

their properties (*Jewish Wars* 7.8.1 §§ 117–118; *Jewish Antiquities* 20.5.2 § 102).
4. Carter, *Matthew and the Margins*, 440.
5. Derrett, *Law in the New Testament*, 336, n. 2.

CHURCH AND CAESAR

Jesus clearly recognizes that there are two separate realms – God's and Caesar's – each with its own roles, though God is Lord and sovereign over all. So, Christians will obey the laws of the land and pay taxes which are due, but will worship only Yahweh. This theme of two realms can be seen in the OT when Daniel was willing to work in King Nebuchadnezzar's palace but he would not bow down to the statue that the king had made.

Christians have dual citizenship: they are citizens both of an earthly nation, their passport country, as well as of the kingdom of God. These two roles demand different responsibilities. As far as possible Christians will obey the laws of the land, carrying out their duties which may include conscription in the army. As citizens of God's kingdom, Christians will only worship God and not Caesar.

There are many ways in which Christians and the church can live in peace in their lands. Bearing in mind the cost of discipleship mentioned above, Christians are to be salt and light in their communities. In places where Christianity is a legally recognized religion, being a Christian could include standing up against injustice and exploitation of the marginalized. In parts of India and Sri Lanka, Christians are those who provide care for the poor. But in societies where it is illegal to be a Christian, or those which are openly antagonistic to the Christian faith, standing up for Christian values and principles as well as the opportunity to worship God is more challenging. In parts of communist China, Christians chose to disobey some of the laws prohibiting mass assembly in order to continue their meeting. Both contexts require wisdom and courage to live out.

Being an individual Christian or a cell group is different from being a church. The corporate body of Christians, the church, also needs to negotiate her relationship with the state. Here in Asia, church-state relationships are different from that in the West as there is no history of Christendom; and the church is generally a small minority and in a position of weakness. Asian Christians need to dig deep into Scripture to find ways of living out the scriptural commands to render to Caesar what belongs to him.

While in Singapore and South Korea there is freedom of religion to believe and to form churches and build church buildings, the church is not a legally recognized body in all parts of Asia. In China and Vietnam, there are official churches which are sanctioned and controlled by the government, and underground house churches which do not have legal recognition. Believers in both these bodies need wisdom to negotiate the path between allegiance to Caesar and to God. Malaysia and Indonesia are Muslim-majority countries with complex histories of church-state relations and to this day dealing with state can be difficult because of the arbitrariness of relevant regulations. The situation in the vast subcontinent of India is also complex as the body of believers interacts with state as well as national authorities. That complexity is compounded because many Christians are from the Dalit or lower castes and so are given little, if any, recognition.

The later parts of the NT give us guidance as to how the church can and should relate with secular authorities. The apostles Paul and Peter in their letters exhort Christians to submit to the governing authorities since they have been established by God (Rom 13; 1 Pet 2:13–17). Peter goes further in telling his readers that though they are strangers in the world (1:1) they are to do "good you should silence the ignorant talk of foolish people. Live as free people, but do not use your freedom as a cover-up for evil; live as God's slaves. Show proper respect to everyone, love the family of believers, fear God, honor the emperor" (2:15–17). This is a clear call for Christians and the church to be involved in society, and not to stay within the walls of the church.

To be salt and light in society means that Christians must be engaged in the community. That engagement could be formal as in the way in the Catholic Church in the Philippines has spoken out against the injustices of the government. In Singapore, the Presbyterian Community Services provides meals to elderly people living alone. In more informal ways, the church can organize activities such as a picnic or fun time for the neighborhood. Not only do such activities provide an opportunity for the surrounding community to bond together, non-Christians can see Christians and the church in action. In these ways, non-Christians can see that Christians are interested in life and the whole person.

Therefore, though Caesar and the Church are two different realms, God is Lord and sovereign over both these realms. The Asian church can certainly do more to engage in the wider society, in contextually appropriate ways and so live under that lordship in everyday contexts.

Kiem-Kiok Kwa

22:23–33 QUESTION #2: RESURRECTION AND LEVIRATE MARRIAGE

The Sadducees approached Jesus with second question on "that same day" (Matt 22:23). In Jesus' parable of the wicked tenants (21:33–46), the wicked tenants represent the chief priests (including the Sadducees who belonged to the priestly clans) and the Pharisees, and both groups knew that Jesus was talking about them (21:45).

The Sadducees may have considered Jesus' silencing of the Pharisees an advantage for them, so they came to Jesus and asked him a somewhat ridiculous question about the resurrection, a question they may have successfully used against the Pharisees prior to this encounter with Jesus. The Sadducees did not believe in the resurrection (Acts 23:8); and they were known to be tactless in speech even towards each other.[6]

They asked Jesus a hypothetical question about a woman who married a man who died without having a son. The man's brother married the woman, but he also died before having a son. The same went for their younger brothers, until seven brothers died without bearing a son, and eventually the woman died. They then asked Jesus whose wife the woman would be in the resurrection (22:24–28). This story is clearly fictitious,[7] but obviously intended, like the Pharisees' question about taxes, to discredit Jesus. If Jesus chose one or more among the seven brothers as the woman's legitimate husband or husbands, his answer would raise more complicated problems concerning the Law.

The Sadducees appealed to the provision in the Law that requires a younger brother to marry his sister-in-law if his brother died without having a son (Deut 25:5–10; Matt 22:24). The first son that they bore would be considered the son of the deceased brother, and this was done in order that the deceased would also have descendants to carry on his name. This practice was called the "levirate marriage." This was one of the cultural practices of ancient Middle Eastern people that was accommodated into the Law.[8] The exact origin of this practice remains unknown, but prior to the giving of the Law, there are stories that show that this is already being practiced (Gen 38:8–11); it continued even during the time of Ruth (Ruth 1:11–13), and apparently until the time of Jesus. Some Jewish rabbis considered it a form of incest, and therefore did not agree with its practice.

Instead of focusing on the petty details of the Sadducees' question, Jesus exposes their ignorance behind their mockery. Thus, he said, "You are in error because you do not know the Scriptures or the power of God" (Matt

---

6. Josephus, *Jewish Wars* 2.8.14 §165.
7. The Sadducees' story may have been based on the story of Sarah, Tobit's daughter-in-law, who had been married to seven husbands prior to marrying Tobias, Tobit's son. In this story, Sarah's seven husband were killed by demons, but the people accused the woman of killing her husbands. She prayed to God to end her life, but the Lord took her disgrace away through her marriage to Tobias (Tobit 3:8–17).
8. Dale W. Manor, "A Brief History of Levirate Marriage as It Relates to the Bible," *ResQ* 27, no. 3 (1984): 129.

22:29). The problem is not with the provision in the Law, nor in its application, but the Sadducees' lack of understanding of the Law and their lack of faith in God.

The resurrection is a symbol of the restoration of Israel as a nation (Ezek 37), but it is also related to the belief that life continues even beyond the grave.[9] Jesus' reply to the Sadducees provides a glimpse of what the resurrection looks like, namely, some of the typical practices of humans do on earth like marriage will discontinue (22:30–31). More importantly, Jesus provides the basis for believing in the resurrection, namely, God is "not the God of the dead but of the living" (Matt 22:32).[10] Once again, Jesus silenced those who wanted to trap him, and instead of discrediting him before the crowd, the crowd was even more astonished at his teaching (22:33).

22:34–40 QUESTION #3: THE GREATEST COMMANDMENT

Jesus had silenced his interrogators twice: (1) the Pharisees who questioned the legality of paying taxes to pagan rulers, and (2) the Sadducees who tried mockery when asking about the resurrection. When the Pharisees saw how Jesus turned the Sadducees' ridicule against them, they gathered together once again to look for other ways to discredit Jesus, but this time, an expert of the Law from among them represented the group in order to test Jesus (Matt 22:34–35). The lawyer asked Jesus what was the greatest commandment in the Law (22:36). Like a building structure that requires a foundation, there is an essential principle upon which all moral and ethical teachings are built. The lawyer was asking about this basic and foundational principle.

Jesus' replied by quoting Deuteronomy 6:5 and Leviticus 19:18 (Matt 22:37–39), saying that "All the Law and the Prophets hang on these two commandments" (22:40). Interestingly, the lawyer asked for only one commandment, but Jesus cited two commandments. Jesus was not the first to combine these two great commandments. These two commands are inseparable, and every pious Jew during Jesus' time would have known them.

Jesus said that the greatest commandment is to "Love the Lord your God with all your heart and with all your soul and with all your mind" (22:37–38).

---

9. Ancient Jewish rabbis have used several OT texts to prove the resurrection. For examples, see Dan Cohn-Sherbock, "Jesus' Defense of the Resurrection of the Dead," *JSNT* 11 (1981): 70–71.

10. It is the belief in the resurrection that empowers the martyrs like Eleazar the priests to suffer persecution in this life (4 Maccabees 13:17).

The passage quoted by Jesus in Deuteronomy 6 included God's command to the Israelites to teach the Law to their children (Deut 6:1–2), requiring them total obedience when they were already living in the Promised Land (6:3–4), to remember the Law (6:6–9), not to forget the LORD in the midst of their blessings (6:10–12), not to follow other gods (6:13–19), and remember their slavery in Egypt (6:20–25). Loving the LORD, for the ancient Israelites, meant a total devotion to God alone (heart), living with absolute obedience (soul), doing everything that God requires (strength), and remembering what he did and passing these to the next generation (mind).

Jesus also said that the second greatest is like the first, "Love your neighbor as yourself" (22:39). This command is echoed by other writers of the NT (Rom 13:8–10; Gal 5:14; Jas 2:8). Paul says that this command could be applied by doing "no harm to a neighbor" (Rom 13:10). Leviticus 19, from where Jesus quoted (Lev 19:18), also provides multiple example on how this command can be expressed. Aside from keeping the last six of the Ten Commandments (19:3, 11–13), loving one's neighbor may also mean not harvesting everything so as to leave a portion of the harvest for the poor and foreigners (19:9–10), paying workers their rightful due (19:13a), not cursing and slandering others especially people with disabilities (19:14, 16a), not showing partiality to the rich or to the poor (19:15), not endangering other person's life (19:16b), frankly rebuking those who do wrong (19:17), and not seeking revenge (19:18). The application of this command, for sure, is not limited to these.

This story may seem out of place in the series of interrogations, but it clearly shows that Jesus was not only able to silence those who tried to discredit him using controversial and ridiculous questions, but he was able to answer essential moral and ethical teachings concerning the Law. The point of these stories is that none of the religious leaders, whether Pharisees or Sadducees, was able to "trap him in his words" (Matt 22:15).

22:41–46 QUESTION #4: THE MESSIAH AS SON OF DAVID

After answering the three questions of his interrogators, Jesus turned to the Pharisees and asked them whose son the Messiah was to which they replied, the Son of David (22:41–42). The Jews expected a Messiah who would rule on God's behalf, and for the Jews, this would happen only after the nation was liberated from the foreign rule. When Jesus entered Jerusalem, he was welcomed as the "Son of David" (Matt 21:9, 15), and the religious leaders may have been expecting him to initiate a revolution. So, it is no wonder they had him watched closely. Their question about paying taxes suggests that they were expecting him to show an anti-Roman sentiment (22:15–22).

The title "Son of David" is associated with Jesus' healing ministry (see comments for Matthew 9:27–31), but it is also a reference to him as a political figure, a descendant of David who would rule in his place. Jesus then asked the Pharisees why David, who was speaking under the inspiration of the Spirit, calls the Messiah "Lord," quoting Psalm 110:1 (Matt 22:43–44). Psalm 110 talks about the enthronement of the king (110:1). God promised him security in his rule (110:2), power to defeat his enemies (110:2–3), and even the ministry of priesthood (110:4).[11] Moreover, God promised that by his power, he would crush their enemies (110:5–7). Jesus' question may be interpreted as his attempt to show that the "Son of David" was not a political figure who would lead an uprising against their Roman colonizers, and that there was no such plan. As the Messiah, he was not just one of the descendants of David, he was greater than David. The real answer to Jesus' question "Whose son is the Messiah?" is not "David," because the Messiah was the "Son of God."[12] After the conversation, no one dared to ask Jesus further questions (Matt 22:46).

The parable of the wicked tenants is a turning point in the Gospel of Matthew. The chief priests and the Pharisees understood that Jesus was referring to them in this parable (Matt 21:45). So they attempted to trap him by asking difficult questions hoping he would say something that would discredit him, but all these attempts failed. Finally, Jesus asked them a question that they could not answer, and it stopped the religious leaders from asking any more questions.

---

11. The significance of this promise of priesthood is to show that just as Melchizedek was the channel of blessing to Abraham (Gen 14:18–20), the Messiah would also be a channel of blessings to the descendants of Abraham (Ps 110:4). Robin L. Routledge, "Psalm 110, Melchizedek and David: Blessing (the Descendants of) Abraham," *Baptistic Theologies* 1, no. 2 (2009): 15.
12. Jack D. Kingsbury, "Title 'Son of David' in Matthew's Gospel," *JBL* 95, no. 4 (1976): 593.

MATTHEW 23:1–25:46

Jesus Pronounces Judgments against the Pharisees and Jerusalem

In the previous chapters, Matthew includes several stories illustrating the unbelief of the Jews in Galilee and Jerusalem, and especially the religious leaders. Jesus' claim as the Messiah/king climaxed with his entry to Jerusalem and was met with strong opposition. By this time, the religious leaders were already planning to kill him. The judgments Jesus would pronounce in the next three chapters against the Pharisees and against Jerusalem should be understood as the consequence of their defiance against God, which is expressed in their rejection of him, the Christ, and resulting in his death. Aside from their rejection of Jesus, the judgment against the Pharisees had also to do with their character and ill practices.

23:1–39 JESUS PRONOUNCES JUDGMENT AGAINST THE PHARISEES

There are at least three sayings attributed to Confucius that show similarities between his expectations of a teacher and that of Jesus.[1]

> *The gentleman makes demands on himself; the inferior man makes demands on others.* (Confucian Analects XV:20)
>
> *The gentleman seeks to enable people to succeed in what is good but does not help them in what is evil. The inferior man does the contrary.* (Confucian Analects XII:16)
>
> *When it comes to acquiring perfect virtue, a man should not defer even to his own teacher.* (Confucian Analects XV:35)

After Jesus' debate with the religious teachers in Jerusalem, and having silenced them, Jesus addressed the crowd and his disciples (Matt 23:1), exposing the hypocrisy of the Pharisees and pronouncing judgments against them.

---

1. Based on De Bary, *Sources of Chinese Tradition* (1st), 1:23, 31.

23:1–10 Jesus Addresses the Hypocrisy of the Pharisees

In history, there are numerous examples of a religious group, which comes out of a parent group, and then seek to expose the errors in teachings and/or the moral and ethical flaws of the parent group. Some of these disclosures may be exaggerated and incorrect stereotyping, but some are accurate representations of the other group. When Matthew was writing this Gospel, the distinction between Christianity and Judaism was becoming clearer, and one cannot deny that the worsening relationship between the two groups is one of the reasons Matthew included the story of Jesus' condemnation of the Jewish teachers which happened decades earlier.

Jesus addressed his disciples (those who were already following him) and the crowd (those who might potentially follow him), and not the religious leaders (those who had already rejected him) (Matt 23:1). He acknowledged that the scribes (or the teachers of the Law) and Pharisees "sit in Moses' seat" (23:2). Some interpreters suggest that "Moses' seat" refers to an actual piece of furniture where teachers of the Law would seat while they taught, while some take it metaphorically to refer to the authority or the social position of the Pharisees as those who taught the Law.[2] Either way, the authority of the Pharisees as teachers of the Law is acknowledged. The difficulty is that earlier, Jesus warned the disciples against the teachings of the Pharisees and Sadducees (see discussion on Matthew 16:6). What we see in this Gospel is that there is neither wholesale rejection of the religious leaders, nor a wholesale recommendation of them; this is the quality of objective criticism.

Jesus told his disciples and the crowd to do what the Pharisees taught them to do, but not to follow their examples (23:3). Those who teach are usually the ones from whom much is expected (Jas 3:1), and in ancient times, teachers who do not live according to their teachings are the ones hit the most by criticisms.[3] It is clear that Jesus was not against the moral teachings of the Pharisees, as he encouraged the people to "do everything" that they were told (Matt 23:3). It is the conduct of the Pharisees that was not worth imitating. He explained that the Pharisees required some things from their students that they themselves were not doing (23:4). The illustration Jesus

---

2. Noel S. Rabbinowitz, "Matthew 23:2–4: Does Jesus Recognize the Authority of the Pharisees and Does He Endorse Their Halakhah?" *JETS* 46, no. 3 (2003): 424, nn. 6–10.
3. Seneca calls teachers to practice what they teach (*Moral Essays* 20.2) Epictetus who castigates teachers who are not living according to what they teach (*Discourses* 2.9.17). See also Steve Mason, "Pharisaic Dominance Before 70 CE and the Gospels' Hypocrisy Charge (Matt 23:2–3)," *HTR* 83, no. 4 (1990): 380.

used is that of a heavy object that needs to be moved which the Pharisees tied to the back of their students, but were unwilling to help them move it. Objects carried on a person's back or shoulder is usually those that are too heavy to be carried using only the arms or hands, let alone one's finger. There is a sharp contrast between those carrying heavy loads on their back and those who are not even willing to lift a finger.

Ancient teachers from other parts of Asia also understood the importance of setting an example through the teachers' way of life. Confucius admits that even teachers have their flaws and students cannot look to them as examples of perfection (see Confucian Analects XV:35 above). This is what sets Jesus apart, for he dares to say, "learn from me" (Matt 11:29); his authority to say this is also affirmed by Paul who says, "Follow my example, as I follow the example of Christ" (1 Cor 11:1; see also 4:16; Phil 3:17; 1 Thess 1:6; 2:14; 2 Thess 3:7–9). Confucius also defines a gentleman as one who makes demands on himself and not on others (see Confucian Analects XV:20); or to rephrase this, he is one who would not demand from others what he had not first demanded from himself. This is the point of Jesus' criticism.

Aside from their demands on others, the Pharisees were accused of doing religious acts in order to show off, "Everything they do is done for people to see" (Matt 23:5). In Jesus' Sermon (Matt 5–7), he contrasted actions done to gain God's approval and those done to gain honor before humans. Jesus brought up the same topic again here, and mentioned several examples on how the Pharisees do things for the purpose of receiving honor from humans.

First, through the use of wide phylacteries and tassels on their garments (23:5). The phylactery (sometimes called the *tefillin*) is a small leather box containing passages from the Law worn by pious Jews on their forehead.[4] This practice is based on God's command to Israel that they should have a visual reminder of God's commands, "a sign on your hand and a reminder on your forehead" (Exod 13:9). These are visual reminders, like the passages written on doorposts (Deut 6:9; 11:20), or in modern time wall decors, bookmarks, or desktop backgrounds with Bible verses, so that the believer will not forget

---

4. There are hints that as early as the 2nd century BC, the Jews were already using the phylactery (*Letter of Aristeas* §159), although the origin of such practice remains unknown. The way it is used also vary even among the various Jewish religious groups. For example, according to the Mishnah (*Menahot* 3:7; *Kelim* 18:8; *Sanhedrin* 11:3 *Sifre* on Deuteronomy §35), only four OT passages (Exod 13:1–10; 13:11–16; Deut 6:4–9; 11:13–21) should be placed inside the box. However, in the Qumran, more passages are included (Géza Vermès, "Pre-Mishnaic Jewish Worship and the Phylacteries from the Dead Sea," *VT* 9, no. 1 [1959]: 67). Later Christian writers also affirm such practice (Justin, *Dialogue with Trypho* 46.5).

the teachings from the Scripture. The use of tassels was also based on God's instruction (Num 15:37–41). The use of visual reminders was not the problem because they could be used to acknowledge God's kingship.[5] The purpose why the Pharisees used them was the problem, because they used them, not only to remember God's teachings, but mainly to look pious.

Second, they sought places and titles of honor in order to exalt themselves (23:6–7). Jesus cited a couple of examples wherein this is evident, the banquets and the synagogue (23:6). The words translated as "place of honor" at banquets and "most important seat" in the synagogues are *prōtoklisia* and *prōtokathedras*, respectively. The words are synonyms and can both be translated "first seat." This suggests that even among themselves, they were debating who was entitled to take the most important seat, like James and John (20:24–28). Jesus' message of humility and servanthood is also emphasized here, that the greatest is the one who serves (23:11).

Aside from places of honor like the "first seat," they also sought titles of honor like "Rabbi." Whether it is a formal title used during the time of Jesus, his point remains clear, seeking honor for the sake of having honor and exalting oneself is not what he wants his followers to desire. He was not against one person honoring another. People called him "Teacher" at times. In the OT, prophets are addressed as "father" as well (2 Kgs 2:12; 6:21; 13:14). Calling teachers "teacher" and treating them as if they are our own fathers is not the issue (Matt 23:8–10). Showing respect is a virtue that Asians value even until now, and such practice is consistent with the teachings of the Bible. Jesus, however, was addressing a situation wherein people place excessive value on honor rather than service. Some serve without receiving any honor, while other serve receiving the honor due them, but still others desired honor even without serving. Hence, Jesus stressed, "The greatest among you will be your servant" (23:11). At the core of this willingness to serve is the attitude of humility (23:12), which Jesus wanted all his followers to have.

23:13–39 Jesus Pronounces Eight Woes against the Scribes and the Pharisees

The earlier comments Jesus made about the Pharisees and teachers of the Law were clearly addressed "to the crowds and to his disciples" (Matt 23:1), and so he would refer to the religious teachers as "they" or "them" (23:1–7). Beginning from Matthew 23:8 there is a change from "they/them" to "you,"

---

5. Haskel Lookstein, "Tefillin and God's Kingship," *Tradition* 4, no. 1 (1961): 72.

which may be interpreted as Jesus directly instructing the crowd and the disciples based on what can be seen in the lives of the religious teachers. But from 23:13 onwards, "you" refers to the Pharisees and teachers of the Law, as if Jesus is addressing them directly even though he was not talking with them. In the same way Jesus pronounced eight words of blessings to the disciples (5:3–12), he pronounced eight woes against the scribes and Pharisees. The eight woes Jesus pronounced concern the hindrances the religious leaders make to prevent people from joining Jesus (woes 1–3 in 23:13–15), their interpretation and practice of the Law (woes 4–5), and their concern for appearance and involvement in the death of the prophets (woes 6–8).[6]

First, Jesus addressed the hindrances placed by the religious leaders to prevent people from coming to him in the first three woes (23:13–15). His description about the Pharisees' diligence in traveling "land and sea" to find new trainees provides a glimpse of how their group continued to grow (23:14). This commendation only highlights their shortcomings. This is like saying, "Such-and-such is good, but (negative comment)." Praises can sometimes be used to highlight the criticism.[7] Despite their diligence, their efforts only show their hypocrisy because instead of pointing their converts to the right way, they hinder them from seeing the right way (23:13), making their converts "twice as much a child of hell" as they are (23:15).[8] For as the students see their teachers saying one thing and doing something else, they not only follow their bad examples, they may do even worse.

Second, Jesus addressed the Pharisees' interpretation and practice of the Law (woes 4–5), particularly the issues relating to oaths, tithing, and purity (23:16–24). In Jesus' Sermon, he focuses on one's intention expressed in oaths (5:33–37), concluding that oaths are really unnecessary. Here, the focus is not on the one swearing, but on the one approving what was sworn. Jesus' comments do not only show the wrong priorities of the teachers of the Law (for example, the gold of the temple considered more important than

---

6. Seven woes in this section begin with the expression, "Woe to you, teachers of the law and Pharisees, you hypocrites!" Some earlier manuscripts do not have Matthew 23:14; if this verse is to be included, it counts as the second woe. We have a total of eight woes if we consider Matthew 23:16–22 as a separate pronouncement even though it opens with another expression, "Woe to you, blind guides!"
7. Praising one's merit can at times be used for criticism (Quintilian, *Institutes of Oratory* 8.6.54–55). Andrew R. Simmonds, "'Woe to You . . . Hypocrites!': Re-reading Matthew 23:13–36," *BSac* 166 (2009): 336–337.
8. A similar expression is found in the Babylonian Talmud wherein the rabbis discuss about sages whose "inside" is not the same as the "outside," according to one teacher, they are those who "inherit a double Gehinnom" (*Yoma* 72b).

the temple, the gift on the altar than the altar; 23:16–21), but it also provides a glimpse of the social problems they encounter. This is something Luke also made clear when he talked about the teachers of the Law who "devour widows' houses," instead of helping the widows who are in need. Even the little that they have was given as offerings and they do so without receiving any honor from the religious sector because of the little they gave (Luke 20:47–21:4). Aside from the gifts and offerings pledged, Jesus also addressed issues relating to tithes. Although there was no clear system of tithing even during the time of Jesus,[9] the principle of giving a portion of one's goods as "tithe" was clearly practiced. Jesus was not challenging this practice and suggesting that it was unimportant and unnecessary. He pointed out, however, that there are "more important matters of the law" such as justice, mercy, and faithfulness that should not be neglected as one brings their offerings (23:23). The exaggerated statement, "You strain a gnat but swallow a camel" (23:24), shows an image of a person who makes sure that their food does not contain little insects, but is actually eating something much bigger, and is not even aware of doing so. The Pharisees had focused on things that are trivial, such as making sure one tithes, but neglected the bigger and heavier social issues.

Third, Jesus addressed their Pharisees tendency to be more concerned about their appearances rather than a heart transformation (woes 6–8), and he likened them to cups and tombs that are clean only on the outside (23:25–28). This concern for right appearance was seen particularly in their honoring of the dead prophets (23:29–32), but rejecting the one in their midst. Jesus used their own words to show the responsibility they shared with those who killed the prophets in the past (23:30), showing that they are "descendants of those who murdered the prophets" (23:31). Sins are not only done by individuals, there are those that are considered sins of a nation or people group. The Jews would view sin as a shared responsibility. For instance, in Daniel's confession, he asked God for forgiveness saying, "we have sinned" (Dan 9:5; see 9:4–19), when clearly, he was not one of those who practiced idolatry from the previous generations.[10] In Jesus' condemnation of the Pharisees, he also pointed out the responsibility the Pharisees shared with those who killed the prophets in the previous generation. In fact, their

---

9. Even during the time of Jesus, there is no clear system of tithing. See Andreas J. Köstenberger and David A. Croteau, "'Will a Man Rob God?' (Malachi 3:8): A Study of Tithing in the Old and New Testaments," *BBR* 16, no. 1 (2006): 53–77.

10. Susan M. Rieske, "What Is the Meaning of 'This Generation' in Matthew 23:36?" *BSac* 165 (2008): 222.

responsibility is greater for building monuments for the prophets while plotting to kill Jesus.[11] Their participation in killing the prophets brought God's judgment, not only for them (23:33–36), but also for Jerusalem whom God had been wanting to protect (23:37–39), but because of their rejection of Jesus, destruction was about to come, referring to the destruction of the city and the temple in AD 70 (see also 1 Kgs 9:8).

24:1–41 JESUS PRONOUNCES JUDGMENT AGAINST THE JERUSALEM AND PROPHESIES HIS COMING

The "woes" in the previous chapter were pronounced against the Jewish religious leaders, but there is no doubt the section also serves as a warning for the disciples, and the Christian community in general, against hypocrisy.[12] The next two chapters (Matt 24–25) must be seen as a continuation of Jesus' pronouncement of judgment against those who rejected him as Messiah. In Matthew 21, Jesus entered Jerusalem as king. There were people in the crowd who acknowledged his kingship (21:9, 15), but many rejected him. His authority was questioned by the religious leaders (21:23–27). The tension escalated as they plotted to kill him (21:46), sending delegates to find something wrong with his teachings which would, at the very least, discredit him as a teacher, or be used as a basis for executing him (22:15–46). Jesus then pronounced judgment against those who planned to kill him by exposing their hypocrisy (23:1–39), followed by this section on Jesus' judgment against the city that rejected him.

24:1–28 Jesus Prophesies about the Destruction of Jerusalem

The people's continuous rejection of God's messengers is the clearest evidence of their rejection of him. Jesus repeatedly mentioned this (5:12); this is also implied in his parables (Matt 21:33–39; 22:5–6). In the same way that the religious leaders were participants in the sins of the previous generation who killed the prophets (23:29–36), those who refused to believe were also in solidarity with them. Although Jesus desired to protect his people as a hen would her chicks because of their obstinacy, he could not protect them (23:37–39). This discussion of judgment against Jerusalem continues as Jesus and his disciples left the temple. The disciples were still marveling at the temple structure when Jesus prophesied about its destruction (24:1–2).

---

11. Hans Scharen, "Gehenna in the Synoptics (Part 2)," *BSac* 149 (1992): 466.
12. Frankemölle, *Matthäus*, 2:366–371.

Matthew

During this period, Jesus and his disciples had been traveling back and forth between Bethany and Jerusalem (21:17–18; 26:55; see also Luke 19:47; 21:37; 22:53). While they were at the Mount of Olives (near Bethany), the disciples asked him two questions concerning two events: (1) when will the destruction of the temple happen; and (2) what would be the sign of his coming and the end of the age (Matt 24:3). The expression "the end of the age" (*sunteleias tou aiōnos*) used by the disciples is the same expression Jesus used in his explanation of the parables of the weeds (13:39–40) and the dragnet (13:49), and in his commission to his disciples to preach the gospel (28:20). Jesus' reply in Matthew's account distinguishes between the destruction of the temple and the "end of the age."

Jesus mentioned three things in relation to the destruction of the temple. First, he mentioned the events that would occur prior to AD 70. False messiahs would appear (24:4–5), and there would be wars and rumors of wars (24:6–7). Prior to the destruction of the temple, wars (both among the various Jewish factions and against the Romans) were led by those who claimed to be the liberators of the Jewish people. Josephus reports that there were three Jewish factions that fought against Rome (and against each other). Each was led by influential individuals that seemingly fit the Jews' expectation of a Messiah (political/revolutionary leader), including Menahem son of Judas the Galilean, John of Gischala, and Simon son of Gioras.[13] However, Jesus said that these false messiahs are those who "will come in my name" and "deceive many" (24:4–5), someone similar to Simon Magus (Acts 8:10) who worked among the believers. Moreover, Jesus mentioned about natural disasters like earthquakes and famine that would occur in various places, many of which were recalled by some ancient writers.[14] These events are too common for us to find specific fulfillment in them of Jesus' prophecy. In Jesus' words, "All these are the beginnings of birth pangs" (24:8). Like a woman in labor, the birth pains signal that the baby will be born soon but the exact time is unknown, therefore, the need to be ready.

Second, Jesus warned the disciples about the coming persecution, and how some of them will grow cold, but Jesus also described the work that they would be doing. He informed them how some of the disciples would be persecuted and others put to death (24:9). Luke describes the kind of

---

13. Josephus recounts the revolt led by Menahem (*Jewish Wars* 2.17.8 §§ 433–56), John (2.21.1–10 §§ 585–646), and Simon (2.22.1–2 §§ 647–654).
14. Acts 16:26. Also Tacitus, *Annals* 12.58.3; 14.27.1; Seneca, *Natural Questions* 6; Pliny, *Natural History* 2.84.86.

persecution the believers went through (Acts 8:1b–3), and how some of them like Stephen (7:54–8:1a) and James (12:1–2) were executed because of the faith they proclaimed. Jesus also told them that many believers would grow cold and turn away from the faith (Matt 24:10–12), something that describes some of Paul's co-workers (2 Tim 4:10) and some of the believers known to John (1 John 2:19). Jesus also warned them against false prophets who would deceive many (Matt 24:11), about which Paul also warned Timothy (1 Tim 4:1), and something which the church continued to see even after the temple was destroyed (2 Pet 2:1–3; 2 John 7–11). Despite the persecution of the true believers and the prosperity of the false teachers, the preaching of the Gospel would continue before the temple's destruction.

Third, Jesus described the circumstances surrounding the destruction of the temple. Jesus mentioned the "abomination that causes desolation" (Dan 9:27; 11:31; 12:11), which is a reference to the altar of Zeus that Antiochus Epiphanes erected on the sacrificial altar in the temple, and was later torn down by zealous Jews.[15] In Matthew's account, Jesus used the language of Daniel to refer to a comparable event that happened at a later time, namely, the desecration of the temple. Luke explains this desolation in connection with the armies surrounding Jerusalem (Luke 21:20). Josephus reports how Emperor Vespasian and the army commander Titus, the emperor's successor, led the Roman troops to Jerusalem and defeated the Jewish fighters trapped inside the temple. The Romans entered, looted, and burned down God's temple. Jesus expressed the urgent need to flee Jerusalem, telling the Jews to go to the mountains[16] and not to go back to their houses to get anything (Matt 24:16–18). He also described the extent of horror that Jerusalem would experience that having to flee while pregnant or nursing, or during winter or Sabbath would make the flight even more difficult (24:19–20); then he concluded, "For then there will be great distress, unequaled from the beginning of the world until now – and never to be equaled again" (24:21). The situation would be very difficult, as Jesus said, and if the days were not cut short, there would be no survivors (24:22). Once again, Jesus warned them against those who claimed to be messiah, especially those who seemingly replicated his miraculous works (24:23–26).

---

15. See 1 Maccabees 1:54; 6:7.
16. The mountain is a typical first place of refuge of people escaping from disaster, regardless of their final destination (Gen 19:17; 1 Maccabees 2:28; 2 Maccabees 5:27; 10:6; Josephus, *Jewish Wars* 2.18.9 §504). Luz, *Matthew 21–28*, 196.

At this point, Jesus began to transition from the temple to his second coming, which he said would be "visible" (24:27), in contrast to those who say that he is "in the inner room" (24:26). Before leaving the discussion about the temple's destruction, Jesus made a final comment, "Wherever there is a carcass, there the vultures will gather" (24:28). The word translated "vulture" is *aetos*, which can also be translated "eagle." Although there are instances wherein the two birds are confused in ancient writings, ancient writers distinguished between the two.[17] The eagle is the symbol for Rome.[18] Hence, one cannot avoid interpreting this passage in connection with the temple's destruction. Josephus recounts the day when Vespasian entered the temple while it was being burned by the soldiers and he found the corpses of the Jewish fighters heaped near the altar.[19]

---

17. For examples, see Gertraud Harb, "The Meaning of Q 17,37: Problems, Opinions and Perspectives," *ZNW* 102, no. 2 (2011): 283–286.
18. It is considered the holy animal of Mars and Jupiter (Pliny, *Natural History* 10.4), used in ancient Roman banner (Josephus, *Jewish Wars* 3.6.2 §123), and symbolizes Rome (4 Ezra 12:11, 22–27) and Roman soldiers (Babylonian Talmud, *Sanhedrin* 12a). Michael Peppard, "The Eagle and the Dove: Roman Imperial Sonship and the Baptism of Jesus (Mark 1.9-11)," *NTS* 56 (2010): 447.
19. Josephus, *Jewish Wars* 6.4.6 §259.

EVANGELISM AS A MEANS TO HASTEN CHRIST'S RETURN

Many Christians would cite Matthew 24:14 to encourage other believers to be involved in the work of evangelism because, as they argue, the passage says all nations must hear the gospel first before the end comes. In addition, they would cite 2 Peter 3:11–12 which mentions the hastening of the coming of "the day of God." Arthur Tappan Pierson (1837–1911) and Albert Benjamin Simpson (1843–1919) are two of the most influential missionaries in the nineteenth century who made this view popular, and this is something we continue to hear even today.[1] This raises the question whether the two passages cited above really say that evangelism can hasten the return of Christ. The unspoken assumption of this view is that the timing of Christ's return is dependent on the Church's diligence in its evangelistic efforts. Thus, the Church has, to some degree, control as to when Jesus should return. The consequence is that human salvation becomes secondary reason for evangelism, and speeding up Christ's return becomes the primary motivation.

First, we need to consider the passage from 2 Peter 3:12, "as you look forward to the day of God and speed up its coming." Second Peter 3 warns about the scoffers who mock believers because of the seeming delay of Jesus' coming, and with the way they live they show that they have disregarded Jesus' promise that he will come back (3:3). The author explains that this delay is not because God is slow in keeping his promise, but because he is giving non-believers additional time to change their minds (3:9). The delay in Jesus' return is evidence of his mercy for non-believers, but this inevitably prolongs the time of suffering for believers, so they are comforted with the fact that the Lord will come soon (3:10), and because judgment will also come definitely, they ought to live holy and godly lives (3:11), as they "look forward to the day of God and speed its coming" (3:12). In other words, the delay is evidence of God's mercy for the non-believers; and the hastening is evidence of God's mercy towards believers in order not to prolong their sufferings. Godliness, and not evangelism, is the means to achieve this.

Second, Matthew 24:14 is about the destruction of the temple, not the Second Coming of Jesus. The expression "gospel of the kingdom" (Matt 4:23; 9:35; 24:14) recalls the "good news" Isaiah pronounced in the midst of Babylon's threat to conquer Jerusalem, "Go on up to a high mountain, O Zion, herald of good news; lift up your voice with strength, O Jerusalem, herald of good news; lift it up, fear not; say to the cities of Judah, 'Behold your God!' Behold, the Lord God comes with might, and his arm rules for him; behold, his reward is with him, and his recompense before him" (Isa 40:9–10). The good news or the "gospel" is that God remains king despite the fact that the enemies of the Jews were threatening to rule over them.

Moreover, the expression "the whole world" (Greek, *oikoumenē*) is typically used to refer to the Roman territories (Luke 2:1). Jesus warns his disciples that this proclamation would happen amidst Christian persecution (Matt 24:9–13), something we see fulfilled in the early church (Acts 8:1, 4). When referring to the "end of the age," Matthew uses the word *hē sunteleia* or "end" (Matt 13:49–40, 49; 24:3; 28:20). Although *to telos* (the word used in Matt 24:13–14), which can also be translated "end," is also used in the expression "end of the age" (1 Cor 10:11), the verses that follow Matthew 24:14 requires us to understand *to telos* as a reference to the "end," not of human history, but of the temple's existence. The destruction of the temple is an assertion of Rome's absolute authority over Jerusalem. Jesus is essentially saying that even before that happens, the persecuted disciples are going to proclaim God's absolute authority within the territories of Caesar. In short, before Caesar declares his kingship in God's house (*oikos*), God's servants would declare his kingship in Caesar's territories (*oikoumenē*). In one sense, Jesus' prophecy is a statement of hope, that although the Jews would have to submit to their Roman rulers, they can find comfort in the fact that God, and not Caesar, is the real king.

Going back to the question, can evangelism be a means to hasten the Second Coming of Jesus? The answer is clearly *No*. The Father is the one who decides when this will be (Matt 24:36). Nonetheless, the preaching of the gospel *must* continue until this day comes, not to speed up the day of his coming, but because of Jesus' command (Matt 28:18–20).

Samson L. Uytanlet

---

1. Arthur T. Pierson, *The Modern Mission Century Viewed as a Cycle of Divine Working* (New York: Baker & Taylor, 1901), 43–45, 355; Albert B. Simpson, *The Coming One* (New York: Christian Alliance, 1912), 220–222.

24:29–41 Jesus Prophesies about His Coming

The expression "immediately after" suggests that the focus of Jesus discussion moved from the temple's destruction to the events that come after it. The word "immediately" suggests the nearness of time, but how soon after is not specified; the only thing that is clear is that it will be "after" the events described in the previous verses.

The ancient Chinese believed that unusual signs in the sky happen as a result of poor governance, "misgovernment in the high places incite dislocations in natural order, causing the appearance of comets, eclipses, drought, locusts, weird animals."[20] In the OT, however, these unnatural occurrences in the skies are symbol of God's judgment. Isaiah expressed God's judgment against the Babylonians (who destroyed the first temple), "The stars of heaven and their constellations will not show their light. The rising sun will be darkened and the moon will not give its light" (Isa 13:10). God's judgment is not only against Babylon, but also against "the nations," and the prophet declares, "All the stars in the sky will be dissolved and the heavens rolled up like a scroll; the starry host will fall like withered leaves from the vine, like shriveled figs from the tree" (34:4). Matthew's quotation from these two passages is an expression of hope (24:29), that although the Romans (like the Babylonians) also destroyed God's temple, he will bring judgment to the nation that desecrated his house. Moreover, God will judge the nations that will not submit to his kingship. No wonder Jesus said that "all the peoples of the earth will mourn" (24:30) when the day of judgment comes; but there is assurance for the "elect" of his salvation (24:31). The "lesson from the fig tree" is straightforward (24:32–33); in the same way that tender twigs and leaves of the fig tree signals the coming of summer, so also the destruction of God's temple signals the nearness of God's coming judgment. The expression "this generation" does not necessarily refer to Jesus' contemporaries (23:34), but those who remain unbelieving and unrepentant (see also comments for Matthew 23:39–42).[21]

Jesus stressed that the only thing that is certain is the nearness of these events (24:32–34), not the exact timing of his return (24:35–36). He compared the day of his coming to the day when the great flood came during the time of Noah, an ordinary day when no one expected that disaster would arrive (24:37–38). During the time of Noah, those who were "taken away" were those who were judged (24:39a); Noah and his family were left behind, and they were saved. Jesus' statement should be understood in the same way. He clearly said, "That is how it will be at the coming of the Son of Man" (24:39b). The expression "take away" is an idiom that means "to receive judgment/punishment," as Jesus' statement about Noah's contemporaries makes clear (24:39a). Hence, there is no reason to assume that the following verses are talking about the "rapture." The man in the field and the woman grinding with a hand mill who will be "taken away" are *not* those who will be caught up to be saved (24:40–41). On the contrary, those who will be "taken away,"

---

20. De Bary, *Sources of Chinese Tradition* (1st), 1:170.
21. Neil D. Nelson, "'This Generation' in Matt 24:34: A Literary Critical Perspective," *JETS* 38, no. 3 (1995): 375.

as in the days of Noah, will be "taken away" for judgment. Like Noah and his family, the other man in the field and the other woman grinding with a hand mill who were left behind will be saved. The day will be an ordinary day, and therefore we must be prepared.

24:42–25:46 JESUS CALLS FOR PREPAREDNESS

Jewish groups during the latter part of the first century responded in various ways to the destruction of the temple. Some became "forward looking" and focused primarily on the judgment in the end-time, hence, many apocalyptic writings (books similar to the Book of Revelation) were produced during that time. Others, the spiritual descendants of the Pharisees, began to emphasize the study of the OT Law (or the Torah) and they developed a system for interpreting the Scripture. The Christians shared some things in common with each of the "rival" groups above, holding on to the traditional teaching of Jesus who was recognized as the authorized interpreter of the Scripture, and at the same time looking forward to the coming of the Messiah.

Many interpreters recognize that Jesus' condemnation of the Pharisees (Matt 23) reflects some of the tensions between the Christians and the Pharisaic groups and these tensions are also seen in the illustrations about preparedness and God's judgment (Matt 25). Regardless of this historical backdrop, Jesus' exhortation on readiness is clear. The exact time of Jesus' return is unknown (24:36), but he made clear that it would be soon. Hence, he called his followers to be like the faithful servant (24:42–50), the wise maidens (25:1–13), and the good stewards (25:14–30), because the day for separating the sheep and goats will come soon (25:31–46).

24:42–50 The Wise and Faithful Servant

Jesus made clear the certainty of his return and its nearness, even though the exact time remains unknown. The logical conclusion to Jesus' revelation is, "Therefore keep watch" (24:20). The comparison of his coming to that of a thief is done by other NT writers (1 Thess 5:2–4; 2 Pet 3:10; Rev 3:3; 16:15). The point is that just as no thief will give a prior notice of his coming and will make sure to come at an unexpected time (Matt 24:43–44), Jesus will come when it is least expected.

Jesus illustrated what it means to be prepared by contrasting the wise and faithful servant with a wicked servant. The wise servant is appointed to provide food for the other servants at the proper time (24:45), like what the sheep had done for the "least of these brothers and sisters" (25:35; see discussion for Matthew 25:31–46). In contrast, the wicked servant took advantage of his master's absence to beat the other servants (24:49), like the goats who ignored the needs of the others (25:41–43), and the gentile masters who "lord it over" the others (20:25), the wicked tenants who mistreated the land owner's slaves (21:35–37), and the ungrateful subjects who not only ignored the invitation of the king to his son's wedding banquet, but also beat up his messengers (22:6). Moreover, the wicked servant indulged in his eating and drinking with drunkards (25:49), suggesting that he had not done the work his master entrusted him.

The wise and faithful servant was put in-charge of the master's possession (24:47), like the two other faithful stewards in another parable (25:21, 23); while the wicked servant was cut into pieces and assigned a place among the hypocrites where there was weeping and gnashing of teeth (24:51). Hypocrisy is Jesus' charge against the Pharisees (23:13–32), and here he pronounced that the place for them is the place "where there is weeping and gnashing of teeth" (24:51), which is a description of hell (13:42, 50; see also 8:12; 22:13; 25:30).

25:1–13 The Wise and Foolish Virgins

In Matthew 13, Jesus compared the kingdom of heaven to a sower of good seeds (13:24), a mustard seed (13:31), treasure hidden in a field (13:44), and a net (13:47). In all instances, he used the present tense which suggests that he was referring to a characteristic of the kingdom that can already be observed. Here, in 25:1, Jesus said, "At that time the kingdom of heaven will be like ten virgins." The future tense suggests that he was talking about a characteristic of the kingdom that will be manifested in the future. Nonetheless, this description of the future is the inevitable result of present actions and decisions (25:13).

Jesus discussed about ten virgins who were waiting for the bridegroom to come. Five of them were wise and took jars of oil with them, and the other five were foolish and did not bring extra oil for their lamps (25:2–5). All of them fell asleep, and when the bridegroom came at midnight, the wise virgins still had oil in their lamps, but that was not enough to share with the foolish virgins (25:6–9). While the foolish ones went to buy oil, the ones who were prepared entered the wedding banquet. The foolish ones were shut outside (25:10), and even though they came back, they were not allowed to enter (25:11–12).

The unusual nature of this wedding has been observed by many interpreters.[22] The time of the wedding is not a normal time for people from any culture to conduct a wedding ceremony. The groom is present, but there is no mention of the bride. The virgins seem to be aware of the possibility that the groom would arrive late. There is no sign of celebration. The "selfishness" of the wise virgin is presented as something honorable. The foolish virgins went out to buy oil in the middle of the night as though night markets or 24-hour convenient stores were common during Jesus' time. Also, if the virgins were part of the wedding entourage, they were not expected to keep the oil exclusively for themselves.

This is the second parable in Matthew about a wedding (22:1–14; 25:1–13), used as an image of the end time judgment. However, there is an essential difference between the two parables. The parable of the wedding banquet is part of a series of parables (two sons, 21:28–32; wicked tenants, 21:33–46; wedding banquet, 22:1–14) illustrating the Jews' rejection of God, while the parable of the ten virgins is part of another series of stories (wise and faithful servant, 24:42–50; ten virgins, 25:1–13; talents, 25:14–30; sheep and goats, 25:31–46) calling people to be prepared for his coming and for the coming judgment.

In this parable, the groom was delayed in his arrival to his wedding, and because of this, the ten virgins who were waiting for him already fell asleep (25:5). Paul encouraged the believers not to fall asleep (or to be prepared) for Jesus' coming (1 Thess 5:2, 6). Even Jesus called his audience to "keep watch" (Matt 25:13), but the ten virgins were not reprimanded for falling asleep. Clearly, remaining awake in this parable is not about being prepared. Sleeping is another way to refer to death (9:24; 27:52), and waking up for the resurrection (Rom 13:11; Eph 5:14). With the coming of the bridegroom, the ten virgins are awakened from sleep (Matt 25:7). This could be a reference to the resurrection prior to the day of judgment.

The ancient Jews used oil as a symbol of good deeds,[23] and this may be the case here as well. Both the wise and foolish virgins have it, but the supply of the wise virgins lasted until the coming of the groom while the

---

22. J. Massyngberde Ford, "Parable of the Foolish Scholars: Matt 25:1–13," *NovT* 9, no. 2 (1967): 107; Karl P. Donfried, "Allegory of the Ten Virgins (Matt 25:1–13) as a Summary of Matthean Theology," *JBL* 93, no. 3 (1974): 417; Godfrey William Ernest Candler Ashby, "The Parable of the Ten Virgins," *JTSA* 10 (1975): 62; Dean O. Wenthe, "Parable of the Ten Bridesmaids: Matt 25:1–13," *Spring* 40, no. 1 (1976): 12.
23. This is seen in their commentary on Numbers 7:19 (Numbers Rabbah 8:15–16). Donfried, "Allegory of the Ten Virgins," 427.

foolish virgins used up whatever they had. In his Sermon, Jesus talked about those whose good deeds would be given long-lasting rewards by the Father and those who would have temporary rewards from humans (6:1, 2, 4, 5, 6, 16, 18). The consequence of this is that the foolish virgins are shut outside, like the hypocrites in the previous parable (24:51), and in the light of Jesus' distinction, one may say that the main difference between the wise and foolish virgins is the genuineness of their piety. In the same way that the wise servant in the previous parable did what the master required from him while waiting for his master's return (24:46), the deeds of the wise virgins have an effect that last until the coming of the groom (25:7). The effect of this piety is non-transferrable; hence, the foolish virgins are not given oil of the wise virgins (25:9). Jesus concluded the parable with the command, "Therefore keep watch" (25:13), by making sure ones' "righteousness surpasses that of the Pharisees and the teachers of the law" (5:20).

25:14–30 The Good and Faithful Stewards

Jesus continued with another parable about a man going on a journey and entrusted his wealth to his servants (Matt 24:14). One was given five "bags of gold," another two bags, and the third one only a bag. He explained that the amount is based on the servants' ability (24:15). The first two servants invested the money and doubled it, while the third one hid the money in the ground (24:16–18). As a result, the first two servants received the master's approval and were given more responsibilities (24:19–23). The third one accused the master of taking advantage of his workers (24:24–25). He received the master's disapproval (24:26–27), and was eventually brought to judgment (24:28–30).

In a number of parables of Jesus, the "master" in the story is absent: the absentee landlord (21:33–34), the master who went away for a long time (24:48), and the tardy groom (25:5). These parables share two important aspects: they are found after Jesus' prediction of his death (20:17–19), and in these parables, the people are still held accountable for their deeds while the "master" is absent. The people experienced God's presence while Jesus was physically with them, teaching and preaching, healing and casting out demons, and even in his confrontation with the religious leaders. His ascension marks the beginning of the temporary period of Jesus' physical absence from his people; nonetheless, Jesus promised his continuous presence (28:20). In short, even in Jesus' absence, the divine presence remains with his people.

In this parable, the master who went on a journey entrusted "bags of gold" to his servants. "Bags of gold" may not be the most accurate translation for the Greek word *talantōn* (see also comments for Matthew 18:24), but it clearly avoids the confusion that can be caused by translating *talantōn* as "talents," which is used in many earlier English translations. The English word "talent" can refer to special abilities, and the statement, "each according to his ability" (25:15), only adds to the confusion. The *talantōn* is equivalent to a huge amount of money which is more or less equivalent to the amount that a daily wage earner could earn in a lifetime, and three servants were entrusted various amounts.

Ancient Jews would illustrate God's dealings with his people using business transactions. Even the language of debt as referring to human sin reflects this notion as well (6:12). The expectation of earning 100 percent is legal in ancient times,[24] whether it is morally right is another story. What is clear is that Jesus used an illustration with which people of his days could identify, but without raising ethical questions. The story was told not to condone the system, but for the sake of illustrating good stewardship. Thus, when the servants who were given five and two "bags of gold" doubled their master's money, they received the approval of their master, "Well done, good and faithful servant! You have been faithful with a few things; I will put you in charge of many things" (Matt 25:21, 23). The rewards for faithfulness was not a pay raise or promotion, but added responsibility. The master's confidence was part of the reward they received. The greater blessing, however, was the master's invitation, "Come and share your master's happiness" (25:21, 23). These two servants' "entrance" into their master's joy is the direct opposite of the third servant being "thrown out" to the darkness (25:30). In short, the reward for the faithful servants was to be continuously in their master's presence, which the unfaithful servant would not have enjoyed.

In contrast to the first two servants, the third servant did not invest the money, but simply hid the "bag of gold" in the ground, and later returned the amount to the master fully intact. Burying the bag of gold underground was not necessarily easier than investing the money, considering the amount of work required to do so (finding a location to bury the gold, time spent in digging, scheduling the work and marking the spot while making sure no one could discover the hidden treasure). The highlight of what the third servant

---

24. J. Duncan M. Derrett, "Law in the New Testament: The Parable of the Talents and Two Logia," *ZNW* 56, nos. 3–4 (1965): 190.

did, however, was not the burying of the talents entrusted to him, but his returning of the full amount intact, which is a metaphor that ancient Jewish teachers would understand as a reference to keeping the Law.[25] Keeping the Law for the sake of keeping the Law was not what Jesus wanted for his disciples. On several occasions, Jesus distinguished between true and false piety (for example, Matt 6); he also used metaphors to illustrate real piety such as producing fruit (13:23; 21:19, 43), or the doubling of the talents (25:19, 22). The master's giving the one talent that was not invested properly by the third servant to the first servant was not unexpected (25:28), for if the first servant could double five talents, he would now have more to trade. This parable, like the three other illustrations in this section, is clearly against the Pharisees and teachers of the law.

The third servant accused the master of being "a hard man, harvesting where you have not sown and gathering where you have not scattered seed" (25:24). There is no question that this description reflects the system of exploitation during Jesus' days. However, this does not imply that the first two servants represent those who were devoured by this system and have become corrupt themselves, while the third servant serves as the whistleblower who exposed the corruption of the master. Again, Jesus did not raise ethical questions about the master's unjust practice, which the Bible clearly condemns. The assessment of the third servant as a "wicked, lazy servant" (25:26) and his punishment of being thrown out "into the darkness where there will be weeping and gnashing of teeth" (25:30) are enough to associate him with those who practice false piety (24:51).

25:31–46 Separating the Sheep and Goats

The first three illustrations talk about the future judgment (24:51; 25:1, 10; 25:30). Jesus' story about the separation of sheep and goats is no different. The occasion will be the arrival of Jesus (25:31a). When that time comes, Jesus said, the Son of Man "will sit on his glorious throne" (25:31b). The same scenario is presented by Daniel wherein the kingship and authority of the Son of Man will be universally recognized (Dan 7:13–14). Matthew transitions smoothly from his reference to the "Son of Man" who separates the two kinds of animals (Matt 25:31–33) to the "King" who addressed God as Father and eventually declared judgment (25:34, 40). The "Son of Man" and "King" are clearly referring to one person, namely, Jesus. In Matthew, Jesus'

---

25. For example, Mishnah, *Avot* 14.

lordship will also be universally recognized, and with the authority given him, he will separate the sheep from the goats (25:32).

Although the sheep and goats are recognizable based on their physical appearance and behavior, they have many similarities that at times can still be confused. In Chinese, both sheep and goats can be called *yáng* (羊). Only when they are being distinguished from each other are sheep called *miányáng* (綿羊) and goats *shanyáng* (山羊). In this story, the sheep represent the "righteous" ones (25:37); and the goats, by implication, represent the wicked. The sheep are "blessed" and are the recipients of God's inheritance, which is the "kingdom prepared for [them] since the creation of the world" (25:34), while the goats are "cursed" and will receive only the punishment of "eternal fire prepared for the devil and his angels" (25:41). The deeds of the sheep and goats before the day of judgment distinguish one from the other; the sheep fed the hungry, gave water to the thirsty, sheltered the homeless, clothed the naked, took care of the sick, and visited those in prison (25:35–36; see also Isa 58:7); none of these were done by the goats (Matt 25:42–43).

The sheep in this parable recalls the wise and faithful servant who gave food to the other servants at the proper time (24:45). Their deeds were the exact opposite of what the Pharisees and teachers of the law were doing, who gave tithes but forgot the more important things such as justice and mercy (23:23). Like the parable of the talents which is about stewardship of money but with broad application, the story of the separation of sheep and goats based on their acts of justice, is applied more widely than just concern for the underprivileged or those who are suffering from various forms of injustice.[26] Jesus clarified that the actions done for "the least of these brothers and sisters" were essentially done to him (25:40, 45). The "little ones" who receive a "cup of cold water" could be a reference to the persecuted disciples (10:42); the "little ones" in the other passages in Matthew also refer to disciples (11:11; 18:6, 10, 14). The description of the condition of the "least of these" – hungry, thirsty, naked, in prison – suggests some kind of persecution. Who are in a better position to help suffering believers than other believers? This statement also provides another picture of God's presence, namely, his presence with those who are suffering because of their faith. Of course, the believers' involvement in such action need not be limited towards fellow believers.

---

26. The story is not solely about social justice; neither does it exclude this issue. One must avoid both extremes. For examples, see Lamar Cope, "Matthew 25:31–46 'The Sheep and the Goats' Reinterpreted," *NovT* 11, nos. 1–2 (1969): 44; John R. Donahue, "The 'Parable' of the Sheep and the Goats: A Challenge to Christian Ethics," *TS* 47, no. 1 (1986): 18–19.

Matthew 23:1–25:46

After Jesus condemned the Pharisees and teachers of the law for their hypocrisy, their desire for self-glorification over true piety, the wrong priorities they gave to offerings, their injustice and lack of compassion, and their solidarity and direct involvement in the death of God's prophets (including the death of Jesus), he turned to the city of Jerusalem and pronounced the destruction that was about to come. God's judgment against Jerusalem is inseparable from his judgment against the rest of the nations, which will come when Jesus returns. He promised to come back soon, but the exact time was not given, so he called his followers to be prepared. Even in his call to his disciples to be prepared, the condemnation of the Jewish religious leaders continued indirectly as Jesus talked about those who show no compassion towards others (the wicked slave, 24:48–49; the goats, 25:41–45), those who lack genuine good deeds (the foolish virgins, 25:8), and those who practice false piety (the one entrusted with one talent, 25:18–27). God's judgment, however, is universal in scope (25:32); hence, it includes not only the religious leaders Jesus condemned but also those who lived like them, or in Jesus' words, those whose righteousness does not "surpass that of the Pharisees and the teachers of the law" (5:20). God's judgment is not only universal, it is also eternal (24:51; 25:11–12, 30, 46).

MATTHEW 26:1–28:15

The Sufferings of Jesus and His Victory over Death

The Holy Week is a very important event in the Philippines, and is observed more religiously than in other Asian countries. The suffering of Jesus is remembered in various ways. Some do so using artistic plays such the *Moriones Festival* in Marinduque (a play based on the legend of the half-blind Roman soldier Longinus) and the *Senákulo* (a reenactment of Jesus' passion at Golgotha). Others do so by attending the mass in a church or the community's *pabasa ng pasyon* ("the reading of the passion" where readers are assigned to read texts about Jesus' suffering). Still others perform various acts of sacrifice including fasting, abstaining from eating meat, and the practice of *penitensya* (public penance when the person with the *panata* or "devotion" would whip himself and be nailed or tied to a cross for public display).

The death of Christ is something to be remembered, and one does not have to wait for the Holy Week to remember his sufferings (1 Cor 11:23–32). More important than remembering *how* he died is remembering *why* he died, and the Gospels provide us the explanation about the significance of his death.

26:1–16 THE PLOT AGAINST JESUS

26:1–5 The Chief Priests and Pharisees Plotted Jesus' Death

Several incidents in the earlier chapters of Matthew point forward to the sufferings of Jesus leading to his death. Aside from Jesus' hints (Matt 12:39–40; 16:4) and predictions of his own death (16:21; 17:22–23; 20:17–19), incidents like his baptism (see comments for Matthew 3:16), Jesus' healing of Peter's mother-in-law (8:14–17), his response to the question of John's disciples about fasting (9:14–17), and the Transfiguration (17:1–13) also hint about his sufferings.

After Jesus' ministry in Galilee (4:12–20:16), he started his journey to Jerusalem (20:17–34), entered Jerusalem as king, was welcomed by some people (21:1–22), but had confrontations with the religious leaders

(21:23–22:46), whom he condemned together with those who rejected him (23:1–25:46). The religious leaders had already been planning his arrest even during their confrontations, but were afraid that it would create unrest (22:45–46). The story of Jesus reached its climax with the story of his sufferings, death, and resurrection.

The transition from the account of Jesus' teaching in Jerusalem to the story of his suffering is clearly marked with the statement, "When Jesus had finished saying all these things" (26:1), and once again he announced his death to his disciples just before the Passover began (26:2). The death of Jesus is closely associated with the Passover, an event celebrated on the fourteenth day of the first month of the Jewish calendar (Lev 23:5; Num 28:16; 33:3; Deut 16:1; Josh 5:10). For the Jews, it recalls God's liberation of Israel from bondage in Egypt. The conflict was not just between human powers, because during the first Passover, God did not only bring judgment on Egypt through the death of every firstborn male Egyptian, but God also brought judgment on the "gods of Egypt" (Exod 12:12). Every Israelite family whose house was marked with the blood of the sacrificial lamb was spared (12:27). This also highlights the importance of the shedding of Jesus' blood.

The Lord required that the Passover sacrifice be offered at the right location (Deut 16:2, 5–6). During the reign of Hezekiah, he called people from other tribes to go to Jerusalem so the whole nation could celebrate the festival together (2 Chr 30:1–5), but he celebrated it in the second month (30:15); but during the reign of Josiah, Jerusalem became the center of this celebration, and once again it was celebrated in the first month (2 Kgs 23:23; 2 Chr 35:1). This practice continued when the Jews returned from exile (Ezra 6:19–21). Thus, it is important that Jesus died in Jerusalem, and not elsewhere.

Matthew informs us how the chief priests and elders conspired to kill Jesus in the palace of the high priest (26:3), suggesting that the highest religious official was fully aware of their plan and agreed with it. Moreover, they "schemed" (Greek, *dolos* or "with deceit") to arrest and kill Jesus (26:4), and this added to their culpability. The plan was not to do it during the festival, referring to the week-long celebration of the Feast of Unleavened Bread (26:17). The reason was that they feared that this would cause a riot (26:5). Some of the Jews regarded Jesus as a prophet (20:11), in the same way that they acknowledged John the Baptist as one (21:26), and with many more people going to Jerusalem during this period because of the Feast, one wrong move could potentially create disorder, something that might have pushed the Romans to use force against the people.

26:6–13 Jesus Anointed at Bethany

While the chief priests and elders were plotting Jesus' death in Jerusalem (26:3), Jesus was dining with some of his disciples and friends in the house of Simon the Leper at Bethany (26:6–7), during which a woman came with an alabaster jar of expensive perfume and anointed him with it. John identifies the woman as Mary sister of Lazarus and Martha (John 11:2). He also identifies the disciple who was indignant as Judas (12:4–5), who was angry not because of his concern for the poor but because, as John reveals, he was a thief (12:6), suggesting that Judas may have seen the sale of the perfume as an opportunity to steal. The estimated price of the perfume was three hundred denarii (12:5), which was equivalent to a daily wage earner's income for working ten months without a day off. In Matthew, however, "the disciples" (plural) were indignant (Matt 26:6), which suggests that all of them were guilty of "bothering this woman" (26:10). Although they may have understood Jesus' teaching about compassion by thinking about the poor (23:23), they had not understood the significance of the woman's action, which, for Jesus, was "a beautiful thing" (26:10).

Jesus commended the woman's action by saying, "The poor you will always have with you, but you not always have me" (26:11). The point is not about caring less for the poor, but about the urgency of her actions because his burial would happen in a couple of days. In ancient Jewish custom, dead people were usually buried the same day that they died. The corpses were washed,[1] and in Jesus' case, myrrh and aloes were used before the body was wrapped in linen (John 19:39–41). The anointing of Jesus with perfume anticipated what was about to happen (Matt 26:12), and like the scent of perfume that can be smelled long after it was applied, what the woman did would be remembered long after she did this "beautiful thing" (26:13).

26:14–16 Judas Betrays Jesus

The woman was not the only one whose deed was to be remembered even centuries later; Judas' betrayal of his teacher is also remembered until now. The name Judas is supposedly a beautiful name (it means "praise"); Leah named her fourth son Judah, because of her gratitude for another son and

---

1. See Mishnah, *Shabbat* 23:5; John 19:40.

she said "I will praise the LORD" (Gen 29:35); but because of what Judas did to Jesus, the name "Judas" became associated with evil.

In Matthew's account, Judas took the initiative to see the chief priests to ask, "What are you willing to give me if I deliver him over to you?" (Matt 26:15). Among the Gospel writers, Matthew is the only one to specify the amount and says it was a fulfillment of prophecy (27:3, 9; see also Zech 11:12–13; Jer 19:1–13; 32:6–9). Why would Judas want to betray Jesus? Perhaps he was dissatisfied with Jesus, thinking first that he would be the liberator of their nation, but later realizing they did not share the same principles. Perhaps he assumed that Jesus would be able to find a way to free himself while being interrogated by the priests and the elders. If this happened, it seemed like a win-win situation – Jesus would be set free, and he would get his thirty pieces of silver – but, alas, it ended with his execution. The only thing that is clear in the Gospel accounts is that Judas did it for the money.

26:17–35 JESUS' FINAL MEAL WITH HIS DISCIPLES BEFORE HIS CRUCIFIXION AND HIS PREDICTIONS

26:17–30 The Last Supper and Prediction of Judas' Betrayal

Matthew tells us that Jesus and his disciples shared the Passover meal on the first day of the Feast of the Unleavened Bread (Matt 26:17).[2] The Passover is the beginning of a week-long celebration of this festival (Exod 12:11, 17, 21, 27; Lev 23:5–6; Num 28:16–17; Deut 16:1–3). Jesus and his disciples were not residents of Judea, and so they would have had to borrow or rent a room there. In this case, they used the house of an unidentified man (Matt 26:18–19). Hospitality was one of the good traits of the ancient Jews, and they willingly welcomed even strangers. Although it is possible that this "certain man" (26:18) was someone who knew Jesus and his disciples because they had visited the city often, his identity was not disclosed. Jesus instructed the disciples to say to the man, "The Teacher says, 'My appointed time is near'" (26:18). On the first Passover, the Israelites were instructed to roast the meat and use unleavened bread (Exod 12:8). Roasting meat and preparing unleavened bread would normally take less time than boiling meat and making leavened bread. The meal had to be eaten with cloak tucked under

---

2. For a discussion on the day Jesus celebrated the Passover with his disciples and issues relating to the Jewish calendar, see Étienne Nodet, "On Jesus' Last Supper," *Bib* 91, no. 3 (2010): 348–369.

the belt, sandals on the feet, and staff in hand; and they had to eat in haste (12:11). The first Passover pointed to the urgency of their flight from Egypt and the nearness of God's salvation. In the same way, Jesus' meal with his disciples also pointed to the nearness of God's salvation.

While they were eating, Jesus revealed that one of them would betray him; and when each took turns to ask if Jesus was referring to him, Jesus explicitly said that the one who dipped his hand into the bowl with him was the betrayer (Matt 26:22–23). The statement should have made clear to the disciples who would betray Jesus, but the disciples remained clueless. Jesus also said that his death was inevitable, and although the betrayal was necessary, the gravity of the betrayer's offense could not be minimized. Hence he said, "The Son of Man will go just as it is written about him. But woe to that man who betrays the Son of Man! It would be better for him if he had not been born" (26:24). Jesus' statement is similar to the complaint of Job and the observation of "the Teacher" (Job 3:1, 11; Ecc 4:2–3), who compared those who were born only to experience sufferings and those who were never born. The OT sages suggested a third option, namely, to be born and enjoy life. In Jesus' statement, the comparison is between those who were born only to be instruments of evil and later suffer the consequences of it, and those who were never born at all. A third option is also implied here, namely, to be born and be instruments of good, like the woman who anointed Jesus with perfume (see comments for Matthew 26:6–13 and 26:14–16).

Even Judas asked Jesus whether he was the one who would betray him (26:25), and this only highlights the evil of the betrayal. Jesus' exposing the sin without identifying the person involved should have deterred the betrayer from continuing in his sinful plan. This method of indirect confrontation is what Asians would still do even today. For Judas to even say, "Surely you don't mean me, Rabbi?" (26:25), was shameless; and for him to address Jesus as "Rabbi" added to gravity of the offense, because even though he respectfully addressed Jesus, the evil he was planning shows his disrespect towards his master.

Matthew also recounts the meal itself. While they were eating, Jesus first took the bread, gave thanks, broke it, and distributed to his disciples (26:26a). Breaking of bread was a normal part of their meal, but it gained a new significance when Jesus used it as a symbol of his body, "Take and eat; this is my body" (26:26b). Likewise, the passing of the cup was normal part of the meal, but gained new meaning after Jesus used it as symbol of his blood, "Drink from it, all of you. This is my blood of the covenant, which is poured out for many for the forgiveness of sins" (26:27–28). John recounts the instance during Jesus' ministry when he referred to his body and blood as bread and drink (John 6:48–58), but for the first time, the meaning of the death of Jesus was made clear. It was for the forgiveness of sins (Matt 26:28).[3] The mention of the covenant recalled the incident wherein Moses, after reading the Law to the people, sprinkled the blood of a young bull on the people and declared, "This is the blood of the covenant that the LORD has made with you in accordance with all these words" (Exod 24:8); this covenant did not only result in their cleansing, but it was the act through which Israel had entered into an agreement with God to be subject to him, and in the process established their identity as the people of God. Through Jesus' act, not only was forgiveness of sins made possible, but the "people of God" were redefined because it was no longer based on ethnicity. In fact, Jesus' statement, "I will not drink from this fruit of the vine from now on until that day when I drink it new with you in my father's kingdom" (26:29) recalls the earlier reference to the future banquet for the wedding of the king's son (22:1–14; see also 25:1–13), the banquet which will be joined by many "from east and west" (8:11). Moreover, the mention of forgiveness recalls Jeremiah's prophecy about the new covenant (Jer 31:34). Matthew makes clear, that Jesus is not only the one who has the authority to forgive sins, but the one whose suffering is necessary for the forgiveness of sins. Yieh summarizes this correctly, "Jesus may look like a victim of religious conspiracy and political expediency, but his death is voluntary and vicarious – the righteous Messiah who lovingly and courageously dies on the cross to save the sinful, and whose death will bring the new creation."[4]

The meal was concluded with a hymn (26:30). Singing is part of Jewish worship; it was part of Jesus' worship practice with his disciples (26:30; see also Mark 14:26), and of the early Christians (Eph 5:19; Col 3:16). After the meal and singing, Jesus and his disciples went to the Mount of Olives once again.

26:31–35 Jesus Predicts Peter's Denial

While they were at the Mount of Olives, Jesus predicted that the disciples would "fall away" or be scattered when he was arrested, and he did so by quoting from Zechariah (Matt 26:31; Zech 13:7). Zechariah's prophecy included God's promise of cleansing for his people (13:1, 9), removal of idols

---

3. Ham, "The Last Supper," 56–59.
4. Yieh, *Matthew*, 8.

and impurity, and an end to false prophecies (13:2–4). The prophet also announced that Jerusalem would be plundered, but added that the LORD would punish the nations that plundered Jerusalem (14:1–8). After which, "the LORD will be king over the whole earth" and there will only "be one LORD" and people will acknowledge only him as God (14:9). This suggests that even after Jerusalem's fall, which might seem as if God had abandoned them, the reality was that God remained present with them.

The quotation from Zechariah points to the reality that God remained king despite the disciples' abandonment of Jesus, and God's sovereignty would be seen particularly in Jesus' resurrection (Matt 26:32a). The certainty of Jesus' resurrection is seen in his instruction to his disciples to meet him in Galilee (26:32b). At this point, Peter, followed by other disciples, promised that he would not abandon Jesus; and in response, Jesus predicted his denial (26:33–35).

26:36–56 JESUS ARRESTED WHILE PRAYING AT GETHSEMANE

26:36–46 Jesus' Prays in Gethsemane

After Jesus' prediction about the disciples abandoning him, he went to Gethsemane taking with him only Peter, James, and John (26:37). These three disciples were also with him during the Transfiguration (17:1). The Transfiguration pointed to his sufferings (see comments for Matthew 17:1–13), and his prayer in Gethsemane marked the beginning of the suffering leading to his death. In both instances, the three disciples had the privilege of being present with Jesus at significant points of his life.

Jesus did not call the three to accompany him *because* he was overwhelmed with sorrow. Matthew is clear that "he began to be sorrowful and troubled" only *after* he called these disciples to be with him (26:38; see also Mark 14:33). Nonetheless, the humanity of Jesus remains clear, especially as he requested the three disciples to "keep watch" or pray with him (Matt 26:38). His prayer, "My Father, if it is possible, may this cup be taken from me. Yet not as I will, but as you will" (26:39), is an expression of his obedience. What he taught his disciples to do (6:10), he exemplified through his willingness to receive the "cup" of suffering (see also comments for Matthew 20:22). When Jesus found his disciples sleeping instead of praying with him, he reprimanded them, "Couldn't you keep watch with me for an hour?" (26:40). Jesus was about to be arrested, hence, the urgency to pray, and sleeping was not an option for his disciples. Jesus also warned them, "Watch and pray so that you will not fall into temptation. The spirit is willing, but the flesh is weak" (26:41). In this account, the temptations the disciples faced include the temptation to betray their teacher for money (26:14–16), the temptation to abandon and deny their teacher to save their own lives (26:31–35, 69–75), and the temptation to prioritize their physical needs when they could be in solidarity with their teacher in his time of sorrow (26:38–41). Although it is clear what kinds of temptations the disciples faced during this period, the principle of praying in times of temptation is applicable whatever the temptation one faces.

Eventually, Judas arrived, accompanied by the soldiers who came to arrest Jesus. Jesus immediately called his disciples, "Look the hour has come, and the Son of Man is delivered (Greek, *paradidōmi*) into the hands of sinners" (26:45). Jesus' statement recalled his earlier prediction that he would be delivered (Greek, *paradidōmi*) to the chief priests and scribes who would condemn him, and to the Gentiles who would mock, scourge, and crucify him (20:18–19). For the first time, Jesus referred to the religious leaders and the Romans as "sinners," and their sins would be made clearer in the events that followed.

26:47–56 Jesus Arrested at Gethsemane

When Matthew first introduced Judas as one of the Twelve, he disclosed the latter's identity as the betrayer (Greek, *paradidōmi*) or "the one who delivers" (Matt 10:4; see also 26:46, 48). In this story, Matthew explains how he did it. After agreeing to deliver Jesus to the religious authorities for thirty pieces of silver (26:14–16), Judas accompanied an armed crowd sent by the chief priests and elders to arrest Jesus (26:47). It is unclear in Matthew when Judas left; he was still with them during the meal (26:25). John, however, specifies that Judas left while they were still eating (John 13:26–27). This means Judas was no longer with them when Jesus and the disciples went to Mount of Olives (Matt 26:31–35).

This may not be the first time Jesus went to Gethsemane to pray, so Judas knew where to bring the soldiers to arrest Jesus. The "crowd" that came to arrest Jesus was clearly not the same group that listened to Jesus preach and came to Jesus for healing; if it was, they would have recognized him. Judas pre-arranged a signal with the arresting crowd that the one he kissed was the one they should arrest (26:48–49). For countries in eastern part of Asia, kissing is usually reserved for married couples, children-parents or immediate family members or close relatives. Filipinos show respect by taking the hand of the elderly and putting it on one's forehead; the Chinese bow before the elderly. With Western influence, public hugging and cheek-to-cheek greetings have become socially acceptable. Ancient Jews and their ancestors kissed, not only as an expression of marital affection (Song 1:2; 8:1; see also Prov 7:13), but as a way of showing respect (Gen 27:26–27; Luke 7:38, 45). Kissing was part of their welcome and farewell greetings. This practice was continued in the early church (composed of both Jews and Gentiles) because it was culturally acceptable (Rom 16:16; 1 Pet 5:14). Once again, the gravity of Judas' deceit is highlighted, for what was supposedly a sign of affection became a signal for betrayal, and this was aggravated by his respectful greeting, "Rabbi" (26:49; see also comment for Matthew 26:25). In response, Jesus called him "friend" or *hetairos* (26:50), a term which is used in this Gospel for rebuke (20:13; 22:12).

While Jesus was being arrested, one of Jesus' companions, whom John identified as Peter (John 18:10), took a sword and cut off an ear of one of the high priest's servants (Matt 26:51). Jesus immediately reacted to this violent action of the disciple by reminding them that violence only leads to more violence (26:52). Moreover, Jesus reminded his disciples that he could call twelve legions of angels to help him (26:53). The size of the army of angels is not to be understood as the actual size of the heavenly armies or the size that is available to come to aid Jesus. The point was rather that his arrest was not a sign of his helplessness, but was necessary so that the Scripture might be fulfilled (26:54–56). No particular passage from the Scripture is specified, and it is best to assume that the reference here is to a general fulfillment of OT prophecy – the coming of the Messiah, the renewal of God's covenant, and the offer of God's forgiveness for everyone who acknowledged God as king.[5]

26:57–75 PRELIMINARY INVESTIGATION OF JESUS BEFORE THE JEWISH ASSEMBLY AND PETER'S DENIAL

26:57–68 Jesus before the High Priest

After Jesus was arrested, he was immediately brought before Caiaphas the high priest and the assembly composed of the teachers of the law and elders for preliminary investigation (Matt 26:57). The high priests had great authority over the Jewish people. They received this authority after the death

---

5. Davies and Allison, *Matthew*, 3:514.

of Herod the Great and his son Archelaus,[6] and they exercised this during the initial trial of Jesus. The assembly, as Matthew portrays it, was more of a kangaroo court than an impartial investigating body. They had already been trying to find ways to pin Jesus down even in the earlier chapters (21:45–46; 22:15), and Judas' betrayal was a good opportunity for them to do so (26:14–16). They sent an armed crowd to arrest him (26:47), and they had been waiting for the arrival of the alleged criminal, waiting for the opportunity to pronounce the verdict they made before the investigation.

Peter followed Jesus from a distance, and he was able to enter the courtyard of the high priest, and sat with the guards (26:58). Ordinary citizens are not allowed in the courtyard of the high priest, but John explains that Peter was able to enter because he was accompanied by a disciple who knew the high priest (John 18:15–16).

Matthew points out that the "chief priests and the Sanhedrin were looking for false evidence against Jesus so that they could put him to death" (Matt 26:59),[7] and in order to accomplish this, the accusers sought false witnesses (26:60). What is clear from Matthew's account is that those who are supposed to be guardians of the Law are in this instance the lawbreakers (Exod 20:16; 23:1–3, 6–9). God's indictment against false witnesses is clear, "Have nothing to do with a false charge and do not put an innocent or honest person to death, for I will not acquit the guilty" (Exod 23:7; Prov 19:5, 9; 21:28). The priests were supposed to investigate and do away with malicious witnesses (Deut 19:16–21), but in this case, they were the malicious witnesses.

Matthew does not specify all the charges brought against Jesus, but calls them "false evidence" (26:59). There is, however, one charge that was true, that Jesus claimed to be able to destroy the temple and rebuild it in three days (26:61). John confirms that Jesus made this statement (John 2:19), but explains that those who heard the statement firsthand misunderstood his statement (2:20), and it was only after the resurrection that the disciples understood he was using the temple as a metaphor to refer to his body (2:21–22). Even if Jesus made such a statement, death was not the necessary

---

6. See Josephus, *Jewish Antiquities* 20.10.1 §251.
7. Earlier historians think that the Jewish assembly did not have the authority to sentence someone to death (Richard Wellington Husband, *The Prosecution of Jesus: Its Date, History and Legality* [Princeton: Princeton University Press, 1916], 137–181). This idea is changing in the recent years (J. Spencer Kennard, "Jewish Provincial Assembly," *ZNW* 53, nos. 1–2 [1962]: 44–45, nn. 94–95).

punishment for it. For even if Jesus was a false prophet, his claim to rebuild the temple in three days would be no more than an empty boast.

At this point, the high priest stood up to begin his interrogation (Matt 26:62), but Jesus remained silent (26:63a). Silence can mean a lot of things. Philip explained that in the case of Jesus, silence was a fulfillment of prophecy (Acts 8:32–33; Isa 53:7–8). The high priest continued his interrogation asking, "I charge you under oath by the living God: Tell us if you are the Messiah, the Son of God" (26:63b). This recalls Satan's question when he tempted Jesus (4:3, 6), which associated the religious leaders with evil. Satan was unsuccessful when he attempted this at the beginning of Jesus' ministry, but here he seemed to be gaining some success through the human authorities. The title Messiah (transliterated from Aramaic *mashiach*) or Christ (based on its Greek equivalent *Christos*) is a political title for the one expected to liberate Israel from their gentile colonizers. One should not forget that the Jews' hope for the Messiah was both "a political hope and religious prayer."[8] Claiming to be the Messiah in itself was not blasphemous, but it could potentially create disorder. Even the title Son of God was a royal title (Ps 2). Jesus replied to the high priest's question using Daniel's prophecy about the Son of Man coming with authority to execute judgment (Dan 7:13; Matt 26:64). His answer shows that he was not only claiming to be the Messiah, but also as the divinely appointed ruler who would judge even those who were investigating him. Thus, the high priest responded by charging him with blasphemy, which was punishable by death (26:65–66).[9] After this pronouncement, the people in the assembly began to humiliate him by spitting on him, striking, and mocking him (26:67–68). Capital punishment is the consequence for blaspheming the name of the LORD (Lev 24:10–16; Num 15:30). What the chief priests and elders did not realize was they were the ones committing blasphemy by being treacherous (Ezek 20:27), that is, by refusing to acknowledge the Messiah/king God appointed.

26:69–75 Peter Disowns Jesus

Two of Jesus' disciples had already deserted him (Matt 26:56), while eight others had very likely done so as well, and one had betrayed him (26:14–16, 47–50). Besides, the Jewish authorities had condemned Jesus their leader to death already. In situations like this, there are only two possibilities, either one of the followers would rise and take the leadership or the followers would

---

8. Yieh, *Matthew*, 25.
9. See Mishnah, *Sanhedrin* 7:5.

be scattered (Acts 5:35–37). Only Peter was bold enough to follow Jesus to the priests' courtyard (26:69), and now he was in a dangerous position because one of the servant girls recognized him, "You also were with Jesus of Galilee" (26:69). Galilee was the origin of many leaders who led the revolt against Rome, and for him to be associated with "Jesus of Galilee" who was just sentenced to death might mean that he would be next, and the guards would have no difficulty arresting him because he was already in the priests' courtyard. No wonder his immediate response was to deny any association with Jesus (26:70).

Peter's accent, however, made it impossible for him to deny that he was a Galilean (26:73). This recalls the Ephraimites in Judges 12 who were trying to escape from the Gileadites after the civil war between the two groups. In terms of physical features, they may have looked similar; but the Ephraimites were identified because they pronounce "Shibboleth" as "Sibboleth" (Judg 12:1–6). Unlike the Ephraimites, Peter was able to escape by denying association with Jesus three times (Matt 26:70, 72, 74). Jesus had predicted that before the rooster crew that night, Peter would deny him three times (26:35). The crowing of the rooster meant that the investigation happened between midnight and dawn, which was actually not allowed by the Jews. But the religious leaders were in a hurry to finish the investigation (26:4). Peter's failure shows the weakness of all humans, even of believers. John 21 shows us that even those who fail have a chance to be restored. Unfortunately, not everyone who fails responds to failure by rising again, hence, the story of Judas which follows this episode.

27:1–26 JUDAS' DEATH AND JESUS' TRIAL BEFORE PILATE

27:1–10 Judas Hangs Himself

After the chief priests and elders tried Jesus the previous night, they were ready to bring him to Pilate for execution (Matt 27:1–2). Bringing the accused before the governor was part of the protocol (see also Acts 22:30–22; 24:1–27; 25:1–26:32), and while they were preparing to hand Jesus over to Pilate, Judas came to return the thirty pieces of silver to the chief priests and elders because of remorse (Matt 27:3). The Messiah was sold for thirty pieces of silver which was the price for a slave.[10] Judas was probably not expecting

---

10. Michael Knowles, *Jeremiah in Matthew's Gospel: The Rejected Prophet Motif in Matthaean Redaction*, JSNTSup 68 (Sheffield: Sheffield Academic Press, 1993), 77.

that the trial would end up the way it did, but when he learned that Jesus was condemned to death, he admitted, "I have betrayed innocent blood" (27:4).[11]

For Judas to return the money meant that he did not want to continue participating in the sins of the chief priests and the elders, but they responded by saying, "That's your responsibility" (27:4). In contrast to Peter, Judas went and hanged himself after throwing the money in the temple (27:5). It is unclear how Judas was able to enter the temple (the Greek is *naos* which refers to the sanctuary accessible only to priests, not *hieros*, which may refer to the temple courts accessible to ordinary people). Matthew only informs us that after the incident, the chief priests picked up the money, but refused to *return* it to the treasury. This tells us *where* they got the money to pay Judas, suggesting an even greater responsibility because they used the temple money for evil.[12] They claimed that the law prohibited putting blood money into the temple treasury (27:6), but it is unclear which law is being referred to here. What is clear is the hypocrisy of the religious leaders who did not want anything impure like blood money to be brought into the temple, but at the same time had no qualms in using temple money to shed innocent blood.

The chief priests decided to buy a potter's field and used it as a burial place for foreigners (27:7). This place was called the "Field of Blood" (27:8), and according to Matthew, this took place to fulfill Jeremiah's prophecy (27:9–10). The quotation in Matthew 27:9–10 is actually from Zechariah (Zech 11:12–13), but the mention of Jeremiah recalls his prophecy about the kind of judgment against those who are involved in shedding innocent blood (Jer 19:4).[13]

27:11–26 Jesus' Trial before Pilate

The chief priests and elders brought Jesus before Pilate for trial. His first question, "Are you the king of the Jews?" (Matt 27:11), is essentially the same as the question of the high priest (26:63), but their reasons for asking were different. For someone to claim to be king was equivalent to rebellion against

---

11. The Mishnah prohibits trial before the eve of a Sabbath or a festival, or trial at night (*Sanhedrin* 4:1). It is likely that this rule was already in place during the time of Jesus, and if this is the case, the Jewish authorities had also violated this rule (T. Alec Burkill, "The Trial of Jesus," *VC* 12, no. 1 [1958]: 1).

12. John A. Upton, "The Potter's Field and the Death of Judas," *Concordia Journal* 8, no. 6 (1982): 219.

13. Although Matthew mentioned Jeremiah, the quotation is actually from Zechariah 11:12–13. Some interpreters explain this in connection with Jeremiah's purchase of the potter's field (Jer 19:1–13; 32:6–9), and Zechariah's prophecy (Zech 11:12–13). See Donald Senior, "A Case Study in Matthean Creativity: Matthew 27:3–10," *BR* 19 (1974): 24.

Rome, and this may have forced the colonizers to use their power against the Jews, which of course, would endanger the political standing of the priests. On the part of Pilate, Jesus' response would determine whether Jesus was a real threat to Rome.

The chief priests and elders continued to accuse Jesus before Pilate (27:12), which showed their determination to make sure Jesus would be sentenced to death. Jesus, however, remained silent amidst the accusations "to the great amazement of the governor" (27:13–14). A defiant response, rather than silence, would have been expected of a true rebel, and Pilate may not have considered Jesus as a real threat to Rome so he tried to free him. This does not present Pilate positively, for his response may be understood as arrogance rather than impartiality.

Matthew explains that it was the custom that during the festival, the governor would release a prisoner chosen by the crowd (27:15).[14] So Pilate presented Jesus and Barabbas to them (27:16–17). Matthew explains that Pilate understood that the religious leaders were motivated by self-interest in wanting to execute Jesus (27:18). Moreover, his wife had a dream that bothered her, so she advised Pilate not to have anything to do with the death of Jesus (27:19; see also comments for Matthew 1:20–25). Ancient Jews were discouraged to attend gladiatorial games except to participate in shouting for the loser to be set free instead of being executed.[15] In this case, however, the religious leaders were the ones who persuaded the crowd to have an innocent man executed, and the real insurgent set free (27:20–22). Pilate attempted to free Jesus once again by asking them to specify the crime Jesus had committed, but he realized he was not getting anywhere, and so he eventually gave in to the demands of the religious leaders made through the crowd (27:23).

Pontius Pilate is often remembered for his handwashing, after which he claimed, "I am innocent of this man's blood . . . It is your responsibility" (27:24). In the OT, someone involved in the death of an innocent person is often described as a person with filthy or blood-stained hands (Deut 21:7; 2 Sam 4:11; Prov 6:17; Isa 1:15; 59:3; Ps 24:4), whether the act was done directly (Gen 4:11) or through a messenger (Ps 51:4). The people who agreed

---

14. There is virtually no evidence outside the Bible that shows that there was such a custom. The closest available are evidences showing similar practices of the Assyrians, Babylonians, and Greeks. For examples, Robert L. Merritt, "Jesus, Barabbas, and the Paschal Pardon," *JBL* 104, no. 1 (1985): 59–61. The Gospels, however, should be taken as a historical source as well, and the Evangelists indicate that there was a custom. It may not have been practiced continuously for a long period, hence, the lack of other records.
15. See Babylonian Talmud, *Avodah Zarah* 18b2; Jerusalem Talmud, *Avodah Zarah* 2:5.

to have Jesus crucified were equally liable. The Law also required that the elders of the nearest town where an unsolved murder happened to offer animal sacrifice through which they announced their innocence (Deut 21:1–10). The ritual included handwashing and was accompanied by a declaration of innocence (21:7). However, the elders' confession suggests that there was guilt, even though no one in the town witnessed the crime and they did not know the real killer (21:8–10). Pilate's act and his claim may seem, at first glance, to absolve him from the crime. However, read in the light of Deuteronomy 21, his washing of his hands actually includes him as a resident of a guilty town.

The crowd who shouted for Jesus' crucifixion readily accepted the blame, "His blood is on us and on our children" (27:25). This had been misunderstood in the past and had been used to justify anti-Semitism. Matthew makes it clear, however, that both the Jews and Gentiles would participate in his death (20:18–19). The crowd's admission of guilt explains the evil that would befall Jerusalem decades after Jesus' death (24:1–29). As the story continues, Barabbas was released, and Jesus was crucified (27:26).

27:27–61 THE MOCKERY, CRUCIFIXION, DEATH, AND BURIAL OF JESUS

27:27–44 The Roman Soldiers Mocked and Crucified Jesus

Jesus had earlier predicted that in Jerusalem, he would be delivered to the chief priests and teachers of the Law who would condemn him to death, after which he would be delivered to the Gentiles who would mock, flog, and crucify him (Matt 20:18–19). In the following chapters, we see how the story develops and how these came to pass: (1) they went to Jerusalem (21:10); (2) he was delivered/betrayed by Judas (26:14–16, 46, 48); (3) he was brought to the chief priests and teachers of the Law (26:57); (4) he was condemned by them (26:65–66); (5) he was delivered to the Gentiles (27:1–2); and (6) he was flogged (27:26). The last two elements of Jesus' prediction are now about to be fulfilled – the mockery and crucifixion.

The soldiers of Pilate brought Jesus to the Praetorium (27:27), which may be a reference to the Roman military barracks known as the Antonia tower. The soldiers stripped him of his clothes and dressed Jesus with a scarlet robe (27:28). Being naked in public was considered shameful, and it remains so not only in Asia but also in most parts of the world. Being stripped of clothes was an act of extreme disrespect and humiliation, especially in the case of Jesus who was stripped involuntarily. The soldiers added to his humiliation by replacing his own clothes with a scarlet robe and giving him a crown of thorns (Matt 27:28b–29). Scarlet robes were considered special and luxurious (2 Sam 1:24; Prov 31:21; Jer 4:30; Nah 2:3), but it was used here to insult, not to honor. Crowns are usually made of gold or other precious metals, but they used thorns to inflict physical pain. Spitting was also another way to shame others (Job 17:6; 30:10), and the soldiers did not hesitate to do so after pretending to pay homage by kneeling before him saying, "Hail, king of the Jews" (Matt 27:29–30). After all this, they led him away to be crucified (27:31).

Having gone through agonizing prayer the previous night, followed by the arrest and preliminary interrogation done at a time when people are normally sleeping, the pain of being betrayed and abandoned, the one-sided trial before the governor, and the physical and emotional torture by the soldiers would leave anyone exhausted; and Jesus was no exception. This explains why it was necessary to call someone else to bear Jesus' cross for him. The three Gospel writers identified the man as Simon of Cyrene, a passerby, the father of Alexander and Rufus (Matt 27:32; Mark 15:21; Luke 23:26). It could be that the brothers were known to the believers, and hence, they were identified here. Early Christian interpreters disagree about the identity of Simon and his role in the Gospel; some say he was really the one who was crucified and not Jesus, but this is clearly not the case; some say he is an example of Christian discipleship, as one who carries the cross, while others sees him as an example of a reluctant Christian.[16] The meager information that is available should keep us from too much speculation. Many of the characters in the Gospels are not identified, perhaps for reasons of safety, but others are identified perhaps because they were in some ways associated with some of the believers.

The place where Jesus was crucified is Golgotha, an Aramaic term meaning "place of skulls" (27:33; John 19:17). The reason the place was so named remained disputed, but it was a very appropriate name if executions normally took place there. Matthew also tells us that Jesus was given wine mixed with gall, alluding to David's word in the psalms (Matt 27:34; Ps 69:21). Like David, Jesus cried desperately for help (Matt 26:36–46; Ps 69:3). Although

---

16. For examples, see Mark DelCogliano, "Gregory the Great on Simon of Cyrene: A Critique of Tradition," *ASE* 28, no. 1 (2011): 317–320.

Pilate did not declare him innocent (see Luke 23:4), he could not find anything Jesus did that was worthy of capital punishment (Matt 27:23). In the same way, David claims he was hated without cause by powerful enemies (Ps 69:4). Like David, Jesus was estranged from his brothers (Matt 12:46–50; 26:1–5, 14–16, 31–35; Ps 69:8), yet he remained zealous for the house of God (69:9; John 2:17; see also Matt 21:12–17).

Ancient people did not enjoy the comforts of the modern era, wherein clothes could easily be bought, and so any additional garment was valuable. This explains why the soldiers were interested in having the clothes of Jesus which they divided among themselves by casting lots (27:35); this is something John considered a fulfillment of prophecy (John 19:24; Ps 22:18).

Jesus was crucified with guards stationed (Matt 27:36), and with a written charge placed above his head, "This is Jesus, the king of the Jews" (27:37). In the eyes of the Jewish authorities, this statement was far from accurate (John 19:19–21), but the Romans did not care. In the eyes of the Gospel writers, this less-than-accurate charge against Jesus was an accurate revelation of his true identity, because he was really the king of the Jews. Jesus was crucified with rebels beside him (Matt 27:38), because the charge against him was political in nature.

Matthew also informs us that passersby also hurled insults and shook their heads at him (27:39–40). Shaking one's head could be a gesture of pity or disappointment, but it could also be a sign of rejection, scorn, rejoicing in another's misery, or condemnation (2 Kgs 19:21; Job 16:4; Ps 64:8; Jer 18:16; Lam 2:15). Aside from the passersby, the chief priests, teachers of the Law, and elders were also present there mocking him (Matt 27:41–43). The gravity of their insult is underscored because they used Scripture to insult Jesus, "He trusts in God. Let God rescue him now if he wants him" (27:43; Ps 22:8). The rebels, who were supposed to be ashamed because they were also crucified, joined the others in mocking Jesus (Matt 27:44).

27:45–61 Death and Burial of Jesus

Matthew recounts the darkness that covered the land from noon until three in the afternoon (27:45). This is the time of the day that is typically the warmest and brightest, yet there was darkness, which recalls not only God's judgment against Egypt (Exod 10:21–29) serving as a warning against those who refuse to acknowledge his kingship, but also highlights God's abandonment of Jesus during this period (Matt 27:46). Matthew consistently shows God's presence with Jesus, particularly through his public ministry of teaching and healing, or even through the prophecies he fulfilled. Yet here, for the first time, Jesus cried out about the absence of God, which is aggravated by the religious leaders' insult by quoting Scripture. Theologians explain that at this moment, Jesus was carrying the sins of the world and therefore God could not even look at him, hence the abandonment. This explanation is made in the light of Paul's statement, "God made him who had no sin to be sin for us" (2 Cor 5:21).

It is also clear that Matthew wanted to show in this account that even in his last moments, Jesus' mind remained filled with the Scripture. In contrast to the religious leaders who desecrated God's word by using Scripture to insult him, Jesus, as a pious Jew used Scripture to express even his agony before God (27:46; Ps 22:1). David, whose words Jesus used, continued to acknowledge God's reign (22:3–5), a truth that would be proclaimed in order that "all the ends of the earth will remember the LORD" (22:27), because dominion belongs to him (22:28–29), and so that the succeeding generations would know him as well (22:30–31). Jesus' commission to his disciples shows that his sufferings would eventually lead to the proclamation of God's rule, and the promise of his presence show that God's abandonment was only temporary.

Jesus' cry of agony was misunderstood by some passersby. Matthew preserved the Aramaic expression, *"Eli, Eli, lama sabachthanni"* (Matt 27:46). The language Jesus used explains why not everyone understood his words, but some incorrectly thought he was calling Elijah (27:47). For the second time, Jesus was given something to drink; he was earlier offered the bitter gall (27:34), and now, the sour vinegar (27:48). Both were mentioned by David as the drinks offered by those who scorned him (Ps 69:21); they represent the kind of liquid that is not only useless for quenching thirst, but also add to the agony of a suffering man.

The people who were present continued to hurl insults at him (Matt 27:49), until eventually Jesus died (27:50). Matthew recounts how the curtain of the temple was torn from top to bottom (27:51). Some identify this as the veil at the entrance to the holy of holies.[17] Accounts regarding the torn veil are also found in other Jewish writings, and are understood in relation to the destruction of the temple.[18] Ancient Jews have interpreted this torn

---

17. Daniel M. Gurtner, "LXX Syntax and the Identity of the NT Veil," *NovT* 47, no. 4 (2005): 344–346.
18. Josephus, *Jewish Wars* 6.2.3 §290; also in the Jerusalem Talmud, *Yoma* 6, 43c; Babylonian Talmud, *Yoma* 39b. Marinus de Jonge, "Matthew 27:51 in Early Christian Exegesis," *HTR* 79,

veil in different ways. The author of Hebrews, for example, understands it as evidence that believers now have access to God (Heb 4:14–16; 9:1–28). In this Gospel, however, the tearing of the veil was preceded by an earthquake, followed by the opening of the tombs and resurrection of the dead (Matt 27:52–53), and the gentile centurion's confession that Jesus is the Son of God (27:54). Although there is no question that God is able to raise the dead, as it was already shown in this Gospel multiple times, it is best to understand this incident (27:53–53) as one of the images leading to the revelation of Jesus' identity. Earthquakes (Rev 6:12; 11:13; 16:18) and the opening of holy shrines (4:1; 11:19; 15:5–8) are typical images found in Revelation and other similar works.[19] The display of natural forces (earthquakes) together with unusual occurrences (tearing of veil, resurrection) that eventually lead to the confession that Jesus is the Son of God suggests that Matthew wants us to understand the tearing of the veil as part of God's revelation of Jesus' identity. Interestingly, the pronouncement came from the mouth of a Gentile, which suggests that the nations were now ready to receive God's revelation.

Women have a special role in this Gospel. Matthew informs us that they not only took care of the needs of Jesus and his disciples (Matt 27:55), but even during his crucifixion, they were the ones present. Mary Magdalene and Jesus' mother were present (27:56; see also 13:55), together with the "mother of the sons of Zebedee." This is the second instance the mother of James and John is mentioned; the first is when she asked Jesus to give her sons prominent positions in the kingdom (20:20–28). In Matthew's account, she changed from someone who desired power and prestige, to becoming a true servant.[20]

Jesus died at around three in the afternoon (27:45). A couple of hours later, the disciples were preparing to bury him (27:57). Matthew identified a rich man named Joseph of Arimathea who went to see Pilate and requested for Jesus' body so they could immediately bury him (27:58). The fact that Joseph was able to do so suggests his power and influence, and his wealth may be one of the reasons for this. He buried Jesus according to the Jewish custom in a tomb that was recently cut from stone (27:59–60). Giving a person a

---

no. 1 (1986): 68; Robert L. Plummer, "Something Awry in the Temple?: The Rending of the Temple Veil and Early Jewish Sources that Report Unusual Phenomena in the Temple Around AD 30," *JETS* 48, no. 2 (2005): 301–316.

19. Kenneth L. Waters, Sr., "Matthew 27:52–53 as Apocalyptic Apostrophe: Temporal-Spatial Collapse in the Gospel of Matthew," *JBL* 122, no. 3 (2003): 500.

20. Daniel Patte, *The Gospel according to Matthew* (Philadelphia: Fortress, 1987), 391–395.

proper burial is a way of showing respect. Joseph's courage to approach the governor to ask for Jesus' body was commendable, but offering the tomb he made for himself to Jesus was a gesture of self-sacrifice. Jesus was buried with not many mourners present – only Mary Magdalene and his mother are mentioned as present at that time together with Joseph of Arimathea (27:61).

THE SUFFERING OF JESUS

The Mel Gibson film *The Passion of Christ*, shows graphically the pain and suffering (hence the old English word "passion"), as well as the details of the crucifixion that Jesus went through at the hands of the Romans. The film brings home to the viewer the extent of the physical suffering that Jesus went through.

Many Christians today suffer for their faith. For example, converts from Islam face ostracism and even death. In some parts of Asia, it is illegal to be a Christian; hence believers in those places live in constant threat and fear for their lives and their livelihood. In other parts of Asia, Christian suffering comes in the form of job discrimination; they are given only menial jobs and are not recognized as full members of society. All Christians who seek to live out the commands and example of Jesus Christ must pay a price for discipleship. Suffering for the faith has different facets; and it is inappropriate for one person to suggest that her suffering is 'greater' than another person's. Suffering, especially unjust suffering is hard to bear. Christians know that they follow a suffering Messiah (see Isa 53) and that he profoundly knows, understands and empathizes when his followers suffer.

Buddhists view life as suffering. They recognize that there is much suffering in this world and accept it as part of the law of karma, and that pain and suffering are just part of the human condition. There is a stoic acceptance of suffering. Others, like modern-day hedonists, seek to avoid suffering because they are only seeking the good life of pleasure, and pain and suffering have no place in that worldview. Some Christians have an incorrect theology when they hold the view that God only wants to bless his children and suffering cannot be part of God's purposes.

The whole counsel of God from Scriptures paints a more rounded view about life and suffering; we are not to be masochists who seek out suffering, but rather we recognize that living in a fallen world means that there is evil around us and that a consequence of that evil is suffering. Jesus did not want to suffer and pleaded in the Garden of Gethsemane for his heavenly father to take away the cup, but he still accepted the will of God (Matt 26:39–42). Living in a fallen world has its consequences. For example, a young person full of promise faces a tragic accident which incapacitates him and leaves his family with mounting medical bills, or a mother of young children dies because of cancer. But since Christians believe in God who is both Sovereign, Just and the final Judge, we know that when we can have faith in this God, at the end of time, he will judge fairly and can redeem the suffering for the greater good and for his glory.

However, not all hardships that Christians go through are "suffering." Jesus said that his disciples had to take up his cross and follow him, and the paradox is that those who seek to preserve their lives will lose it but those who lose their lives for his sake will find it (10:38–39). Following Jesus is contrary to the ways of the world, and so today there will be some hardship for all believers. For example, a Christian who chooses not to be swayed by bribes in her workplace may find that she is ostracized by her colleagues or overlooked for a well-deserved promotion. This is what following Christ in a fallen world means, and that is the cost of discipleship.

Jesus also said that his yoke is easy and his burden is light and those who follow him will find rest for their souls (11:28–30). So, in some sense, following Jesus and accepting all the consequences of this discipleship will not be burdensome; but Christ himself will give rest for the weary.

Paul said that suffering produces endurance and character and so did not shy away from it (Rom 5:3–5). Since our Lord Christ has suffered, we know that we too will suffer; and with his strength and presence we can endure. Paul also said that when one part of the body suffers, the whole body suffers (1 Cor 12:26). This is a reminder that Christians need to pray for those who are persecuted and suffer for their faith.

Kiem-Kiok Kwa

27:62–28:15 THE RESURRECTION OF JESUS

The next day, the chief priests and the Pharisees also went to Pilate to request him to assign guards in order that Jesus' disciples would not be able to steal his body (Matt 27:62–64). Matthew earlier shows that Jesus' trial began with the religious leaders' deceitful tactic (26:3–4). Here, this same group called Jesus the "deceiver" (27:63). Their description of Jesus shows their perception of him, and this perception led some Jewish teachers to explain that Jesus was executed because of his involvement in sorcery.[21] The "next day" was the earliest time for the religious leaders to make such a request (27:62), which

---

21. Babylonian Talmud, *Sanhedrin* 67a.

means that they wasted no time to make sure guards were assigned to man the tomb. Pilate granted their request and assigned guards who even sealed the tomb (27:65–66). The guards were Roman guards, and this suggests that even after Jesus died, the Jewish and Roman authorities continue to conspire against Jesus.

After the Sabbath, the two women named Mary went back to the tomb, and once again there was an earthquake, and they saw the angel of the Lord who rolled away the stone sitting on it (28:1–2). The appearance of the angel was similar to Jesus' appearance when he was transfigured (28:3; see also 17:2). Matthew contrasts the response of the two women and the guards; the guards were terrified and became like dead men, while the women, although fearful, readily received the message of the angel who instructed them to tell the disciples to meet him at Galilee (28:4–7). This was something Jesus already told them earlier (26:32), and now the angel reminded the disciples through the two women that the time had come for them to meet there.

Before the women were able to tell the disciples, Jesus met them, and gave them the same instruction (28:8–10). The response of the women can also be contrasted with that of the disciples; the two women worshipped Jesus (28:9), but some of the disciples doubted (28:17). The guards reported what happened to the chief priests, who paid them to spread the news that the disciples came and stole the body (28:11–13). If the disciples were really able to steal Jesus' body, the guards would have faced execution (28:14; see also Acts 16:25–28). Matthew does not explain how the Jewish leaders were able to convince the Roman authorities not to punish the guards, or whether they had been informed about the incident. Matthew's comment, however, explains the origin of the reports about Jesus' stolen body that had been circulating for more than four decades already at the time the Gospel was written (Matt 28:15).

RESURRECTION, AUTHORITY, AND MISSION

The authority of Jesus Christ is seen throughout the gospel: the crowds were amazed at his teaching because he taught (Matt 7:29), forgave sins (9:6–8), and healed as one who had authority. When Jesus first sent out the disciples he gave them authority over evil spirits and to heal disease and sickness (10:1). At the end of the gospel, Jesus' gives his final command to go and make disciples because he has been given all authority in heaven and on earth. This "Great Commission" can be carried out by Christians because we go with the authority of the resurrected Lord Jesus Christ. That authority is necessary because Christians can then baptize those who believe in the name of the Father, Son and Holy Spirit and teach them to obey everything that Jesus has commanded. The promised presence of the risen Lord empowers us to live out life in the kingdom of heaven.

The task of world evangelization continues to be urgent. There are many who still have not had the opportunity to hear the message and to know the Lord Jesus Christ and the life that he gives. Despite the many challenges that face us in this task, Christians go in confidence because they go in the name of he who has been given all authority in heaven and on earth. Jesus promises to be with them always, to the very end of the age and that is comfort and strength. The authority of Jesus is sufficient for us for whatever we face.

That confidence is in Christ and should not come across as arrogance or aggressiveness. Witness and evangelism in Asia has sometimes been accused of being that way; when young, enthusiastic believers disregard their cultural norms in their evangelistic efforts. There is a place for telling the message with firmness and conviction and yet that proclamation must be polite and respectful. While Christians may feel the urgency of sharing the Good News with their loved ones, that is no reason to be forceful. Jesus himself was gentle and humble, and we must be too. If messengers do not have culturally appropriate postures, the message of Jesus may not be heard.

There are still many issues in Asian apologetics. For example, how to present the uniqueness of Christ in a multi-religious world. That Jesus is the only way, the truth and the life (John 14:1) still needs to be proclaimed firmly when other religions and worldviews stress tolerance and acceptance, on the premise that all religious faiths are the same. To the post-modern culture of relativism, Christians need to articulate the absoluteness of Christ. When Christians go in the name of Jesus, we seek to be Jesus to others. We will show his love, compassion and mercy, as well as embody justice, mercy, and truth as personified and lived out in Jesus.

Proclamation of the message is the first step towards conversion, for Jesus calls us to make disciples and not merely converts. Hence much still needs to be done in the areas of growing disciples and building the church.

> Too often Asian Christians merely translate books and other materials from Western sources and so unwittingly adopt those cultural norms, for example, of Western individualism. Rather we need to consider more deeply the contextual and discipleship issues, such as standing against the petty bribery that confronts us in everyday life; spiritual warfare in this very religious milieu; and developing Spirit-led leadership structures which are less hierarchical and patriarchal. Even though many churches in Asia are self-propagating, self-governing and self-financing, the Asian church can do more self-theologizing. That is, on the one hand studying the many issues which face Asian Christians and on the other hand studying Scripture and tradition and proposing theological answers to these issues. These will be important steps to making disciples and thus growing the church in Asia into maturity.
>
> **Kiem-Kiok Kwa**

28:16–20 THE GREAT COMMISSION

The resurrection is the clearest proof that God had not abandoned Jesus (Matt 27:46; Ps 16:10 in Acts 2:31). After God raised him from the dead, Jesus instructed the disciples through the two Marys to meet him at Galilee after his resurrection (Matt 26:32; 28:7, 10); so the eleven remaining disciples went to Galilee to wait for him there (28:16). Unlike Luke, who indicates the beginning of Christian mission from Jerusalem (Acts 1:8), Matthew points to Galilee as the starting point of mission. This need not be seen as conflicting accounts, for while Luke shows the Jewish *origin* of gentile missions, Matthew shows the gentile missions that *result* from Jesus work among the Jews. Matthew earlier refers to Galilee as "Galilee of the Gentiles" (4:15), and the work among the Gentiles anticipated Jesus' command given here (8:11). Thus, Galilee is the most appropriate launching pad for mission to the Gentiles.

Matthew has no qualms in saying that when the disciples saw Jesus, although some worshipped, some still doubted (28:17). In the other Gospel accounts, when Jesus appeared to his disciples after his resurrection, some disciples were not able to recognize him immediately (Luke 24:30–32), while others could not believe that he was indeed raised (24:37–39). This could explain why some among the eleven remained doubtful.[22] Regardless of the reasons for their doubt, it is clear that Jesus did not commission people with perfect faith, and this is hope for us who lack faith at times.

Jesus claimed that "all authority" was given to him (Matt 28:18). This is not the first time he made this claim (see 11:27). His birth, his public ministry of teaching and healing, even his confrontations with the religious leaders all pointed to the authority that he possessed; and with this authority he commanded his disciples to make disciples by going to all nations, baptizing, and teaching them to obey (28:19). His command to "*go* and make disciples" was only given after he challenged them to "*come* and follow me." For one to be able to make disciples, he/she must first be a disciple of Jesus.

Jesus' instruction was to make disciples of "all nations." The word *ethnos*, which is translated nations, can also be translated "Gentiles," and some have indeed argued that Jesus' commission is for the disciples to go to the Gentiles. This does not suggest, however, that today's mission should exclude the Jews. Matthew closes his work with Jesus' promise of his presence with his disciples (28:20), which suggests that the divine presence at work through Jesus is also available to the eleven who would be doing the mission. Moreover, the mission that will continue until "the end of the age" suggests that the work must be continued by those who claim to be his disciples with the assurance that the same divine presence will be available.

---

22. E. Margaret Howe, "But Some Doubted, Matt 28:17: A Re-appraisal of Factors Influencing the Easter Faith of the Early Christian Community," *JETS* 18, no. 3 (1975): 173.

RECOMMENDED WORKS

Bauer, David R. *The Structure of Matthew's Gospel: A Study in Literary Design.* JSNTSup 31. Sheffield: Almond Press, 1988.

Betz, Hans Dieter. *The Sermon on the Mount: A Commentary on the Sermon on the Mount Including the Sermon on the Plain.* Hermeneia. Minneapolis: Augsburg Fortress, 1995.

Bornkamm, Günther, Gerhard Barth, and Heinz Joachim Held, eds. *Tradition and Interpretation in Matthew.* New Testament Library. Philadelphia: Westminster Press, 1974.

Bruner, Frederick Dale. *Matthew: A Commentary.* 2 vols. Grand Rapids: Eerdmans, 2004.

Buchanan, George Wesley. *The Gospel of Matthew.* Mellen Bible Commentary 1. 22 vols. Lewiston: Mellen Biblical Press, 1996.

Burgess, Joseph A. *History of the Exegesis of Matthew 16:17–19 From 1781 to 1965.* Ann Arbor, MI: Edwards Brothers, 1976.

Carter, Warren. *Matthew: Storyteller, Interpreter, Evangelist.* Peabody: Hendrickson, 2004.

_____. *Matthew and the Margins: A Sociopolitical and Religious Reading.* The Bible and Liberation Series. Maryknoll: Orbis Books, 2000.

Charette, Blaine. *Restoring Presence: The Spirit in Matthew's Gospel.* Journal of Pentecostal Theology Supplement 18. Sheffield: Sheffield Academic Press, 2000.

Crowe, Brandon D. *The Obedient Son: Deuteronomy and Christology in the Gospel of Matthew.* Beihefte zur Zeitschrift für die neuentestamentliche Wissenschaft und die Kunde der älteren Kirche 188. Berlin: De Gruyter, 2012.

Culas, Laurence. *Good News amidst Crises: Antioch and the Gospel of Matthew.* Delhi: Indian Society for Promoting Christian Knowledge, 2010.

Davies, W. D., and Dale C. Allison. *A Critical and Exegetical Commentary on the Gospel according to Saint Matthew.* 3 vols. International Critical Commentary. Edinburgh: T. & T. Clark, 1988–1997.

Duling, Dennis C. *A Marginal Scribe: Studies in the Gospel of Matthew in a Social-Scientific Perspective.* Matrix: The Bible in Mediterranean Context 7. Eugene, OR: Cascade Books, 2012.

Evans, Craig A. *Matthew.* NCBC. Cambridge, NY: Cambridge University Press, 2012.

Fiedler, Peter. *Das Matthäusevangelium.* Theologischer Kommentar zum Neuen Testament 1. Stuttgart: Kohlhammer, 2006.

France, Richard T. *Matthew.* NICNT. Grand Rapids: Eerdmans, 2007.

_____. *Matthew: Evangelist and Teacher*. Grand Rapids: Academie Books, 1989.

Frankemölle, Hubert. *Matthäus Kommentar*. 2 vols.; Düsseldorf: Patmos, 1994.

Goulder, M. D. *Midrash and Lection in Matthew*. London: SPCK, 1974.

Hagner, Donald A. *Matthew 1–13*. WBC 33A. Dallas: Word Books, 1993.

_____. *Matthew 14–28*. WBC 33B. Dallas: Word Books, 1995.

Hilary of Poitiers. *Commentary on Matthew*. Fathers of the Church 125. Translated by D. H. Williams. Washington, DC: Catholic University of America Press, 2012.

Keener, Craig S. *A Commentary on the Gospel of Matthew*. Grand Rapids: Eerdmans, 1999.

Kingsbury, Jack Dean. *Matthew: Structure, Christology, Kingdom*. Philadelphia: Fortress, 1975.

Kupp, David D. *Matthew's Emmanuel: Divine Presence and God's People in the First Gospel*. Society for New Testament Studies Monograph Series 90. Cambridge, NY: Cambridge University Press, 1996.

Levine, Amy-Jill. *The Social and Ethnic Dimensions of the Matthean Salvation History*. Studies in the Bible and Early Christianity 14. Lewiston, NY: Edwin Mellen Press, 1988.

Luz, Ulrich. *Matthew 1–7*. Hermeneia. Minneapolis: Fortress, 2007.

_____. *Matthew 8–20*. Hermeneia. Minneapolis: Fortress, 2001.

_____. *Matthew 21–28*. Hermeneia. Minneapolis: Fortress, 2005.

_____. *The Theology of the Gospel of Matthew*. Translated by J. Bradford Robinson. Cambridge: Cambridge University Press, 1995.

Moses, A. D. A. *Matthew's Transfiguration Story and Jewish-Christian Controversy*. JSNTSup 122. Sheffield: Sheffield Academic Press, 1996.

Moss, Charlene McAfee. *The Zechariah Tradition and the Gospel of Matthew*. Beihefte zur Zeitschrift für die neuentestamentliche Wissenschaft und die Kunde der älteren Kirche 156. Berlin: De Gruyter, 2008.

Neyrey, Jerome H. *Honor and Shame in the Gospel of Matthew*. Louisville, KY: Westminster John Knox, 1998.

Osborne, Grant R. *Matthew*. Zondervan Exegetical Commentary Series: New Testament. Grand Rapids: Zondervan, 2010.

Pattarumadathil, Henry. *Your Father in Heaven: Discipleship in Matthew as a Process of Becoming Children of God*. Analecta Biblica 172. Rome: Editrice Pontifico Instituto Biblico, 2007.

Patte, Daniel. *The Gospel according to Matthew*. Philadelphia: Fortress, 1987.

Powell, Mark Allan. *God with Us: A Pastoral Theology of Matthew's Gospel*. Minneapolis: Augsburg Fortress, 1995.

Saldarini, Anthony J. *Matthew's Christian-Jewish Community*. Chicago: University of Chicago Press, 1994.

Recommended Works

Schniewind, Julius. *Das Evangelium nach Matthäus*. Neue Testament Deutsch 2. Göttingen: Vandenhoeck & Ruprecht, 1936.

Sigal, Philip. *The Halakhah of Jesus of Nazareth according to the Gospel of Matthew*. Studies in Biblical Literature 18. Atlanta: Society of Biblical Literature, 2007.

Simonetti, Manlio, ed. *Matthew 1–13*. Ancient Christian Commentary on Scripture: New Testament 1A. Downers Grove, IL: InterVarsity, 2001.

_____. *Matthew 14–28*. Ancient Christian Commentary on Scripture: New Testament 1B. Downers Grove, IL: InterVarsity, 2002.

Stock, Augustine. *The Method and Message of Matthew*. Collegeville: Liturgical Press, 1994.

Talbert, Charles H. *Matthew*. Paideia Commentaries on the New Testament. Grand Rapids: Baker Academic, 2010.

Weaver, Dorothy Jean. *Matthew's Missionary Discourse: A Literary Critical Analysis*. JSNTSup 38. Sheffield: Sheffield Academic Press, 1990.

Westerholm, Stephen. *Understanding Matthew: The Early Christian Worldview of the First Gospel*. Grand Rapids: Baker Academic, 2006.

Wilson, Carol B. *For I Was Hungry and You Gave Me Food: Pragmatics of Food Access in the Gospel of Matthew*. Eugene, OR: Pickwick, 2014.

Wilson, Walter T. *Healing in the Gospel of Matthew: Reflections on Method and Ministry*. Minneapolis: Fortress, 2014.

Yang, Yong-Eui. *Jesus and the Sabbath in Matthew's Gospel*. JSNTSup139. Sheffield: Sheffield Academic Press, 1997.

Yieh, John. *Conversations with Scripture: The Gospel of Matthew*. Anglican Association of Biblical Scholarship Study Series. Harrisburg, PA: Morehouse Publishing, 2012.

Asia Theological Association
54 Scout Madriñan St. Quezon City 1103, Philippines
Email: ataasia@gmail.com Telefax: (632) 410 0312

OUR MISSION
The Asia Theological Association (ATA) is a body of theological institutions, committed to evangelical faith and scholarship, networking together to serve the Church in equipping the people of God for the mission of the Lord Jesus Christ.

OUR COMMITMENT
The ATA is committed to serving its members in the development of evangelical, biblical theology by strengthening interaction, enhancing scholarship, promoting academic excellence, fostering spiritual and ministerial formation and mobilizing resources to fulfill God's global mission within diverse Asian cultures.

OUR TASK
Affirming our mission and commitment, ATA seeks to:

- **Strengthen** interaction through inter-institutional fellowship and programs, regional and continental activities, faculty and student exchange programs.
- **Enhance** scholarship through consultations, workshops, seminars, publications, and research fellowships.
- **Promote** academic excellence through accreditation standards, faculty and curriculum development.
- **Foster** spiritual and ministerial formation by providing mentor models, encouraging the development of ministerial skills and a Christian ethos.
- **Mobilize** resources through library development, information technology and infra-structural development.

To learn more about ATA, visit www.ataasia.com or Facebook /AsiaTheologicalAssociation

This highly insightful and useful commentary comes from skillful and multi-competent scholars. Samson Uytanlet and Kiem-Kiok Kwa attend to literary dimensions of this Gospel as well as displaying sensitivity to, and competence in, both the ancient setting of Matthew's Gospel and modern Asian contexts. They seamlessly and brilliantly weave these elements together (along with some insights from the history of Christianity). Uytanlet and Kwa properly highlight relevant issues of honor, shame, kinship, colonial contexts, and so forth and provides insights on Matthew's Gospel from which readers in many cultures, including Western ones, will learn much. All this in a work that is well-laid out and very understandably written!

Craig S. Keener, PhD
F. M. and Ada Thompson Professor of Biblical Studies,
Asbury Theological Seminary, USA

Matthew the Evangelist was spiritually sensitive and multiculturally fluent, so he was able to use Hebrew Scripture and Greco-Roman tradition to introduce and explain Jesus' extraordinary identity and world-changing mission to his Jewish and Gentile readers in the first century with great adeptness and profound impact. In his commentary on Matthew, Dr. Uytanlet and Dr. Kwa have demonstrated the same spiritual sensitivity and multicultural fluency in clarifying the significance of Jesus Christ, underscoring the messages of Matthew, and even more impressively, highlighting the relevance of the Gospel to Asian people, both in the embedded essays and in the running comments.

Dr. Uytanlet's expert knowledge of current Matthean scholarship produces many exegetic insights on Matthew's text and his immersed experience in Asian life and culture, Chinese language, and Filipino customs in particular, brings Asian readers into exciting and creative conversations with this Christian Scripture, yielding much wisdom and faith challenges. This commentary is engagingly written, easy to read, and hard to put down. Lay readers, seminarians, preachers, and scholars will all find it informative and valuable. I highly recommend it.

Rev. John Y. H. Yieh, PhD
The Molly Laird Downs Chair, Professor of New Testament,
Virginia Theological Seminary, USA

Samson Uytanlet and Kiem-Kiok Kwa admirably assist readers of the Gospel of Matthew with their faithful attention to the Gospel narrative and keen awareness of similarities between the first-century New Testament world and twenty-first century Asia. This splendid study serves well the aims of the Asia Bible Commentary Series.

Joel B. Green, PhD
Provost, Dean of the School of Theology,
Professor of New Testament Interpretation,
Fuller Theological Seminary, USA

Samson Uytanlet and Kiem-Kiok Kwa have gifted us with a different kind of commentary on Matthew. Emphasizing a cyclical relation among the commentator's tasks of "observation, interpretation, and application," their commentary not only acknowledges that readers come to Matthew with their present contexts but also addresses how Matthew may speak to the particularities of today's Asia. This contextual-specific commentary will be a great resource to those who are interested in Matthew and committed to Asia.

Tat-siong Benny Liew, PhD
Professor, Religious Studies Department, College of the Holy Cross, USA

Langham Literature and its imprints are a ministry of Langham Partnership.

Langham Partnership is a global fellowship working in pursuit of the vision God entrusted to its founder John Stott –

> **to facilitate the growth of the church in maturity and Christ-likeness through raising the standards of biblical preaching and teaching.**

Our vision is to see churches in the majority world equipped for mission and growing to maturity in Christ through the ministry of pastors and leaders who believe, teach and live by the Word of God.

Our mission is to strengthen the ministry of the Word of God through:
- nurturing national movements for biblical preaching
- fostering the creation and distribution of evangelical literature
- enhancing evangelical theological education

especially in countries where churches are under-resourced.

Our ministry

Langham Preaching partners with national leaders to nurture indigenous biblical preaching movements for pastors and lay preachers all around the world. With the support of a team of trainers from many countries, a multi-level programme of seminars provides practical training, and is followed by a programme for training local facilitators. Local preachers' groups and national and regional networks ensure continuity and ongoing development, seeking to build vigorous movements committed to Bible exposition.

Langham Literature provides majority world preachers, scholars and seminary libraries with evangelical books and electronic resources through publishing and distribution, grants and discounts. The programme also fosters the creation of indigenous evangelical books in many languages, through writer's grants, strengthening local evangelical publishing houses, and investment in major regional literature projects, such as one volume Bible commentaries like *The Africa Bible Commentary* and *The South Asia Bible Commentary*.

Langham Scholars provides financial support for evangelical doctoral students from the majority world so that, when they return home, they may train pastors and other Christian leaders with sound, biblical and theological teaching. This programme equips those who equip others. Langham Scholars also works in partnership with majority world seminaries in strengthening evangelical theological education. A growing number of Langham Scholars study in high quality doctoral programmes in the majority world itself. As well as teaching the next generation of pastors, graduated Langham Scholars exercise significant influence through their writing and leadership.

To learn more about Langham Partnership and the work we do visit **langham.org**

www.ingramcontent.com/pod-product-compliance
Lightning Source LLC
Chambersburg PA
CBHW060555230426
43670CB00011B/1830